Margaret Landon

# Anna and the
# King of Siam

*illustrated by Margaret Ayer*

**Buccaneer Books**
**Cutchogue,  New York**

International Standard Book Number: 0-89966-753-8

For ordering information, contact:

Buccaneer Books, Inc.
P.O. Box 168
Cutchogue, N.Y. 11935

(631) 734-5724, Fax (631) 734-7920
    www.BuccaneerBooks.com

To the memory of

my sister

**EVANGELINE MORTENSON WELSH**

*Her spirit burned away the flesh*
  *Until its calm and lovely light*
*Became a beacon on the way*
  *Where pilgrims warmed their hearts at night.*

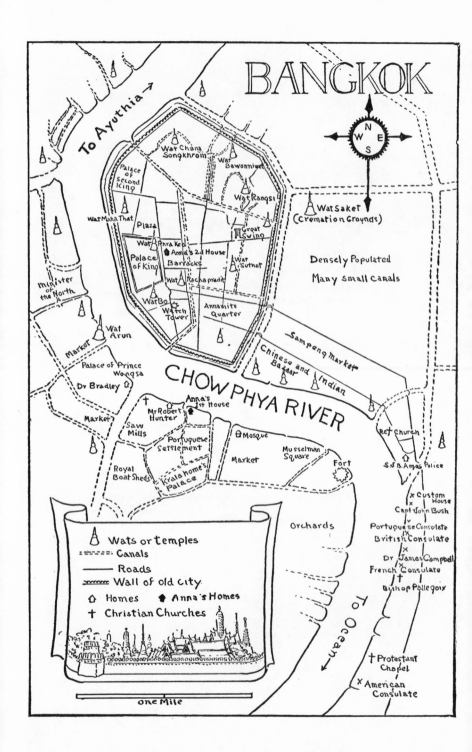

# CONTENTS

# ANNA AND THE KING OF SIAM

Margaret Ayer

I

## BANGKOK, 1862

THE Siamese steamer *Chow Phya,* most modern of the ships plying
between Singapore and Bangkok, came to anchor outside the bar at the
mouth of the River Chow Phya. A troupe of circus performers were hanging over the rails trying to catch the first glimpse of the country whose
king had invited them to entertain his extensive family. Their trained dogs
were barking and snarling at the two dogs belonging to the captain of the
ship, George Orton, but Jip and Trumpet were disdainful and superior.
Somewhat apart from the rough and laughing group an English-

woman was leaning against the rail. Her dress of lavender mull had a neat high collar and modest wrist-length sleeves. She was slender and graceful as she stood there with a light breeze ruffling her full skirts. Chestnut curls framed a face that was pretty except for the rather prominent nose. Her dark eyes were turned toward the line on the horizon that was land. She stood almost motionless, fingering a curious brooch on her breast, a gold brooch into which were set two tiger claws. Beside her a Newfoundland dog stood as quiet as she.

The circus dogs came close, sniffed and barked, but the Newfoundland did not return their greeting. She was aloof, reposeful, dignified, not to be cajoled into confidences with strange dogs. She kept her eyes fixed on her mistress' face as it looked across the water to the distant shore.

The sun rose higher. Golden rays danced and sparkled on the slow blue swells of the gulf. The laughter and shouting on deck continued. The dogs raced about. But the woman was as remote from the confusion as if she were separated from it by an invisible wall.

A carefully dressed boy of about six came up from below deck, followed by a Hindustani nurse in a richly patterned sari. He had the same look of good bones, the same delicate air of breeding that distinguished the woman at the rail. His brown hair was curly and his brown eyes danced.

"Mama, Mama," he cried, dashing up to the still figure. "Are we there? Are we there?"

She turned to him with a smile. "Yes, Louis. We are there. In a little while we'll be in Bangkok. Shall we not, Captain Orton?" she inquired of the bronzed young man in an immaculate uniform who had stepped up behind her son.

"We'll go over the bar with the tide," the officer answered, "and you'll sleep on shore tonight."

Louis ran shouting with the news to the circus performers, and the Newfoundland gravely padded after him. "Stay with him, Beebe," the woman directed in Malay.

"Beebe and Bessy take good care of you and Louis, don't they?" asked the captain.

"Yes, they're very faithful." She smiled faintly, her eyes on the hurrying back of the *ayah*. "Beebe and Moonshee have been with me since before I was married, you know. And good old Bessy is a member of the family, too. She'd guard us with her life."

Captain Orton stood silent a moment. A puff of fresh wind blew the woman's curls back. "Mrs. Leonowens, that ought to be a man's job," he said in a low voice to the pink ear that hardly reached his shoulder. "A maid, a dog, and an old Persian professor aren't enough. I don't like your going in there. For some women, yes. For you, no. People go in there and never come out again." Dark color moved under the clear tan. "Forgive me for saying so much, but you can't even imagine what it will be like."

"You forget that I've lived in the Orient ever since I was fifteen."

"Yes, in British colonies with British soldiers to protect you. This is Siam!"

The woman bit her lip, but did not turn her eyes toward him. "I can't go back now. I've given my word."

"You will not go back now?"

"I cannot!"

He paused, hesitating, then forged ahead. "There's always Mr. Cobb. He's a gentleman and rich!"

She flushed deeply. When she did not speak, he went on in a savage voice, but low. "There is also myself, as you know. Perhaps not a gentleman, and certainly not rich!"

She turned to him then, the deep brown eyes full of tears. "Dear Captain Orton, don't belabor yourself so! To me you are a gentleman, a kind gentleman who has made this difficult trip endurable. But—please try to understand, that for me there has only ever been one man—Leon—and now that he is—gone—there will never be anyone else." She looked out across the water, but her eyes were unseeing. A tear ran down her cheek and she dried it hurriedly with a handkerchief. The man leaned on the rail beside her.

"Mrs. Leonowens, you're too young to bury your heart in a grave." There was a note of pleading in his voice. "Believe me, I would not ask much. Just to take care of you, and Avis, and Louis."

She answered slowly, "But I can't give even that little. I don't know why, but I haven't it left to give." She lifted her face toward his and for a long moment he looked deeply into her eyes, then turned away scowling. Halfway down the deck he wheeled and came back. "I'll be in port every month. If ever you need me, the *Chow Phya* and I are at your service." And he was gone without waiting for a reply.

The sun was hot now. Sighing, but a little reassured, the slight, graceful woman went below.

## FROM WALES TO INDIA

SHE HAD been born in Carnarvon in Wales on November 5, 1834. No one is left there now who remembers Anna Harriette, the daughter of Thomas Maxwell Crawford and his wife. But half a world away in one of the strangest and loveliest cities of Asia, she is remembered still.

Carnarvon was a good place to begin life, a clean town with narrow regular streets. There was a fresh wind from the sea, and ships coming and going in the blue and spacious bay. On a summer evening it was pleasant to walk out along the terrace at the north end of the city wall and watch the sun go down in a paradise of clouds back of the Anglesey Hills. On the opposite side of the town crouched Mount Snowdon, brooding over it. Storms roared down its rocky defiles in winter, and in the spring a child could pick snowdrops and pale primroses at its foot.

There was much in that countryside to remind one of the heroic past: remains of encampments, lines of circumvallation, fortresses, castles, cromlechs, abbeys. Into this land the ancient Britons had retreated before successive invaders. The Romans had never fully subjugated them, for all the many garrisons they had kept on Welsh soil. One of the most powerful of these military stations was still clearly visible hardly half a mile from town—Segontium, now only a shadow of vanished pomp. From there

Suetonius Paulinus had set out with his cohorts to exterminate the Druids at the command of the Emperor Claudius. The Druids were fanatic lovers of their country's freedom and the uncompromising foes of Roman rule. The stern general had fed the bearded priests to their own altar fires, cut down the sacred oaks draped with mistletoe, and destroyed all visible evidence of the faith except the cromlechs—those round altars of sacrifice—and the huge sepultures of the dead called carnedds. But the Romans had not stamped the love of freedom out of Welsh hearts.

Nor could the English do that through the centuries that followed, not even in the thirteenth century when they drove Llewelyn-ap-Gruffyd foot by foot back to the mountain-holds where, deserted by his friends and betrayed by his confederates, he perished alone, last of his race to hold the scepter of Cymri. The city walls which Edward I had built to secure his conquest were little changed in the nineteenth century, although the Castle of Carnarvon, his seal of triumph on defeated Wales, was crumbling into dust.

A hundred years ago in Carnarvon people still talked of these things, and of others. They talked of Din Sylwy where a double circle of stones was believed to be King Arthur's Round Table. They talked also of Pont Aberglaslyn on the Beddelgert Road, which—it was whispered—the Devil had built in return for the soul of the first one to pass over it, and of how the wily villagers had driven a dog across the bridge when it was finished and so kept their bargain and cheated the Dark One.

Reared in this land of elf and Merlin, it was not strange that Anna Harriette Crawford remembered vividly all her life how as a child she had posted letters in trees to fairies and wood spirits and had received the most flattering replies. Nor was it strange that she carried away from it through the years a profound love of freedom, a deep religious faith, a courage and a pride that never deserted her.

She was only six years old when her parents sailed for India. Captain Crawford and his regiment had been ordered to reinforce the troops there in the face of impending war. His little daughter was left with a relative who conducted a school for girls. She was not quite seven when this relative, Mrs. Walpole, called her to the parlor and, taking her gently into plump arms, told her that her father had died a soldier's death in that far-away country where he had gone to serve the Queen.

In the most delightful of all Indian months, the cool month of November, in the year 1849, a steamer came to anchor in the harbor of Bombay, bringing Anna Harriette Crawford among its passengers. She was fifteen, fresh from school, and eager to rejoin her mother, who had married again.

The sun shone through the mists of early dawn as the young girl looked from her cabin window with mingled curiosity and wonder. She was a pretty girl, small-boned and delicate in appearance, with brown eyes and wavy brown hair parted in the middle. In the foreground she saw the

5

stone quays and the great flight of stone steps along the waterfront. Beyond were strange shapes of temples, Hindu, Parsee, Jain, and Mohammedan; the remains of old Maratha forts; and a line of European and native mansions. In the distance was the dim outline of the mighty ghats towering into the clouds.

As the boat docked everything was confusion. Shrieking porters quarreled over luggage. A number of officers, civil and military—some in light-brown coats of China silk and wide-brimmed straw hats, others in frogged blue tunics and military caps—pressed through the crowd and boarded the ship. A young cadet who had been standing near the gangplank rushed into the arms of a handsome officer, very like himself but older by twenty or thirty years. Anna looked anxiously about for her mother, half afraid that she would not recognize her after the long years. But when she found her mother the years did not seem to have mattered. Her mother looked a little older, a little frailer, but that was all. They drove away from the quay happily, Anna almost hanging out of the carriage in her eagerness not to miss any of the new and strange sights. Her mother told her that they would stay with friends at Colaba for a few weeks, and would then go to Poona. Her stepfather held a prominent position in the Public Works Department and was needed in Poona to supervise certain government projects there.

In the meantime they would see as much of Bombay as time permitted. One of their early drives was to the fort, another to the dockyard. It was Anna's first glimpse of the commerce of the world. Her life had been so sheltered that she had hardly bought so much as a ribbon for herself in the shops of Carnarvon. The great square at the dockyard in Bombay was full of merchants, both dark-faced and white, jostling and contending with each other in a dozen languages. There were pompous Englishmen, suave Parsees, Arabs and Hindus, and mixed with them a motley collection of fakirs and beggars hoping for a few pice.

For six hours this mass of humanity bartered, bought and sold, haggled, and fought in a strangely exciting warfare. At four o'clock a long line of carriages drove up to the stone warehouses and dashed away with the white merchants. Almost instantly not a human being was to be seen except a few Indian watchmen and some armed white sentinels. Anna had refused to be dragged away until it was all over. She was intoxicated with the drama of it. So this was commerce! She felt an insatiable curiosity to see and know more.

A day or two later her mother and she drove through the markets and bazaars of the Parsee section. They visited the Bhendi Bazaar, and the Arabian horse-market. They saw the landing of pilgrims from Mecca, a dirty ill-looking set of men. And they watched the arrival of some beautiful slave-women who had been bought for private sale among the rich Indians.

6

But the experience that made the most profound impression on the young girl newly arrived from the simple life of Carnarvon was a dinner party. It was given by a rich widow whose house was near Parel, a beautiful part of the island. Her husband had been an "uncovenanted officer." In the East of those days so great was the prestige attached to the word "officer" that every white man was an officer of some sort, from brigadier to private. A civilian was an "uncovenanted officer."

The carriage bringing Anna Harriette and her parents to the dinner drove through a long avenue of trees to a pillared building of stone with a spacious flight of steps leading to it. On the steps half a dozen servants were waiting, in flowing white robes, crimson and gold turbans, and blue and gold cummerbunds. Anna Harriette looked at this princely assembly in awe. They salaamed the guests, and then with stately dignity advanced to help them alight from their carriages. Another group of flunkeys, equally magnificent, moved forward to conduct them to a sumptuously furnished apartment where they were to lay off their wraps. A third company then led them to the drawing room in the middle of which sat the widow, like a queen, on a yellow satin ottoman, surrounded by her guests.

Anna Harriette found herself little interested in the guests, although the men were for the most part in handsome uniforms, and the women in low-necked dresses of exquisite Chinese crepe and silk, or Indian gauze and mulmul. It was the regal Indian servants who drew her attention. At dinner they glided about, so quietly that their feet seemed hardly to touch the floor, offering the guests costly foods and wines, setting down plates and removing them without making the faintest sound. The punkahs overhead moved softly to and fro. Light fell from coconut-oil chandeliers on the flowers, the glass, the silver. Everything went forward with ease and perfection. The servants who were not at the moment waiting on the table stood with arms folded across their breasts under the shadow of door or pillars, until their turn came. They were so still that, except for the glitter in their eyes, they might have been statues cast in bronze.

The talk at the table was full of expanding British power. It flowed around the young girl in a sea of words. She listened and said nothing. No one considered it strange that she was quiet, because it was the proper thing. But the thoughts in her head were anything but quiet. She heard the officers, whose faces were red with wine, exulting over the accomplished fact of British supremacy in India, and she wondered a little. They discussed campaigns and victories, and spoke contemptuously of the "natives," who everyone agreed had to be put in their place periodically. "Their place?" Anna Harriette pondered, strangely troubled. "And what is their place in their own country?" The laughter, the pomp, the arrogant assertion of racial superiority grated on the young Welsh girl unpleasantly. She watched the Indians moving silently about. She had a feeling of leashed power emanating from the mute and motionless figures under the arches and pillars. It came to her for the first time that it was a very solemn affair for Britons to be in India, luxuriating on her land and on her spoils.

Abruptly the delicious dinner, the music of fountains playing through the windows, the movement and color about the table seemed incongruous, almost revolting! What were they thinking, the dark and sinister men waiting in the shadows, watching every turn and expression on the white faces around the table? Did they hate the conquerors of their ancient land? Did they say to themselves with scorn, "A little while, you fools, and our knives will slit your throats!" The ominous illusion became so strong that suddenly Anna Harriette wanted only to escape this impassive scrutiny. If she laughed at a joke made by the young soldier next to her, if she merely leaned closer to hear better, those obsidian eyes seemed to observe her, even when they remained fixed on vacancy. She could hardly restrain the impulse to stand up and run away from the overpowering sense of animosity and resentment that came to her over the chatter of the table. But this would have been a shocking breach of etiquette. She sat still, trying to hush her secret heart.

The lively conversation turned to the home government, and every man at the table had his own theory of how it should be administered. All of this Anna Harriette knew herself to be too young to comprehend. But she was not too young to perceive that no one around the long table except herself was aware that those dusky, silent figures were flesh and blood. To the other guests they apparently had no more significance than automatons carved out of wood or stone.

When she came out of the house at last she drew a deep breath of relief. She felt as if she had escaped imminent danger.

From that day on she began to think much about India, and the white man in India. She was less volatile than before as she drove about the city with her mother. She did not speak of the groping doubts that troubled her, for what she was thinking seemed utterly different from the thoughts of the people around her. They accepted without question the right of the British to rule, to control commerce for their own benefit, to grow rich on the base of terrible poverty that supported the framework of empire. Gradually the delight that had stirred in her during the first drives through Bombay lessened as she saw how complacently her countrymen were establishing themselves in a land where they were out of harmony in form and color.

During these weeks her intellectual independence was born. It came with a stirring of the conviction that was never to leave her: that a human being, whatever his color or creed or sex, had certain inalienable rights which other human beings had no right to violate. Years later she called the Indian Mutiny "the just retribution that seems to have overtaken our nation."

After a few months in Bombay Anna set out with her parents for Poona, the former capital of the great Indian kings. The country was full of extravagant contrasts—gorgeous temples of gods and squalid dwellings of men; fertile plains and arid wastes; towering hills crowned with ancient forts, now lonely and deserted; deep caves in the hearts of isolated mountains where lay written in stone the romantic culture of long-past ages.

As the *dak,* drawn by horses, trotted briskly along, her mind was busy with many thoughts. And as days later they jounced up the ghats in *palkis,* or palanquins, the thoughts were still with her.

Two things had emerged from the brief time in Bombay as important. First and foremost, she was in love, with a young British officer she had met there and who seemed already essential to her life. He was Major Thomas Louis Leonowens, who held a staff appointment in the Commissariat Office. They had agreed to correspond and it was understood between them that when Anna was a little older they would marry.

The other fact was that she did not like her new stepfather. With every day of the journey her dislike for him grew stronger. He was a domestic tyrant. Unfortunately, too, by the terms of her father's will he—with Colonel Rutherford Sutherland—was her guardian and the executor of the estate her father had left her.

He had begun to hint that he had plans for her future, and they had not been long in Poona before the tension grew serious. His plans included a husband whom he had already picked out, a rich merchant more than twice her age, and objectionable to her in every way. He would not countenance her friendship with young Major Leonowens, who after all had very little beyond his commission. But Anna had her own store of independence, and the friendship continued clandestinely by correspondence.

At last Anna's mother brought about a compromise between her domineering husband and her high-spirited daughter. The chaplain of the East India Company in Bombay was the Rev. George Percy Badger. He and his wife were close friends of Anna's mother. Mr. Badger, a well-known Arabic scholar, had been commissioned to visit the primitive churches of the Nestorians of Kurdistan and other Eastern Christians. He and Mrs. Badger invited Anna Harriette to go with them on their tour of Egypt and the Near East. She was delighted, her stepfather did not disapprove, she had an independent income which made travel possible, so the matter was arranged.

In 1850 she sailed from Bombay with the Badgers. In Egypt she wrote, "We sailed down the Nile, which flows through old hushed Egypt and its sands like a grave and mighty thought threading an unravelled dream; ascended the First and Second Cataracts; in fact, went to visit everything that was worth seeing, the Pyramids, Luxor, Thebes, Karnak, everything!" For a girl imbued with the love of travel it was a wonderful experience. In addition, Mr. Badger undertook her education and she began to study Arabic with him. For her study of Persian she hired a teacher, Moonshee. He and his wife, Miriam Beebe, were to be with her for many years.

Working with Mr. Badger, taking notes as he directed, listening to his explanations of what they saw, opened up a world that Anna Harriette had not known existed. He taught her how to observe, how to perceive more than was indicated on the surface, how to analyze, how to enjoy serious study. It was a rich education for an impressionable girl, better than any the schools of her day had to offer. And during all her travels she wrote to "her own Leon" in Bombay.

When she returned to Poona after nearly a year's absence her mind was made up. She would be married as soon as matters could be arranged, in spite of her stepfather's opposition. Leon wrote that everything was ready for her:

I have taken a large airy house in an excellent healthy situation near Government. It is a long way from the fort, but that is of no consequence compared to the advantage of a splendid house on reasonable terms and a good situation with pure air. I have also purchased a Shijram and horse and completed the furniture as far as I shall be able to go with the exception of a few articles. Our house will be neatly furnished, but not very amply, as it would take an awful lot of money to furnish a house in complete style. As it is I have expended up to date about eleven hundred Rupees, from which you can judge that setting up house is no joke. There are very extensive grounds and gardens attached to the house which you will be pleased with. . . .

The charge for license is very heavy, and we can be "called" (I believe that is the term) at the Poona Church. We had better perhaps avoid incurring an unnecessary expense. You must, however, consult your own tastes and wishes in the matter, and let me know how you decide. As for myself, I am too happy and too delighted to make you, my darling Annie, my wife, to care much whether it is by banns or license, although I attach every importance and weight to that ceremony which will make us one for life. Do not fail to write early on the subject.

They were married in 1851, very quietly. As she wrote later to one of her grandchildren, "This marriage my stepfather opposed with so much rancor that all correspondence ceased from that date." The resentment on her side was as deep. She never mentioned the name of her hated stepfather to her children and grandchildren. None of them knows it to this day.

## 3

## THE ASTROLOGER'S PROPHECY

THE NEW home was on Malabar Hill completely isolated from the rest of the world. The hill was a rocky promontory on the south side of the island of Bombay. It was covered with beautiful houses, many of which were almost palaces. At its highest point, detached and alone, stood a lofty tower. It was a Tower of Silence where the followers of Zoroaster deposited their dead.

On the other side of this much-dreaded spot and not far from a forest of palms which descended in undulations to the base of the hill stood a solitary house, called by everyone "Morgan's Folly." Its builder had returned to England ten years before, broken in fortune and health, and it had stood unoccupied ever since. It was this house to which Major Leonowens took his bride.

The original owner had loved birds and had built his residence to accommodate them. The young couple immediately named it "The Aviary." There were only two stories. The lower was built of stone pillars united by screens of fine open wire wrought in patterns of the Persian rose and the Buddhist lily. Most of the rare birds that had originally been kept there were gone, but there were still the *sooruk,* or scarlet breast, an exquisite singer; the *maina,* or Java sparrow; the *bulbul,* or Indian nightingale; and the *zeenah,* a little quarrelsome brown and red-spotted bird. The upper story was of fine-grained teak. An elaborately carved balcony ran all around it. The eastern end of the house was a tower which commanded the widest and most beautiful view to be found anywhere on the island.

The house had been built to accommodate not only birds but trees. One gigantic *baobab,* which had stood there perhaps for centuries, had been carefully preserved when the house was planned by allowing an opening through both stories and the roof. As a result the house had the singular appearance of having been built around a great tree. The ground floor was covered with weeds and a perfect jungle of brushwood. The gardener told Anna that it abounded in all kinds of reptiles, but she never saw any signs of them until several large cobras were called out one morning by a party of snake-charmers.

The tower chamber was the favorite sitting room of the young Leonowens. It was simply furnished, a table, a few chairs—mostly of cane— a couple of sofas and a Persian carpet, with gauze netting on every door and window to keep out the gnats, flies, and mosquitoes. The rest of the house was furnished with the same moderation. There were no curtains, no blinds, no carpets. The floors and the walls were painted in subdued half-tints.

To keep this unpretentious household there was an army of servants, none of whom would do a duty not his own. The *khansamah,* or Hindu butler, was supposed to keep all the servants in order, but he invariably started revolution in the camp if the Mem sahib wanted anything done her way instead of his. There was a cook who got drunk whenever guests were coming to dinner and a cook's mate who was inclined to be musical just when the master and mistress had retired. There was a lamplighter who asked three times in the course of as many months to go and bury his mother. There was an *ayah,* or lady's maid; a *dhobi,* or washerman; a *bheesti,* who filled the tubs in the bathroom with water, and did nothing else; a *jharu-wala,* who came each morning and swept the house and grounds, and then disappeared until the next morning; a coachman, a groom, and a tailor. Anna wished she could dispense with some of them; but whenever she suggested it *dastur,* custom, was thrown in her face and the whole group combined to force her to keep them all.

In addition to the servants there was a teacher or *pundit,* named Govind, who came morning and evening to teach Sanskrit and Hindustani.

Major Leonowens' work involved a good deal of travel, and the young couple visited the cities of India one after another. When they were not traveling they were studying or seeing the endless sights of Bombay itself. There was much to see and learn. It was a full life.

Once they went to have their horoscopes read by a famous old Fire-priest and astrologer. It had been hard to arrange. They had finally managed it through a Parsee friend of their nearest English neighbor.

The old priest would not receive strangers until his coreligionist intervened.

They started out about six o'clock in the evening, and after a long drive through the Parsee district their carriage drew up before a high, dilapidated wooden building. The balcony projected into the street, supported by rickety wooden pillars, under which there was a small garden of herbs. Their English neighbor, who had often visited the house, led them through the garden and up a flight of wooden steps into a corridor. He tapped at a very old door, slightly ajar, and a feeble voice told them to enter. In another moment they were standing before the Fire-priest. He did not move or speak, or even turn his eyes upon them.

An aged Ethiopian servant indicated that they were to be seated on some cushions near by until his master had finished his evening prayers. They took their seats silently and looked on. In the center of the shabby room was a three-legged stand, and on it a round earthen lamp filled with coconut oil containing depressions at the sides for wicks, of which there were seven burning. Before it stood the Fire-priest, his dress a long, dingy robe which flowed down to his emaciated feet. As his lips moved in prayer, his thin fingers passed over and over a sacred thread, mystic emblem of his faith. The reflection of some inner light made his pallid features luminescent. The watchers were less conscious of the fact that he was incredibly old than of the serene and beautiful expression of peace on his face.

The floor was of planks roughly hewn and rudely put together. A number of old parchments were piled up on one side; pots, earthen lamps, vases, flowers, shawls, carpets, bedding, and embroidered silk cushions lay in seeming confusion on the floor. The Ethiopian attendant, who looked almost as old as his master, grinned at the white strangers from his corner, showing plainly that he had lost nearly all his teeth.

When his prayers were over the Fire-priest put off his long robe and dark conical hat, and put on a gray coat and skull cap, which revealed a few locks of scanty gray hair. He then turned to the Englishman, took both his hands kindly, and saluted him by raising them to his forehead three times. He did the same to the younger people, and then sat down to talk with them.

After an hour they ventured to ask him to read their horoscopes. He rose at once, as if pleased by their request, and led the way with alacrity through a passage and up an old wooden staircase to a small chamber. It was open to the sky by a curious contrivance, a sort of trapdoor, which could be let down in rainy weather. There was a bench in one corner. In the middle of the room stood a circular table, which revolved on a pivot, painted with curious hieroglyphics, and beside it a three-legged stool.

As soon as they had taken their seats on the bench the priest drew out from under the table a board, checkered black and red, and a piece of chalk. He took a dim horn lantern from a niche in the wall and set it on the table. This done, he turned to Anna and questioned her closely in Hindustani about the day, year, hour, and moment of her birth. All such questions as she had power to answer he put down in what seemed to be signs and figures in one of the squares on his peculiar black and red board.

This was the work of some time, for every now and then he seemed doubtful, rubbing out and replacing the signs and figures in new squares. When he had scrawled on the board to his satisfaction he began to compare it with the hieroglyphics on his revolving table, deciphering and studying the stars on each of his tablets with the utmost care. He then turned up his wan face and began to gaze alternately at the bit of sky seen through the open trapdoor and at the hieroglyphics on his table. The stars presiding at Anna's birth were evidently unpropitious. He foretold for her many deaths among relatives and friends, long and hard separations by seas and oceans from loved ones. But he softened his prophecy by predicting a long life, a happy old age, and a numerous progeny of grand- and great-grandchildren.

He then foretold her husband's future, which was even less propitious, since the shadow of one of the great planets crossed his path in middle life. The old priest shook his head. "But if you survive that," he concluded, "you will live to old age in happiness and prosperity with your grandchildren around you."

It was not what the old astrologer said that impressed the English couple so much as his perfect faith in his own rendering of the position of the stars and their implacable meaning. The floating locks of gray hair, the serious brow, the deep, contemplative look on his face, were all very striking. His head seemed full of the mystery of the stars while his heart revolved the secret destiny of human lives.

As they drove away into the warm night they were all silent, each one following his own train of thought, a little amused, a little tolerant, and yet more than half impressed. They could not guess that within a few short years all that the old man had prophesied would begin to come to pass.

Margaret Ayer

## 4

## A KING'S LETTER

IT WAS life, not death, that engrossed Leon and Anna. When they were expecting their first child they decided that Anna should go to be with her mother in Poona. Leon made the trip with her but could not stay until the child was born. Before her eighteenth birthday he was writing excitedly:

My own darling, my beloved Annie,

I have just received Dr. Nohoe's letter informing me of your safe delivery of a little girl. With what anxiety have I, ever since I left Poona, looked for this intelligence, and oh, my darling, my beloved Annie, what feelings of delight and deep gratitude to God did I experience when I learned that our long and ardently expected baby had come home, and that you both are doing well. The consciousness of your deep love for me and my own affection for you always afforded me delightful employment for my thoughts, and it only wanted this intelligence to complete my happiness. I trust, my love, that you did not suffer much, and that you are now all right. Be careful of yourself and our darling baby. How I long to see you, dearest, to press you in my arms once again and to imprint my first kiss on the virgin brow of my child.

We thought we should have a boy. We shall, however, be none the less happy or love our child the less that it is a girl. . . . You say, truly, my beloved, that we must never part again. In the future whatever either of us may have to endure, it will be together, when we can support and comfort each other. . . .

Your own devoted and ever affectionate husband,     LEON.

A few days later he wrote again to say:

You often expressed a wish to have a black satin dress on your twentieth birthday, and I made up my mind long since to get you one. I have been enquiring of late but could not come across a good satin. Today I met with one which I send you. There was only twenty-one and a half or three-quarters yards in the piece, which will perhaps be enough. I send the parcel by Bharyz today and trust that you will like it. Accept my love as a gift from your own Leon and I only regret that I cannot on your birthday clasp you to my heart and wish what I do ever and always, all the happiness that this world can afford.

Again, he wrote:

I have just now returned from a wedding party. Miss Howell was this morning married to Mr. Henderson & I sincerely hope she will be happy. She was very sorry you were not in Bombay to be present at her wedding & desired me to convey to you her kindest regards.

During the breakfast although I talked and made the most fun at table I was very anxious to get away to read your expected and wished for letter. How little did any of them think as pun and story rolled from me making all laugh that I had not a thought or feeling in common with any one of them, that my thoughts were far away, with you, beloved of my heart, and of you. The more I know of these people of Bombay the greater my contempt for them. They are a dull, stupid, inert race without a sentiment above the commonest occurrences of everyday life, and unable as higher and purer minds are to extract a holier feeling out of those mere daily occurrences to which others are able to add such charm.

I never contrast you with others, my beloved, because it would be absurd. My love is yours, is fixed unalterably on you, and I never for a moment think how I could associate with such people in the intimate relations of domestic life, because it would be *impossible*. But I often feel when I look around and form an estimate of the actual worth of those I meet with that, had I not known you, I *never would have married*. You, darling, are after my own heart. You realize all my earliest and brightest dreams of what I would wish my wife to be. As I peruse your dear letter of Sunday night how full of happiness I feel. Yes, darling, the days are long and the times hang heavy to us, loving ardently and passionately as we do, and longing to fly to each other's arms. O my beloved, my own sweet wife, brightest and dearest treasure of my heart, how I long to hold you to my heart, to drink the bliss, the highest bliss from your dear lips, to realize the highest, the most exalted and passionate delight in your arms. How inadequate are all the expressions of fondness and affection I can command to describe my love, my devotion for you, darling. As I write I lack words to tell you how I love you. I worship and adore you, my own darling, and my very feelings of the fondest love and adoration are to

16

me happiness because I know how worthy, more than worthy, you are of that love and adoration. . . .

I hope to go for you by the end of this month. Have your dress made up to receive me in it. I cannot, dearest, tell you how ardently I long to see your dear face, to have my cherished wife again by my side. Kiss our dear Pussy for me. God bless you both forever, prays your fond and

devoted husband
LEON.

But Death was not to be cheated. Within a few short months it had claimed their "dear little Pussy," and Anna's mother, too. The double blow prostrated Anna completely. The doctor told Leon gravely that she probably would not live unless she had a change of climate. Anna lay white and still and pathetically weak. Officialdom, as always, moved with its slow unwieldiness. Months passed, and by the time leave was granted, Anna's healthy young body had asserted itself again.

They took passage on a sailing vessel, the *Alibi,* for England. The leisurely trip of several months would restore her health completely, they thought. But the *Alibi* went on the rocks before they reached the Cape of Good Hope. They were rescued by another sailing vessel and taken to New South Wales.

By that time Leon and Anna were expecting their second child. They decided to wait in Australia until after the child was born, since Anna was still not strong. The little boy, when he came, lived only a few hours. His death brought about a relapse, and Anna grew so desperately ill that she no longer cared whether she lived or died. Leon engaged passage on the next steamer for England and watched over her during the long trip with untiring devotion. By the end of 1853 they were settled in London.

Two children were born during the three years of their London stay— Avis Annie Crawford Connybeare on October 25, 1854, and exactly a year later to the day, Louis Thomas Gunnis. Whether on account of a more favorable climate or better medical care, these two children throve. Their young mother took them into the park herself for their airings, an unheard-of thing for an officer's wife, but she walked happily about among the "nannies" oblivious of a fashion that did not please her. She was glowing again with good health and happiness, and prettier than ever. The English climate had brought color back to her face, and her brown hair curled sweetly around it.

She was delighted and amused when one afternoon with Avis on her hand and Louis in his pram a dashing young man loitered close to her and contrived to open a conversation. She did not tell him who she was but met him with equal gaiety and frankness, secretly delighted at the thought of his confusion should he ever happen to meet her at a dinner table. Finally, when she was preparing to go home, he asked when he might see her again, to which she demurely replied, "My mistress does not allow gentlemen callers."

"Then when will you walk with me again?"

"Neither will my mistress permit me to walk with you again." And with a little swish of her crinoline she hurried off lest he see the smile she could no longer suppress, bending her head in the bonnet lined with lace ruffles to look at the babies in the pram.

In 1856 Leon was ordered to Singapore. There the family was living when, in the spring of 1857, the Indian Mutiny broke out at Meerut. Every newspaper that arrived from Calcutta brought them distressing news. Officers with whom Leon had served were being killed in the fighting. They found on the lists of those who had been massacred the names of their friends—men, women, and children—and the names of several of Anna's relatives. Anna was torn by these losses and harrowed by the persistent thought that since the British had taken India by force the Indians could not be blamed for trying to recover it by the same means. How could anyone justify the cruelty of British commanders who had stamped out the Mutiny of 1764 by blowing sepoys from guns and who had ordered British artillery to annihilate an Indian regiment in 1824 because it refused to invade Burma? How could anyone justify the annexation of Oudh?

The lands of Oudh were rich and prosperous. Lord Dalhousie accused the King of Oudh of encouraging religious feuds. Yet it was common knowledge that the inflammatory papers circulated in Oudh had been printed in Calcutta, the seat of the English government. Lord Dalhousie further accused the king of misgovernment and of oppressing his people. But after all, who had made him judge of such things? Now Oudh and other territories taken on such slim pretexts were costing innocent lives.

When the Mutiny subsided and Queen Victoria signed the Act transferring India to the Crown, Anna had lost not only friends and relatives, but also her fortune. As one after another of the banks failed all over India she found herself penniless. Her little family was suddenly dependent on Leon's salary, which had never been large.

Hardly a year later misfortune struck again. Leon and some of his brother officers had organized a tiger hunt. It was the hot season and Anna had begged him not to go, but he was fond of hunting and the preparations for the hunt were all made. Beaters had been engaged and provisions assembled. He teased Anna by saying that she would make a house pet of him, and promised to be back by the next night.

The tiger led the men a long chase. It was nearly noon before they bagged it. To keep his promise Leon would have to ride through the hea: of the day. The other officers urged him to wait until evening, but he laughed at them. What after all was a little sun to a man accustomed to it? He reached home at the appointed hour and dropped unconscious at his wife's feet.

All night long she knelt beside him praying. Even after the doctor told her that the end had come she continued to pray that he might be restored to her. But when morning dawned and there was no change, she knew at last that he was dead.

People did what they could. His brother officers in Singapore raffled his ponies and tack and gave her the proceeds. They had two of the tiger's claws mounted in gold for a brooch.

For a while it seemed as if her reason would go under with the strain of grief. "It is too much! Too much! Too much!" she thought. Her father, her mother, her two babies, her friends, her relatives, her fortune, her husband. Why try to live at all if life was so cruel? Her stepfather had gained possession of the old homestead in Carnarvon. She had nothing left. No, that was not true—there was Avis and there was Louis, five and four. Faithful Miriam Beebe and Moonshee had looked after them during the terrible days when Anna was prostrated with sorrow. But who was there if she should die or go insane? For the sake of Leon's children she must try to rally herself.

She had never expected to have to earn her living. Fortunately she had a good education. Encouraged by her friends, she opened a school for officers' children, and tried listlessly to resume normal life.

Everyone was kind. Her next-door neighbor was an American, Francis D. Cobb, from Boston. He had come to Singapore on the advice of his doctor because he had lost one lung from tuberculosis. Miraculously he grew stronger. He was associated with an older man in the exporting business. While Leon was alive Mr. Cobb had become friendly with the young couple and had loaned them a copy of Emerson's *Essays*. Anna found that she could lean on him in the months following her husband's death. He often came in during the evening with a new book from the States. He introduced her to the works of Longfellow and Whittier and Hawthorne and Harriet Beecher Stowe. He talked of William Henry Garrison and the rising storm of anti-slavery feeling. He told her about Abraham Lincoln, that strange, gaunt man from Illinois on whom he pinned his faith. Almost in spite of herself she grew interested in the cause of abolition.

Her days were full of the school and of her own children. A year after Leon's death the substratum of sadness was still there, underlying everything she said or did, but without the overwhelming stab of grief that she had known at first. The two children absorbed her thoughts increasingly. They were very different. Avis was gentle and affectionate. Louis was like a shaft of sunlight or quicksilver.

"I remember Papa best," Louis shouted one day in the garden. "I remember everything about him."

"Well," said Avis with quiet persistence, "I remember how he used to ride and how he used to take us for walks."

"Why, that's nothing," Louis countered excitedly. "I remember how Papa used to jump when he was a little boy."

Anna, watching them from above, burst into laughter, then stopped short. She had thought she could never laugh again.

Her greatest worry was that the school was proving a failure financially. The officers sent their children willingly but often forgot to pay the fees. What was she to do to support the three of them? Her stepfather had written that she and the children might return to Carnarvon if she would admit that she had been at fault in defying him and marrying Leon. But could she live in the beloved old house with her stepfather now that her mother was dead? No, she told herself passionately, that she could never do.

Before she had come to a decision her school had attracted the attention of Mr. W. Tan Kim Ching, the Siamese Consul at Singapore, who had been instructed by the King of Siam to secure an English governess for the royal children. After protracted negotiations Anna had received a letter from the King himself:

> English Era, 1862, 26th February.
> Grand Royal Palace, Bangkok.

To Mrs. A. H. Leonowens:—

Madam: We are in good pleasure, and satisfaction in heart, that you are in willingness to undertake the education of our beloved royal children. And we hope that in doing your education on us and on our children (whom English call inhabitants of benighted land) you will do your best endeavor for knowledge of English language, science, and literature, and not for conversion to Christianity; as the followers of Buddha are mostly aware of the powerfulness of truth and virtue, as well as the followers of Christ, and are desirous to have facility of English language and literature, more than new religions.

We beg to invite you to our royal palace to do your best endeavorment upon us and our children. We shall expect to see you here on return of Siamese steamer Chow Phya.

We have written to Mr. William Adamson, and to our consul at Singapore, to authorize to do best arrangement for you and ourselves.

Believe me

Your faithfully,

(Signed)                                         S. S. P. P. MAHA MONGKUT.

## 5

## THE FIRST NIGHT

IN THE early afternoon the *Chow Phya* began its slow and careful passage up the winding river. Tables were set on deck and the passengers ate and talked. The reddish-brown water curved between banks of lush green. Monkeys swung from bough to bough. Birds flashed and piped among the thickets.

After half an hour the ship anchored again at a squalid little town where the captain went ashore to report to the governor and the customs officials. The passengers occupied themselves with watching the life of the village. In the open shed of the Custom House interpreters, inspectors, and tidewaiters lounged on mats, chewing betel and tobacco, extorting money, goods, or provisions from the owners of the various craft anchored at the wharf. Under the flimsy houses of bamboo, pigs and dogs and dirty babies played together in the mud. Across from the town on a small island was the delicate spire of a marble temple. It shone like a jewel on the breast of the river and was duplicated in the quivering shadows of the waters below. A fitful breeze stirred.

When the *Chow Phya* resumed its journey up the river, the English-woman and her son were standing against the rail. The nearer they came to the city the more frequent were the houses, thatched with atap palm, the pyramids and spires and turrets of the larger buildings. The sun was already setting when they caught sight of a roof of English pattern. Presently a white chapel with green shutters appeared beside two houses standing among shade trees, evidently the compound of the American missionaries. The swaying of the trees over the chapel, the peaceful and homelike quality of the scene, stole into the heart of the Englishwoman. Ahead was the glamour of the approaching night, the darkness and mystery of the land to which she had come. The thought filled her suddenly with indefinable dread. She wished for a brief instant that she had listened to her friends in Singapore. Then she put fear away resolutely.

For another half hour the ship moved on into the darkness, dropping anchor near several rotting hulks of Siamese men-of-war. A little farther up the river Anna could discern a long white wall over which towered dimly, tier on tier, the roofs of the Royal Palace. She stood looking at them absorbed, oblivious of the innumerable rafts, boats, canoes, gon-dolas, junks, and ships that filled the river, the pall of black smoke from the steamer, the roar of the engine, the murmur and jar. Here she was, and there was the Palace where she was soon to take up her work. Would they take her there tonight? Would anyone from the British Consulate meet her?

The circus people were preparing to leave. Siamese officers had already come to conduct them to the place where they were to stay. Over the side of the ship went their bundles and trunks into small boats. Off went the dogs, barking and whining. Off went the people. The hatches were opened. The cargo was being unloaded. And still no one had come for Anna, either from the Siamese government or from the consulate. She began to feel a little frightened and very forlorn.

Then out of the deepening shadows flashed a long gondola, beauti-fully carved like a dragon, with torches reflected on the rhythmic dip of rows of wet paddles. On its deck was a small gilded cabin, hung with curtains, and in it lay a Siamese official on a carpet and cushions. In front of him a slave crouched with a fan.

This official mounted the side of the *Chow Phya* swaying with an air of unconcern. A length of rich red silk folded loosely about his person did not reach his ankles. He wore no coat. His brown skin gleamed in the torchlight. He was followed by a dozen attendants who sprawled on the deck like toads, doubling their arms and legs under them. As if at a signal every Asiatic on the ship, coolies and all, prostrated themselves. Only the Englishwoman, her Hindustani nurse, and her bearded Persian Moonshee were left standing. The startled Moonshee gazed at the haughty man in the red skirt, and began to mumble his prayers, exclaiming as he finished each one, "Great God! What is this?"

The Englishwoman stood composedly and waited. The official, equally composed, also waited. Out of the shadows stepped Captain Orton.

"Mrs. Leonowens, may I present His Excellency, Chao Phya Sri Suriyawong, Prime Minister of the Kingdom of Siam? Your Excellency, Mrs. Anna Leonowens."

The Englishwoman bowed slightly with hauteur. The torches flickered across the firmly modeled face of the prime minister. Although he was half naked and without any emblem to denote his rank, Anna knew at once that this Siamese noble compelled respect. There was about him an air of command and latent power oddly at variance with his attire.

He beckoned a young attendant, who crawled to him as a cur approaches an angry master. A rapid flow of unintelligible syllables, and the man on the deck turned to Anna and addressed her in English:

"Are you the lady who is to teach the royal family?"

She inclined her head slightly. "I am."

"Have you friends in Bangkok?"

"I know no one in Bangkok at all."

There was a quick flow of the Siamese language after this. The Englishwoman could not know that the owner of the proud black eyes, which watched her so intently, understood perfectly what she said. His face was without expression other than arrogance. The interpreter spoke to her again: "What will you do? Where will you sleep tonight?"

A muscle moved convulsively in her face. "I don't know," she replied, holding her voice steady by an effort of will. "I am a stranger here. But I understood from His Majesty's letter that a residence would be provided for me on my arrival. And he has been informed that we were to arrive at this time."

Interpreter and lord surveyed her insolently. The lord spoke, the interpreter translated. "His Majesty cannot remember everything," he said indifferently. "You can go wherever you like."

The prime minister strode off and down the gangway, followed by his slaves and minions. The dragon boat with its flickering torches and flashing paddles disappeared into the night.

Anna Leonowens was stunned by the callousness of her reception.

"Do you see now what I mean?" asked Captain Orton. "How much consideration can you expect from men like that?"

Anna could not answer. In a kindly tone he continued: "You may stay here, if you wish. But we'll be unloading all night, and the Chinamen and the smoke will make it unpleasant."

"Thank you," she said in a low voice.

The captain turned and walked off, then came back. "And my other offer is still open."

Blankets and pillows made a bed for Louis on deck. In the darkness Anna sat beside her child, more frightened than she would admit. Again and again the idea which returned to mock her was that it was by her own will that she had placed herself and her child in this position. None of her friends had approved. But what else could she have done? Unless she were to marry Francis Cobb or George Orton? "Leon, dear Leon!" she whispered through stiff lips, half drunk with grief. "I couldn't. I couldn't." She was shaking with sobs she made no effort to stifle.

At a little distance from her in the shadows the captain paced the deck, back and forth, back and forth, cursing softly under his breath. Occasionally he glanced at the figure of the sleeping child, and the bent head of the woman. The crane screamed overhead and the thick black smoke from the engine blotted out the stars. The chattering of the coolies was like the cawing of some strange night crows. An hour passed.

Then a boat approached the *Chow Phya*. In a moment it was at the gangway.

"Captain Orton?" came a loud and cheerful shout. The captain bounded forward in relief. A jovial Englishman with graying hair and a round, ruddy face sprang aboard laughing.

"Did you bring any word from the consul?" asked the captain.

"Sir Robert? No, he's out of the city for the hot season. I just thought I'd drop around to see you."

Everything was arranged in a few minutes. Captain John Bush, the harbor master, would be glad to look after Mrs. Leonowens until the King sent for her. He had a room at his house, plain, you know, but clean. Certainly, certainly, anything you say, sir. Glad to oblige, sir, certainly, certainly.

Louis, half asleep, Beebe and Moonshee, Bessy the Newfoundland, the trunks and boxes, and last of all Anna herself were soon in the boat with Captain Bush. Captain Orton waved them away, shouting farewells and best wishes over the rumble of the unloading. Four men leaned on the oars and the small craft shot out into the dark river. The friendly side of the *Chow Phya* dropped away and with it the last vestige of the familiar.

Under the steady sweep of the oars the boat moved through a dream-like scene: high ships with lofty prows, tapering and elaborately carved, pretty little gondolas and canoes that passed continually. Yet in all the life and motion it was the sweet underlying murmur of the water that filled the ears of Anna Leonowens. At the bottom of her pit of despair the simple medicine of sound was good. No rumbling of wheels, nor clangor of bells, nor scream of engines. Only the fairy-like boats and the singing river.

"By-the-by," broke in her new friend cheerfully, "you'll have to go with me to the play, ma'am, because my wife is there with the boys, and the house key is in her pocket."

"To the play!"

"Oh, don't be alarmed, ma'am! It's not a regular theater, only a catchpenny show got up by a Frenchman who came from Singapore a fortnight ago. And having so little amusement here, we are grateful for anything that may help to break the monotony. The playhouse is in the palace grounds of Prince Wongsa. I'll introduce you to the prince if he's about. He's the King's younger brother. Great chap!"

She did not answer. The news was anything but pleasing to her. A Siamese noble had too lately disturbed her equilibrium.

A few more strokes of the oars in the silent current and the boat ran alongside a wooden pier surmounted by two lanterns. Captain Bush handed her out gallantly. Louis, startled from deep sleep, would not stay with Beebe, but wailed over and over, "I want my mama, I want my mama!" With him in her arms she struggled up the steps to the landing, where a form was coiled on a strip of matting. In the wavering light of the lanterns it looked alarmingly like a bear. The clumsy mass untangled itself, extending a fat human arm at the end of which dangled a fat human hand.

"His Royal Highness Prince Wongsa," said Captain Bush in a matter-of-fact way, rolling the strange syllables easily off his tongue. "Mrs. Leonowens, the new governess, Your Royal Highness." A soft hand closed on hers and a not unpleasant voice greeted her. Near by stood a silent figure. A flicker of the lantern showed a sardonic face. There in the same costume that he had worn earlier in the evening, with a pipe hanging out of the corner of his mouth, looking at her with enigmatic eyes and an aspect of secret pleasure at her obvious terror, was the prime minister.

Wordless and more upset than ever, she hurried after Captain Bush, who squeezed through a narrow bamboo door, then through a crowd of hot people, to seats fronting a sort of altar. A number of Chinese men of respectable appearance sat in the more distant places, while the seats immediately behind Captain Bush and Anna were filled with men and women of the foreign community who looked at her curiously. On a raised dais hung with kincob curtains, embroidered with gold flowers, some Siamese ladies reclined. About them their children, shining in silks and ornaments of gold, laughed and prattled and gesticulated. Under the eaves on every side human heads were packed, each with a tuft of hair like a stiff black brush inverted. In every mouth there seemed to be a cud of areca nut and betel, for Anna observed that these human cattle were ruminating with industrious content.

A juggler appeared. He was a keen little Frenchman who plied his art nimbly. His ventriloquial doll talked, his empty bag became full of eggs, his stones turned into candies and his candies into stones, and his stuffed birds sang. The audience was delighted. There were applauding murmurs and occasional shrieks from behind the kincob curtains.

The Englishwoman in the front row held her small son tight. His head drooped against her breast. Sleep closed his eyes. She was weary and disheartened, waiting with agonized patience for the end of the performance. It came at last. Captain Bush arose and, with her in tow, passed out of the theater. In the confusion he had not been able to locate his wife. "She'll be home before us, no doubt," he said.

The glare of many torches fell on the dark and silent water as they climbed down into the boat. It made the swarthy bodies of the boatmen weird and Charon-like. The landing fell away, and the boat swept out into the river, quieter now than before.

In half an hour they drew up at a small landing. The tired and forlorn little group climbed out. The boatmen unloaded the trunks and boxes. Across a sandy yard, smooth and clean, up wooden steps to a verandah they straggled wearily. Mrs. Bush stood waiting for them, a sleeping baby in her arms. Unruffled and unsurprised by the arrival of strangers, she welcomed them with a pleasant smile. Her gentleness and simplicity dispelled a little their feeling of forlornness.

"It's wonderfully kind of you to have us," Anna said, realizing that for all Captain Bush's bluff heartiness it was asking a great deal of the mother of six children to take in four unexpected guests in the middle of the night.

"Not at all. It's a pleasure," Mrs. Bush replied comfortably, handing her baby to a nurse, and taking them in charge. In a calm manner she led Anna and Louis to a room, lighted a lamp for them, pushed out the shutters. There was a clean iron bed covered with a clean net, white sheets and a round white bolster. Unhurriedly Mrs. Bush arranged mats on her back verandah for Moonshee and Beebe. Bessy took up her position at the door.

A boatman brought up the trunks and Anna chose one for the night. Louis hardly wakened as she undressed him and got him into his sleeper. She laid him on the bed and pulled the net tight. Mrs. Bush had gone. Though she was undressed and ready for bed, sleep eluded Anna. The strange scenes of the day chased each other in confusion across her mind. She was profoundly discouraged by her reception. It confirmed the worst fears of her friends. Perhaps Captain Orton was right, she was making a mistake. The prime minister's refusal to assume any responsibility for her welfare had left her resentful and frightened. Her future was again precarious. Fear of the unknown rose in a tidal wave and washed over her reason. She lay tossing, unable to be still. Then she arose, and wearily knelt by the window where she could see the stars, the only familiar sight in this strange land. Her head slipped to her hands. And as she prayed, a troubled sleep came upon her. When she awoke the dawn was climbing a low wall and creeping in through the half-opened windows.

# 6

## THE KRALAHOME

ANNA STARTED up, all the gloom of the night before descending upon her like a flock of vultures. Louis was still asleep. Dressing quickly and combing her hair, she braced herself for the day ahead. There was water in a pitcher, there was a basin, soap, a towel. She scrubbed her face vigorously, but the mirror told her that no water and soap could wash away the shadow of fear and loneliness. Louis awoke as he heard her stirring. His eyes were eager and questioning, his smile bright and rested. A sudden ray of sunshine caught in his soft hair.

"Mama, we're here! Where's the Palace, Mama? I want to see it. Can we see it today?"

She smiled and drew him to the window.

"Kneel down, Louis, and we'll ask our Heavenly Father to take care of us in this new place."

His childish voice joined hers: "Our Father which art in heaven, Hallowed be thy name. Thy kingdom come. Thy will be done in earth, as it is in heaven." The smooth old words rolled out with their endless comfort, and she prayed silently in her heart: "Lord, Lord, have mercy! Boy is so young! The shadows are so black! Does it need this bitter baptism to purify his young soul?" . . . "For thine is the kingdom, and the power, and the glory, for ever. Amen."

When they were ready they went into the outer room where Mrs. Bush met them *en deshabille,* not beautiful as she had seemed to them the night before, but with the same pleasant smile. She led them to a breakfast table spread with a cloth and set with fruits and tea. As they sat down a servant brought bowls of steaming rice and soup. The hot food was good.

Before they had finished Captain Bush joined them.

"Well, well, and how are you?" he asked heartily. "Another day, eh? Do things look better this morning? Of course they do, of course they do. The prince had you pretty badly frightened, didn't he?" Anna smiled wanly and Captain Bush went off into a long description of what had happened. His wife listened attentively, only interpolating a word now and then, and smiling at them reassuringly. In the yard below two of her sons in wet sarongs were running about laughing and shouting, then plunging into the river that flowed past the house. Louis could hardly wait to join them.

"Really, though," said the captain, turning back to Anna, "he's not a bad sort, Prince Wongsa. The foreigners here like him. He has a reputation for decency and liberality. You'll see after a while."

"That may be," said Anna uncertainly, "but in the darkness he looked like a bear. The real question is, what shall I do next?"

"Do!" expostulated the captain. "Don't do anything. This is Siam. You mustn't be rushing out and doing things. The important point here is to be able to wait until things come to you. Don't worry! The King's put out money for your passage. He'll demand your services in good time."

"But the King doesn't even know where I am," she objected.

"Of course he does. The King knows everything that goes on here. You didn't expect him to meet you personally, did you? No, no, of course not. The Kralahome will send for you in due time."

"The *who* will send for me?"

"The Kralahome, you know. The premier who met you on the ship yesterday. The most important man in the kingdom. Everybody calls him by his Siamese title. He'll send for you when he's decided what to do with you!"

Breakfast was hardly over when this prophecy came true. The Kralahome's boat drew up at the landing. The interpreter told her that she was to bring her servants and her luggage and come to his master's palace at once.

The work of packing was quickly finished, and the little party stowed in the long swift boat.

"Now don't worry," Mrs. Bush urged Anna, patting her on the shoulder. "Everything is going to be all right. Just you give it time."

"Thank you so much for all you've done for us," Anna said gratefully. "I can never tell you how much I appreciate your graciousness to a stranger."

"Good-by. God be with you." The captain waved a plump red hand, and the boat with its many rowers shot out into the river, which was even busier in the daylight. Boats of all sorts and sizes were darting back and forth. Big junks with staring eyes pulled at their anchors.

In about a quarter of an hour the Kralahome's boat had crossed the river and drawn up at a stone quay in a small canal. Staying close together, Anna in the lead, Beebe with Louis, Moonshee and the dog Bessy, the little party walked across the quay to a low gateway, which opened into a courtyard paved with rough-hewn slabs of stone. Two stone mandarins of ferocious aspect, mounted on horses, guarded the entrance. Farther on, a pair of men-at-arms in bas-relief challenged them. Near these stood live sentries, dressed in European uniforms but barefoot. On the left was a pavilion for theatrical performances, the whole back wall of which was covered with a mural. On the right was the Kralahome's palace, with a large semicircular façade. In the background was an extensive range of buildings.

Awed a little, they climbed the stairs to the palace. They moved softly after the interpreter, through spacious saloons in ascending tiers, all carpeted. At the windows were luxurious draperies. Crystal candelabra hung from the ceilings. A superb vase of silver, embossed and burnished, stood on a table inlaid with mother-of-pearl and chased with silver. Flowers of great variety and beauty filled the rooms with a languorous and slightly oppressive fragrance. On every side were rare vases, jeweled cups and boxes, burnished chalices, statuettes, Oriental and European, antique and modern.

They came at last to the audience chamber where their guide stopped. Anna caught sight of a number of young girls peeping at them from behind the velvet curtains which hung from ceiling to floor. A large group of male attendants crouched in the antechamber. Some were in the poor clothing of servants or slaves. Others were handsomely dressed and seemed to be younger relatives of the Kralahome. There was a subdued bustle of excitement, the peering of many dark eyes, and the little party of aliens stood in the middle of it, uncertain, apprehensive, and wholly bewildered by the magnificence and strangeness of what they had seen.

Suddenly the curtains parted and the Kralahome stood before them, semi-nude as on the night before. The murmuring ceased instantly. A wave of unreasoning fear overwhelmed Anna. She gritted her teeth. This man was powerful and what he decided would affect all her future life. He was acting for the King, that was obvious. But while she needed to concentrate her faculties on what was to be said a mist of repugnance clouded her mind. She found herself unable to think clearly. Then, too, she was uncomfortably aware of his naked torso. She had never before done business with a half-clothed man. Some sixth sense acquired from long years in the Orient suggested that the absence of a jacket indicated an absence of respect for her and for the position that she was to fill. In all that room there was not a friendly face. In all Siam there was no one to whom she could appeal for help. An impulse to bolt came over her. She half turned to run, back through the antechambers, tier on tier, out through the garden to the quay—but then where?

The Kralahome held out his hand. "Good morning, sir," he said in careful English. "Take a seat, sir."

She grasped the proffered hand, and smiled involuntarily at the "sir." Its incongruousness diverted her from her fears for the moment and restored a measure of balance to her thoughts.

"Thank you," she said, and sat down a little stiffly on a carved bench.

The noble, oblivious of the embarrassment that his scanty costume created in the Englishwoman, approached her with an expression of pleased curiosity, and patted her small son on the head.

"What is your name, little boy?" he asked.

But Louis cried in alarm, "Mama, come home! Please, Mama, come home!"

"Be quiet, Louis! Hush, dear! This is no way to act. Tell the prince your name!" But the child was in a paroxysm of frightened weeping. When he was calm at last Anna said nervously to the interpreter who crouched beside her on the floor: "Will you ask your master if he will be so kind as to present my request for a quiet house or apartment to His Majesty as soon as possible? I should like to settle my belongings before my work begins. The King has promised me a residence near the Palace. I should like a place where I could be free from intrusion before and after school hours."

When this request was interpreted to the Kralahome, seemingly in monosyllables, he stood smiling and looking at her as if surprised and amused that she should have ideas on the subject of freedom. This look changed quickly to one in which shrewdness, inquisitiveness, and puzzled conjecture blended. After a careful study of her face and person he spoke directly to her, "You are not married?"

She bowed slightly. "My husband is dead."

"Then where will you go in the evening?"

"Not anywhere, Your Excellency," she answered shortly, pricked by the insinuation. "I simply desire to secure for myself and my child some privacy and rest when my duties have been fulfilled."

"How many years your husband has been dead?" he insisted, apparently unconvinced of her virtuous purpose.

A cold still look passed over her face. Any lingering fear had been frozen into icy resentment. She turned to the interpreter. "Tell your master that his rights do not extend to the point of prying into my domestic concerns. His business with me is in my capacity of governess only. On other subjects I decline conversation."

When the interpreter translated this a look of amazement passed over the face of the Kralahome, a look that gave her a short and bitter moment of pleasure, even though she doubted instantly the wisdom of having struck out so sharply. Her instinctive reaction had blinded her momentarily to the knowledge that Orientals usually opened a conversation with a series of personal questions, and that the Kralahome's seeming impertinence may have implied nothing more than a conventional desire to be polite. Still, the words were said. It was important to establish her position at once, and her right to respect and privacy were integral parts of that. The Kralahome shrugged his shoulders slightly, "As you please."

He began to pace back and forth, but without turning his eyes from her face, as if he would discover for himself what she would not tell him. Apparently satisfied at last, he said something to his attendants. Five or six of them raised themselves on their knees with their eyes fixed on the carpet and crawled backward until they reached the steps, bobbed their heads and shoulders, started spasmodically to their feet and fled from the apartment. Anna was startled. Louis, awed and upset again, began to cry.

There were more harsh gutturals, and another half dozen of the prostrate slaves arose and ran. The Kralahome resumed his promenade, still carefully keeping an eye on them, still smiling to himself, like a mysterious Buddha, all-seeing and all-knowing. So they sat for half an hour, until Louis, tortured beyond endurance, clutched Anna's skirts and cried, "Come home, Mama! Why don't you come home?" and dropping his voice, but not enough to escape the Kralahome's ears, "I don't like that man!"

The Kralahome halted suddenly; sinking his own voice ominously he said, "You no can go!"

He was teasing the child. But Louis clutched his mother's dress in utter terror, and hid his face in her lap, where his sobs were somewhat smothered. And yet, attracted and fascinated, the child looked up, only to shudder and hide his face again. His mother, almost as frightened as he by the appalling vista of the work she had undertaken, still maintained her smoothly controlled exterior. She patted his head and comforted him with shreds of words.

After what seemed an eternity the interpreter returned. He came across the floor on all fours, pushing one elbow out before the other as he crept along. As he reached his master he made such an abject salutation as might be offered deity. There were a few unintelligible sentences. The Kralahome bowed, turned, disappeared behind a mirror. All the curious peering eyes that had been directed at the central group from every nook and corner where a curtain hung vanished. At the same time sweet, wild music like the tinkling of silver bells could be heard in the distance.

The interpreter stood up and yawned. With a swagger he approached one of the mirrors and gazed intently and admiringly at himself. He arranged the tuft of hair on the top of his head with cool coxcombry. This done he approached the Englishwoman.

"Hello. Good morning. How are you?" he said with his bold eyes on her face.

"Good morning," she replied coldly. "I thought you were a servant."

He drew himself up offended. "I am the Kralahome's half-brother." He leered at her meaningly. "I think you should be nice to me."

She stood up. "I don't ask any man to grovel at my feet as you do at your brother's, but kindly remember that I do demand respect. I will not tolerate any familiarity from you."

"My brother often listens to what I say." His look was malicious. "Come this way, please. Rooms have been prepared for you."

The little group followed him down long and beautiful corridors. There was again the bewildering collection of statues and vases, Persian rugs, flowers.

"My friends, his friends. My enemies, his enemies," their guide went on, grinning slyly. "I not ask much. I think you give."

Anna made no motion toward her purse, and he led them to two large rooms which had been prepared for them in the west end of the palace building. Their boxes and trunks had already been brought from the boat and were disposed around the wall. The rooms opened on a quiet piazza, shaded by fruit trees in blossom, and overlooking a small artificial lake stocked with colored fish. The Kralahome's half-brother entered the rooms with them. As Anna stepped from the first into the second he crowded close to her. Her temper, already stretched taut by his impertinence, snapped. She stamped her foot and her face flushed scarlet: "Go! Go! You filthy creature! Get out of here!"

The next instant he was kneeling in abject supplication in the half-open doorway. Rage, cunning, insolence struggled in his face. She stopped, astonished at the effect of her own words. He groveled before her as he had before his brother: "Mem, you will not tell my brother. I promise I not bother you again. Promise you not tell, Mem!"

He was not so powerful as he claimed then! Anna was glad that she had not stooped to bribing him. "I promise," she said, not bothering to disguise the loathing in her voice. "But go now, right away!" With a backward glance of half-smothered resentment he ran.

Hardly had he disappeared when the ladies of the Kralahome's harem descended on her in force. Crowding in through the door she had neglected to shut, they came with eager curiosity, all trying to embrace her affectionately, all chattering in Siamese like a bedlam of parrots. They were young, nearly all delicately formed, attractive even to the fastidious Englishwoman, except for their black teeth and clipped hair.

The youngest were children hardly more than fourteen years of age. All were dressed in rich materials, although the fashion of their clothes did not differ from that of their slaves, numbers of whom were behind them prostrate on the floors of the room and down the halls outside. Some of the girls satisfied Western ideas of beauty with their clear olive complexions and their dark almond-shaped eyes.

One wretched crone shuffled through the noisy throng with an air of authority and, pointing to Louis, who had taken refuge in his mother's lap, cried in the familiar syllables of the Malay language, *"Moolay, moolay!"* (Pretty, pretty.) The known words fell pleasantly on Anna's ears. She addressed the woman in Malay: "It is good to hear the Malay language again. But how does a Malay woman happen to be here in a Siamese palace?"

Instantly the visitors stopped their chatter and waited with interest. The old crone settled herself comfortably on a couch with the air of the confirmed raconteur.

"I am a native of Kedah," she began. "Sixty years ago my sister and I were working in the fields one day when we were captured by a party of Siamese adventurers. We were brought to Bangkok and sold for slaves, along with many other Malay girls who had been taken in the same way. At first I mourned my father and mother. Ah, that was bad, very bad! I was unhappy. But I was young and beautiful then. And I had been bought for the household of the Somdet Ong Yai, the father of my lord, the Kralahome. The prince noticed me, and I became his favorite. I bore him two lovely sons just as beautiful as this *moolay, moolay* boy. But they are dead. Alas, they are dead!" She wiped her eyes with the end of a soiled silk scarf. With the furtive tears in her eyes she seemed less ugly to Anna, who felt a quick surge of pity. She, too, knew the anguish of lost children. How alike women were everywhere!

"And my gracious lord is dead also. See, he gave me this beautiful gold betel-box!"

Anna admired the box with a smile. "But how is it that you are still a slave?" she asked.

"I am old and ugly and childless, and therefore to be trusted by my dead lord's son, the beneficent noble upon whose head be blessings!" She clasped her withered hands and, turning toward that part of the palace where her lord was no doubt enjoying his siesta, bowed. "So now it is my privilege to watch and guard these favored ones, to see that they know no man bt my lord." The harem cycle, Anna thought with a shudder. Slavery, physical and spiritual!

Now that her story was ended the old woman extracted some betel from her box and leaned back comfortably to chew it. The younger women, who had been quiet throughout, although they did not understand the Malay language that she spoke, could no longer suppress their merriment nor preserve the decorum that was apparently due her age and authority when she was speaking. They swarmed around Anna like bees, plying her with questions, which the old Malay translated.

"How old are you?"

"Have you a husband?"

"Have you more children than this one?"

"How many boys do you have?"

"Are you rich?"

"What country do you come from?"

One pert minx leaned forward suddenly and said something quickly that made the rest laugh. The Malay woman translated faithfully:

"She says, 'Would you like to be the wife of our lord here? Don't you think that would be better than being the wife of the Lord of Life?' That is the King?"

At this monstrous suggestion the Englishwoman was quite dumb. Did these stupid, vulgar girls think she was here to enter the King's harem? With a shock she remembered that one of the solicitors in Singapore had long had a standing order for "an Englishwoman of beauty and good parentage" for the harem, which already was known to include, besides the Siamese girls of good family, many Chinese and Indian girls, purchased annually by agents stationed at Peking, Foochow, and different points in India. Without a word Anna stood up and retired into the inner chamber.

But the girls pursued her without compunction, repeating over and over the insulting question, laughing and nudging each other, dragging the Malay duenna along willy-nilly to interpret the reply. The intrusion provoked her. Sharp words rose to her tongue. Then she remembered the poverty of their lives, the lack of liberty, of hope, of education, of love, and she choked the words back. But they were persistent. They would not leave the room without an answer. She did not dare to open her boxes and begin unpacking for fear that they would pounce on every little treasure. Desperately she turned to them at last. In a controlled voice she said, "And if I give you an answer, will you go away like good girls and leave me to myself for a while?"

They nodded. All their eyes were fixed on hers eagerly. Her answers tumbled over each other within her. Leon. Her religious scruples. Slavery. Polygamy. What could these children understand?

Slowly she spoke, the duenna interpreting a sentence at a time: "The

Kralahome, your lord, and the King, the Lord of Life, are Buddhists. A Christian woman like myself would rather be put to the torture, and chained in a dungeon for life, than enter the harem of either!"

They were silent in unbelieving astonishment. One, bolder than the rest, cried, "What? Not if he gave you all these jeweled rings and boxes, and these golden things?"

When the old Malay woman, fearing to offend, whispered the test question to her, she laughed at the earnest eyes around her, and replied gently: "No, not even so. I am only here to teach the children of the royal family, not to enter the harem. You see I am not like you. You have nothing to do but to play and sing and dance for your master. But I must work to support my children since my husband is dead. One of my children is on the ocean going far away from me to England to school. She is a girl, only seven years old, and I am very sad now that I must be separated from her."

Shades of sympathy flitted across the faces pressed close to hers. Then softly repeating, *"Phutho, Phutho!"* (Dear Buddha, dear Buddha!) they quietly left her. A minute more and she heard them laughing as they retreated down the corridors of the palace.

## 7

## THE KRALAHOME'S HOUSEHOLD

**AFTER HER** visitors had gone Anna began to unpack. The apartment was comfortably furnished in the European manner. Apparently the chests, beds, wardrobes, and chairs had been imported from Singapore or Hongkong. Louis was happily playing in the little garden near the pond while Beebe and the dog Bessy kept guard. Suddenly all the weariness of the day before, the sleepless night, overcame Anna. The unpacking could wait. She lay down on the bed, grateful for the quiet of the spacious rooms, and fell into a deep and dreamless sleep.

She was awakened, how much later she could not tell, by piercing shrieks. "Mem, Mem! Mem sahib, help! Oh, help!"

It was Beebe calling. Had Louis fallen into the water? With alarm Anna leaped from the bed, just as Beebe rushed wildly into the room. Her head was uncovered. Her fine muslin sari had been trampled under her feet. Her face was green with terror. Louis came running behind her.

"Beebe, quiet! Quiet! Tell me what has happened." The trembling Beebe sank to the floor.

"Mem sahib, my husband, the honored Moonshee, Mem's good teacher, has fallen into the hands of these barbarians. Mem sahib, help us, help us!" Her voice rose in an anguished wail.

"Come, Beebe, come! Calm yourself and tell me what has happened or how can I help you?"

"Mem sahib, he meant no harm, he did not know. How could he know, Mem sahib?"

"Know what, Beebe?" Anna insisted.

Beebe swallowed her sobs as best she could. "He did not know that it was the harem. It was not walled off as in India, Mem. How could he then tell? It is his kismet! He has walked into the quarters of the favorite, and he has been arrested by two great ugly women and dragged to court."

Anna did not stop to do more than adjust her collar and smooth her dress. This was serious! She did not even comb her rumpled hair, but followed the shaking *ayah* headlong to an open *sala* that served as court.

Moonshee, respectable servant of the Prophet, stood there with his hands tied behind him. His turban had come off in the scuffle that accompanied his arrest. His face was woebegone but resigned. Faithful Moslem that he was, he waited patiently to have his throat cut, since it was his kismet that had brought him to this land of *Kafirs,* infidels. His eyes as he turned them toward his mistress were calm and hopeless.

"Moonshee, Moonshee!" she exclaimed. "Don't look like that! And don't worry. There's been a mistake. I'll find the interpreter and we'll fix everything."

Moonshee said nothing, and Anna ran off in search of the Kralahome's half-brother. She dared not go too far, fearing to err as had her servant by entering some part of the palace grounds to which she was forbidden. The interpreter was nowhere to be found. Hurrying back to the *sala,* she saw that the judge had arrived, an imposing and irascible person. Frantically in signs and gestures she tried to tell him that her old servant had offended unwittingly. The judge could not, or would not, understand her. He stormed at the old man in a tone easily understood, even though his words were not. But Moonshee bore the abuse with a calm indifference. He did not understand the language in which he was being cursed, and he expected neither intelligence nor mercy of these *Kafirs* among whom the Mem sahib was so unaccountably determined to live.

The loafers in the yards and porches shook off their napping and surrounded the group in the *sala.* Among them came the interpreter. Anna rushed to him at once: "Oh, there you are! I've been looking for you everywhere. Come quickly and explain to the judge that my Moonshee did not know where he was going, and that he got into the harem quite by mistake and meant no harm."

The young man eyed her insolently, then turned away with a shrug. "It's the judge's business. I can't interfere. Your stupid servant must take his punishment."

Grins went around the crowd of squatting loafers, who did not miss the significance of the sideplay, although they understood no English. It added zest to see the queer white woman getting so excited and making a fool of herself.

Anna wondered briefly if she had been wrong after all not to have bought the interpreter's good will. Then the judge paused dramatically and in a solemn voice pronounced what must have been the sentence. A long whip was brought by a ragged lackey. Other slaves stepped forward and suddenly stripped the old man's clothes from his back.

Anna's eyes blazed. Her mauve muslin swished. She walked straight up to the judge and looked him squarely in the eye: "Let one single lash fall on the back of that old man and I'll see to it that you suffer tenfold. I am going this very minute to lay the matter before the British Consul, so take care what you do!"

Although she spoke in English the words "British Consul" had meaning even for the judge. He stayed the lackey with the whip, and turned toward the interpreter, speaking to him in Siamese. The interpreter moved forward and a long conversation began.

Anna watched anxiously. The judge was asking, the interpreter explaining. There was nothing to reassure her in either cruel face. Suddenly they both fell on the ground as did every other person in the *sala* except Moonshee and Beebe and herself. Behind her stood the Kralahome unannounced.

Calmly he took in the situation. Calmly he motioned to the slaves to untie Moonshee's bonds. From the corner of her eye Anna could see the interpreter inching away on his knees and elbows until he was out of the crowd, and out of the way of his brother's eyes. As soon as Moonshee's hands were free he picked up his turban and, advancing with the dignity that had never left him, laid it at the feet of his deliverer.

"Peace be with you, O Vizier of a Wise King," he said in Hindustani.

The mild and venerable aspect of Moonshee with his snow-white beard falling low upon his breast must have dissipated any lingering doubts that the Kralahome had about his character and purpose.

"You may go to your wife's room, old man," he said in English, and the little company broke up.

Anna went back to her apartment and resumed the unpacking. Her fright over Moonshee had upset her, and the putting away of things steadied her, restored her jangling nerves a little. She was occupied with this work until five o'clock when dinner was brought. It was set on a table by little pages. Louis and she seated themselves and began, rather uncertainly, their first Siamese meal. It seemed to be a mixture, European foods probably prepared especially for them, and curries and sauces that were obviously Siamese. The little pages waited on them with brown cheroots hanging out of pouting lips. From time to time they hopped over two large porcelain heads of Medusa set in front of the windows, and spit into the yard. When she pointed reproachfully at this double peccadillo, they only laughed and scampered away. They were soon replaced, however, by another set of pages, bearing fruits. These were set in their baskets on the table by the boys, who then retired to the sofas to lounge and watch with interest while she and Louis dined. She shook her head at them. They giggled, jumped off the sofas, did several acrobatic stunts on the carpet and took themselves off. The second day in Siam was over.

It was twilight on the piazza. The sun was setting in long pencils of rose and gold from a palette of painted glass. The blended gloom and brightness without entered and mixed with the blended gloom and brightness within. Lights and shadows lay half asleep, and life seemed to be breathing itself sluggishly away, drifting along a slumberous stream toward the ocean of death.

Below in the garden Beebe and Moonshee were preparing their evening meal. The smoke of their pottage was borne slowly upward on the hot still air, which was stirred only by the careless laughter of some girls plunging and paddling in the golden lake.

Moonshee was unperturbed by his misadventure. Anna, on the other hand, was still troubled by it and its implications. "Perhaps I should have conciliated that wretch," she thought. "He's vindictive and dangerous." Angry color came and went in her cheeks. "No, I couldn't have made the situation better by trying to placate him. He would merely have grown more demanding. He *had* to be shown his place! Even though he may cause us trouble. But when we have our own home everything will be better." And it was comforting to remember that the Kralahome had been just.

She determined to press for the fulfillment of the King's promise without delay. She must try to establish her home before her work at the Palace began. And that surely could not be long now. Even an Oriental monarch with the wealth of Croesus would hardly want to pay her salary to sit idle.

The next day was full with unpacking and several callers. In the morning Anna was surprised on answering a knock at the door of the room she had just finished arranging as a parlor to find a Eurasian man standing there. He bowed slightly.

"I am Mr. Robert Hunter, ma'am. His Excellency's English secretary. Is there anything that I can do to help you?"

A wave of relief filled her at the knowledge that she need not depend upon the half-brother as an interpreter. "Mr. Hunter, I am so glad to meet you. Won't you sit down? I don't need anything now, but I shall certainly be calling upon you for help later."

He bowed gravely. "My duties as harbor officer quite frequently take me out for many hours of the day, but I am always in for at least a while." His manner of speaking was stilted but friendly. "I shall be delighted to be of service. If there is nothing you want now, I shall be going."

"Do you have any idea when the King will send for me, Mr. Hunter?"

The secretary looked thoughtful. "It's hard to say, ma'am. It may be several days or several weeks. His Majesty is busy with two important ceremonies, which started the day you came here and will last until the twenty-first. He is performing the tonsure on his oldest daughter and he is raising his oldest son, Prince Chulalongkorn, to official rank. It's all quite complicated, you see. The boy is to be presented with a gold tablet engraved with his royal name—it's a kind of christening, in other words. And then he's to be invested with official position and title."

"You mean he's to be installed as crown prince?" Anna asked with interest.

"Well, no, not exactly that. There isn't any such office. But he will have a grade of forty thousand *sakdina*. I hardly know how to translate it but a common man has only six *sakdina*—ranks or points you might call it—so naturally forty thousand will place him above everyone else in the kingdom. And in a way it does make him the same as the crown prince."

"The heir presumptive, perhaps," Anna suggested. "And will he be one of my pupils?"

"I think he will," Mr. Hunter assured her. She was pleased with this news. Her decision to come to Siam had not been dictated entirely by the need for employment. She had felt a sense of destiny. Death had left her without ties except those that bound her to her children.

The movement in the United States to free the slaves had struck in her a sympathetic chord. Perhaps the opportunity to teach in the harem meant that she would be able to inculcate into her pupils her own deep sense of the sacredness of the human soul, and the evil of any system which violated it by permitting one person to own another. It was possible, she thought, looking back over her twenty-seven years, which had started so promisingly and withered so quickly, that like Queen Esther in the Bible she had come into the world "for such a time as this." If the young heir was to be her pupil she could hope, at least, to mold him a little. All this flashed through her mind as she asked Mr. Hunter: "And you think I'll be sent for as soon as the ceremony is over?"

"It's impossible to say, ma'am," he hedged carefully. "Mr. Alexander Loudon is here to exchange the ratifications of the Netherlands Treaty with the Siamese government. He will be received in audience several times and there will be a state dinner. Then New Year starts on the twenty-ninth and there is always a great to-do with fireworks on the river and on the royal plaza, and theatricals in all the palaces, and gambling for the people. And after that there is another festival called the *Songkran*. And His Majesty is getting ready for the public cremation of his late queen consort, Prince Chulalongkorn's mother, who died last September. That will be in April sometime and will take a week or two. I think you may count on having some time to yourself."

He bowed again in his grave and courtly way and left.

Shortly after a page came with a card which read "Mr. George Orton." Behind him was the captain, smiling. He had a pleasantly familiar look in the new and strange surroundings and Anna's greeting was warm.

"We're sailing with the tide," he explained. "And I wanted to ask you if you had anything to send back to your friends in Singapore."

"Captain Orton, how kind of you! Do sit down. Will I have time to send Beebe out for fruit?" And learning that he could wait, she dispatched Beebe at once. "Get some pomeloes, Beebe, and mangoes, if you can."

While she waited, she sat down to write to Avis. What could one say to a child? Terror, the darkness, the sense of being tossed about on a sea of unpredictable people, the fear. She sighed. None was for a child. But when she began, the letter wrote itself:

My own Avis,
  Birds sing sweetly and brightly. The sun beams as Mama reads again her darling's dear little note. Be good brave child and never cry when kind friends are near, for that will make them and Mama sad. Look up to the fair blue sky every evening, for Mama looks there then; and think how much comes from there—sunshine and rain, cool winds and breezes, dew drops and rainbows, while one, only one thing brings these bright visitors to us, that is love, God's great love, which is small in the dew drop but how large in the sunshine.
  So be good in the smallest and brave in the largest act of your young sweet life. Louis sends his love and this flower which he has picked from the little garden below our window. We often speak of our dear Avis and miss her now. We feel her very near, not before our eyes but in our hearts. O Father, bless my Avis in and with Thy love.
                                                    YOUR MAMA.

The tears were close to Anna's eyes as she signed and sealed the note and handed it over to the captain, with the basket of fruit for Mr. Cobb and the other Singapore friends. He held her hand just a moment longer than was necessary as he asked, "You're staying, then?"

"I'm staying," she said in a low voice.

"God bless you," he said, and was gone.

The unpacking and putting to rights was harder than ever after that. The face of the child now perhaps on the ocean seemed to have been evoked by the mere act of writing the letter. Anna felt the little arms around her neck like fetters as they had been that last day in Singapore when she was about to leave for the *Chow Phya.* "Mama, Mama, I won't let you go," Avis had said. And Anna had seemed to herself insensible and cruel as she disengaged the arms and entrusted the small soft body to strangers—friends, yes, but strangers who could not know or care, kind as they were, for the private lovelinesses of the child's heart. Tears, which seemed to come now so easily and to make her a constant Niobe, rose again to her eyes and fell unheeding on her lap, turning the mauve muslin to purple where they struck.

How long she sat there she did not know. A knock at the door aroused her. A Siamese woman entered. She was perhaps forty, stout, dark, heavy of feature. She was followed by a large retinue, which proclaimed her the chief woman in this establishment filled with women. She was not pretty, but for all its plainness it was a mild face that came toward Anna, and the hands that took hers between them were gentle. The duenna of the day before interpreted.

"Mem, this is Khun Ying Phan. She is the head wife of the Kralahome. She bids you welcome and asks if there is anything that you will need."

"Thank her for me, and invite her to be seated."

The Khun Ying took a seat upon one of the low sofas, bringing her feet up and behind her. One of her maids crawled to her on elbows and knees with a gold tray on which were several small gold containers. With deliberation she chose a piece of areca nut, a siri leaf, a tiny pinch of tobacco; waxed the inside of her lip carefully, put the lime on the siri leaf, and then the whole into her mouth. It was not until this cud was thoroughly resolved into a single red mass that she spoke again. "Are you comfortable here?" she asked through the duenna.

"Please tell her that I'm quite comfortable and also that I'm grateful to her for these pleasant apartments and the good meals her servants have been bringing me and my son."

The Khun Ying looked gratified at the praise of her meals. "How many children have you, Mem?" she asked.

"I have two, a girl and a boy. The girl is on her way to England to school."

The Khun Ying's expressive face showed sympathy. "Ah, that is hard, that is hard indeed."

"How many children does the Khun Ying have?" asked Anna in her turn.

"My lord is childless," she replied.

And the duenna whispered an explanation: "She is my lord's second wife. He put away his first wife because he believed that her child was not his. And he named the boy, when he was born, 'It is not so.' But the good Khun Ying brought this son back and raised him here. She changed his name to 'My lord endures.' And now he is an important man and his father's assistant. But he is my lord's only son." She shook her head at this calamity, obviously the result of some terrible sin in a former life.

"Offer her some gift, Mem," the duenna prompted.

Anna selected from a basket an excellent little pair of scissors of which she was fond. "Will Lady Phan accept this small gift as a token of my appreciation of her generous hospitality?"

Lady Phan was enchanted with the gift, turning it over and over in her palm. One handle was delicately fashioned like a stork.

"Some day soon you must come and see my garden," she said. "Of flowers I have many, and they take the place of the children I do not have."

"I have noticed the lovely flowers in vases in every room in the palace."

The Khun Ying smiled again, pleased. "And tonight we are having theatricals," she said. "If the Lady Leonowens cares to attend I shall send a slave to fetch her."

Anna bowed her acceptance, hardly knowing what else to do.

"It will be the *Ramayana,* the section where Rama comes for Sita."

"Ah, then I am more than delighted, for I have often seen the *Ramayana* in India and have grown to understand and admire it."

And now that her business was over the Khun Ying and her retinue retired to go on with the business of the palace, which kept her occupied from dawn to dark.

It was after eight o'clock and Louis was in bed and asleep with Beebe sitting beside him, when the slaves came to conduct Anna through a series of long corridors to the saloon in which the drama was taking place. The slaves indicated a low bench where she seated herself in a vast room dimly lighted, around the edges of which shadows played. Candelabra on the remote ceiling shed a soft illumination like mist. As her eyes grew accustomed to this half-light, she saw the Kralahome himself, the only man present in a room filled with women.

He sat like an idol of ebony with his feet crossed under him, erect and silent on a bench covered with a Persian carpet. He seemed like a natural king among the dusky forms that surrounded him, semibarbaric but comely. His body was vigorous, the neck short and thick, his nose was large, the nostrils wide, his eyes inquisitive and penetrating. The force of some tremendous intellect reached across to her through the disgust and fear that still hung in her mind from the first terrifying interview on board the *Chow Phya,* when his indifference to her welfare had so shadowed her arrival.

Apart on a dais lay the Khun Ying Phan, surrounded by waiting maidens. Nor did she turn her head from busily creaming her lips when Anna entered.

From the folds of a great curtain a single flute opened the entertainment with low tender strains. Twelve girls appeared from curtained recesses, bearing gold and silver fans. They seated themselves on the floor before the central group and began fanning the Kralahome and his consort. Another group of girls, graceful and laughing, were seated behind musical instruments of so great a variety as to recall to Anna's mind the "cornet, flute, harp, sackbut, psaltery, and dulcimer." They picked up the theme of the flute in a swift ruffle of rhythm and melody.

In the center of the hall the dancers appeared, a long line of girls with skins of olive. There were some twenty, naked to the waist, with golden girdles and transparent draperies, obviously the chorus. Their heads were modestly inclined, their hands humbly folded, and their eyes drooping timidly beneath long lashes. Their only garment was a skirt that floated around their legs in light folds, of some costly material bordered with gold. On the ends of their fingers they wore gold nails six inches long, like the claws of some mythological bird.

Now the dancers responded to a burst of joyous music and formed in two lines. Simultaneously, with flawless precision, they knelt, folded their palms together, and bowed until their foreheads touched the carpet before their lord. He watched them indifferently, no trace of approval or recognition of their graceful gesture upon his face.

When they had retired, still dancing, to the background, the principals of the drama appeared, Rama and his followers in jeweled clothes, the monkey king and his followers in hideous masks. The war began. Anna could not understand the words that were sung, but the story was easy to follow because she was familiar with it. The grace of the actors was exquisite. Each movement of a finger or foot was obviously traditional, conventional, with meaning. For two hours she watched intently until the battle was won and Sita had been recaptured at last.

In the triumphant finale the chorus sprang to their feet and described a succession of rapid and intricate circles, tapping the carpet with their toes in time to the music. The soft rain of light sparkled on their bare breasts, their gold ornaments and the gold of their clothes. Their arms flashed with heavy bracelets of gold. Their dance was a miracle of grace, poetry in motion. Every attitude was an expression of love, the eloquence of passion overcome with its own fervor. On and on, on and on they danced, and the hypnotic mystery of the music kept pace.

The dim lights, the shadows blending with them, the fine harmony of colors, the rhythmic symphony of sound, the fantastic steps of the dance, the overwhelming sentiment—all the poetry and pity of the scene, the formless longing, the undefined sense of wrong, were overpowering.

Half-shocked, half-fascinated, Anna tore her eyes from the dancers to look at the stony figure for which this exotic thing was done. He sat like an idol of ebony, cold and grim, his huge hands resting on his knees in statuesque repose. Whatever the fire raging within him, he was to all appearances as calm as night, affecting contempt for these trifles of humanity offered on his altar. There was about him the look of some sable Moloch in whom the flame burned fiercely, even though no ardor was visible through any crevice in the outward man.

The music swelled into a rapturous crescendo that seemed a prelude to a choral climax. The dancers raised their delicate feet, curved their arms and fingers in seemingly impossible flexures. They were withes of willow swaying before a wind. All the muscles of their bodies were agitated like leaves in a breeze. Their eyes glowed, their lips were parted, as they floated round and round in the slow eddies of the dance.

And there sat the Kralahome, carved of basalt, while the elfin worshipers with flushed cheeks and flashing eyes, tossing arms and panting bosoms, postured their adoration.

Then they were at his feet, blown there by the winds of desire, and so left, like brown leaves of humanity after a storm. Was it all *maya*—delusion? The utter unreality overcame Anna. She closed her eyes against the sensation of floating away out of time and space, opened them, closed them again. It was not *maya*. It was incredible reality.

There they lay, living puppets, their young bodies panting on the floor, not daring to look up into the face of their silent god where scorn and passion contended for place. Then expression died out. He yawned. Automatically he arose, abruptly retired, bored.

The third day in Siam—was it really only the third?—had ended.

## 8

## THE MATTOONS

THE WEATHER began to be very hot. No rain had fallen for months and the grass in the gardens was brown. Some of the trees were shedding their leaves. Even at night there was little relief from the suffocating heat. As one stifling day after another dragged itself out Anna waited more and more impatiently for her interview with the King. But no summons came, nor did she get any word that a house had been prepared for her.

She had devised a temporary schedule. In the mornings she taught Louis his lessons. Afternoons they both rested until the worst of the heat was past. Then letters were written. Evenings after dinner Moonshee brought his books and settled down with them at her table. She enjoyed these hours of study, one evening in Persian and the next in Sanskrit. She felt an intense pleasure as nugget after nugget of ancient knowledge was turned up to lie shining in her thoughts.

Every day or so her apartments suffered a tumultuous invasion from her intimate enemies of the harem. They came upon her like a flight of locusts and rarely left without booty in the form of trifles which they had begged or taken. To them this was not thievery. They regarded it as their due. Sometimes they dragged with them the old Malay duenna and then they pelted Anna with a storm of childish questions.

Morning and evening she and Louis strolled in the gardens or along the quay that faced the river. Sometimes Anna called at Khun Ying Phan's pretty house, in the women's quarters of the Kralahome's palace. Here were the same half-tints and subdued lights that gave such an air of graciousness to the saloons of the palace. Here, however, there were neither carpets nor mirrors, nothing indeed of foreign origin. The only articles of furniture were sofa-beds, low marble couches, tables and a few chairs. The forms of these were antique and delicate, like nothing that Anna had seen in any other country. The combined effect was one of delicious coolness, retirement and repose, and this in spite of the hot March sun that shone along the satin floor through silken window nets.

Around this charming home bloomed an equally charming garden. The shrubbery, fountains, nooks, walks, and lawns had been laid out by a consummate artist. There was none of the excessive use of dwarf trees in big Chinese jars that gave to the usual Oriental garden the stiffness of a cemetery. There were instead flowering trees, ferns, shrubs, all harmoniously arranged. A cool and shaded walk ran to an even larger garden, bordered with latticework, and filled with flowering shrubs of extraordinary beauty.

"These are the children of my heart," said the Khun Ying, as she and Anna walked there. And in a whisper, "For as you know my lord is childless."

But Khun Ying had little time to spare for visiting. Around the palace and within it more than a thousand of the prince's retainers lived. There were also several hundred slaves to be directed. This miniature city was the Khun Ying's responsibility.

As the days passed Anna grew to admire her more and more. She was mild in her manner, but very efficient. The big establishment moved easily with something of the calm which distinguished its mistress. Anna was especially impressed with her unfailing kindness to the younger women of her husband's harem. She lived among them as happily as if they were her daughters, sharing their confidences, comforting their sorrows, pleading their cause with her lord and theirs. And over the Kralahome himself, unyielding and aloof as he seemed, she yet managed to exercise a cautious but positive influence.

Every day or so Mr. Hunter called to see Anna and to inquire about her health or her needs, and to report the progress of negotiations for her presentation at court. She found him a harried little man, serious when sober, and very volatile when, more often, he was otherwise. Once he brought his wife, a pleasant woman, part Siamese and part Portuguese, with the musical name of Rosa Ribeiro Alvergarias Noi Hunter. She was interested in Louis and his games, for, as she said, "I have two boys myself. Robert is eleven now, and John is nine."

"Louis is only six," Anna said, "and my little daughter Avis is seven. She is on her way to London to enter a school there."

The shadow of compassion flitted across Mrs. Hunter's face. "Ah, it is hard, is it not, to be separated from the little ones? Our boys are going, too, but I think I cannot endure to have them away." And she sighed.

Sometimes it was the interpreter who came from the Kralahome instead of Mr. Hunter. His visits were always unwelcome. The combination of fawning humility and arrogant pride, of which he seemed to be fashioned, never failed to annoy Anna. And try as she would she could not make herself cover up the repugnance which he aroused in her, even though policy dictated the wisdom of making as few enemies as possible in this strange country.

Late one afternoon she had a call from Mr. and Mrs. Stephen Mattoon of the American Presbyterian Mission. Mr. Mattoon had twinkling eyes above a beard. Mrs. Mattoon was very plain with pronounced features and hair drawn back straight under a netted cap. But something about her reached across to the young Englishwoman with comfort.

They were friends at once. Anna could ask them the questions pent up in her. She learned that they had been in Siam for fifteen years except for the time they had spent in the United States on health furloughs. Anna was especially interested in the teaching that Mrs. Mattoon and two other mission women had done in the Palace ten years before.

"We were invited by the King himself to start teaching the women of the Palace—let me see—that must have been the very year that he came to the throne, 1851. You will find as we did, I think, that it is hard to hold their attention for more than a few minutes at a time. You see most of them have never been trained to use their minds at all. But many of them have an inherent nobility of character on which you can build."

"I think," Anna said, "that I am to have the teaching of some of the young princes, too."

"So we have heard, and that is of course your greatest opportunity, for one of them will be king."

"The women here at the Kralahome's have filled me with terror of the King himself. They call him the Lord of Life, which is certainly an awesome title for a human being and very suggestive of his power. Is he really as capricious and vengeful as they say?"

Mrs. Mattoon hesitated. "Yes. It wouldn't be fair to make you think that he's anything else. But he's an extremely intelligent man, and he's done more for Siam than all his predecessors. Those of us who have known him over a period of years admire him very much. You must remember that the King is really absolute only in name. He is very advanced in his ideas, but he must work against intrigue and suspicion on the part of the more reactionary nobles and against the inertia of the mass of the people, who do not want any change. He is the head of what you might call the Young Siam Party. And he has with him his younger brother who is Second King, and the Kralahome, and Prince Wongsa, whom you will meet . . ."

"I have already met him," Anna interrupted.

"Oh, have you? Good. Well, and a few others. But the mass of the nobility are afraid of the opening of the country to trade with Europe. And you can understand that, I'm sure. They're suspicious of the colonial aspirations of both France and England and would have preferred a policy of seclusion. Think of the King like this then—he has one foot in the past, in the middle of ages of feudalism, perhaps we may call them, in which he grew up, and he has one foot in the modern world of civilization and science. He is two people. And it is hard to say on any given occasion which one he is going to be, the Oriental despot, or the learned man of science. First he's one and then the other. But never underestimate him! He's a very brilliant man. I've known him to be very cruel, and again to be very tender-hearted."

"You see," explained her husband, "he should've come to the throne when his father died in 1824, but his older half-brother was very powerful at the time and really usurped the throne with a vague promise that he would relinquish it to Prince Mongkut when he was of age. But Prince Mongkut saw the handwriting on the wall, not to mention the danger to his life, and left his wife and two small children to enter the priesthood. He had a natural inclination toward learning anyway. He became a scholar of note in Pali and Sanskrit as well as his native language. He rose to be high priest. The priesthood gave him a freedom that he would not have had in palace life. He used to come often to the homes of the missionaries to borrow books and ask questions. He even took up the systematic study of English with one of them, Jesse Caswell, and studied French and Latin with Bishop Pallegoix. He's a fine mathematician and amateur astronomer, too."

"He sounds formidable," Anna laughed.

"He is really," Mr. Mattoon went on. "For instance, he is the first Siamese to set up a printing press. He did this while he was still in the priesthood. And he ordered for it two fonts of English type, and two of Pali, and one of Siamese. He has even prepared a new character for the Pali, which he calls the Ariyak. The Cambodian character commonly used in Siam requires a thousand matrices, while the King's new Ariyak requires only forty-one. Yes, he's an amazing man! He started a reform movement within Buddhism here, too, and reorganized the whole Buddhist church while he was in the priesthood."

Mrs. Mattoon continued, "And now that he's King he has his press with him in the Palace. Have you seen any of the products of his press yet?"

"No, I haven't," Anna replied.

"Well, he has an amazing use of the English language. Not that he uses it with grammatical accuracy, but he does use it with force, and he never seems to run out of copy. We'll have to give you some samples when you come to see us."

"I'd be glad to see them, but tell me—how did you happen to give up your teaching in the Palace?"

"That's quite a long story," Mrs. Mattoon said. "There's one thing about the King that you must always remember. He is very sensitive to criticism. Of course he is surrounded by adulation and flattery, so it's natural enough. Well, he subscribes to the Singapore papers and combs them for any reference to himself. If there's one that he doesn't like he goes into a regular transport of rage. Several years ago an article appeared in one of the papers criticizing him for his conduct of negotiations with various European countries. He immediately shut the doors of the Palace against us without any explanation. We found out that he suspected one of the Baptist missionaries of having written the offending article. Now all of the missionaries were innocent, naturally, for it would have been the height of stupidity to have done any such thing, but it took more than a year to convince him that none of us had done the deed. I think that eventually he was convinced, but he has been suspicious of us since. But, as I said before, he is an intelligent man. Only one does have to tread lightly."

As they gathered their things to go Mrs. Mattoon added, "If we can help you in any way, you must call upon us. Our house is only five miles down the river."

"I saw it as we came up the river," said Anna. "It looked like a bit of home transplanted."

Margaret Ayer

9

## THE FIRST AUDIENCE WITH THE KING

ON THE fateful afternoon of April 3 Anna dressed with more than usual care. Over her mauve muslin she wore a black lace shawl from the India days. After several weeks of negotiations with the Kralahome, through the medium of Mr. Hunter, it had been decided that she should be presented at court by Captain John Bush. The British Consul, Sir Robert Schomburgk, was out of town for the hot season and Captain Bush seemed the next best person. He was British, and his official position as harbor master had brought him the Siamese title of Luang Wisut Sakharadit. This made him eligible to present himself at the semi-weekly audiences of the King. Before the matter had been settled and the day selected, however, March had slipped away and April had begun.

With her best bonnet framing the smooth brown curls around her face, and long black silk gloves, Anna was ready an hour before the appointed time. Then a complication arose. Louis refused to be left behind. He wailed so at the prospect that even Beebe's offer to take him for a walk and make him some *couay* could not quiet him. He had to be dressed and prepared to accompany his mother.

Promptly at five o'clock Captain Bush arrived, puffing a little in his high-necked suit of white duck, but ruddy and cheerful as always. The little party moved out of the canal and across the river in his boat. Louis, tired and fretful from the unrelenting heat, maintained an ominous silence. Once he leaned against his mother and whispered, "Mama, I'm afraid of the King!"

"There's nothing to be afraid of, dear," she whispered back, willing herself to believe it. "You've never even seen him."

But a spasm of fear squeezed her own heart at the prospect of the interview with the strange king about whom she had heard so many sinister things. There might be much to fear. And she was alone, in a strange country where there were no broad-backed soldiers of the Queen. Siam was not India or Singapore. She must make just the right impression on this mysterious Oriental potentate, whom his subjects called "The Lord of Life"—appear neither servile nor presumptuous. The only question was how.

She mused on this as the boat moved steadily across the river to the Palace landing. It was teeming with activity. A large party of priests were bathing in the river. Other priests, standing on the bank in wet yellow robes, were wringing out garments they had just finished washing. Graceful girls with vessels of water balanced on their heads were passing along the road that bordered the quay, while others carried bundles of hay or baskets of fruit. Noblemen in gilded sedans, borne on the backs of sweating slaves, were hurrying toward the late afternoon audience. In the distance Anna caught a glimpse of a troop of spearmen, the sun glittering on their long weapons.

Captain Bush, Anna, and Louis climbed out of the boat and walked through the covered gangway of the landing to a clean brick road, which took them away from the river and down a narrow street bounded on either side by high brick walls. The wall on the left, whitewashed and crenellated, enclosed the Royal Palace, while the one on the right surrounded Wat Bo. Captain Bush told them about Wat Bo, especially about its famous colossus, a reclining figure of Buddha one hundred and fifty feet long and forty feet high, overlaid with gold plate. The soles of its monstrous feet were covered with bas-reliefs inlaid with mother-of-pearl. "You must see it for yourself, ma'am," he urged. "I doubt that India has shown you anything more awe-inspiring."

"I will, I surely will!" cried Anna eagerly, with the pleasure that the strange and bizarre always aroused in her.

Leaving the temple behind they turned left with the palace wall and walked for some distance until they reached a circular fort, like the model of a great citadel, with bastions, battlements, and towers. They entered its heavy wooden gate, bossed with huge, flat-headed nails, and found themselves on a stony path close to the stable of the White Elephant. Louis wanted to stay and see the great beast, albino rather than white, but there was no time.

They came next to the Wat Phra Kaeo, Temple of the Emerald Buddha, most fabulous of all the gorgeous temples of Siam, and the King's private chapel. Anna stopped delighted. The tall, octagonal pillars that stretched skyward, the spire that tapered far aloft, reminded her of the Temple of the Sun as she had seen it at Baalbec, of the proud fane of Diana at Ephesus, of the shrines of the Delian Apollo. The quaint doors and windows suggested the Gothic, but Brahminical symbols predominated. Strange, she thought, that the Buddhists who had suffered ruthless persecution at the hands of the Brahmans should have returned in this great monument of their faith to Brahmin pantheism.

Louis was entranced with the many statues and would have dragged his mother and the captain to look at each one, if they had been willing. There were beautiful Italian marbles on pedestals—even one of Ceres and one of the Apostle Paul—oddly out of place in the midst of many-armed deities of bronze, birds with human heads, and strange four-footed beasts.

Beyond the temple they passed into a paved courtyard. The fantastic roofs of palaces and still more temples, soaring tier on tier, sparkled and gleamed. A short walk brought them to the Amarind Palace. They paused uncertainly at the entrance, but there was neither guide nor page waiting. Slaves who passed looked at them with indifference. So they walked in unescorted, and through several antechambers until they came to one larger than the rest that gave entrance to the audience hall itself. They hesitated on the lowest of the marble steps, expecting some sign from whatever functionary presided at the door above.

A flood of late afternoon sunlight swept through the spacious hall from high, crowned windows, upon a throng of noblemen dressed in gold-encrusted silks of various colors. All were crouched on their elbows and knees with their heads down, facing the golden throne at the far end. On it sat the King. He was of medium height and excessively thin, dressed in what from that distance seemed to be cloth of gold. As he sat cross-legged and motionless, he appeared to have been carved of a piece with the glittering throne.

The little group on the steps waited and watched with deep interest for perhaps five minutes, but, when it appeared that no one intended to pay them the slightest attention, Anna whispered to Captain Bush, "Please do present us at once. Louis is beginning to be quite tired and hungry."

"Better to wait, ma'am," Captain Bush demurred.

But Anna's patience was exhausted. She shook her curls and took Captain Bush by the arm. Together they mounted the steps with Louis dragging on her hand and entered the hall unannounced. Ranged on the deep red carpet were the prostrate, mute, motionless forms of hundreds of courtiers and noblemen. Anna felt a wild childish impulse to play leap-frog down those lines of squatting figures and so arrive triumphantly before the man in whose hands her destiny lay, sitting impassive and remote, like Buddha on his throne.

The King caught sight of them at once. He bounced erect and advanced rapidly down the length of the hall, screaming petulantly, "Who? Who? Who?"

When he reached them, Captain Bush, on his knees like the other courtiers, performed his office: "Your Majesty, the new English governess, Mrs. Anna Harriette Leonowens, and her son, Louis."

Anna curtsied deeply, and then balanced herself as best she could with bent knees in the froglike position she had been told would be acceptable. "At least," she thought, "I'm not a worm like those poor reptiles on the floor!"

The King shook hands with her, watching her all the while out of hard shrewd bird's eyes. But he said nothing at all. With his appraising eyes still on her he began to march up and down the carpet in front of her in quick steps. He put one foot before the other with mathematical precision, as if bent on performing accurately the steps of some intricate drill. His feet were encased in gold slippers turned up at the toe and crusted with gems that refracted little gleams of light as he moved.

Captain Bush whispered in a quick aside out of the corner of his mouth, "The fireworks'll begin in a minute, ma'am. Best to be prepared!"

Suddenly the King took one long final stride and brought himself to a halt exactly in front of her at a distance of three feet. He stretched his arm at full length and pointed his forefinger at her nose.

"How old shall you be?" he asked in a stentorian tone.

Anna was taken completely by surprise. In all her worrying over this interview she had never imagined it beginning like this. She was hardly able to suppress a smile. Yet she was annoyed, too, at the prospect of a cross examination into her private life in front of the hundreds of kneeling men. Her sense of propriety made her feel that such intimate questions should have been asked before she was employed or in private. Still she did not wish to offend the King at the outset. Her mind made several quick revolutions. She answered demurely, "One hundred and fifty years old, Sire."

The hand dropped. Surprised, puzzled, the King resumed his march, back and forth, back and forth, in quick even steps. His beady jet eyes scrutinized her face minutely, then lighted with quick understanding. He coughed, laughed, coughed, and in a high sharp key returned to the attack. "In what year were you borned?"

Instantly she struck a mental balance and with a grave and serious expression replied, "I was born in 1712, Your Majesty."

At this reply the expression on the faintly withered countenance of the King was indescribably funny. Captain Bush, who had begun to rumble ominously, slipped behind a pillar without ceremony to have his laugh.

The King coughed again with a significant emphasis that startled Anna into wondering whether he was angry with her for her boldness in evading his questions. Then he addressed a few quick words to the nearest courtiers, who smiled at the carpet beneath their noses—all but the Kralahome, who turned and studied her, frowning.

In the meantime the King had taken up his quick march with vigor, studying Anna's face as if he would get it by heart. Then he stopped, wheeled, and lunged with a swift thrust, "How many years shall you be married?"

"For several years, Your Majesty," parried the new governess, determined not to be outwitted, and not to reveal any of the simple facts of her private life in this public place except as they dealt with her qualifications for the post of governess. She had begun to enjoy the battle, which was like a child's game of wooden swords.

The King took six steps, paused, and fell into a brown study. After several minutes of careful thought he turned again. Then, laughing, he rushed at her and demanded triumphantly, "Ha! How many grandchildren shall you have by now? Ha, Ha! How many? How many? How many? Ha, ha, ha!"

Everyone laughed heartily, King, governess, Captain Bush emerging from his pillar, and those of the courtiers who knew enough English to understand the exchange. The King had won the engagement.

In excellent fettle at having beaten her at her own game, he seized Anna's hand and dragged her rapidly down the length of the Audience Hall past the ranks of kneeling men and through a curtained door at the back. Louis clung desperately to her skirt. At this undignified pace they flew along a succession of covered passages, in which crouched shriveled and grotesque duennas, and a few younger women. All had modestly covered their faces with their scarves, as if the sun of the King's presence was to their merely human eyes unendurably bright. When Anna and Louis were quite out of breath the King stopped at last before one of a series of curtained recesses. He pushed open the velvet hangings.

There on the floor was the kneeling form of a woman. Like the women in the corridors her face was covered with her scarf. She had a childlike body as finely made as a Dresden figurine. The King drew aside the pleated silk that she held in front of her face. Her features were as delicate as her figure, and very beautiful. Stooping he took her hand and placed it in the one of Anna's that he still retained. It lay there softly, unresisting as a dead bird.

"This is my wife, the Lady Talap," he made the introduction. "She desires to be educated in English. She has had some lessons from the ladies of the mission. And she is as pleasing for her talent as for her beauty. It is our pleasure to make her a good English scholar. You shall educate her for us."

Something about the young woman won Anna completely. Her eloquently modest and gentle bearing was very charming. "That would give me great pleasure, Your Majesty," Anna said.

As the King translated the reply to Lady Talap, she laughed in a clear ripple of sound like temple bells. She cast in Anna's direction a look of such genuine joy that Anna was startled. Was it so much to ask, to study English? The Lady Talap apparently thought it was. She appeared so enraptured with the graciousness of the King's act, so overjoyed at the granting of her wish as she prostrated herself before them, that Anna left her with a mingled feeling of affection and pity. How revolting to be dependent for one's innocent desires upon the caprice of this withered grasshopper of a King! She cast a sidelong glance at the rigidity of his features and shuddered a little.

The Palace—marble and gold and rich fabrics, jewels and glistening tiles—seemed filled with gloom. Anna could not tell whether the shadow of its slavery and oppression had suddenly fallen across her spirit or whether the sun was setting.

Back through the corridors toward the great hall the King led her. Dozens of children had come out of the inner precincts of the Palace. The King addressed them indulgently, but it was Louis who drew them. They descended upon him, chattering, laughing and shouting. He pulled back shyly as they reached out to touch him, but they only pressed closer. They fingered his clothing, his hair, his skin, his shoes, and his strange white hands. It was agony to Louis, torture almost beyond endurance. He looked beseechingly at Anna, but there was nothing she could do except keep on walking. The King laughed, pleased by the spectacle of the children.

"I have sixty-seven children," he said proudly, as they reached the Audience Hall, and Louis was free at last. "You shall educate them for me, and as many of my wives also as may wish to learn English. And I have much correspondence in which you must assist me." Leaning closer to her he went on *sotto voce,* "And, moreover, I have much difficulty for reading and translating French letters, for French are fond of using gloomily deceiving terms. You must undertake, and you shall make all their murky sentences and gloomily deceiving propositions clear to me. And, furthermore, I have by every mail foreign letters whose writing is not easily read by me. You shall copy on round hand for my readily perusal thereof."

Anna was appalled at the prospect of such a multiplicity of duties, but thought it best to reserve any protests for the future.

"I will send for you later," the King finished with a wave of his hand.

Anna curtsied, and even Louis managed a bob of the head. Then with Captain Bush they withdrew and were shortly out in the evening air. Anna breathed deeply. The Palace had been stifling in the great heat

56

of April. She was profoundly thankful that her agreement with the King included a home outside its walls. To go in and out of that unbelievable place and teach would be one thing; to live in it would be quite another! But the interview had not gone badly, although it had been strange. The King had seemed kindly disposed, and he was certainly not without a sense of humor. But he was a curious man, obviously unpredictable and autocratic to a degree, and he might be hard to please, especially if he expected her to be private secretary as well as governess. She did not mind hard work; in fact, she welcomed it as an anodyne.

Captain Bush was still chuckling as they passed through the gate of the Palace. "He had you there, didn't he, ma'am? 'How many grandchildren do you have?' That was a good one, all right. Though I can't say that he got the best of you, either, when it comes to that."

## 10

## THE CREMATION OF A QUEEN

THE SUMMONS to start the new school did not come. The King, it seemed, was busy initiating the first civil police force that the city of Bangkok had ever had. Two young Englishmen from Singapore were the new commissioner and deputy-commissioner, S. J. B. Ames and S. Bateman. The fifty-five officers and constables were mostly Malays and Indians.

Then the cremation of the queen consort began. The ceremonies were to last from April 10 to April 18, when the King would ignite the pyre. The Kralahome in his official position was responsible for a large pavilion in which any foreign residents of Bangkok who cared to attend were to be accommodated. This meant a great deal of work for Lady Phan. The day before the ceremonies were to start boatloads of furniture had to be taken across the river to the pavilion, curtains hung, and rugs laid. Long before daylight on the first day of the rites the household was astir. Flowers were cut and put in vases and much food was cooked. It was the custom to serve an elaborate collation to guests at whatever hour they came. The fat prince at whose palace Anna had seen the circus was charged with the entertainment of the priests and Siamese officials. The common people, of course, would not presume to enter the fenced square in which the ceremonies took place.

Anna was glad of the invitation to go with the household. It was her first glimpse of a royal cremation and she was much interested in every detail.

The mausoleum had been erected on a great concourse that extended north from the Royal Palace. The base was sixty feet square and the apex of the roof seventy feet from the ground. It rose tier on tier with something of the same lacy, upward-lifting effect of Gothic architecture. The catafalque was approached by long flights of stairs on the east and west. The body of the queen had been placed in a golden urn around which the scented wood used for the cremation was already piled.

On one side of the square enclosing the mausoleum was the King's pavilion, on another that of the Kralahome. Outside the square tens of thousands of the common people milled about. Anna was surprised to see that there was none of the solemnity that Western minds associated with occasions of this sort. Instead, there was an air of festivity. All over the concourse theatrical performances were in progress, free to the people. There were pugilistic combats and tight-rope exhibitions. In the evening there would be grand displays of fireworks.

Within the enclosure people came and went. Chapters of priests from all over the kingdom chanted in course, one group succeeding another. Many grotesque figures of great size had been set up near the approaches to the mausoleum, apparently guardian giants from the Hindu mythology. There was a rock garden, with fountains and a pool. Anna was amused to see some of the priests bathing there, indifferent to passers-by.

For several days she went back and forth with the Kralahome's household. On the three afternoons before the day of the cremation the King sat in state surrounded by his nobles. Toward evening he amused himself and them by tossing among them handfuls of limes in which small coins and gold rings had been embedded. He seemed to enjoy the undignified way they scrambled after these prizes on their hands and knees. The third day there were tickets in some of the limes, which entitled the finders to handsome boats that the King was giving away.

Anna met many of the foreign residents at the Kralahome's pavilion. There was a great deal of suppressed excitement and speculation among them about the all-too-apparent absence of the Second King. Some even whispered that his flag still flew at its masthead, and that he was incensed at the pretentiousness of the cremation on the ground that the queen consort had not been of high enough rank to deserve it, especially since it was even more splendid and costly than the cremation of the two kings' brother the year before.

"Oh, well," one of the gossipers said to another, "the King does as he pleases, and why not? Everyone knows how fond he was of the queen."

"It's probably just another move to settle the succession on her son. I don't believe this woman ever was raised to the full rank of queen, was she? The real queen died ten years ago, if my memory serves. But a full royal cremation like this would establish her position in the public mind. Therefore, the position of her son, too. And scotch any remaining hopes the Second King may have of succeeding his brother."

"It could be," the first speaker agreed.

"Oh, I don't know," a third put in. "It sounds to me more like the old jealousy between the two brothers. Besides, the Second King is powerless. What fun does he get out of life except annoying his brother with a little occasional disrespect?" They drifted away.

It was the first Anna had heard of the feeling between the two kings, although the strange institution of the dual kingship was familiar to her from Sir John Bowring's account. It had been customary in Siam for hundreds of years to have two kings simultaneously. Only the first had actual power. Often they were father and son, and the son usually succeeded his father. Now they were brothers. The Second King's palace could be seen at the northern end of the concourse on which the cremation was taking place. It was almost as large, although not so magnificent, as the First King's, which was at the southern end.

Anna did not attend the igniting of the pyre. It came on the afternoon of Good Friday and she decided against it.

When the cremation was over and she still received no call to start the school in the Palace, she determined to begin her study of the Siamese language. Mr. Hunter supplied her with a teacher, a withered old man who had once been a priest. Sometimes Mr. Hunter himself stopped by to help her with difficulties that were beyond the ability of the teacher, who spoke no English.

She found that she liked the study. As she gradually mastered the curious letters, and then some of the words, she saw that her knowledge of Sanskrit was going to be useful. She could recognize occasional Siamese words from their resemblance to Sanskrit words. *Bida,* for instance, was *father,* and *krot* was *anger.*

When she returned the Mattoons' call one afternoon they gave her an elementary book called *Tables & Lessons in the Siamese Language,* and a *Gospel of Matthew.* Mr. Mattoon had revised and printed the *Gospel* several years before. And Mrs. Mattoon, whose personal copy the book was, had written into the margins and spaces between the lines translations of the more difficult words. Armed with this, Anna made rapid progress. By comparing it with her English Bible she was able to get the meaning of many Siamese words and phrases which her teacher could explain only vaguely. Again, the Mattoons sent her about fifty pages of a partially printed Siamese-English dictionary which another of the missionaries, Dr. Dan Beach Bradley, was compiling. It proved a great boon.

She began halting conversations with the women of the harem when they called on her. These were necessarily limited to words and the simplest of sentences—"Are you well?" "What do you call this?" and so on. They entered into the new game with enthusiasm. They told her the names of all the objects in her room and she pronounced the words after them. Her memory was good and she soon knew many common nouns, adjectives, and many action verbs. She began to be able to detect here and there a word when it was spoken rapidly in ordinary conversation. Once in a while she caught a whole sentence. The fascination which languages always held for her made the dull hot days interesting. Living as she did in the very midst of the Siamese people, she found that she was acquiring the language even faster than she had Hindustani and Malay, and that was a source of satisfaction.

Francis Cobb wrote from Singapore that Avis had sailed with Mr. and Mrs. Heritage and Susan on April 16:

I saw the travellers on board, and Avis was gay, talkative and merry as a lark—seemed in high enjoyment of the novelty and could not remain motionless one second. The ship *Ranu* did not dissipate my former character of her and I prophesy a slow but safe voyage. By October 16 you should expect to hear from her in England.

Captain Orton personally delivered the letter, a small package from Mrs. Heritage with a new picture of Avis that brought tears to Anna's eyes, and a little note from Avis herself saying, "Mama good-by now good-by for Louis, your own child, Avis Leonowens."

Her old house in Singapore was about to be reoccupied. Mr. Cobb's partner was going to the United States and Mr. Cobb was to act as vice-consul for the United States beginning in May. Anna sighed. Everything moved forward except her work in the Palace.

Apparently the King had forgotten that he had hired her at all. Mr. Hunter told her that His Majesty was about to set off for Petchaburi, a city three days' travel distant to the south on a river of the same name, which was a great favorite with the King. There on a low range of mountains the King had had a retreat constructed. Five hundred slaves had been working under the supervision of the Kralahome for many years. Now the palace was ready for dedication. A prominent part of the services to be performed would be the installation in a shrine of a sliver of bone said to be a genuine relic of the Buddha.

"How does the King know that it's genuine?" Anna asked curiously.

"Well," Mr. Hunter's voice was deprecating, "it is said that when lime juice is dropped on it, it is agitated a little. And if it is placed under the eyelid and carried there it does not irritate the eye. That is, er—hem, supposed to be the final test."

So May began and the King and his entourage went grandly by on the river. Louis and Anna still took their morning and evening walks. On them they caught glimpses of the lives of the simple people of Bangkok, meals being cooked over charcoal braziers, crowds of youngsters laughing and splashing about in the river like brown porpoises. Once they ventured to buy cakes of banana dipped in batter and toasted over open coals. Anna was delighted to realize that she knew enough of the language to count out the proper amount for these when the woman asked it.

There was a never-ending fascination about the river for both of them. It was as if the whole panorama of the life of Bangkok passed them there as they stood watching hand in hand. In the morning the sun flickered on the silver ripples of the water and gilded the hundreds of little boats in which the market people moved up and down to the swing of a single oar. Tied to the riverside were rafts and hundreds of floating shops in which much of the population lived. These shops offered curious things for sale. Sometimes Anna and Louis bought trifles to be sent to Avis. If they were up early enough, they watched priests in saffron robes moving from door to door of the floating houses in tiny boats, receiving without thanks the alms with which the pious laid up merit. Swinging at anchor in midstream were junks from Amoy and Swatow, some green, some red, with enormous staring eyes. Swarms of coolies crawled over them like flies. Slaves, half naked or in rags, hurried by on errands for their masters, paddles flashing. Worshipers on their way to the temples balanced dainty trays of cakes that they bore as offerings. And over the whole sparkling scene fan-shaped temple bells scattered Aeolian melodies. It was like the Burma of Ann Judson's poem:

On the pagoda spire
The bells are swinging,
Their little golden circlets in a flutter
With tales the wooing winds have dared to utter;
Till all are ringing,
As if a choir
Of golden-nested birds in heaven were singing;
And with a lulling sound
The music floats around
And drops like balm into the drowsy ear.

One tempting morning when the air was almost cool they ventured beyond the bounds of their usual cautious promenade, which had previously kept them close to the quayside of the Kralahome's palace. They stopped to watch forty or fifty carpenters building boats under a long shed. Louis was entranced. "Let's come every day, Mama," he urged, as they strolled to a canal where a stone bridge was being built. The laborers were half-clothed convicts wearing heavy iron collars which were joined together by lengths of thick chain. They seemed to move only with the greatest effort, even with positive pain. It sickened Anna to watch them, and she would have turned away quickly, if Louis had not pulled on her hand. The men were bringing cut stones from a barge tied to the bank of the canal. Each man picked up a stone and then the line moved slowly up the bank sweating and panting to where masons fitted the stones into the structure of the bridge. Most of the prisoners had hard defiant faces. But there were several with sad and gentle eyes.

"Poor things!" Anna thought. "I wonder if Pharaoh's slaves worked like this on the Pyramids."

She and Louis watched them for some time. Then the leader of one of the columns, which had just disposed of its stones, approached Louis and held out his hand, grinning. Louis recoiled, but reaching into his pocket drew out the few coins he had and dropped them into the filthy palm extended to him.

What happened then was so unexpected that Anna had not a second to prepare for it. With a shout the whole gang was upon them, hands outstretched, chains clanking, bodies pressing, grabbing at them and screaming, "Give alms, give alms, give alms!" The men crowded around Anna and Louis on all sides, wrangling and yelling and snatching at them. Frightened almost out of her senses Anna could do no more than seize Louis and hold him against her breast where the wild rabble could not trample him. She tried to break through the press, again and again, and could not.

The men were in front of her and behind her. She had no money with her to satisfy their menacing, "Give alms, give alms, give alms!" The disgusting odor from their bodies sickened her. For a moment she lost footing and thought that she and Louis must both go down. A brown mist floated before her eyes and she was afraid she was going to faint. Then, suddenly, as if struck by lightning the men were lying flat on their faces around her. She swayed and caught her breath. Officers flew among the prostrate convicts swinging heavy thongs against the human flesh that a moment before had seemed menacing, and now seemed only pitiful.

This scene was as nauseating as the other. With another deep breath Anna stepped quickly over the bleeding slaves to the open ground. She set Louis carefully down. He was white and shaking, but unharmed. Anna snatched his hand and grasping her skirt she ran—ran until she had no breath left in her, with Louis skimming along beside her. Then without a backward glance they walked as fast as their panting lungs permitted to the palace gate, back into the courtyard and were safe in their rooms. These rooms that Anna had grown to hate nevertheless now seemed like a gracious sanctuary.

After Louis and she had taken off their clothes, stained by the sweaty hands of the prisoners, had bathed and dressed in fresh garments, they sat down quietly to breakfast. As was their custom, Anna opened her little prayer book and read the lesson for the day: "I had fainted, unless

I had believed to see the goodness of the Lord in the land of the living. Wait on the Lord: be of good courage, and He shall strengthen thine heart." She closed the book with a feeling that the verses had been written especially for her.

Beebe brought in breakfast. She had taken over the serving from the mischievous pages. But breakfast tasted earthy and the atmosphere was choking. Their hearts were sick with the morning's experience and they could scarcely swallow.

"Let's go away, Mama," said Louis with a pleading look. "Let's go back to Singapore, please!"

Anna sighed. She, too, had been thinking of their home in Singapore, but she was not ready to give up yet. So she summoned a false cheerfulness and answered, "You'll like it here, Louis, when we have our own home. We'll get the piano out and the pictures of Avis, and all our books, and it will be just as nice as Singapore."

## IN THE KING'S HAREM

THE HEAT was still intense, although it would break any day now with the coming of the monsoon. At night Louis tossed on his bed calling, "*Ayer sujok,* Beebe. *Ayer sujok.*" (Cold water, Beebe. Cold water.) And Anna gasped for a cool breeze, turning back and forth beneath her mosquito netting. She had a fancy that the air of this Eastern prison house in which she lived was like the life within it—heavy, stifling, stupefying; and that the air of her own home, if she could only get it, would be fresher.

But what could she do? The King had returned from Petchaburi and had not sent for her. She could not go to him until he did. She would not return to Singapore and admit defeat. Her heart recoiled from marriage. Whenever she lay down to sleep her thoughts ran in an endless circle: she must do something, and there was nothing to do. She had been in Siam for two full months, and the inaction was eating her heart. If only it were not so hot—if only her work would begin, to absorb her thoughts—if only she had a home of her own where she could be busy—if only . . . Then somehow the night would be gone. Another leaden day would start.

Finally one morning Mr. Hunter came from the Kralahome to tell her to be prepared to commence her duties at the Palace at once.

"The Kralahome's sister, Lady Piam, will take you this time," he explained. "She'll call for you tomorrow morning with her boat."

The Kralahome's sister was a broad, motherly woman who greeted Anna with, "Good morning, sir."

"Good morning," Anna replied. "It's kind of you to come for me. Shall we start at once?"

The lady answered amiably, "Good morning, sir. Good morning, sir."

Taking this to mean "yes," Anna put on her cloak, bonnet, and gloves. Beebe settled Louis's hat on his curls, for he had insisted on going, and picked up the books that had been carefully prepared and waiting for weeks. Lady Piam led the way to her boat, walking slowly. Behind her came the procession of slave girls who always accompanied her. One bore a golden teapot upon an embroidered cushion of satin. Another, a gold tray on which were set two tiny porcelain cups without handles but with covers. A third carried a betel-box, also of heavy gold, intricately wrought. Two brought up the rear with large fans. These were all emblems of the noble lady's rank and were not to be left behind.

After the whole party was seated in the covered basket boat, Lady Piam caught sight of the books and took one up with interest. When, in turning over the pages, she came upon the alphabet, she gave Anna a look of pleased surprise and started to say the letters, pointing at each with her finger. Anna helped her, and for a while she seemed gratified and amused. But presently she closed the book abruptly and offered Anna her plump hand, saying, "Good morning, sir."

Anna replied, "Good morning," and after a moment's thought added "sir." As the boat proceeded in a leisurely fashion up the river her ladyship repeated the greeting every time her attention returned to Anna, which was not less than a dozen times.

They landed at a showy pavilion that projected into the river with a roof rising tier on tier. Parts of the elongated structure looked ancient and dilapidated. But some of the interlocking roofs were gay with new colored tiles. To the slender Englishwoman approaching the landing for the first time it seemed as if the rotting pillars groaned and protested against the architectural anachronism that piled so many young heads upon their time-worn shoulders. The fancy pleased and diverted her.

Through several covered passages they came to a barrier guarded by Amazons. These were strongly built women, a little taller than Anna, with the usual short hair of the country. They wore tight-fitting jackets of scarlet buttoned to the neck, with sashes tied diagonally across their breasts. Their lower garments were a sort of woven plaid that reminded Anna of kilts. The old lady was evidently well known to them, for they threw open the door quickly and then squatted with their hands folded before their faces until she and her party had passed. A hot walk of twenty minutes brought them to the inner wall, which shut off the Forbidden City, the *Khang Nai* (Inside), from the rest of the palace grounds.

A curious oval door of polished brass in an ornate frame opened noise-lessly to admit them to a courtyard.

On their left were several lofty temples set among groves of old trees; on their right was a long dim gallery. The floor of the open pavilion on which Lady Piam led them was of marble. The shade from the trees and the coolness of the *sala* were a relief after the heat through which they had come.

A number of women lounging in and around the pavilion started up to greet Anna's guide. They seemed to be of superior rank, for she prostrated herself before them. Perhaps they were her sisters, at least several of these held high positions in the harem, Anna had been told. When the formali-ties were over, they all fell into animated conversation. Children sat or sprawled upon the marble floor. Babies slept or frolicked in the arms of their nurses.

Almost immediately slaves appeared with silver trays. These were cov-ered with scarlet netting stretched over light frames of bamboo, in the shape of beehives. After the beehives were removed, the trays were found to be filled with a variety of foods that were strange but appetizing look-ing. Anna would have liked to try them, but no forks or spoons were fur-nished and she could not bring herself to use her fingers as the others did. She and Louis had to content themselves with oranges. She was troubled a little by the fear that her refusal would be considered rude, especially if the food had been prepared in her honor, but no one paid the slightest attention to her. Lady Piam and the women of the harem ate, laughing and chatting without a glance in her direction.

When she and Louis began to peel their oranges the children came close to watch with interest and amusement. They laughed and pointed and talked, though she and Louis could not imagine what was odd about their manner of eating. Later she was to observe that Siamese peeled all fruit with a whittling stroke away from themselves and considered for-eigners indescribably foolish for cutting toward their own thumbs. The children were attractive, with parchment skins, liquid brown eyes, and well-formed bodies. But when Anna had finished her orange and held out her hand to them, the smiles disappeared and they drew away.

Soon Lady Talap, who had so charmed Anna at their first meeting, appeared. After saluting the sister of the Kralahome profoundly, and talking with her for a few minutes, she lay down upon the cool stone floor with her gold betel-box as a pillow.

She beckoned to Anna with a swift downward gesture, almost the exact opposite of the English equivalent, and smiled with the sudden sweetness of expression that distinguished her from the other women. Anna got up and went over to her. As she sat down beside the pretty relaxed figure, Lady Talap said in quaint clear English, "I am very glad to see you. It is long time I not see. Why you come so late?" to all of which she apparently expected no reply. Anna addressed her with several simple sentences, but she shook her head laughing. Anna then tried baby talk in an effort to make a few amiable sentiments intelligible to her, but in vain. When she saw that Anna was really disappointed and embarrassed by this failure, Lady Talap smiled again, the same evanescent sweet smile and began to sing:

"There is a happy land,
   Far, far away,
Where saints in glory stand,
   Bright, bright as day . . ."

and then said, "I think of you very often. 'In the beginning God created the heavens and the earth.'"

Anna looked at her in astonishment. If she was trying to display her knowledge of English, the performance was meritorious, but disjointed, to say the least. Louis, lying with his head in Anna's lap, stared at this strange woman with frank curiosity. Was she speaking English or wasn't she? A long silence followed, to Anna a trying one. She could not think of any way to show her friendliness, and she wanted to, for she would need to make friends if her work was to be a success. But Lady Talap was lying stretched out, unaware of the torment in Anna's mind, looking up blankly at the carved and gilded rosettes of the pavilion roof.

After perhaps half an hour Lady Talap rose to her knees and looked cautiously around. Lady Piam had strolled away with her friends and the children were scampering about in the sun. There was no one near and she moved quickly very close to Anna and whispered in her ear: "Dear Mem Mattoon! I love you. I think of you. Your little boy dead— you come Palace—you cry. I love you!" And she moved quickly away again and lay down with her head on her betel-box. She placed her finger on her lips, removed it, and began to sing again in her clear treble:

"There is a happy land
   Far, far away, . . ."

Anna sat silent and alert. The furtiveness of Lady Talap's act had meant something. Suddenly she understood, and was profoundly touched. How stupid she had been to have supposed that it was a random performance! This childlike woman locked away behind the high walls of the Forbidden City was trying to send a message to the outside world. She wanted to tell Mrs. Mattoon of her sympathy for the other woman's sorrow in the loss of a child, to express her affection, to let Mrs. Mattoon know that she still remembered what had been taught her. She had devised this unique way of sending love and comfort to the woman she counted friend. How clever! How humane! Anna smiled and nodded her head and Lady Talap smiled back. It was agreed between them. But it meant more than just that to Anna. She was thrilled with the knowledge that Lady Talap had trusted her with the message, evidently sure that she would not disclose it to the King. This was a matter for women, something that women's hearts understood, and the Siamese woman had trusted the Englishwoman with a message for the American woman. Anna looked at Lady Talap with renewed interest. There she lay, imprisoned by walls and customs, which made her hardly more than the plaything of a king, but for all that she bore the marks of Mrs. Mattoon's character. Anna fell to dreaming. How many minds enchained by age-old fetters would she set free?

The day wore on to noon, then to afternoon. Some of the women went, others came. The children continued to play. Anna rested against one of the pillars of the pavilion and felt herself to have fallen into an enchanted world out of an old fairy tale. It seemed impossible that only twenty minutes' walk could bring her to the outside stir and bustle of Bangkok.

She was aroused by a slight noise from the covered gallery. An old woman appeared bearing a candlestick of gold, with branches supporting four lighted candles. The effect was instantaneous and amazing. All the drowsy indolence of the afternoon vanished. Lady Talap started to her feet and fled unceremoniously. The other women and even most of the children followed suit. Anna was left alone with the Kralahome's sister and her attendants, and Louis, who was sleeping comfortably in his mother's lap.

It was easy to guess that the King was in some way connected with the candles. But it was not until much later, when she understood the customs of palace life, that she came to understand what the candlestick signified. It was the offering invariably sent by the King to the Chapel Royal of Wat Phra Kaeo as soon as he awakened from his nap; and it meant that his appearance was imminent.

In a very few minutes a straggling procession began to move past— hundreds of women and children, some pale and downcast, others bright and blooming, more moody and hardened, all walking quietly in one direction. None stopped to talk. None loitered or so much as looked back. Lady Talap reappeared among them, dressed now in dark blue silk that contrasted becomingly with the rich olive of her skin. She did not pause to speak, did not even glance at Anna, but hurried after the others with a certain anxious alacrity in her smooth young face. She was the favorite, but others had been so before her.

Anna began to feel uneasy as her ordeal approached. All this hushed and careful bustle set in motion a contagion of fear. She was determined to take up with the King personally the question of a house. He had promised her a brick house in his letter, but as the Kralahome had said on that first never-to-be-forgotten night, "His Majesty cannot remember everything." Perhaps he needed to be reminded.

She took out the two letters from the King that had come to Singapore, and re-read them. In addition to the letter which had been addressed to her personally, she had a copy of the King's letter to Mr. W. Tan Kim Ching, which was very specific:

Bangkok, 26th, Feb. 1862

In regard to the Lady whose name you have said Mrs. Leonowens whom you pleased mostly to have in our employ for being school mistress here I have refused her application on last occasion because she required monthly salary more than how much we thought was proper, and on hearing that she wish to live at Missionary establishment far from this palace her pleasure might cause a trouble to us in conveying her to and fro every day, and her appearance is in pleasure with Missionaries of Christ religion I fear lest she in doing her education may endeavour to convert our Children to Christianity more than education for knowledge of English language and literature like American Missionaries and their wives have done here before then our expense may be considered our countrymen whom English called inhabitant of Benighted land. We need not have teacher of Christianity as they are a bundant here.

But if the Lady Leonowens accept to receive salary for every month but $100 and promise to live in this palace or in vicinity hereof, and that she will do education of language and literature more than endeavour to convert our Children to Christ religion I shall be glad to have her our school Mistress according to your favourable opinion.

I have written to Mr. Wm. Adamson who and whose wife have introduced the application of this Lady to you before, on this subject and have ordered him that the said Lady shall place good arrangement with you before she would come up here. I beg to authorize for doing best arrangement with her who may be not out of my aforesaid rules.

When she would come up here I will give her a brick house in nearest vicinity of this palace where she can live with her husband or manservants freely without rent or lessening payment the monthly salary will be $100 firstly—but afterwards when I observe her labour greater than expected or her scholars will be increased or her scholars may become in facility of language and literature very soon, I will reward her some time more than salary or add her monthly salary according to her labour.

Please state my statement to her, and let her believe me.

The letters were not unfriendly. Why then was she apprehensive? Anna folded them away again and roused Louis. The straggling procession of women and children had stopped. She stood up to await the King's arrival.

70

For an hour she stood, expecting him to appear at any moment. The wait was trying, and as time passed her apprehension grew. She found herself steeling her will against the impact of the King's waspish personality, though she hardly knew why. After all, the agreement was clear. Only details remained to be settled. True, he had won the last engagement, but she had not lost. She had kept her innocent secrets.

Then there was a general frantic rush. Attendants, nurses, slaves vanished through doors, around pillars, under stairways. And at last—preceded by a sharp cough—behold the King himself!

He was not smiling. He approached the little group that waited for him in the pavilion, coughing loudly and, it seemed to Anna, crossly. It was an ominous introduction to the interview. Louis, always sensitive to the moods of those about him, buried his face in the folds of his mother's dress to escape the notice of this person who announced himself so strangely.

The trail of women and children following the King prostrated themselves as he paused before the Kralahome's sister. She, too, had dropped to the floor. Only the Englishwoman with her child and the King were left standing.

The King shook hands with Anna coldly, and, looking at Louis whose face was invisible, remarked indifferently, "The child's hair is beautiful."

He then turned to the Kralahome's sister and engaged her in a long conversation. Anna waited, but the King paid no further attention to her. As she waited several of the women inched themselves close to her and hissed something at her. She could not understand them, if they were trying to talk to her, and so remained with her eyes fixed on the King's face in an effort to catch the drift of the conversation he was carrying on with Lady Piam.

It was not a particularly pleasing face, although the features were regular and the complexion fair. The nose was broad at the base and the eyes narrow and hard. The right half of the face was on a slightly lower plane, and there was a peculiar falling of the under lip on that side, as if the King had once suffered from partial paralysis. But it was a strong face, imperious and shrewd.

Again the hissing of the women interrupted her scrutiny. She looked at them curiously, but their eyes were on the ground as they squatted on their elbows and knees. What could they be trying to say? The whisper came more insistently. Evidently, whatever it was, they considered it important enough to run the risk of a rebuke from their lord. Didn't they know that she could not understand them?

They said nothing more, but suddenly without warning four of them reached out and took hold of her skirt. Before she could guess what they planned they had pulled together vigorously. The movement was so quick that she lost her balance. Triumphantly they jerked her over backward and she landed full length on the pavement, stunned, Boy beside her. Tears of pain and anger started to her eyes. Furiously, she attempted to struggle to her feet, but they held tight until the King saw her dilemma. He said a few rapid sentences in an insolent tone and Anna was allowed to resume her upright position, rumpled and shaken.

"They not understand European custom," said the King to the flushed Englishwoman who was trying to smooth her dress and quiet Louis, who had a big bump on his head and was sobbing wildly.

The King spoke to the women and they crawled backward a little and left Anna standing in an open space. Then with a wave of his hand the King went on, "It is our pleasure that you shall reside within this Palace among our family."

Only half recovered from the shock of the fall, Anna was struck dumb. Live here? How could she live where the sense of tyranny was so strong she could smell it, and the shadow of slavery so deep that even the sunlight was full of gloom? Live where she could find no privacy and no respite from the harem and its life, no freedom to come and go, where every gate was guarded and every movement of those within watched by spies, where she would have no home of her own in which she could bring up Boy in the beloved tradition of English childhood? She closed her trembling lips firmly. Never! She would never consent to live shut away from the help of the British Consul and the American missionaries.

"Your Majesty," she said with a quietness she did not feel, "it is impossible for me to live here. I shall be happy to work here during the school day, but I need some little home of my own outside the Palace where I can retire when my duties are done. I do not speak the language yet, and I should feel like an unhappy prisoner locked away here when the gates are shut in the evening."

A sudden suspicion gleamed in the King's eyes. "Where do you go every evening?" he demanded.

"Not anywhere, Your Majesty," she replied indignantly. (How dare he?) "I am a stranger here."

"Then why shall you object to the gates being shut?"

"I do not clearly know," she answered slowly—with a secret shudder at the idea—"but I am afraid that I could not do it. I beg Your Majesty to remember that in your gracious letter you promised me 'a brick residence adjoining the Royal Palace,' not within it."

He advanced toward her several short steps, his face contorted and purple with sudden rage.

"I do not know I have promised. I do not know former condition. I do not know anything but you are my servant"—the voice was climbing higher and higher toward a shriek—"and it is our pleasure that you must live in this Palace, and YOU SHALL OBEY!" The last three words were screamed in her very face.

She backed off a little, trembling, and for seconds she could find no words to say nor the strength to say them. "If I give up now," she thought, "I'm lost. I will not live in this Palace! Not if it means going back to Singapore. No! Dear God, help me, I couldn't do that! But I will not live here, as if I were a member of his horrid harem myself!" She gathered the vestiges of her courage around her and managed to say in a voice so cold and calm that it surprised her: "Your Majesty has perhaps forgotten that I am not a servant, but a governess. I am prepared to obey all Your Majesty's commands within the obligation of my duty to your family, but beyond that I can promise no obedience."

"You shall live in the Palace," he roared, "you shall live in the Palace!" Then the roaring stopped. The purple faded from his face. He blinked his eyes rapidly several times and spoke in a moderate tone. "I will give women slaves to wait on you. You shall commence royal school in this pavilion Thursday next. That is the best day for such undertaking in the estimation of our astrologers."

Anna drew a deep breath. He had begun to bargain. She was having an effect. Slaves! If he knew how she abhorred slavery with every atom of her being, how she would do everything within her power to destroy it, he would not think she could be bought over for a few pitiful human beings. Astrologers! So that was why there had been a delay in starting the school! The astrologers had not found a propitious day. The King turned away as if the matter were settled and began to address commands in a staccato voice to some old women about the pavilion.

Louis, who could contain himself no longer, was crying in loud shaking sobs. The Kralahome's sister raised her head and threw him several fierce glances. Anna felt tears gathering in her own eyes. After all, who was she, one frail Englishwoman, to pit herself against this relentless despot and his crawling minions? She would not live in the Palace. She had better not stay and burst into undignified tears. That would reveal weakness, and here one could not afford to be weak. She could not wait for the King to terminate the interview! Better rude than weak! Taking Louis by the hand she turned and walked quickly back toward the brass door.

Voices behind her began to call. "Mem, Mem, Mem." The King was beckoning and shouting. The tears were close to the surface now and she was shaking with nervousness. She bowed profoundly and hurried on through the oval door, head held high.

The Kralahome's sister came bouncing after her in a distraction of rage, tugging at her cloak, shaking her finger in Anna's face and crying, *"Mai di, mai di."* Anna knew enough Siamese now to understand that simple phrase—"Bad, bad!"

But she walked on, outwardly serene, toward the farther gate which led to the river, ignoring the excited woman beside her. Her father and her husband had been soldiers of the Queen. She could not be bullied and coerced.

All the way up the river in the boat there were more *"Mai di's"* and none of the "Good mornings" of the earlier trip. Even up to the very door of her apartment Anna was followed by the outraged noblewoman who continued to pelt her with a hail of words she could not understand, interspersed with *"Mai di, mai di, mai di."* But Anna's mind was made up. She shut and locked her door firmly. Anger had burned out fear. Let them do what they would! She could resign her new position if she must! She would not live in the Palace.

Margaret Ayer

12

## THE NEW HOME

ANNA SENT Louis off for his evening bath with Beebe, and sat down heavily to think. But the more she thought the more apparent it became to her that the unfortunate interview with the King could not have been avoided. He was quixotic and unpredictable, and those about him expected to adapt themselves to his whims. This she could not and would not do. She felt a pang of regret for the comparatively happy home she had left to come to Siam. But she put regret out of her mind and concentrated on the problem at hand.

Against her will she found herself in conflict with the King, and at the very outset. She had been warned by the Mattoons, but she did not see how she could have done other than she had. Still she could hardly expect to get the better of the King on the issue of her home as matters stood—

75

unless . . . Yes, of course, that was it! She must enlist the help of the Kralahome.

It would be a good idea to see him soon, as soon after his sister as possible. The more she knew of him the more enigmatic he appeared, but already she felt his power in the kingdom. It was plain that those who came in contact with him both feared and loved him. The reason for the fear she had felt instinctively at the first meeting on shipboard—a kind of suppressed and ominous force. The reason for the respect and love he inspired she could not fathom, unless it came from his reputation for justice. He was known for a rigid sense of right, which was never swayed by passion as was the King's.

He had at all times a kind of passive amiability, of which he seemed fully conscious and which was his forte. Anna could not discern by what means he exacted the prompt obedience that met his low-spoken commands, nor how he controlled the country with reins apparently held loosely, even carelessly. There was a curious aura of greatness about him. She had seen even in her first month in Siam that his influence and prestige penetrated to every nook of the vast and undeveloped kingdom. There was never a week, hardly a day, that provincial officials from remote corners of the country did not wait upon him. As each week passed she had been impressed more and more by the homage the Siamese rendered him, and by the casual remarks of the Europeans she met. Mr. Thomas George Knox, the interpreter of the British Consulate, who knew Siam intimately from long residence, told her that the Kralahome alone had kept the King on the throne in the face of a strong conspiracy to supplant him with his much more urbane and popular brother, the Second King.

These reflections settled the matter. She would appeal to the Kralahome again, relying on his rectitude to bring about the fulfillment of the King's contract with her. As if in answer to her thought Mr. Hunter knocked on her door and asked whether there was anything that he could do for her.

"Oh, yes, Mr. Hunter, there is! If the Kralahome is disengaged, I should like very much to speak with him about what happened at the Palace this afternoon."

In a few minutes Mr. Hunter was back to say that the Kralahome would receive her in his private sitting room. He was smoking a pipe when Mr. Hunter ushered her in—sitting in front of a litter of papers in the Siamese language.

"Yes?" he said, looking up and taking the pipe out of his mouth.

"Your Excellency has heard of the interview this afternoon?"

A faint smile relieved the impassivity of his face. He nodded.

"Nothing was farther from my thoughts than such an unpleasant conversation with His Majesty. But it is impossible for me and my child to lodge within the Grand Palace. As you know there was some correspondence about this before I was engaged." She drew out the two letters she had carried to the Palace with her and laid them before him. "I have accepted the King's terms and expect to fulfill my part of the bargain, but I feel strongly that His Majesty is bound in honor to make good the conditions by which I was induced to close my school in Singapore and come here."

The Kralahome picked up the letters and read them carefully. When he put them down and looked at her again she saw that she had succeeded in arousing his interest.

"What for you object to live in Palace?"

She hesitated. How could she make him understand her need for privacy? It was something the Siamese did not seem to want or even like. "Your Excellency," she began slowly, "I shall need a quiet home where I shall be free from intrusion when my day's work is over. My work will be difficult. It will take many hours and when it is finished I shall be very tired indeed." She paused, hunting for the best way to explain what she feared was inexplicable to the man before her. "There is no privacy in the Palace. That is why I want a home outside where I can retire for the evening, and where I can be assured of peace and seclusion. And then, too, the Palace gates are shut early. As you know, Europeans do much of their visiting over the tea and the dinner table. I want to be free to go and come, and I want a place to entertain my European friends. I couldn't do this in the Palace. I shall be very happy to work there, and even to assume the secretarial duties that the King has decided to add to my school work, but I feel that I'm entitled to a place to live where I shall be free to follow the customs of my own people without offense to anyone."

The Kralahome listened attentively, then asked several questions of Mr. Hunter in Siamese.

"Very well, sir," he said. "I shall try to arrange."

A few more days passed draggingly. Anna taught Boy, studied Siamese, visited Khun Ying Phan—anything to relieve the monotony of waiting. The girls of the harem continued to descend on her like locusts, but she suffered their depredations with the thought that now since the Kralahome was on her side it would not be for long.

Finally one morning almost a week later Mr. Hunter came to her to say that the King had consented. A house had been selected for her at the King's express command and a messenger was that moment waiting at the door to conduct her to it. Her boxes and trunks would be sent after her later in the day, if she cared to go on ahead. The house, he added, was furnished.

Anna was overjoyed. She put on her walking clothes and rushed out with Louis, leaving Beebe and Moonshee to start the packing. An elderly man in a *panung* and a dingy red coat with yellow satin facings, such as a grenadier might have worn, was waiting for her. His faintly sinister look dampened the first ardor of her enthusiasm, but he started off briskly without a word, and she and Louis fell in behind. On their way out of the palace they met the Kralahome coming in through the gate. He studied them with a quizzical smile as he said, "Good morning, sir." Was he amused at the look of relief in Anna's face? Or was it merely his customary air of omniscience?

Anna shook off her misgivings and stowed herself and Louis under the high uneven pavilion of wood in the center of the boat that had brought the messenger. Anna's appearance seemed to afford infinite amusement to the ten rowers as they plied their oars. Her guide stood in the entrance to the boat's shelter chewing betel and spitting methodically into the river. He looked even more ill-omened in the full light of the sun, a shrunken, dirty old man with a leering expression.

They crossed the river to the King's pavilion and climbed out. The guide set off quickly along a circuitous and unpleasantly dirty road. They picked their way after him. In half an hour they came to two tall gates and passed into an even narrower and dirtier street. From the offensive odor that immediately overwhelmed them they knew that they were in the fish market. On the counters of the open stalls that lined the street were sun-dried fish of many sorts—fresh fish, prawns and crabs, and purple balls of rotten prawn called *kapi*.

The stench gagged them. The sun burned and the air stifled. Dust choked them. The ground blistered their feet. They were half-suffocated and very bewildered when their guide stopped abruptly at what seemed to be the end of this execrable lane. Their way was barred by a wall in which was a single door. The guide made a sign to them to follow him up the three broken steps of brick that led to it. Then from a pouch in his dingy coat he produced an enormous key. He applied it to the door, where it grated in the rusty lock. Surely this was not their destination? The end of a fish market! Anna hoped wildly that the door gave access to a courtyard and pretty garden—what matter if a little overgrown and neglected?—with a quiet house in the midst of the garden at the river's edge, as far as possible from the smells and noise of the market.

But when the door opened creakingly they found themselves looking into a small room. Anna stepped across the threshold and all her hopes collapsed. The room was very dark for there was no window. As her eyes adjusted themselves she began to pick out details. The half-light from the door revealed a remnant of filthy matting in the middle of the floor. On it stood a table, minus one leg, and propped up by two chairs. The arms of the chairs were broken.

With a shudder she passed on into the second room. It, too, was windowless, and even darker than the first. In it was only a cheap excess of

Chinese bedstead filling all available space. And on the bed a mattress. Anna recoiled in disgust. A mutilated epitome of some Lazarine hospital! It brought into her mind a picture of twisted and emaciated bodies rotten with sores, and she could scarcely breathe. The walls were leprous with mold. There was a smell of disease and decay. There was no kitchen, no bath-closet. Anna retched involuntarily. And this was the residence sumptuously appointed that the King had assigned to the English governess of the royal family of Siam!

Her nausea was succeeded by such blistering anger as she had never known. She understood now the Kralahome's strange smile. But even in her rage her mind worked clearly enough to realize that this outrage was not his doing. No, this was the King's own idea. She had thwarted him, and he had countered. Very well!

Her stock of Siamese words was still small, but she gratefully recalled the emphatic monosyllables of the premier's sister. She turned with blazing eyes on the King's messenger, who was standing behind her, grinning and holding out the key.

"*Mai di! Mai di! Mai di!*" she said and with an imperious movement dashed the key from his hand. Then she turned and caught Louis in her arms and bounded out of the house, clearing the three steps in a leap.

Without a backward glance she fled—anywhere, anywhere! She was stopped by a crowd of men, women, and children. They gathered around her wondering, mouths half open. They were barefoot, half-naked, fetid, animal. She paused then, remembering all too clearly her experience with the chain-gang. With a quick revulsion of feeling she turned to retrace her steps. Her insulted escort came panting up and she motioned him haughtily to lead them back to the boat. This he began to do. The people pressed close as they started to move. Some of them timidly stretched out their hands to touch Anna's skin. When this happened she actually found herself grateful for the protection the presence of the King's messenger gave her.

"Hurry, hurry!" she said to him and he quickened his pace. Ten minutes later they repassed the gates and left the suburb of disgust behind.

All the way back to the Kralahome's palace in the boat her guide stood at the entrance of the wood pavilion staring at her. There seemed to be no human intelligence or feeling in the mask that time had made of his face. It was carved in a senseless and fiendish grin like a gargoyle's. Anna could not tell whether it expressed apology or ridicule, or whether it had petrified in a shape that meant nothing. But to her immense relief the guide did not get out of the boat at the Kralahome's landing. The rowers pushed off and Anna and Louis saw his grin disappearing in the distance.

Without a pause Anna went straight to the Kralahome. His sly amused smile provoked her anger again. In a few sharp words she told him what she thought of the lodging provided for her by the King's munificence, and announced firmly that nothing would induce her to live in such a slum.

He looked at her coolly from his seat on the floor, and without taking his pipe from his mouth told her that there was nothing to prevent her from staying where she was. She started from her low seat with an exclamation. His insolence and complete indifference to her wishes stung her to fury, nor did she have the control after the emotional strain of the morning to prevent his seeing the fact. With some difficulty she found her voice and told him that neither his palace nor the den in the fish market would suit her, that she insisted on her contract, and that she demanded suitable and independent accommodations in a respectable neighborhood.

With a leisurely movement he stood up, smiling a little. She saw that her rage had succeeded only in amusing him. Who was she after all but an Englishwoman of no particular importance in a country of which he was the unacknowledged ruler? Her knees shook with sudden weakness and depression. In a tone that he might use to a petulant child the Kralahome said, "Never mind, sir! Never mind! By and by it will be all right." And with that he retired to an inner chamber.

Her head was throbbing with pain and she could not keep back the tears. Defeated and half-sick, she dragged herself to her rooms and told Beebe and Moonshee to abandon their packing. Her pulse bounded and her throat burned. Fever! She threw herself across the bed exhausted by emotion and gathering illness.

The next week was a nightmare. She lay prostrated with fever and tortured day and night with hideous fancies. Sometimes she dreamed that she saw the Kralahome standing beside her bed and looking at her as he had the first time they met on shipboard. There was the same sardonic look on his face, as if he personified all the forces arrayed against her. She would scream and reach out her hands to push him away, only to encounter space. Sometimes the stone images of the mythological creatures in the courtyard seemed to gather around her bed where they stood shaking their gray and hoary heads, mocking her for coming to a country where she would never be anything but an alien. She would cry out in her troubled sleep and Beebe would come running with water. Several times she woke to find Khun Ying Phan bending over her, anxiously bathing her face with water in which jessamine had been steeped.

Gradually the fever began to leave her and with it the dreams. She slept for long hours and ate a little. Finally one day she awoke with her head perfectly clear to find the Khun Ying sitting beside her. Anna reached out weakly and took the soft brown hand in her own, caressing it gratefully. "Khun Ying," she implored, "help me!" And partly in Siamese and partly in English she begged Lady Phan to intercede on her behalf.

The Khun Ying smoothed her hair and patted her cheek, as though Anna were a little girl, and agreed to do her best. But she urged Anna to be patient. This was impossible. Persistence was both a virtue and a fault with Anna. She could not see the Kralahome even in passing without pressing her case, telling him that the life she was leading was insupportable, although she was grateful for the many offices of affection and kindness she had received during her illness from the women of the harem.

She saw that she was accomplishing something—not what she wanted but something. She had made an impression on him, even though she could not be sure just how. In a country where the idea of *noblesse oblige* was unknown and where the great demanded the exact amount of homage that was their due, her insistence upon what she believed to be her rights was probably having its effect. The Kralahome continued courteous but imperturbable. He promised little, yet she had the distinct feeling that he was working in her behalf.

Nevertheless nothing happened. When Anna grew warm on the irrepressible topic the Kralahome would smile slyly and tap the ashes from his pipe saying, "Yes, sir! Never mind, sir! You not like, you can live in fish market, sir!" And she would chafe at his *sang-froid*, and even hunt for little ways of enraging him without compromising her own dignity. But he endured them all with a nonchalance that irritated her the more because it was not assumed.

Two months passed in this fruitless struggle. Desperately she settled down to her studies, content at last to snub the Kralahome with his own indifference. But this made no more impression on his granite surface than her importunings. Rather, he seemed to ignore her existence blandly.

Then suddenly one afternoon he paid her a visit, something he had not done before. He complimented her on her progress in the language and on her *chai yai*, her "magnanimity." He told her that the King had been highly incensed by her conduct in the affair of the fish market, and that it was not possible to make any progress until His Majesty got over his pique. Then he said that he had found something for her to do. He had decided to start a school in his own palace, which she could teach until she was summoned by the King.

"Thank you. Thank you very much!" she said with such enthusiasm that he looked surprised.

"Siamese lady no like work. Love play. Love sleep. Why you no love play?"

She assured him that she did like play very well when she was in the humor for play, but that at present she was not disposed to it. She was weary of her idle life in the palace and sick of Siam altogether. He received her candor with his characteristic smile and a good-humored "Good-by, sir."

Next morning ten Siamese boys and one girl filed into her room, marshaled by a harem duenna. Gracefully they knelt. Solemnly they raised their small hands and salaamed her. Her first school in Siam! Most of them were half-brothers and nephews of the Kralahome. A few were dependents, selected for seeming promise. The little girl was a half-sister. Anna began her work gratefully. It was a comfort and a wholesome discipline.

And so June passed and July began.

Anna realized as the days went on that she had given up the unequal struggle with the King and abandoned her expectation of having a home. The acknowledgment of defeat brought no feeling of resignation, however. She felt thwarted by her inability to exact fulfillment of her contract, and wrote Francis Cobb that she might return to Singapore after all. He did not press her, but he did write to say that he was having a picture of Avis painted on ivory for her from a photograph that Mr. Heritage had made before Avis sailed, and that he would hold the miniature until he heard what she had decided to do.

She had come to Bangkok full of high hopes and great plans. After the two difficult years in Singapore since Leon's death, she had welcomed the thought of regular paid employment. She had anticipated life in new surroundings, for familiar ones kept alive the aching pain of her loss. And above all she had craved hard work. She loved to teach. She had imagined herself helping an enlightened monarch found a model school that would set the pattern of education for a country just emerging from medievalism. She had looked forward eagerly to influencing a nation through its royal family. She believed so passionately in human freedom, in human dignity, in the inviolability of the human spirit, that she had thought when the chance came to penetrate the harem, the very heart of the Siamese system of feudalism and slavery, that God had meant her for a liberator. Perhaps—she had dreamed—she would teach some future king, shaping his child mind for a new and better world.

Thus she had left Singapore with a sense of mission that was strong enough to resist the objections of her friends who considered the whole venture wild and dangerous. She was a woman, slight, almost frail in appearance; not someone who could fight with guns to free the slaves, as in the United States, but someone who could fight with knowledge in the corner of the world where she found herself. But now all her multicolored bubbles of hope were gone, shivered to fragments on the floor of two squalid rooms at the end of a Bangkok fish market.

Nor could she rouse herself from the apathy that had overtaken her. She found the children in the Kralahome's palace responsive and interesting. But she continued to feel despondent. Every morning she whipped up her energies anew to begin the day's lesson. And the very effort of will wearied her. She wished to make the most of the opportunity, and fought the engulfing discouragement, only to realize that day by day she was growing more and more dispirited. Go or stay—did it matter?

Then one morning as school was about to commence Khun Ying Phan walked into Anna's room unannounced.

82

"Mem *cha*," she said, "I have found a house for you."

Anna sprang up with such an influx of joy that her heart almost burst.

Lady Phan smiled at her radiant face and begged her not to expect too much. "But it is on the river and has a small garden. And you may have it if you like. Do you want to go and see it now?"

Anna was amazed to discover that she could be happy again. Listlessness and depression vanished. She thanked the Khun Ying for her kindness with such enthusiasm that the Siamese woman laughed, protesting that Anna must not thank her until she knew whether there was any reason for gratitude. But Anna's excitement could not be dampened. She snatched Louis from his chair and covered his small face with kisses until he protested.

School was dismissed before it began. Anna hurriedly dressed for the street and collected a few things to take with her. A young brother of the Kralahome was appointed guide to the new home.

"Come, Boy," Moonshee said in Malay, "we'll go, too. The house must be a paradise since the Great Vizier bestows it upon the Mem sahib, whom he delights to honor."

Since the house was not far from the palace, the little procession started out on foot. They passed through several narrow streets and came at last to a walled enclosure, which they entered. At first glance it was not promising. The yard was covered with a rubble of broken stone, bricks, lime, mortar, as if from some demolished building. A tall dingy storehouse occupied one side of the compound. The opposite side was a wall with a low door opening on the river. At the far end of the yard stood the house itself, shaded by several fine trees that drooped over the piazza and made it almost picturesque. This was a thousand times better than the fish market!

When they entered the house, however, their enthusiasm faltered. They were in the presence of overpowering filth. Rotten matting covered the floors. Gory expectorations of betel stained the walls. Moonshee began to curse in a low monotone, and Anna did not rebuke him for he expressed the sharp disappointment they all felt. Out of his extensive vocabulary he execrated his own fate, damned in vivid detail this land of infidels, and reviled all viziers. Anna grew conscious that so superlative a performance implied an audience, and turned to see to whom the old Persian's lamentations were addressed. There, seated on the floor in the corner, was a second Mohammedan. No one seemed to know how he had got there. Apparently he had materialized from a crack in answer to Moonshee's need for a sympathetic listener! Many times Anna and Louis had seen Moonshee pontificating to just such an appreciative fellow· Moslem when things had gone wrong. The familiar drama in this unfamiliar scene brought back sharply other years and other places, and they both burst out laughing. Filth or not, home was beginning to fall into a familiar pattern.

With renewed courage they explored further. The house had nine rooms, including bathrooms and a kitchen. Some of the rooms were pleasant and airy. There were two stories. In Oriental style the bathrooms, kitchen, and storehouses were separated from the main body of the house by a court—open to the sky, but walled in on the ends. In this bank of rooms were quarters for servants.

Except for the dirt the house was livable, and soap and water would remedy that. Beebe and Boy were very optimistic. They hurried back to the front room and put an end to Moonshee's rhetoric by ordering him to enlist the services of his audience and some Chinese coolies, if he could find them, in fetching water and scrubbing. He protested that there were no buckets. But Anna gave him a few dollars and packed him off to buy some. With the philosophical resignation of the good Moslem he stopped his discourse and set out, his new friend in tow. Louis was tied into a pinafore by Beebe. He had announced that he would help clean while Beebe returned to the palace to pack their belongings. Almost without discussion they had decided to stay.

In this interim of quiet Anna sat down on the only chair in the house, a broken one of Chinese design, to plan the attack. The first question was where to begin. There was so much filth, and it was so monstrous in quantity and kind. The Kralahome's brother, who had settled himself negligently on the railing of the piazza, wandered into the room and stared at Anna with interest. She stood up and shook her head at him firmly until he retreated outside. Then she marched through a broken door into an inner room. She hung her bonnet and mantle on a rusty nail in the wall and slipped out of her neat half-mourning. She had brought an old wrapper and this she put on. Then she flung open the door and dashed at the matting, tearing it up fiercely. After months of boredom there was sheer joy in the use of physical energy.

In due time Moonshee and his new friend returned with half a dozen buckets, but no coolies! Furthermore, Moonshee had been beguiled into assuaging his grief with a cheap variety of the wine of Shiraz. He sat maudlin on the steps, weeping piteously for his beautiful home in Singapore. But Anna refused to be discouraged.

"Get up, Moonshee!" she said unfeelingly. "Go and fetch Beebe. And you can bring the bedsteads and boxes yourself while she helps me. Ask some of the Kralahome's slaves to help you if the boxes are too heavy. We're going to clean at least two rooms, and we're going to stay. So hurry along. Come on, now, get up!" The old man looked at her sadly. He stood up uncertainly and shuffled off sniveling.

As Anna stood on the piazza rearranging her plans in annoyance, Mrs. Hunter arrived. She was neat and pleasant as always. Her husband had told her of Anna's contemplated move. She had brought with her a half-dozen slaves, buckets of whitewash, and rolls of sweet China matting for the floors. In an hour the house had been swept throughout. Three of Mrs. Hunter's slaves were busy whitewashing the walls. The rest were down on their hands and knees scrubbing the floors with half coconut shells. Mrs. Hunter moved unhurriedly about, seeing that water was emptied often, that plenty of soap was used, that every floor was scrubbed twice.

By late afternoon the house was immaculate. The matting, which smelled like new-mown hay, was laid and the furniture carried in and set in place. There was not much of it for so big a house, but there was a table and two armchairs. There were some candlesticks, and many books. Anna thought with pleasure that they came out of their boxes like old friends. There was a piano with remembered songs pent up in it. And in the bedroom Louis' cot had been spread with white sheets and set next to Anna's bed. Snowy white nets were ready to be lowered against the mosquitoes. On the table beside the bed Anna set a picture of Avis. That was the final touch. Anna and Louis were at home.

Mrs. Hunter smiled at the picture and at them. Then she said good-by and set off with her slaves, loaded with Anna's gratitude and a promise that Anna would visit her often and write letters for her in English to her boys who were being sent to England. As she went out Beebe came in through the gate with soup and dainties, prepared with the help of a "Bombay man" she had somehow managed to find.

It was quiet. There was only the lap of the river against the bank and the sound of some children splashing and swimming in it. Boy? Where was Boy? Anna and Beebe found him asleep in one of the empty rooms, dirty but with a look of content on his face. Anna carried him to his bed and laid him on it. Then she washed and put on her muslin, combed her hair, and prepared to queen it at the first meal in her own palace.

All at once it seemed a very solemn moment. As she stood smiling into the mirror memories crowded thick about her. She was home again! The very word was an organ singing through her mind in perfect chords. She did not know why her request for a home had been suddenly granted. It was as mysterious and quixotic as the original refusal. But the wall was down. She had entered her Jericho to the fanfare of unseen trumpets. And that was enough! Whatever the future, she could face it now. The strictures that had bound her heart were gone.

She had her home, her refuge, her integral being. Home! The word kept re-echoing in her mind. It carried her to other places where she had known the same deep peace, back to her mother, and the lap in which she had rested her head when she was a little girl, looking up into eyes whose deep and quiet light had never sparkled with unkindness or anger. She thought of her mother's lips and how they had loved to croon the songs of a far-off and happy Wales, of the comfort and hope and strength and courage and victory and peace that there had been in her mother's presence.

The tide of emotion rising in her heart overcame her. She dropped on her knees beside Louis and threw her arms around him. He awoke as she covered his grimy face with kisses, unable to understand why there were tears in his mother's eyes and why she vowed so passionately that he, too, would have a home to remember, and a mother.

"I'm hungry," he said.

## 13

## THE SCHOOL IN THE PALACE

THE NEXT morning Beebe had a good breakfast ready for Anna and Louis as soon as they were bathed and dressed. It was luxury to be free of the bustle of the great house. They sat down to their leisurely meal with ceremony and mock solemnity, for it was a feast of their glorious independence.

They were not allowed to finish uninterrupted. A vacant chuckle— mere sound unrelated to mirth—announced a presence on the piazza. It was none other than Gabriel of the fish market, in his shabby red coat with the yellow facings. He had an order from the King. Mrs. Leonowens was to present herself at court immediately. This was Thursday, the day of the week sacred to the god of wisdom, Brihaspati, and therefore suitable for the formal opening of the school in the Grand Palace.

"Well," Anna said with some asperity, "it does seem as if I might have been told in advance!"

She had again the sense of being a pawn moved about on a chessboard by unseen giant players. The pattern of the game eluded her, but that there was a pattern she did not doubt.

Nothing must spoil this first breakfast in their own home, however. Boy and she lingered over it until there was no further excuse to dally. Then they prepared to follow their ancient guide. Boy hugged Bessy fondly by way of good-by. Anna left money with Beebe for food, charcoal braziers and other kitchen equipment, and told her that someone was to remain in the house all the time. "If you go to market yourself, Beebe, Moonshee must stay to watch things," she called as she waved good-by.

The same long, narrow, and very crank boat that had taken them to the fish market received them once again. Although it was still early the sun was hot. The oarsmen tugged grunting against the strong current while rivers of sweat ran down their bare backs. At the ornate river landing Gabriel turned Anna and Louis over to slave girls, who conducted them to the Palace through the gate known among the common people as "The Gate of Knowledge." A company of Amazons, smartly dressed in green and gold, then conveyed them to the entrance of the "Inside" where other slave girls waited to take them to the pavilion that had been designated as the new school.

The approach to the pavilion was through a grove of orange and palm trees so thick that Anna and Boy moved in sun-flecked twilight. The slave girls signaled them to wait at the outer portico of what seemed on closer view to be a temple. While the slaves went in to announce their arrival, Anna stood wondering among the tall golden pillars that reached up through shadowy distance to the room. The mysticism of the place descended upon her like a blanket of tranquillity.

At a sign from one of the slaves Anna took Boy by the hand and moved on a little hesitantly into the temple itself, not knowing what was expected of her, nor what to expect. A colossal golden image of the Buddha dominated the great chamber. And in the center of the tessellated floor stood a long table, finely carved, and some carved and gilded chairs. The King and most of the noble ladies of the court were present, with a few priests. A flutter of interest stirred the richly dressed women as Anna and Boy entered, but the priests in their simple yellow robes, barefoot and with shaven heads, continued their silent contemplation of infinity.

The King received Anna and Louis very kindly, with no hint of the ill-temper of their previous meeting. He pointed to two seats that had been prepared for them. An interval of silence followed. Then the King clapped his hands lightly and the lower part of the hall filled with female slaves. A word or two from the King and every head bowed in assent as the group dispersed. When they returned crawling expertly across the floor they were carrying boxes of slates, pencils, ink, pens, and the familiar Webster's blue-backed speller, which they shoved up onto the long carved table. Other women entered, also creeping, with burning tapers and vases of white lotus, which they set on the table in front of each of the twenty or more gilded chairs. Everything seemed to have been prepared in great detail. The formality and perfection of the arrangements were impressive.

At another indication from the King the priests took up a chant. During the calm half hour that the religious service afforded, Anna looked around her. On one side of her and in front of the Buddha was an altar enriched with the most curious and precious offerings of the goldsmith's and jeweler's craftsmanship that she had seen in her travels in the Far East. Beyond this was a gilded rostrum on which the chief of the priests sat, a vigorous man of about fifty. She recognized him as His Lordship, Chao Khun Sa. The anonymity of shaven head and yellow robe could not conceal the strength of intellect and personality for which he was famous. She had already heard much of this man, who had been a follower of the King during the twenty-seven years that the King had been in exile from the throne in the priesthood. She had been told that His Majesty required the priest's attendance on all occasions of importance.

Near the preaching chair on which the learned abbot sat cross-legged was the strangely carved trunk of an old bo tree, and on the tree an image of Indian design, the god Brihaspati, deity of mind and wisdom. Anna wondered with amusement what the silent impressive Buddha high above the altar thought of this interloper from the Hindu pantheon.

The floor was a mosaic of marble and semi-precious stones, so rich in color as to seem almost gaudy. The golden pillars, the friezes above them, and the remote vaulted roof of gilt arabesques, however, served to tone down the whole to their own chaste harmony of design. Anna thought the effect of the temple indescribably beautiful.

When the chant was ended there was a ruffle of music from an unseen orchestra. This announced the entrance of the princes and princesses who were to be her pupils. They advanced in the order of their age. First in line was a girl of about ten. Anna was struck with the rich satin of her skin, the delicacy of her form, and the subdued luster of her dreamy eyes.

The King took her gently by the hand and presented her to Anna, saying simply, "The English school mistress. Princess Ying Yaowalak, first-born among women." The child's greeting was quiet and self-possessed. Taking both of Anna's hands between her own small ones she bowed, touching them to her forehead. Then at a word from the King she retired to her place on the right. One by one, in like manner, all the royal children were presented and so saluted Anna. As the last child inched away along the floor to his place in the kneeling line the music ceased its tinkling and plaintive melody.

The King then spoke briefly to his children, translating for Anna as he did so. "Dear children," he said, "it is our pleasure that you shall be educated in English as well as in your own language. Now as this is an English school, you will have to learn the English modes of salutation, address, conversation, and etiquette. Each and every one of you shall be at liberty to sit in my presence in your chairs when I come to inspect the school. Unless, of course, it is your pleasure not to do so. In this I do not command you. But to study hard and make the best of your opportunities I do command you. This is a privilege no royal children have had before, and you are to make best use of it." The children all bowed, touching their foreheads to their folded palms on the floor in token of acquiescence.

This ended the ceremony, and His Majesty departed with the priests. The moment he was out of sight the ladies of the court were up from their knees and about the table. With much noise and confusion they began to ask questions, turn over the leaves of the spellers, examine pens and pencils, chatter, giggle. Some were interested in Anna's clothing, especially her skirts and the hoops that held them in place. She turned to find two of them standing just back of her, in deep discussion of her person.

As she was beginning to wonder whether she should try to organize her school, slaves arrived and bore the royal children off. She was astonished to see, not only the tiny children, but the bigger boys and girls of eight, nine, and ten, apparently quite unaccustomed to walking even short distances. They were carried away in the arms of women, who were their slaves and human vehicles, as unconcernedly as if they had been infants. "Well!" thought Anna in disgust. It seemed another and revolting manifestation of the hydra-headed slavery of the Palace.

She realized that school was over for the day, and that the ceremony had been merely the formal initiation. No one bothered to tell her when she was to begin the actual work of teaching. Apparently she was expected to hold herself ready at all times. "The King will send Gabriel when he wants me again," she thought with a shrug, and set off to finish moving from the Kralahome's palace to her own new home.

Anna and Beebe spent the next few days making the house habitable. It had been built where the palace of the Grand Duke, late father of the Kralahome, once stood, and material from the palace had been used in its construction. It was comparatively new for all its dirt.

While the two women bought furniture, hung curtains and pictures, and outfitted the kitchen, Moonshee pottered about in the yard clearing away the mass of rubble that still littered it. Occasionally he paused to bring into the house for Anna's inspection some piece of stone with a Thai or Cambodian inscription, or a fragmentary carving in bas-relief from the mythology of the Hindus.

One of the upstairs rooms overlooked a long row of conjoined houses of the Eastern sort, disfigured by the stains and wear of many wet seasons. They were the property of a Mohammedan of patriarchal appearance, who stored sugar in them waiting for a rise in the market. This worthy paid Moonshee a visit every afternoon. His coming was the signal for Moonshee to stop carrying loads of debris to the river and withdraw to the small eastern chamber that had been set aside for his studies and meditations. There the two Moslems propounded solemn questions from the Koran and discussed the neighbors.

From his window Moonshee could see the roofs of most of the houses in the vicinity, huddled together with forms more or less fantastic according to the purse and caprice of the owners. It did not take the old Persian long to learn from his new friend the names of the people who lived under each one, their means and social standing. All of this information he carefully garnered and passed on to Anna. He was childishly pleased to find that they were in a very aristocratic quarter. Most of their neighbors were either members of the powerful Bunnag family, of which the Kralahome was head, or were descendants of Chao Tak, the "Mad King," whom King Mongkut's grandfather had driven from the throne because he claimed to be a reincarnation of the Buddha. The only unpleasant aspect of their situation was that the hated interpreter lived almost next door.

By the time Anna was called again to the Palace, the family was established in their home. Beebe already knew at what hour the fat Chinese butcher would paddle by in his narrow boat, and which of the women in their broad hats sculling slowly along had the best mangoes for sale. She hailed them expertly and haggled with them from the narrow quay at the river's edge as if she had been doing it for years. The family slipped easily into a familiar routine: on awakening, morning tea and fruit, then baths, breakfast and work; at twelve, tiffin, mid-day siestas, and more work; at four, tea, followed by study, dinner, and then bedtime, with stories and songs for Boy.

Just a week from the day of the formal opening, the serious business of school began. Gabriel put in his chuckling appearance and Anna and Boy set out across the river with him. On this second Thursday a crowd of half-naked children followed them from the dock to the Palace gates. There Gabriel turned them over to a consequential female slave, who was squatting on the ground chewing betel while she waited for them.

When they reached the wall of the Inside the ponderous gate swung open grudgingly to the slave's shouted command, and only wide enough to admit a single person. They squeezed through one at a time and it closed behind them. Before the opposite gate on the inner side of the thick wall was opened, the Amazons of the guard scrutinized them carefully. There was a heated discussion lasting several minutes. One of the guards seemed to question the propriety of admitting Boy. A second countered with a sharp remark, coarsely jocular, for guffaws greeted it, and then they were allowed to enter. Once again they went through the long covered passageways and the oval door of brass into the orange grove. A little breeze riffled the tops of the palm trees making them sigh gently. In the dim cool pavilion the chairs were arranged as before, at the center of the hall.

Several old women, who had evidently been posted near the door to await Anna's arrival, flew off in various directions when she appeared. About an hour later they returned with twenty-one of the King's children. Anna was given a list of their names written in the King's own hand. The names were so difficult that she felt it would be some time before she would remember them, and she copied them carefully into a notebook:

Princess Ying Yaowalak
Princess Thaksincha
Princess Somawadi
H.R.H. Prince Chao-fa Chulalong-
korn
Princess Sri Phatana
Princess Praphat
Princess Phak Phimonphan
Princess Manya Phathon
H.R.H. Princess Chao-fa Chan-
thara Monthon
Prince Krita Phinihan

Princess Srinak Sawat
Prince Khakanang Yukhon
Princess Kannika Kaeo
Prince Suk Sawat
Prince Thawi Thawanya Lap
Prince Thongkon Yai
Prince Kasemsan Sophak
Prince Komalat Loesan
H.R.H. Prince Chao-fa Chaturon
Ratsami
Prince Unakan Ananda Norachai
Prince Kasem Sri Suphayok

The youngest of the royal children was only five, the oldest ten. It was not long before they were ranged around the long table with a Webster before each one, open at the first page. Anna placed Louis at the foot of the table while she went to the head.

The lesson began. Anna said the letters of the alphabet and the children recited them after her. Boy's face was serious with responsibility. He had mounted a chair, the better to command his division. He mimicked his mother with a fidelity of tone and manner that amused and pleased her. Out of the corner of her eye she could see him pointing with his small finger to one letter after the other as his class looked on, letters that were so strange to them and not perfectly familiar to him.

About noon a number of young women were brought to Anna to be taught like the children, but no list of their names was given. She received them with smiles, and began to note their names in her book as they repeated them to her. For some reason this simple action created a panic. She did not know their language well enough to discover why, but she put down the memorandum book and continued the lesson. "Ba-be-bi-bo," she said loudly and clearly. And "ba-be-bi-bo" the royal children chanted in unison. Gradually as the lesson proceeded the concubines recovered from their alarm.

When their confidence was restored they began boldly to take an inventory of Anna's person that was anything but agreeable. Evidently their teacher was much more interesting to them than their lessons. They fingered her hair and extracted some of the hairpins to examine them. One tried to put a hairpin in her own locks, but it dropped out and they all laughed, for her hair was cut in a short brush not more than three inches long, as was that of all the women. They felt Anna's dress, particularly the belt and collar, and then her rings. She discovered two of them flat on their stomachs trying to peek under her skirt.

"For goodness sake! What is the matter?" she asked in annoyance. "What do you want to know about my feet?" From one who spoke Malay she finally learned that the Palace had been seething with excited discussion of her figure ever since her first appearance. The bell-shape of her hoopskirts had convinced some of the harem ladies that she belonged to a totally different species from themselves, with a body that grew larger and larger downward and ended in pedal extremities big enough to fill the vast circle of her skirt.

"Mercy!" Anna exclaimed with a laugh, and lifted her hoops far enough for them to see that her feet and legs were like theirs, except for the boots and hose she wore.

"Ah-ah-ah!" they all breathed, entranced by this new knowledge. Then a slave crouched down in front of Anna and pointed at the Englishwoman's nose. She wanted to know, it seemed, whether Anna's nose had grown long from much pulling, and also whether it had to be arranged every morning to keep it so. Anna assured her that the size of the nose was not a matter of exercise or volition on the part of its owner, but a work of nature. The slave clucked in sympathy and turned away fingering her own flat nose gratefully.

In the meantime one of the girls had put on Anna's cloak and bonnet and was making a promenade of the pavilion, mimicking teacher's walk with considerable success to the delighted shrieks of the rest. Another had pounced on her veil and gloves and disguised herself in them. The children abandoned their studies and laughed boisterously.

The laughter brought a grim duenna from the outer porch. Her wrathful expression was in itself enough to restore order. Instantly bonnet, cloak, veil, and gloves were flung right and left and the young ladies of the harem and their slaves dropped to the floor repeating shrilly "ba-be-bi-bo." The old woman looked balefully around and then squatted near the door and the lesson was resumed.

One young consort, whose artlessness made her seem hardly more than a child, had evidently studied English before. She scorned the alphabet and demanded to be steered at once into the mid-ocean of the speller. But when Anna abandoned her in an archipelago of hard words she soon raised signals of distress.

A few of the concubines began to drift away, already bored with the effort of learning. But at the far end of the table one was studying with rapt attention. She was a pale young woman, dejected and forlorn. She bent over a little prince, obviously her son, with her eyes riveted on the letters that Louis was naming to her. Anna had noticed her first during the commotion that had interrupted the lesson. She alone of the whole group had paid no attention to the hubbub around her. Instead she had kept her eyes on her book, repeating to herself the strange names of the letters, as if the merriment of the others had no meaning for her. Now she stood apart and alone, concentrating on mastery of the alphabet with the help of her small teacher. When the hour for dismissal came she repeated the entire lesson to Boy, who sat listening with imposing gravity. She finished the lesson correctly and Louis pronounced her a "very good child indeed," and told her kindly that she might now go.

A flush of pleasure stirred in her face, but when she saw that Anna was watching her with curiosity, she crouched almost under the table, as if to admit that she had no right to be there and was worthy only to pick up such crumbs of knowledge as fell from the feast of the others. Anna looked at her more closely and saw that she was not so young as she at first appeared. Nor was she pretty, except for her eyes, which were dark and profound. They were expressive eyes, full of reserve and sadness, and they were looking at Anna now in an agony of alarm.

Anna decided that it was the part of prudence, as well as of kindness, to appear unconscious of the other woman's presence, and so encourage her to come again. She put on her hat, veil, and gloves, and took Louis' hand. They walked out past the crouching woman, still half under the table in pathetic eagerness to remain unnoticed, and left the Palace before the King awakened from his afternoon nap. Anna guessed that the concubine had somehow fallen under his displeasure. In the universe of the harem with its thousands of moons circling the single great sun of the King, such disfavor was a terrible calamity. All the way home Anna thought about the concubine. Here, perhaps, was someone who would welcome a new world of knowledge to replace the pomp and circumstance that had collapsed about her.

## 14

## THE RED SNAKE

WHEN THE first confusion was over, the school was quickly organized. Classes began immediately after the nine o'clock service of worship in the temple. Anna had to attend this in order to muster her pupils. The long table, inlaid and heavily gilded, at which the little princes and princesses would presently take up their studies, was the same on which were laid offerings of food for the priests of Buddha. There also were placed bronze censers and golden vases, from which rose clouds of fragrant incense and the perfume of flowers. For the brief period of the service the gloom of the vast temple was relieved by the rich colors of the silks and satins, the gold and jewels of the regal worshipers, and by the deep saffron of the priests' robes. When the priests, looking neither to right nor left, had withdrawn, and the ladies of the harem had retired, school began.

Mornings were devoted entirely to the royal children, some of whom quickly showed promise of becoming excellent scholars. In the afternoons any of the women who were interested were encouraged by the King to be present at the classes. They were never regular, however, as were the children—with the exception of the pallid young woman whom Anna had noticed on the first day. She came every afternoon without fail and squatted behind her son or leaned over his shoulder, studying with an intensity and absorption that would have set her apart if her dejected appearance had not done so.

95

It was some time before Anna won her confidence enough to ask her her name. When she did, she found it inexpressibly charming. For it was "Son Klin," which meant "Hidden Perfume." Anna was conscious of a sweetness under the sober exterior of the concubine and thought the name wonderfully apt. But she was too wise to single the woman out for special help or attention until she could do so unobtrusively. She realized that such attention would be noted instantly by the jealous eyes of the harem, and would add somehow to the crushing load of sorrow that Lady Son Klin carried. The concubine needed no special help, however. Her keen interest carried her along as rapidly as the best pupil in the class.

Once the routine of the school was established Anna had time to examine her surroundings. The Palace, and especially the harem, was a world in itself. When Anna and Louis entered the great double portals each morning they left the ordinary realm behind and stepped into a glittering kingdom out of *The Arabian Nights*.

The first places that Anna explored were the three temples around which the city of the *Nang Ham,* the Forbidden Women, had taken root and gradually grown. They were remarkable. The one in which Anna taught was called "The Temple of the Mothers of the Free." (The name *Thai* means "free.") It had formerly been dedicated to the mother of Buddha as its ancient name of *Manda Maha Gotama* showed. The second was dedicated to *Buddha Thapinya,* Buddha the Omniscient, and the third and most beautiful to *Buddha Annando,* or Buddha the Infinite.

The general effect of these buildings was not unlike that of some great cathedral in southern France. Each was a square two hundred feet long with double rows of windows all around. The windows were flanked by pilasters and crowned with spiral canopies. At the center of each side rose a lofty anteroom terminating in an immense gabled façade. These vestibules converted the temples into vast Greek crosses. The roofs rose in diminishing terraces to pyramidal steeples like Hindu *shivalas,* and these in turn were crowned by spires of gold rising more than a hundred and fifty feet from the ground.

The interiors were two concentric corridors with large recesses for the images, some standing, some sitting, and some in the attitude of preaching from a high lotus-shaped pulpit made of the great snake, the Naga, whose cobra head formed a shade for the preacher. The vaulted cell in the main chamber of each temple, where the central figure was seated, reached to the second or third level of the roof. From a small window in the roof itself there streamed downward on the head of the colossus a flood of sunlight with wonderful effect.

No one seemed able to satisfy Anna's curiosity about the origin of the three magnificent temples. Even the name of the builder had been forgotten. People whom she asked said vaguely that according to tradition the temples had stood there for more than a thousand years, embedded in what had once been a sacred grove of olive, palm, and bo trees. Long before Bangkok had been founded in 1782 as the capital of the kingdom these temples had attracted pilgrims from all parts of the East, particularly women, who came to perform vows or to offer votive sacrifices at the shrines.

The first king of the Chakri dynasty, whose claim to the throne left vacant by the ravages of the Burmese wars had been ability rather than royal blood, chose the site of the triad temples as the seat of his government. He ordered the Chinese trading village that surrounded them cleared away and removed his palace from the west to the east bank of the Chow Phya to found the city of Bangkok. He had surrounded it with triple walls and called it the "great city of the angels."

As often as Anna was to sit in the porches of these temples while the chanted prayers of the worshipers re-echoed through the aisles, she was to be filled with a sense of deepest awe. The character of the buildings was nothing short of sublime. The architect had wrought "in a sad sincerity" and the stone had grown to beauty. Anna was to know every inch of the temples in the years she was to teach there, and yet she was never able to penetrate their meaning and power. Whenever she passed along the dim and silent corridors, and came unexpectedly in front of one of the great golden images amid the gloom of the never-ending twilight—the head and shoulders illuminated by a halo from the unseen source above—she was impelled to stop. The Buddha, motionless with folded arms and drooping eyelids, looking down upon her in monitory sadness, had the wisdom of ages stamped upon his brow. Each time this happened Anna felt again a strange mystical sense of the solemn and profound thought of the unknown builder.

Among her pupils none attracted Anna so much as Prince Chulalongkorn and his pretty little sister Princess Chanthara Monthon, whom everyone called "Fa-ying," or Celestial Princess. They were both exceptionally bright children. Prince Chulalongkorn, the Fa-ying, and their two younger brothers lived with an old great-aunt in the Tamnak Tuk, one of the most imposing of the palaces on the Inside. Their pretty young mother, the Queen, had died the year before and Princess Lamom had undertaken their care. She had raised their mother, too, since the Princess Ramphoei had also been orphaned in childhood.

The old princess was a tranquil woman, attracted by everything that was bright and pretty. She was always busy with her flowers, or some poetry, or her niece's children. The little Fa-ying was her favorite, and after the princess the young crown prince. Her establishment was a very large one, full of the daughters of her brothers, her nieces and nephews and friends; for not only was she a very great lady indeed, into whose home it was an honor to have a daughter received, but she was also famous for her goodness and kindness.

Anna and she had many earnest conversations about the education of Prince Chulalongkorn. The old princess astonished Anna from the first by imploring her to instill into the mind of the young prince the tenets of the Christian faith, its principles and precepts. She drew no distinction between her own religion and Anna's, desiring only that her young charge be fortified with all available goodness against what she knew lay in wait for a king. She was most scrupulous in her devotions, with a freshness of religious zeal like that of a young girl. And, although her nature was happy, she loved too well and too wisely not to have been apprehensive all her life, first for the mother, then for the children.

The children themselves were no problem. They were intelligent and charming, and the little Fa-ying was a fairy child. She was not only her great-aunt's favorite, but also her father's. From infancy the King had liked to have her near him. He held her on his lap at meals and took her with him on tours as far away as Ayuthia.

Prince Chulalongkorn, too, was exceptionally attractive, neither tall nor short, but handsome. He was attentive to his studies, and serene and gentle as well-bred Siamese boys were expected to be. He was invariably affectionate to his old aunt and his younger sisters and brothers. He had a warm heart that was aroused to sympathy by the mere sight of poverty or pain. And he studied hard, seeming to overcome obstacles with a resolution that gained strength as his mind gained ideas. Each new idea was an inspiring discovery to him of his actual poverty of knowledge, and the possibilities of intellectual opulence. The shadow of the throne was already upon him. It had deprived him of any childish love of play. Life for him would be full of heavy responsibilities. As Anna watched his swift young mind hurrying along from day to day, she remembered her dreams and doubled her efforts to help him in his eager search for knowledge. He was only a ten-year-old child now, but who could say when vast and limitless power over the lives of millions would be his?

The studies that took the most absolute possession of the fervid Eastern imaginations of all the royal pupils were geography and astronomy. Each of them had his own ideas about the form of the earth, and it needed much patient repetition to convince them that it was neither flat nor square.

The only map they had ever seen was an old one that had been made twenty-five years or so before at the request of the late king, the Usurper, his present Majesty's older half-brother. It had been drawn by the prime minister of that time, who was a better politician than cartographer. It was five feet long and three wide. In the center was a ground of red, twenty by twelve inches. A human figure as long as the red patch was cut out of silver paper and pasted on it. This was the King of Siam. On his head had been placed an enormous crown with many points, indicative of his vast possessions. In one hand he held a breadfruit, symbol of plenty, and in the other what looked like a pitchfork, with which he consigned to destruction all who opposed him. His legs were miserably thin and met sympathetically at the knees.

On three sides and a part of the fourth was a broad margin of blue, representing the ocean. Over it miniature ships, boats, and junks sailed in every direction to and from the land, showing the great amount of Siam's mercantile trade. Just above the patch of red was a smaller one of green, twelve by four inches, intended to represent Burma. In the center of this was drawn in India ink a rude figure without clothes or crown, the King of Burma. His lack of equipment showed the poverty of his domain. Around him sported rude figures of demons and hobgoblins, showing the disorder and misrule supposed to prevail in his little realm. On the north side of the green patch was painted a large Englishman, wearing a cocked hat with red feathers, and clasping in his arms what was meant for an immense tract of land. This was British Burma, and the Englishman holding on to it was Lord Clive.

But however inadequate the children's knowledge of terrestrial geography, their knowledge of celestial geography was amazing. They loved to tell Anna about it with a wealth of picturesque detail concerning the mountains and seas and countries of this far land; the turtle on whose back it all rested; and the fish that had churned the ocean when the world was forming. Whenever a difference of opinion arose among them as to the height of some of the mountains or the breadth of one of the oceans in the celestial world, they would at once refer to a Siamese book called *Trai Phum Lok Winichai,* a book, they explained, which settled all questions about the three realms of the angels, the demons, and the gods.

Anna did not dispute with them. Indeed, she listened to them with interest. But at the same time she sent a request to the King for maps and globes. His Majesty responded promptly with a large English map and globes of the celestial and terrestrial spheres. These created an enormous sensation when they arrived one morning in the Temple of the Mothers of the Free. The King had caused the map to be mounted in a heavy gold frame, and commanded that it be placed with the globes on ponderous gilt supporters in the middle of the temple. For nine days crowds of women came to be instructed in geography and astronomy. It was hard for them to see Siam reduced to a mere speck on the great globe. The only thing that comforted them was that England, their teacher's country, was smaller yet.

After the first excitement had worn off and the women had left the schoolroom to the children again, the royal pupils began to enjoy their lessons with the map and globes. They would cluster around the latter, delighted with the novel idea of a world revolving in space. Some of them became as keen as any Arctic explorer for the discovery of the North Pole. They seemed to think that if it could only be discovered they could sit astride it with perfect ease and satisfy their doubts about the form and revolutions of the earth.

One day, as they were busily tracing the River Nile, an event took place which profoundly changed Anna's status in the harem. She was telling the children about her own long-ago trip through Egypt when there suddenly fell from the vaulted roof above their heads onto the very center of the chart, which she had stretched on the table, a coil of something that looked at first like a thick silk cord neatly rolled up.

In another instant the coil unrolled itself and began to move slowly away. Anna screamed, and forgetting her dignity fled to the far end of the temple expecting the children to follow her. When she turned she was amazed to see all her royal pupils sitting quietly in their seats with hands folded before their faces in the attitude of veneration. Not a child had moved or made a sound. The temple was profoundly still. All the children's eyes were fixed on the serpent as it moved in lazy tortuous curves along the entire table. With a feeling of shame Anna returned to her seat to watch the beautiful creature. She even managed to share a little of the children's fascination as she looked into the clear eyes of the snake. She had never seen one like it. The upper part of it was a fine violet color. The sides were covered with scales of crimson edged with black. Beneath, it was a pale rose, and the tail ended in tints of bluish ash of a singular delicacy and beauty.

The snake moved on its slow way down the table. To Anna each second seemed an hour. She held her breath in terror as it dropped from the table to the arm of the chair of Prince Chulalongkorn. What if the child moved and the snake struck? She had no doubt that her own life would be forfeit in a moment were the young crown prince to die thus under her care. She wanted to call out to him to hold perfectly still, but no sound came. She need not have worried, however, for he sat as motionless as the Buddha gleaming in the twilight behind him. Anna could not swallow or breathe until she saw the serpent glide from the chair and trail itself through the corridor and down the steps, and finally out of sight under the stone basement. Then she almost fainted from relief.

Not a child had stirred, and not a hand had been lowered from the position of salaam. But on the moment of the snake's disappearance the royal children jumped from their seats and clustered around her in what she saw was the wildest joy. They fell at her feet. They salaamed her and caressed her, and chattered at her so fast that she could not grasp a word. As the news spread the women of the harem came hurrying in to greet her affectionately and to salaam her as they had never done before. It was with the greatest difficulty that she finally learned what it was all about. They were trying to tell her that the gods evidently loved her, else they would not have sent such an auspicious token in favor of her teaching. They assured her that the gliding of the snake all over the table was full of happy omens, and that its dropping onto the arm of the Prince's chair was an unmistakable sign that he would one day become famous in wisdom and knowledge.

Nor was it an ordinary snake. This was the Sanskrit *Sarpa Rakta,* the red snake which brings secret messages from the gods. The Siamese called it the *Ngu Thong Daeng,* the crimson-bellied snake, which confers on the beholder all that is good and great.

Anna hardly knew whether to be amused or annoyed or pleased. Even the King, when he heard of the behavior of the visitor, was impressed. He caused the event to be made known to the wise men of the court. They all united in pronouncing it a wonderful and inspiring recognition of favor from on high. Anna herself felt not a little uncomfortable for days after the sudden appearance of the snake, and secretly hoped that she might never again be so signally favored of the gods. But she did not mention her thoughts to the women of the harem. For they, both young and old, continued to come and congratulate her during the week that followed, grasping her hands between theirs and raising them to their foreheads in veneration.

Whatever prejudice they had had against the innovation of an English school in the Royal Palace—and it must have been strong and deeply rooted, for they were inherently conservative and suspicious of change—was gone overnight. From that time on Anna was treated with great consideration and respect. And she was grateful. Another of the intangible barriers against which she worked was down.

15

## THE PALACE CITY

THE PALACE itself, which at first had seemed too complex to be understood, gradually assumed proportion and form for Anna. It was in reality a walled and fortified city, rectangular in shape, covering more than a square mile. Parallel walls running east and west divided it into three sections.

The northern section comprised the seat of government. In it were the armory, the barracks of the palace guard, the government offices, the exchange, and the supreme courts of justice. Here, too, were the buildings of the Chapel Royal in the midst of which stood the gorgeous temple of the Emerald Buddha. Men came and went freely on official business in this northern enclosure.

The middle enclosure was almost as large. It was approached through two sets of double gates in the wall that separated it from the first section. It was semi-private. Men were admitted only for certain work and certain occasions. In it were the mint, the King's private press, and a number of pavilions, theaters, and aviaries, richly gilded and ornamented. It was dominated by two buildings, one of which was the Amarind Winichai Palace, or "Audience Hall of Indra," near the eastern end, where Anna had first gone with Captain Bush. Close to it stood the largest of the aviaries, so large that trees had been planted in it on a miniature mountain. Around this on all sides were ornate pavilions in Chinese style where the court and the nobility sat to watch processions such as those connected with royal tonsure.

At the west end toward the river rose the second important building. This was the majestic cruciform temple of the Dusit Maha Prasat, where kings had been crowned and where their remains had lain in state in golden urns on the high golden altar. The roof was of glazed tile, each of the four wings being covered with a five-tiered roof. Where the roofs met rose a tapering gold spire supported by four enormous Garuda birds. The terraces were studded with sculptures and large incense vases of bronze, the dark color and graceful forms of which stood out in beautiful relief against the shining white of the building.

But both the first and second enclosures were for Anna mere preludes to the wall that separated them from the third, the city of the *Nang Ham,* where her work was. Not only was this area guarded on its northern side by the wide double belt of the two enclosures; it was protected on the east, west, and south by an inner wall running parallel to the outer wall of the Palace. The ponderous double gates of the latter were guarded by men; the hardly less ponderous gates of the former by Amazons.

The heart of the entire royal city was the palace within a palace, where the King lived. It was on the east of the harem behind its own walls. It was so placed that it could be approached from the outside through heavily guarded gates, and from the second enclosure. The most imposing building within was a large audience hall where diplomats were received. Near this was a state banquet hall and a museum, in which the gifts to the King from the heads of foreign states were housed. There were also private dining salons, an audience hall for the women of the Palace, and several residences with sleeping apartments, a chapel, an armory, and a building for the secretariat. Between this elaborate concourse of buildings and the Chapel Royal at the northeast corner of the walled city stood the old palace of the King's father, almost unused now, but preserved by the King for religious purposes as a memorial to his royal sire.

The windows of the King's palace opened on terraced gardens. These were formal, with orange and pomegranate trees growing in costly Chinese pots. The leaves of ilex and oleander cast pointed shadows on the marble pavements. Porcelain jars were planted with water lilies in every form and color, purple and gold, and pale pink, and white. There was the perpetual splashing of fountains. Stone basins caught the overflow and in the basins gold and silver fish glittered like gems.

Anna had found to her delight a description of the inner city in a book by the venerable Bishop Pallegoix, who had died shortly after she arrived:

> In the third enclosure is a remarkable garden, and containing in miniature a representation of the world as they imagine it to be—woods, mountains, cultivated fields; a sea with islands, vessels of war and merchantmen of every nation; a city, a village, a bazaar, a market; all quadrupeds and birds; and all the rare trees and plants they can produce. They call it the "Garden of Delights," or "Terrestrial Paradise." It is on the model of that at Peking.
>
> As there are persons enclosed here who have never seen the world, and who will never see it, they have thus an imperfect notion of what it contains. It is illuminated at night by lamps. The ladies of the harem retire to the garden and amuse themselves there, if they please, till morning.

This had been written in 1828. Anna could find no trace of the "manikins representing all the different nations of the earth." But there was a beautiful garden, close to the King's palace and within the harem, which seemed to fit the description otherwise. In the center of it was a small artificial lake. Morning and evening the great ladies and princesses came there to bathe. They spent many hours splashing about and picking the water lilies.

Not far from the garden were the barracks of the Amazons and the pillared hall where, as in the days of old, female magistrates daily administered justice to the inhabitants of the city of women. Near the court set in a grove was the Temple of the Mothers of the Free where Anna taught, and next to it the theater and gymnasium where the more important women assembled every afternoon to gossip, play games, and watch the dancing girls.

It did not take Anna long to discover that here, as in any other city in the world, there were good residential areas and poor. Immediately south of the wall which divided the inner city from the center enclosures were some of the finest residences. Here were the palaces of the princesses, daughters of the late king, who were never allowed to marry unless the present king desired them, since there was no one else high enough in rank and a foreign alliance was unthinkable. Here also lived the more favored of the royal consorts with their numerous slaves and personal attendants. In this part of the city there were clean regular streets and small parks, groups of fine trees scattered over miniature lawns, and beautiful flower gardens.

A covered passage led from the harem to the palace of the King. At the end where the precincts sacred to royalty began was a bas-relief representing the head of an enormous sphinx, with a sword thrust through its mouth, and this inscription: "Better that a sword be thrust through thy mouth than that thou utter a word against him who ruleth on high." Anna thought when she saw it of the countless women who had paused there for the first time to read the grisly words. And though the day was warm she shivered a little.

In the southern part of the city, the most populous and least desirable area, were the markets, the workshops of the women carpenters and smiths, and the quarters of the slaves. These plied their many trades for the benefit of their mistresses, even going outside the Palace on occasion to peddle their wares. It was whispered that more than one princess in financial difficulties, perhaps from too much gambling, had made cakes from recipes known only to palace women and sent her slaves outside to sell them. In this section the streets were narrow and dirty, the tenements crowded.

No man was ever permitted to enter the harem city, except the King and the priests who came under guard for religious functions. The slave women were allowed to go out to visit their husbands for a certain number of months every year—as well as on business for their mistresses—but the mistresses themselves rarely if at all until they had attained a small degree of freedom through age and position. King Mongkut, more liberal than his predecessors, sometimes allowed his consorts and ladies-in-waiting to go out for such an important occasion as the cremation of one of their parents. But the privilege had to be sought in writing and was not always granted. Even when granted it cost prohibitively in bribes and tips to the Amazons of the guard. So for most of the harem the city was the world—a world of women, nine thousand of them within the confines of its high walls.

The women of the harem seemed an indistinguishable mass of human beings to Anna, but as time went on the mass broke down into individuals, many of whom she regarded as friends. She first became acquainted with the mothers of her pupils. Their position as *Chao Chom Manda*, Mothers of Royal Children, set them apart. Of the nine thousand women only about thirty were so honored. Most of these were the daughters of noblemen and had been offered for the royal service by their families, who chose the prettiest daughter or niece for this important position. Some had lived in the Palace since childhood as maids-in-waiting to one or another of the princesses. Each princess had her own establishment, large or small, with many such little maids, and each must make out of her narrow sphere whatever life she was to have.

Some did exquisite embroidery work, and taught their maids-in-waiting to do likewise. Some made wax and paper flowers for cremations and for temple decorations. Others were skilled in weaving fragile chandeliers, lambrequins, table covers, and even curtains in lacy patterns of rose petals, jasmine, and other natural flowers, threaded and netted in beautiful designs for important festivals. Some read novels, poetry, and plays and taught their small maids to read also. And some spent countless hours in gambling.

The little maids did light tasks for their mistresses in return for their education in the refinements of palace life. Since there were no schools for girls, it was only girls so trained who had any opportunity for education. All the palace arts were highly prized. They were the mark of the cultivated woman. It was considered an honor for a family to have a daughter in the Palace in this or any other capacity. For, if she caught the eye of the King, or the king-to-be, advancement, wealth, position, and power were in sight for her family.

The royal consorts as well as the princesses had the daughters of relatives and friends entrusted to them. They, too, had their own establishments, and possessed slaves few or many according to their means. The allowances made to them by the King were hardly adequate for the simplest living, but many of them were independently wealthy.

Some of the consorts and most of the princesses were very haughty and insistent upon every ounce of respect and honor to which their positions entitled them. Many, however, were gracious and charming. One of these who became Anna's fast friend was Lady Thiang, mother of her pupil Princess Somawadi. Lady Thiang was the most important of the royal wives. She was a woman of about thirty, fair almost to whiteness, with jet black hair and eyes. She was clever and kind, although as compared to some of the more intellectual women of the harem not highly educated.

But she was the mother of more of His Majesty's children than any other woman, even though she had never been his favorite at any time. She had borne four daughters and three sons to the King, and her maternity had brought her pre-eminence. Now that both queens were dead she had become head wife, not by edict, but by common consent and by the veneration in which she was held. She had another distinction. Of all the women in the Palace she alone, according to Anna's observation, really loved the King as man and husband. She contrived to be always in his favor, serving him with an innate gentleness and understanding that endeared her to him.

He in turn had recognized her complete trustworthiness by raising her to the position of superintendent of the royal cuisine. This was an extremely lucrative position, which carried with it many perquisites, among them two houses. One was her home where her children were born and brought up, a quaint stately edifice with stuccoed fronts in the most fashionable part of the inner city in the midst of a pleasant garden. The other adjoined the royal kitchens, and there she spent the greater part of each day, selecting and sometimes preparing costly dainties for the royal table.

Her natural friendliness had made her generally loved, and her im mense wealth and influence seemed only to have broadened her sympathies. She was always ready to help the other women of the harem, whatever their shortcomings or whatever means she was obliged to use to render them service.

She reconciled her little plots, intrigues, and deceptions by saying: "Surely it is better for HIM not to know everything. HE knows too much already with HIS Siamese and English and Pali and Sanskrit. I wonder HE can ever get to sleep at all with so many different tongues in HIS head."

Another woman who interested Anna, although she never succeeded in getting to know her, was the beautiful Princess Tongoo Soopia. She was a Malay, the sister of the Sultan Mahmud, ex-Rajah of Pahang. The King had fallen fiercely in love with her on her presentation at his court and had procured her for his harem against her will as a hostage for the good faith of her brother. She was a Mohammedan, however, and she maintained toward the Buddhist King a deportment of tranquil indifference. The King soon tired of her coldness and dismissed her to a wretched life of neglect within the Palace walls, but this, too, she bore with seeming indifference. Anna used to talk to her in Malay when they chanced to meet in one of the avenues of the Inside, but the acquaintance was confined to mere civilities.

Of the executive staff, which was very large and included four hundred Amazons, twelve judges, stewards, undertakers, and many other officers, none was so interesting to Anna as the chief of the judges of the women's court. Like most of the executive officers, she was not and never had been a royal consort. Her title was Khun Thao Ap, and she was an unusually tall and commanding woman for a Siamese. She was stout also, and very dark, with soft eyes in a heavy face. Her only real beauty was the graceful form of her hands and arms. Her native aloofness prevented intimacy, but she and Anna soon became friends. Both she and Lady Thiang were much interested in Avis and each sent her silk for a dress on her birthday that first October that Anna was in Siam. Khun Thao Ap accompanied her gift with a little note telling Avis that she was studying English with Avis' mother.

She was a religious and scrupulously just woman with a serious bearing. Everything she said or did was studied, not from the desire to create an effect, but from discretion. A certain air of preoccupation was natural to her. She had secured her high office by dint of attention and penetration, and she kept it by virtue of her supreme but unassuming fitness for the position. She knew everything that took place in the harem, and concealed it all within her breast. Her complete integrity and her reputation for silence brought her the confidences of the women. The hideous symbolical sphinx with the sword through its mouth had no secrets from her.

In spite of her enormous power her way of life was simple and even austere. She lived alone in a small house at the end of one of the main streets where she was easily accessible. She was served by four faithful slaves, who constituted her entire establishment. The rest she had freed.

But none of these women interested Anna as much as Lady Son Klin, Hidden Perfume. It did not take her long to devise a means of seeing the frightened, quiet, passionately eager student. One afternoon Anna went quickly up to the woman before she could run away and asked her if she would not like to come for an hour or two after school for English lessons, since she had gone past the place where Boy could help her. A smile lighted her face and made her lovely for a moment.

"You will teach me?" she asked in unbelieving wonder. "But, lady, I'm not worthy that you should waste your valuable time on me."

"That isn't for you to decide," Anna replied firmly. "I'll be the judge of that when I see what you can do."

Lady Son Klin gave a cry of utter rapture, then dropped swiftly to the floor and embraced Anna's feet.

She was a diligent scholar and came day after day and month after month with a perseverance that none of the other women had. Her expression was troubled and old. She had long been out of favor. Without hope from the King, she had surrendered herself wholly to fondness for her son, Prince Krita Phinihan, who was nine, only a year younger than Prince Chulalongkorn. The King was an affectionate father to those of his children whose mothers had pleased him, but he could not forgive any child a mother who had not. So Prince Krita, although he was the second living son of the King, had the same diffident air of being unwanted as his mother. For the shadows of the harem fell even across the hearts of children.

Lady Son Klin was cautious about accepting the friendship that Anna proffered with equal caution. Gradually, however, their daily lessons and talks became her happiest moments. They gave her entrance into a new world from which no catastrophe could bar her. Her clear dark eyes began to grow calmer as time passed. She rarely talked about herself or her troubles, but Anna succeeded in learning a little. She was a Mon, or Peguan, and of royal descent. Her great-grandfather had been brought to Siam as a hostage, and had been placed in charge of the Mon corps of the army by the first Chakri king, who had found him trustworthy.

By the custom of the time there was no army of Siamese except irregular levies raised during war. The only permanent forces were recruited from captives and their descendants, who were required to give four months of military service a year. The Mon corps under Son Klin's great-grandfather and his sons and grandsons had been, during most of a century, responsible for the protection of the river approach to Bangkok. Her father was Governor of Paklat, one of the river towns. The family had grown rich through the years and Son Klin's father had presented Prince Krita with a palace at his birth. It was on the river bank and the little prince would occupy it when he was too old to live any longer in the harem. Many other relatives were in government service, but they also were out of favor with the King, who was strongly prejudiced against both the Mon and the Annamese.

As the acquaintance ripened Lady Son Klin invited Anna to visit her. After that, the lessons were sometimes in her small and unpretentious home. Her reticence did not melt, however, until one day when Anna chanced to call on the Siamese Sabbath. As a slave led her to a little room that they had dignified with the name of "the study," she saw her friend kneeling in prayer in an adjoining room. On the altar before which Lady Son Klin had prostrated herself was a gilt image of the Buddha, while on either side hung pictures of the King and her son.

The room was covered with gay hand-painted wallpaper in the Burmese style. On it were huge trees, some standing, and others uprooted and carried away by the flood of a mighty river. Here and there they drifted along lifeless, or were covered with flowers. The sun shone through a window on the dark, upturned brow of Hidden Perfume. Her eyes were closed and there was a mysterious joy in her plain face that transfigured it completely. She seemed to be holding direct communion with the Infinite Spirit, oblivious of all else. Anna stepped quietly into the study and waited until the devotions were finished.

In a short time Lady Son Klin's clear voice called Anna to join her in the sanctuary. Anna sat down on the floor beside her before the altar. "Did you see my wallpaper?" she asked.

"I noticed it as I came in," Anna said. "It's a very gay one for your little oratory, isn't it?"

"I see you don't understand the meaning of it," Son Klin said, and proceeded to explain the allegory, partly in Siamese and partly in broken English: "That big green tree there," she said, pointing to it, "is like unto me when I was young and ignorant, rejoicing in earthly distinctions and affections. Then you see I am brought as a gift to the King, and only think how very grand I am and how rich I shall become. And there you see that I am drooping and my leaves are all withering and beginning to fall. Here I am shattered and uprooted by a sense of sorrow and humiliation. And there I am drifting along an impetuous river to destruction, but by and by a little flower stops my downward course. See how pretty it is! That little flower is my child. He springs out of the very waters that threatened my ending. And now he grows into a garden of flowers all over the trunk of the tree, to hide away from me that which would make me sad and sorrowful again. And now I am always glad. Do you see?"

The two women sat quietly for many minutes. Each had known deep sorrow. One's loss had been by death, the other's by humiliation and degradation. In a sense they were both widows, and they both had sons who were all the world to them. A deep bond of sympathy was forged between them in that hour that was to last as long as life.

After a little Anna stirred, shifting her legs, which were becoming stiff. Then she asked curiously and a little hesitantly, "Son Klin, you were praying to that idol?"

Lady Hidden Perfume did not reply at once. At length she laid her hand gently on Anna's arm and said: "Shall I say of you, dear friend, that you worship the image which you have of your God in your mind and not your God? Even so say not of me that I worship the golden image that you see, but the Great One who sent me my teacher, the enlightened Buddha, to be the guide of my life."

16

## MOONSHEE DIGS FOR TREASURE

THE PLEASANT work of making home more homelike had been accomplished. Anna was able to return the various dinner invitations that had come to her. Her social contacts were limited, of course, by the fact that the foreign community of Bangkok was small. The British Consulate had become the hub of Bangkok life not only for the British but for other foreigners. On several occasions during her first year Sir Robert Schomburgk had been host to "a series of public meetings of a social and improving character, superintended by the ladies of Bangkok." Sir Robert had even obliged on one such occasion with a long and very dull essay on a trip he had made to Chiengmai. His heavy German accent clung still to his speech though he had been many years in British service. He was Prussian born, a protégé of Prince Albert. His soirees were not brilliant but they were pleasant, as were the dinners he gave on the Queen's birthday. It was natural that during his consulship his own stilted tastes should have set the tone of Bangkok's social life.

Anna did not mind, however. Sir Robert was a scholar of note, and her own tastes were scholarly also. She liked him better than some of the gayer of her compatriots who grumbled about him. Then, too, she had made friends among the American missionaries, and attended church in their chapel frequently. From them she learned much of the progress of the Civil War, in which she was such a passionate partisan. She was especially fond of the Stephen Mattoons.

At home even the work of cleaning up the yard, which had appeared utterly hopeless, was proceeding with astonishing speed. Moonshee, who had at first shirked the task as below his dignity, was now busy every day with spade and rake. As Anna saw him delving among the stone slabs, examining the rubble with care, she wondered if he had become animated with a sudden access of antiquarian enthusiasm. He offered no explanation, but dug away with his spade hour after hour, excavating bricks, stones, tiles, and carvings. Anna was at a complete loss to account for this new quirk in his behavior, so contrary to his usual dilettante approach to physical effort.

She had told him to clear the surface of the yard, but she had certainly never ordered him to dig out the rubble embedded in the earth, as he was doing. Still, it was a harmless pursuit, and one that Boy enjoyed also. He was interested in the snails and grubs and bits of broken figures that came up from Moonshee's diggings. Sometimes he brought an unusually interesting bit of carving for his mother to see and she put it on a shelf that gradually filled with such pieces.

One evening as she sat musing on the piazza with a book open on her lap she heard Boy's clear voice ringing out in peals of laughter from the spot where the excavating was being carried on. She laid her book aside and went to see for herself what the two had found. On the edge of a deep hole, in a corner of the compound, sat Moonshee, an effigy of doleful disappointment, and beside him stood Bessy, wagging her tail, and Boy clapping his hands and laughing. The old child had taken the young one into his confidence and together they had dug a hole in search of buried treasure! At the bottom of their digging they had found what looked like a rusty purse. His hands shaking with excitement Moonshee had reached for it with the spade. And after several empty hauls, he had fished it up. A toad! A huge unsightly yellow toad!

"May the foul fiend fly away with thee!" he cried in rage, as he flung the astonished reptile back into the pit, and bewailed his kismet, while Boy shouted with infidel laughter.

Anna added no words of reproof to the old man's misery, seeing that he had been sufficiently punished by the severity of his disappointment. For several days after this the spade stood neglected in its corner. Then she surmised from the cautious drift of Moonshee's remarks at the close of her evening Sanskrit lesson that his thoughts still clung to the possibility of discovering hidden treasure. Somehow he had become obsessed with the idea that there was gold buried in the compound, gold for the needs of his Mem sahib and himself, if his spade could only find it. Gold would free them all from the grievous necessity of living longer in this land of *Kafirs*. Anna was touched by his concern on her behalf, and tried to disillusion him gently. But her cold sense made no impression on him. The more he dreamed, the more he believed. But the spot? The right spot? "Only wait!" he said mysteriously with a wag of his turbaned head.

For a week he said nothing more. Then one morning before breakfast while Boy was reciting his lessons, Moonshee entered the room with one of his profoundest salaams, and an expression at once so earnest and so comical that Anna asked him anxiously what was the matter. Panting a little from the combination of eagerness and age, he stammered: "I have something of the greatest importance to confide to you, Mem sahib! Now is the accepted time. Now you shall prove the devotion of your faithful Moonshee, who swears by Allah not to touch a grain of gold without your leave, in all those bursting sacks, if the Mem sahib will but lend him ten ticals, only ten ticals, to buy a screwdriver!"

"A screwdriver!" Anna looked at her old servant as if she thought he had lost his senses. "What in the world can you want with a screwdriver, Moonshee?"

"Oh, Mem, listen to me!" he cried, his face glowing with the rapture of possession. Then he lowered his voice to a sepulchral whisper and leaned close to her. "I have found the exact spot on which the old duke, the Somdet Ong Yai, expired. It is a secret, a wonderful secret, Mem sahib. And not a creature in Siam knows it!" He looked at her triumphantly, expecting curiosity, praise.

"Then how did you come by it, Moonshee," Anna asked in mounting amusement, "since you don't speak a word of the language, which you scorn as unworthy to be uttered by the Faithful, and of no use on earth except to confound philosophers and Moonshees?"

"Listen, Mem, listen," he said with a grandiose wave of his hand, ignoring her levity. "No human tongue revealed it to me." He paused impressively. "It was the Angé Gibhrayeel. He came to me last night as I slept, and said, 'O son of Jaffur Khan! To your prayers is granted the knowledge that for all these years has been denied to *Kafirs*. Arise! Obey! And with humility receive the treasures reserved for thee, thou faithful follower of the Prophet!' And so saying he struck the golden palm fronds he bore in his hand; and though I was now awake, Mem sahib, I was so overpowered by the beauty and effulgence of his person that I was as one about to die. The radiant glory of his wings, which were the hue of sapphires, blinded my vision. I could neither speak nor see. But I felt the glow of his presence and heard the rustle of his pinions, as once more he beat the golden palms and cried, 'Behold, O son of Jaffur Khan. Behold the spot where lie the treasures of that haughty *Kafir* chief!' I arose and immediately the angel flashed from my sight. And as I gazed there appeared a luminous golden hen with six golden chickens, which pecked at bits of blazing coal that, as they cooled, became nuggets of pure gold. When suddenly I beheld a great light of *rooshnees* (fireballs), and it burst upon the spot where the hen had been. And then all was darkness again. Mem sahib, your servant ran down and placed a stone upon that spot, and kneeling on that stone, with his face to the south, repeated his five Kalemahs."

Anna threw back her head and laughed. The next minute she was sorry that she had, for Moonshee's face fell. "I tell you, Mem sahib, I saw it. And all I require is ten ticals for a screwdriver and I will find the treasure for you."

"But, Moonshee," she said kindly, "ten ticals is a lot of money for me. And besides, I do not believe that your dream was anything more than a dream. The old duke's treasure became the property of his son, the Krala-home, a long time ago. And if part of it had been hidden someone would have found it when his palace was torn down, anyway."

But the old man's face was stubbornly set. "I tell you, Mem sahib, it was a vision. And this is the part of the treasure that was buried. All these *Kafir* chiefs bury part of their gold against an evil day. And no one has found it yet."

The only part of the story that Moonshee could persuade her to believe, however, was that the old duke might at some time have buried a part of his riches. She knew that Siamese did bury their gold and silver to save it from confiscation by those in power. In such cases a slave was often im-molated on the spot to make a guardian genius. Many Siamese spent years digging for such caches in abandoned temples. It was said that the ruins of Ayuthia were for decades a heap of diggings where families tried to recover treasure hidden during the siege of the city by the Burmese in 1767, which had resulted in its razing. Even in 1862 treasure hunters were still digging for unrecovered caches at the old capital. These treasure seekers first passed a night near the supposed place of concealment. At sunset they offered to the guardian spirit of the site oblations of candles, perfumed tapers, and roasted rice. When they fell asleep a genie was ex-pected to appear in their dreams and indicate precisely the hiding place of the gold. If the spirit offered to permit the sacking he expected the usual fee, "one pig's head and two bottles of arrack." On the other hand, if the genie appeared in an angry aspect, flourishing a club, the dreamer awoke and ran. Perhaps the old duke had buried part of his vast fortune. It was, of course, possible that it had never been found. Even so, the idea that the Angel Gabriel should have made a personal appearance to Moonshee was ridiculous. Anna's failure to believe the tale and to help him, especially after the promise of riches he had made, mortified Moonshee so much that he vowed the next time the angel appeared he would call her to come and witness the miracle for herself.

"All right, Moonshee," she said, glad to escape with so easy a promise. "You call me the next time the Angel Gabriel comes. And I agree that, if I see the nuggets of pure gold which Gabriel's chickens peck, I'll im-mediately give you the ten ticals to buy the screwdriver." Though why a screwdriver? she thought after he had gone. Perhaps Moonshee meant some sort of tool to pry open the boxes of gold and jewels and precious stones he seemed so sure he was to discover. But the most expensive screwdriver would hardly cost ten ticals. Impractical old man, fond of wine and words, no doubt he felt that ten ticals was a small investment for her to make in an enterprise that was to yield such dazzling profit. She was amused to see that Moonshee's faith in his vision was so perfect that he accepted the promise with complete satisfaction.

Anna quickly forgot the matter in the rush of earning what little gold she thought herself likely to obtain, by dint of teaching at the Palace. But not many nights later she was aroused by Beebe and Moonshee calling, "Awake! Awake! Mem sahib! Come and see! Come and see!"

Drowsy with sleep, Anna leaped from bed in alarm, thinking the house must be on fire. She threw a dressing gown around her and ran into the next room with Boy in her arms. The night was dark, a thick mist rose from the river, and gusty puffs of wind swept through the compound. Moonshee and Beebe were by the window. Silently they pointed to a light glowing in a far corner of the compound. In the wind it cast fitful shadows. Moonshee was staring at it with fixed eyes. "In a moment, Mem sahib, you'll see. The Angé Gibhrayeel will rise out of the flame."

It was an eerie night, the sky and the stars invisible. There was no sound but the lapping of the water in the river and the intermittent sighing of the trees. Anna stirred impatiently, but Beebe put a soft hand on her arm as if to plead for patience. Anna grew weary of waiting at last when nothing happened, and went downstairs followed by her awe-stricken household. Cautiously she stepped out across the yard toward the far corner where the glow still flickered.

The fire was real enough. Smoke rose from it in the wind, and low flames whipped back and forth. But no Angel Gabriel, no celestial poultry rose from it, as Anna with Moonshee and Beebe trembling behind her reached it. On a remnant of matting, with a stone for a pillow, lay an old Siamese woman asleep. She had evidently been driven by the heat to sleep out-of-doors, and she had kindled a tiny fire to keep off mosquitoes.

Moonshee regarded her with mouth agape. "There, Moonshee!" Anna said crossly as she started back for bed, "there is your Angel Gabriel! Don't you ever again trouble me for ticals to invest in screwdrivers. Treasure indeed!"

Margaret Ayer —

17

## THE KING'S ENGLISH

AFTER THE school routine was well organized, King Mongkut demanded Anna's assistance with his English and French letters. This work proved no sinecure since His Majesty's correspondence was enormous.

He had begun it long before in the priesthood. During those years of meditation and study his mind had been probing the scientific knowledge of the West, especially astronomy. This interest was the source of many exchanges with learned men all over the world. But the bulk of the correspondence had been undertaken for diplomatic reasons. Almost alone among his Siamese contemporaries, he had realized early that some revision of his country's traditional foreign policy was necessary, if its independence was to be maintained.

Ever since the French had tried to gain control of Siam in the seventeenth century, Europeans had been objects of suspicion to Thai kings. They had driven the French out by force. The Dutch they had starved of trade. The Portuguese they had reduced to the most menial of positions, until the descendants of this once proud race lived in squalor in one of the poorest sections of Bangkok.

In the nineteenth century, however, the acquisitive fingers of both France and England were reaching out for the Malayan peninsula. During the previous six hundred years this long arm of land that early cartographers called the Golden Chersonese had been under the suzerainty of Siam, and Thai rule had not been oppressive. The various principalities had been required merely to render certain goods in time of peace, and troops and supplies in time of war. Their own princes, having received investiture from the King of Siam, ruled them with little or no supervision. At stated intervals gold and silver trees or flowers of gold were sent to the capital in token of allegiance to the feudal lord.

Only Malacca and Johore had slipped out of Thai control before the British arrived. In 1772 the British East India Company made a first attempt to purchase Penang Island from the Sultan of Kedah, but he told the Company agent plainly that he was the vassal of Bangkok and that "the King of Siam has strictly forbidden me ever to let any Europeans settle in my kingdom." Francis Light worked the corruption of the Sultan with gold and the promise of protection, and succeeded in hoisting the British flag over the island in 1786.

When word of this reached Bangkok, the Thai sent a punitive expedition and drove the Sultan from his throne. Light failed to keep his promise of protection, and the disillusioned Sultan made up his mind to ingratiate himself once again with his rightful sovereign by recovering Penang. But Light collected a small force and attacked him on the mainland before his preparations were complete, for Light intended to keep Penang in the name of the Company, by diplomacy if possible, by arms if necessary, or by both.

In a few more years the Company had a foothold on the mainland opposite Penang also. Then they secured Malacca from the Dutch. And when Prince Mongkut was an astute boy of fourteen, news reached Bangkok that two agents of the Company were intriguing to place a pretender on the throne of Johore—for a consideration. They succeeded. Their fee was the Island of Singapore, and their names were Farquhar and Thomas Stamford Raffles.

The very next year the Company, now seemingly ubiquitous, declared war on Burma, Siam's traditional foe. After a disastrous defeat Burma bought peace with her valuable maritime provinces, which Siam also claimed.

All this Mongkut had seen many years before he came to the throne, but he had observed something else. His political acumen had recognized instantly the significance of the Opium Wars. China, the greatest power in Asia, had failed in a policy of isolation and exclusion. She had been forced to admit representatives of Great Britain for trade and intercourse. The old order, therefore, had passed; and certain things about the new were already apparent. First, that England intended to replace China as the dominant power in East Asia; and second, that, since England was a nation of merchants who traded at the point of a gun, exclusion had become untenable as a policy not only for great states like China, but also for smaller states like Siam. Furthermore, it was obviously important for Eastern nations to acquire the general education and knowledge of science that made European nations formidable.

While he was still in the priesthood Prince Mongkut had begun a discreet correspondence with British officials at Penang, Singapore, and Hongkong. He was acutely aware of the danger hanging over his country from the stubborn exclusionism of his half-brother, the King, and he was hardly more than seated on the throne himself before he was writing to Colonel W. J. Butterworth, Governor of Prince of Wales Island—as Penang was now called—Malacca, and Singapore, to say that:

Our people both of capital and dependent districts and tributary countries around Siam, with their principal heads of Governors, were seemed to be unanimously glad to us both for being successors to the throne. Whole Siamese country is now quite well with [out] any suspect of disturbance distress at any where.

I hope on my [part] the affairs of trade &ca. will be well regulated with the foreign and native people, betterly than upon the time of my predecessors, but I hope you will allow me the time for reformation of custom of country and great ceremony of the funeral service to the dead body of my esteemed brother the late King.

I trust you will be most rejoiced on hearing of my news of succession on the throne as you were longly my dear friend, and that you will write the information to my friend Sir James Brooke, K.C.B., who proceeded to England and let him be glad to me for fulfilling my late statement I had done to him. I have no time to write him now.

I intend to send my other messengers to visit you with some golden and silver flowers which, by custom of Siam, are presents for information of new enthronement or recent crown of country, when I already was crowned . . .

I am unwilling to cut off the friendship between you and me at all, though I would be in highest seat of this Kingdom. Please remember me whenever and wherever you may be in the future. Whereas I was changed from priesthood to the seat of President of country now, I have neglected all my tools and intentions of my own use or left the sacred place for the use of priests. I ought to obtain many things newly for use in my own family out of those that for the royal palace or regal residence. I have therefore placed $1000 in the hands of my man Mr. Nai Bhoom who I have ordered to purchase for me many articles of various curious weapons or articles of gold and silver clothes &ca. and some wooden tools of best wood, mahogany, &ca. I hope your Honor will aid him by directing him to obtain best articles for me, what you would think proper for my use when I am on the throne and where such best thing can be obtained.

And again a month later he wrote rather anxiously:

I beg to assure you that I shall be very glad to accept them if some parties of English men come to my country to visit me, but please stay or stop the affair of negociation of new treaty but one year more, until the ceremony of funeral service of my esteemed brother the late King was concluded, on about March or April of the proximate year.

The ceremony of burning of the Royal King's corpse ought to be done with the greatest pomp, which cannot be finished quickly. If therefore in this interval before conclusion of the King's funeral ceremony, the Mission of British Government may come to our country, it might be great troublesome to us, wherefore I beg to solicit your Grace to delay or expect until May or June of next year, when the proper opportunity allow or was made to us.

By 1854 he was deep in correspondence with Sir John Bowring, Governor of Hongkong, who came to Bangkok the following year and wrote the first of the many modern treaties negotiated during Mongkut's reign. Correspondence with Sir John lasted until the King's death.

Shortly thereafter he was writing to "our worthy noble Friend, Right Honorable the Earl of Clarendon, Her Britannic Majesty's Minister Secretary of State of foreign and colonial affairs in London &ca. &ca." And even to "our Royal affectionate Sister, and distinguished Friend, Her Majesty."

It was Sir John Bowring who had encouraged the King to begin the correspondence with Queen Victoria. The King was quite well aware of the irregularities of his English style, but Sir John reassured him. In his memoirs Sir John says that King Mongkut "thought of writing to Her Majesty and asked me about the style of the letter. I answered, that as His Majesty's English was *perfectly intelligible*, an autograph in his own manner, uncorrected, would be more acceptable than any letter in whose composition an Englishman should be called in to assist." So the King began the correspondence with proper formality:

Somdetch Phra Paramendr Maha Mongkut, by the Divine blessing of the Superagency of the Universe the First King of the Siamese kingdom, consisting of Siamese proper both Northern and Southern and the adjacent tributary dependencies, Laos, Cambodia and several provinces of Malay peninsula
&c  &c  &c
To her Gracious Majesty Victoria the Queen of the United Kingdom of Great Britain and Ireland, the powerful Sovereign of British Colonies almost around the Globe of Human world,
&c  &c  &c
Our most respected and distinguished Friend, and by race of the royalty our very affectionate Sister.
Humble and respectfully sendeth Greetings.

One result of this correspondence and the new treaty relations was an exchange of gifts. Of Queen Victoria's gifts to him the King wrote:

We on this occasion have liberty to let our native photographers take the likeness of ourselves, when we adorned with the watch decked with diamonds and the double edged sword, which were honorary royal gracious gift from your Majesty, received by us a few years ago, and seated ourselves by the tables containing the gift silver inkstand and desk together with the revolving pistol and rifle, wholly being royal gracious gift from your Majesty.

Nor was the King to be outdone in the sumptuousness of his gifts to the Queen. According to his own list these included:

1. The Royal official customary letter slightly written in Siamese characters upon a solid golden plate and wrapped in the Royal solid golden envelope and sealed with Royal peculiar seal and enclosed in a golden case richly enamelled.

The translation of this Royal letter in English annexed or appended herewith.

This is made according to the Siamese Royal custom for very respectful compliment to the Sovereign of Superior Kingdom, not to the equal or inferior always—when the superior Sovereign does not allow to be omitted.

2. Two Royal Daguerreotype portraits, one of which is a likeness of His Majesty the First King of Siam dressed in full royal robes and decorations seated on his throne of state.

The other is the Daguerreotype of His Majesty with the Royal consort and two Royal children seated in Their Majesties knees.

3. A Royal Crown beautifully enamelled and set with diamonds.

4. A Royal Ribbon with circular gold brooches richly set with rubies locked together and fixed all round with blue satin.

And so on through thirty-four elaborate and costly gifts, and sixty-four samples of articles of merchandise mentioned in the tariff schedule of the treaty. The correspondence continued and in 1861 in a long letter the King remarked:

. . . We venture to state that we are desirous of presenting your Majesty a Siamese decoration made to show a sign of ourselves or of our country, which would be appeared or known that it was offered from ourselves, whenever your Majesty might graciously decorate with it and show on any assembly or congregation, it will prove greatest honor to our name in that meeting. Also we are very desirous of receiving an honor from your Majesty's gracious favour, by benevolently bestowing upon us any decoration in any suitable manner to be dressed on our body, and to show in principal meeting that it was bestowed on us from your Majesty as a peculiar royal gift, it will prove greatest honor to us here among Eastern Monarchies. Will the desire occurred to us be proper and agreeable or not? We are the only rule of remote or very distant country from Europe and have very different costume and appearance, yet we became an allied to our Majesty and other several rulers of civilized world, but we are afraid that the decoration made by our native artist, jeweler, gold smith, &c will be very ill construction or more titled manufacture than those of European article, so Siamese manufactured decoration may not be acceptable by your Majesty. Also we are very ignorant of the custom in furnish the style of Diploma which was said to be accustomed to accompany the offered decoration, how it shall be formed in proper manner; for this consequence we have postponed our desire to do so in the present occasion. . . .

After the death of Prince Albert he wrote:

We were sincerely grieved to learn of the decease of Your Majesty's royal mother, and of Your Majesty's royal consort, which two sad events happened on the last year.

We sincerely sympathize with Your Majesty's irrepairable losses, nevertheless, we trust that Your Majesty will find consolation in the thought that all mankind must follow this path, even those most dear to us cannot be prevented from leaving us. . . .

We must now beg to express our pleasure and congratulations at learning that Your Majesty's royal family has been increased by the birth of royal grandchildren. We sincerely trust that they may long remain and will prove a source of happiness to Your Majesty. . . .

This correspondence was, of course, no random affair. It was shrewdly calculated to further friendly relations between Siam and England, and to thwart the more rapacious empire builders.

In the year before Anna came to Siam there was an exchange of letters between the King and Abraham Lincoln. It was of an entirely different character. The King had read that in the traveling menageries, which were very popular in the rural areas of the United States, the elephant was regarded as the most remarkable of the animals on display. He had further read that there had been an importation of camels from Arabia. His fertile brain immediately conceived a service that he thought he might render the United States. He wrote:

Somdetch Phra Paramendr Maha Mongkut, by the blessing of the highest superagency of the whole universe, the King of Siam, the sovereign of all interior tributary countries adjacent and around in every direction, viz: Laws of Shiengs on northwestern and northern; Law Kaus on northern to northeastern to southeastern; most of the Malay peninsula on southern and southwestern; and Kariengs on the western to northwestern points, and the professor of the Magadhe language and Budhistical literature, &c., &c., &c., to his most respected excellent presidency, the President of the United States of America, who, having been chosen by the citizens of the United States as most distinguished, was made President and Chief Magistrate in the affairs of the nation for an appointed time of office.

It has occurred to us that if, on the continent of America, there should be several pairs of young male elephants turned loose in forest where there was abundance of water and grass, in any region under the sun's declination both north and south, called by the English the torrid zone, and all were forbidden to molest them, to attempt to raise them would be well, and if the climate there should prove favorable to elephants, we are of opinion that after a while they will increase until they become large herds, as there are here on the continent of Asia, until the inhabitants of America will be able to catch and tame and use them as beasts of burthen, making them of benefit to the country, since elephants, being animals of great size and strength, can bear burdens and travel through uncleared woods and matted jungles, where no carriage and cart roads have yet been made.

We on our part, will procure young male and female elephants, and forward them, one or two pairs at a time.

When the elephants are on board the ship, let a steamer take it in tow, that it may reach America as rapidly as possible, before they become wasted and diseased by the voyage.

When they arrive in America do not let them be taken to a cold climate out of the regions under the sun's declinations or torrid zone, but let them with all haste be turned out to run wild in some jungle suitable for them, not confining them any length of time.

If these means can be done, we trust that the elephants will propagate their species hereafter in the continent of America.

Mr. Lincoln already had a great deal on his hands, what with the Civil War and other difficulties, but his reply was courteous:

I appreciate most highly your Majesty's tender of good offices in forwarding to this government a stock from which a supply of elephants might be raised on our own soil. This government would not hesitate to avail itself of so generous an offer if the object were one which could be made practically useful in the present condition of the United States. Our political jurisdiction, however, does not reach a latitude so low as to favor the multiplication of the elephant, and steam on land, as well as on water, has been our best and most efficient agent of transportation in internal commerce.

I shall have occasion at no distant day to transmit to your Majesty some token or indication of the high sense which this government entertains of your Majesty's friendship.

Meantime, wishing for your Majesty a long and happy life, and for the generous and emulous people of Siam the highest possible prosperity, I commend both to the blessings of Almighty God.

Your good friend,<br>ABRAHAM LINCOLN.

Washington, February 3, 1862.
By the President: William H. Seward, Secretary of State.

On foreign mail days Anna always spent from eight to ten hours with the King's outgoing letters. The work was delicate and difficult because

His Majesty was both fickle and tyrannical. It seemed impossible to please him. He would write letters, sign them, affix his seal, and dispatch them in his own mailbags to Europe, America, or elsewhere. Then, later, he would order Anna to write to the parties addressed to say that the instructions they contained had been an error—*her* error, of translation, or transcription, or anything but his intention. Sometimes she succeeded in slyly wording these second letters in such a way as to reverse the orders without compromising either the King or herself. But not always.

One thing she insisted on. If she was to work in the same room with His Majesty, she must be allowed to stand upright in his presence. The froglike crouch that had been permitted her as a special dispensation was intolerable for more than a few minutes. The King agreed. He specified, however, that she must sit down when he did, on a chair if he sat on a chair, on the floor if he sat on the floor. This was acceptable to Anna. In operation the compromise proved somewhat arduous in spite of its reasonableness, since His Majesty's favorite position was prone with a book propped up before him, his heels swaying to and fro in the air.

Fortunately the King was often busy in other parts of the Palace. While Anna worked, His Majesty's principal private secretary, whose title was Phra Alak, lolled in the sunniest corner of the room, stretching his limbs and nodding. Anna never saw him other than drowsy, for all the sleep he ever managed to get was stolen. The King's working moods were capricious; he was busy while the average man slept and asleep while his secretaries waited with important letters, papers, dispatches. Anna was called in the middle of the night many times to assist in some letter so important that the writing of it could not wait until morning, only to learn the next day that the mail boat had been held at its mooring for hours waiting for the royal correspondence which could not be sent because His Majesty had fallen asleep.

Phra Alak was on twenty-four-hour duty. He and the King had played together as boys, studied and entered the priesthood together. He had been at once slave, friend, and classmate, so it was natural that he should have become confidential secretary as well. But it was not an easy life. The old man was stiff with continual stooping to his task, and subdued by a life of service in which he was threatened and cuffed, then taken into favor the next moment; was kicked and beaten on the head, then restored to confidence and bosom-companionship, as the King's mood veered.

Usually he bore the ills of his employment with patience, but there were times when, goaded beyond endurance, he fled to a home of his own about forty yards from the Grand Palace to snatch some rest and refreshment in the company of his young wife. Then the King would waken and demand him. A messenger would be sent to find him, and Phra Alak would plead that he was ill and could not possibly rise from his bed. Or he would tell his wife to say that he was out and that she did not know where he was, while he hid under a mountain of bedclothes. He had used this trick so often that its very staleness infuriated the King, who invariably sent officers to seize the terrified wife and lock her up as hostage for the scribe's appearance.

At dusk Phra Alak would emerge, rested and contrite, and prostrate himself at the gate of the Palace. The King, who had spies posted in every corner of the city and knew as well as Phra Alak himself what his secretary had been doing, would stroll forth. Seeing his recalcitrant slave stretched on the threshold, he would fly into a genuine rage and order him beaten with sixty lashes across the bare back and decapitated on the spot. While two attendants flew right and left—one for the blade and the other for the thong—His Majesty would seize whatever came handy and belabor his friend on the head and shoulders.

Having thus relieved his feelings, the King would dispatch the royal secretary for ink-horn and papyrus, and begin dictating letters, orders, appointments. The scimitar and lash were slow in arriving on these occasions. The slaves sent after them had played their parts in the masque many times and knew that the King would have forgotten his rage before they appeared. Perhaps in the very thick of dictating, the King would remember Phra Alak's wife and would order someone near to him to release her.

It did not seem strange to Anna, then, that to Phra Alak there was no greater luxury than napping in the sun for an hour or two. "Mem *khrap*," he murmured dreamily on one particular morning, "I hope in the *chat na* (the next birth), I shall be a free man."

"I hope so sincerely, Phra Alak," she answered. "I hope that you'll be an Englishman or an American, for then you'll be sure to be independent."

She was busy that morning with a letter to the Earl of Clarendon. She had found that any attempt at partial correction only made the King's meaning ambiguous and dulled the striking originality of his style. So she had learned to copy his letters with literal exactness. On this occasion she was merely debating whether to leave "wilful" and "well-wishing" out of the sentence, "I hasten with wilful pleasure to write in reply to your Lordship's well-wishing letter. . . ."

In the summer and fall of 1862 the King's correspondence was especially full of the affairs of the Malay provinces. The Governor of the Straits Settlements, which were still officially part of India, had been charged with the power to negotiate treaties with the Malay principalities. These treaties first recognized a Malay state as "independent," which meant independent of Siam, and then bound it by commerce, diplomacy, and force to the expanding British Empire. Colonel W. Orfeur Cavenagh, who was destined to be the last of the Indian governors, was aggressively pushing British control farther and farther up the peninsula.

He refused to recognize Siam's ancient claim to suzerainty, and in his zeal was careless of the niceties of diplomacy where they interfered with his purpose. In 1861 he had sent the sloop *Coquette* and the corvette H.M.S. *Scout* to Trengganu—one of the indisputably Siamese provinces —to compel the Sultan to surrender the ex-ruler of a Dutch island, Mahmud Mozzaffer Shah, who had taken refuge there. Governor Cavenagh's reason for this irregular procedure was that he suspected Mahmud of plotting against the state of Pahang, next-door neighbor of Trengganu. The governor had decided to undertake the "protection" of Pahang himself. When the Sultan of Trengganu refused to yield to Cavenagh's demands until he had received orders from Bangkok to do so, the British dismantled his fort, spiked his guns, and destroyed all the shipping in his harbor.

Not even Cavenagh's associates approved of his arbitrary methods. Sir Richard McCausland, Recorder of Singapore, had long been a friend of King Mongkut's. Through him the King secured information and advice that made it possible to counter somewhat the blind determination of the governor to extend the British Raj at any cost.

In 1862 serious trouble threatened again. The younger brother of the Sultan of Pahang invaded Pahang on his own behalf. Governor Cavenagh became convinced that Trengganu had supplied the pretender, Ahmad by name, with ninety guns and forty barrels of gunpowder, and was continuing to support him with men and supplies. Since Trengganu was tributary to Siam, Cavenagh suspected King Mongkut of complicity. On November 3 he sent an ultimatum to the Sultan in which he threatened that unless in twenty-four hours all aid to Ahmad was withdrawn and Mahmud was expelled he would order Trengganu City shelled, all its shipping seized and destroyed, and its entire coast blockaded. The Sultan proudly rejected so outrageous a demand, violating as it did the treaty between Siam and Great Britain.

The court and city of Bangkok were electrified to learn very shortly that Governor Cavenagh had made good his threat. The *Coquette,* the *Scout,* and the *Tortoise* had fired two hundred rounds into the town. Siamese nobles and people seethed with anger and fear. The helpless city of Trengganu, its guns demolished by the previous British assault, had been unable to make any reply. The foreign community of Bangkok, too, regarded the shelling as a wanton outrage upon Thai sovereignty and speculated on the possibility that Governor Cavenagh was manufacturing incidents to justify further aggression, perhaps aimed at invasion and annexation of Siam itself.

On the ninth of December the *Coquette* and the *Scout* anchored at Paknam, the port of Bangkok. Panic and conjecture were rife in the capital. Even the British Consul, Sir Robert Schomburgk, was alarmed. He hurriedly wrote a letter to the port authorities informing them that Lord John Hay, Commodore of the British fleet in the Indian Ocean, had brought two ships of war to anchor outside the bar and requested permission to come up on one of them to Bangkok, for what purpose the consul disclaimed all knowledge.

When the Ministers of State, the Senabodi, had read the letter, they held a series of hasty consultations. Sir Robert informed them frankly that Lord John Hay was coming up on the eleventh, with or without permission.

The alarm of the Siamese increased when they learned that Sir Robert was hastily warning his friends among the business men and shopkeepers to look well to the disposition of their merchandise. Lord John Hay outranked him both in birth and position and had not deigned to intimate to him what had brought the warships to Bangkok. But if Lord John intended to treat Bangkok as Trengganu had been treated they could judge for themselves what the effect would be upon the flimsy wood and bamboo structures that made up most of the city. The only calm voice was that of Mr. Thomas George Knox, the interpreter to the consulate, who assured the Senabodi that he did not believe that Lord John Hay would presume to usurp the diplomatic function of the consul by attempting negotiations backed by force in regard to the Trengganu affair. And if he did, then Mr. Knox would gladly forward a strong protest on behalf of the Siamese to London where Mr. Knox had excellent connections through Lord Stanley.

The King and Council did not debate long. They hurriedly sent several important noblemen to the bar to escort Lord John to Bangkok. They had decided that refusal might incite the British to spike the guns and dismantle the forts which lined it at intervals. It would be wise to give them no excuse. Thus they would have to make an occasion, if determined to have one. Otherwise they would arrive in Bangkok to begin negotiations, if that was their intention, having been given a reception that would make it hard for them to open conversations on any but a friendly basis.

The noblemen sent were all of high rank. They had instructions to do everything in their power to ingratiate themselves with Lord John, and to disarm any feelings of ill-will he might have. According to the custom of the country they took with them large presents of fresh food for the officers and men of the ships—sugar, bunches of bananas, and chests of tea.

Lord John received the committee of welcome affably, although he declined the gifts they had brought on the grounds that it was contrary to British custom to accept them. He inquired after the health of the King and the members of the council of the Senabodi. The motors of the *Coquette* were started and before dusk she lay at anchor below the British Consulate. The Thai noblemen breathed a sigh of relief. Nothing at all untoward had happened on the way.

Within an hour Sir Robert sent a letter to the King advising him that Lord John Hay had come to present his respects to His Majesty and the government. Would His Majesty be so gracious as to appoint an hour at which Lord John might be received in audience?

The next afternoon the King sent for Anna peremptorily. School was over for the day and she was sitting comfortably in her parlor enjoying a book. It was one of the cool and sunny afternoons, full of the golden light peculiar to autumn in Siam, that make December a pleasant month. She shut her book impatiently, and followed her guide to the Palace. She was conducted to the audience chamber of the inner court, which was used only by the women of the King's household.

The King took no notice of her at first. He was anxiously scrutinizing some pretty young women who were prostrate before him. Each of them was beautifully dressed in a gauzy costume and jewels which displayed to advantage their arms and shoulders. At last he seemed to become aware of Anna's presence and turned to her.

"Mem," he said, "shall it be proper for English Ambassador to make request to see some of our most beautiful women?"

Anna was astonished. She had shared with the rest of the city the intense excitement that had gripped the people at the knowledge that British men-of-war were on their way to Bangkok. She had been turning over in her mind what she and Boy ought to do if shelling started. The two of them with Beebe and Moonshee had stood on the piazza the evening before and watched the slim shape of the *Coquette,* with the last of the sunlight glinting on its uncovered guns, moving up to the British Consulate across the river.

She had heard the rumors that flooded the capital—how the Second King had hurriedly gone up-country more than a week before; and how his officials and close friends had been packing and following ever since. This was regarded as a sign that trouble was expected, for the Second King had long been a close friend of Mr. Knox at the British Consulate. Hadn't Mr. Knox worked for the Second King as drill sergeant when he first came to Siam from India penniless more than ten years before? And hadn't the Second King provided Mr. Knox with a wife from among the girls of his household? What more natural, then, that Mr. Knox should return these favors now by warning the King so he might flee and hold himself available in case his older brother, the First King, should fall a victim to armed invasion? Perhaps the British were even plotting with the Second King to overthrow Mongkut and supplant him with his more popular brother in return for favors and concessions in the Malay provinces.

When Anna received the summons to the Palace she supposed that a serious crisis had arisen, perhaps even that the King was about to flee upriver to Ayuthia and wanted her to accompany his harem. His calm examination of the girls on the floor, and his strange question amazed her.

"What did Your Majesty say?"

"Lord John Hay! Shall it be proper for him to make request to see some of the ladies from the Palace?"

The King's preoccupation with so trivial a thing was reassuring. Somehow he had become convinced that there was nothing alarming about the arrival of the British ships. Anna breathed a sigh of relief and answered guardedly, "Has Lord John Hay asked to see some of the women?"

"No, not yet, but he will. Shall it be proper?"

She did not question the King's source of information, for she knew that even the consulates were full of his spies.

"If Your Majesty were in England or America," she said judiciously, "you would wish to see the prettiest girls in either country, and it's natural that Lord John Hay wishes to see some of the most beautiful women here, since he's never been in Siam before. Of course, he takes it for granted that they are in the Palace."

"But I can't let him see them as they are with black teeth and no shoes on feet," the King countered, throwing her a speculative and cunning look. Apparently he had determined to make a grand impression if he let the unprecedented audience take place. "He will go back to Queen Victoria and tell her that our women are black and without clothes, or stockings or shoes on feet, and she will consider me as barbarian of Sandwich Islands. So, Mem, you must educate some of these young women in European etiquette and costume for presentation to the English Ambassador of Great Britain."

"But, Your Majesty . . ."

He waved his hand imperiously. "I shall appoint women to sew for you, and you will cut out according to proper pattern. And I will have sent to you bolts of Chinese and Indian silks for your selection, and you shall choose the best for making the handsomest gowns. Now you must tell me which of these girls are most like European beauties."

Anna surrendered, although she was apprehensive. The girls were all pretty according to Siamese standards. Even by English standards they were lovely in every respect but two. Their teeth were black from betel, black teeth being esteemed as beautiful by the fashionable ladies at court, but the King assured her that a barber would take care of that. And their noses were flat. Anna did not mention this unalterable fault, but chose among the girls those whose noses were the least irregular.

"And when does Your Majesty require that the girls be ready?"

"Saturday afternoon at two o'clock."

Anna sighed. A day and a half!

The next morning the schoolroom was converted into a sewing room. Silks, jewels, flowers, laces, and every assistance were placed at her disposal by one of the high female chamberlains. Anna had often seen such gifts on the marble pavement before the King's private palace. They were placed there every morning for his acceptance, and he looked them over on his leisurely progress from bed-chamber to breakfast hall. Sometimes there were bales of brocade or velvet on silver trays, boxes of tea in carved and jeweled chests, swords in gold or silver scabbards, calicoes, embroidered muslins, fans, priests' robes, precious spices, silver, gold, and curiosities of all kinds—everything that money could purchase or the most abject sycophancy could imagine as likely to please the King. Each noble, prince, and merchant tried to obtain the royal favor by gifts so presented, for it was fully understood between the donor and the receiver that whoever gave the most costly presents might expect the largest share of the royal patronage. Sometimes there were young girls lying on the pavement, too—guarded by old duennas who waited to make the presentation to the King.

Besides the dozens of bolts of heavy silk and brocade brought from the storehouses for Anna's selection, pocket handkerchiefs, hose, and jeweled slippers were provided. The only omission was material suitable for undergarments. When Anna remonstrated with the chamberlain on her neglect, she simply replied that there was not time to make any.

Fortunately a pretty little English dressmaker named Annie Elliot happened to be in Bangkok, and she came to help. The two women enjoyed handling the gorgeous materials, cutting, fitting, and planning. They trimmed the court robes with costly laces threaded with gold. The effect was most satisfactory. The Princess Phanrai, half-sister of Prince Chulalongkorn's late mother, had been chosen as most suitable of the women to receive the commodore. The five pretty girls whom Anna had selected were to be her maids-in-waiting. They were both excited and fearful, flattered by having been chosen, and alarmed at the ordeal ahead of them. But they thought it great fun to have hoopskirts like the Mem, and each paraded up and down the temple in hers as soon as it was finished.

True to his word, the King sent the royal hairdresser and barber to scrape the teeth of the six until they were as white as milk. On Saturday morning a Chinese artist arrived at the temple to paint their skins white also. Their heads were covered with wigs of European hair, curled in the latest fashion, and bound with ropes of pearls, rubies, and diamonds. With the addition of jeweled brooches, necklaces, and bracelets, they were really a dazzling sight.

Then it was time for their drill in European etiquette. All that was required of them was that they sit behind a magnificent crimson curtain, wrought with gold, that had been hung across the temple at the King's command. When the curtain was drawn and His Majesty made the presentation, they were to rise, bow, and retire backward. Somebody had told the King that no one ever turned his back when presented to Queen

Victoria, but withdrew face forward. His Majesty was imperative, therefore, in requiring this on his own behalf and that of the English Ambassador.

The girls promised strict obedience; but they were excited and inattentive and Anna was soon in despair. None except the princess was more than fifteen. Each had a small looking-glass. They were so delighted with themselves that even while Anna made them walk in and out of the temple, bow to her in the Western fashion, and then retire, they would be peering at their faces in the mirrors they held in their hands. Over and over Anna made them practice the simple maneuver, while they laughed and grimaced and jabbered all the time until she almost lost hope of making any kind of impression on them.

She was nearly exhausted as two o'clock approached. At last a distant bugle announced the arrival of the grand visitor. Anna gave up further coaching and seated her charges on the row of gilt chairs that had been brought in for them. She could do nothing to quiet their giggling, but they looked charming in their hooped skirts of rich blue and rose and green with the jewels sparkling on their wigs and necks, arms and fingers. Anna knew a brief pang of regret that there had been no time for undergarments, although a critical examination reassured her that the heavy brocades were so thick that no one could possibly have guessed the omission.

By the time Anna succeeded in marshaling them to their chairs in proper order, Lord John and the King were already in conversation. The public audience, at which the nobles of the court and the officers of the ship had been present, was over. The King had withdrawn to his private chambers where he had been followed at a discreet interval by Lord John and Sir Robert. The King was questioning Lord John about his purpose in coming to Bangkok. Lord John replied that in his three years in the Orient he had visited every other court but Siam's. Now that he had completed his tour of duty and was to return to London in five months he had embraced this opportunity of calling to pay his respects to the King. He said that he had heard of His Majesty's remarkable accomplishments in the use of the English language, and had rejoiced to know that the King's regard for the English was so great as to have induced him to master this most difficult foreign tongue. He went on to add that it had occurred to him that he might further the cause of Siamese-British amity if he could report to Her Majesty Queen Victoria that he had waited upon her good friend, the King of Siam, before taking his leave of the East. From this the King was able to deduce that the visit of the two warships and the commodore was a tacit apology for the recent shelling of Trengganu in which the King had learned that Lord John had had no part. It had been ordered by Governor Cavenagh and carried out by a subordinate. Lord John went on to say that he had planned to come to Siam earlier, but had not been able to do so. And he understood that in the interval Her Majesty Queen Ramphoei had passed away. He wanted to know if another queen had been elevated to the throne, and if so, he requested the privilege of paying his respects to her also.

The King replied that no one had been elevated to the position as yet. Sir Robert interposed smoothly, "It is surely most regrettable, Lord John, that you did not visit Bangkok during the lifetime of Her Majesty, but I believe that her younger sister is still living. And it may be that she can be prevailed upon to receive you, with His Majesty's consent."

Lord John turned a questioning eye on the King and added that he would be delighted to present his compliments to the Queen's sister, if she would be so gracious as to receive them. His Majesty frowned, thought a moment, and said that it could be arranged. He then dispatched a slave to tell Anna to have the girls in their place in about fifteen minutes.

The giggling and chattering of the girls had gradually subsided, only to be replaced by nervousness. There were bursts of hysterical laughter mixed with agitated questioning. One girl, trembling from head to foot, turned to Anna and inquired, "What kind of men are *farangs?*"

Another, obviously pale under her paint, clasped her hands tightly on her lap and asked, "Is it true that they have hair on their chins like goats, and are cannibals?" There was a rumor in the harem that all Englishmen were bearded—very repulsive to a beardless people—breakfasted off little children, and carved up young girls for dinner. And furthermore, that many of them had evil eyes, terrible blue eyes that could look straight into their victims' souls and trap helpless spirits forever. The girls had remembered these stories at the critical moment, and it was as much as Anna could do to keep them from running away.

A second time the silver bugle sounded. His Majesty entered at the other side of the temple with Lord John and Sir Robert. A ruffle of flute music followed and the curtain vanished. The Englishmen and the Siamese beauties were face to face.

Unfortunately Lord John did wear a full beard and a heavy mustache, which mingled and flowed down upon his breast, leaving only his eyes and nose visible. This was a profound shock to the Siamese girls, who sat frozen in their chairs. It was what they had feared and expected, however, so it was Lord John Hay who was taken most completely by surprise. He was quite unprepared to find what seemed in the half-light of the temple to be European ladies in the royal harem of Siam. As if to make sure, he raised his monocle to his right eye and began to examine them from head to foot as the King made the presentation.

Then he bowed profoundly in his most courtly manner. The girls instead of rising and bowing, all uttered little shrieks of terror, clapped their hands over their faces, and peered between their extended fingers at what they regarded as an awful goat-headed monster out of some unbelievable

European mythology, and not a human being at all, since human beings did not have hair on their faces.

Seeing that the creature continued to gaze at them calmly through his glass eye one of them cried, "The evil eye!" No doubt he was enmeshing their helpless spirits with his stare. Another screamed, "I won't let him look at my face! I won't! I won't!" And with one accord they started up from their seats, threw their skirts over their heads to protect them, and fled from the temple.

Anna ran after them desperately. Frantically she tried to bring them to a sense of the childishness and impropriety of such conduct before a stranger, to explain that many European men were bearded, that the monocle was no different from the King's spectacles.

"No, no," they cried in an agony of terror, "we can't let him look at our faces." She argued, cajoled, pleaded. But it was useless. Not even fear of the King's wrath could dispel their unreasoning horror of the monster in the temple and persuade them to go back. They scampered off hither and thither like a flock of frightened sheep.

Anna went dejectedly to the temple alone, prepared to face the music. The ambassador and the King had gone. The curtains had been removed. Some of the elder ladies told her that the King was furious with her for not having taught the girls better manners. In a short time a dozen or more women came running breathlessly into the temple, saying, "Make haste, make haste, the King calls you!" With something of the sense of misgiving the girls had felt Anna entered the King's presence. She could guess the vitriolic things he would have to say at this ignominious end to his attempt to make a grand impression. But he was mild in his rebuke.

"Wherefore have you not educated those girls more scientifically?" he demanded. And she knew what he meant, since good manners were almost a science among Orientals. Then as she braced herself for the specific charges of failure and omission that she thought were coming, he added, "And wherefore have you not acquainted them with English custom of spying-glass? They were quite unprepared, and our women are too modest to let a strange man look on their faces."

Margaret Ayer

18

## LADY SON KLIN IN THE DUNGEON

ONE AFTERNOON a few weeks later, when Anna went to Lady Son Klin's house for the semi-weekly private lesson in English, she found Prince Krita sitting in the window, his face unusually sad.

"Where's your mother, dear?" Anna inquired.

"With His Majesty upstairs, I think," he answered uncertainly, without looking at Anna. His eyes were fixed on the corner of the street, as though he expected his mother to appear there at any moment.

"Will she be back soon?" Anna persisted.

"I don't know," he replied. "She's been gone a long time."

Anna was puzzled and vaguely alarmed. This was a strange circumstance! It seemed unlike Lady Son Klin, who was most punctilious in all her engagements. The only possible explanation was that she had been summoned by the King so unexpectedly that she had had not even a moment to send one of her slaves with a message for Anna. There was something ominous about her failure to return or to send reassurance to Krita. The King's hatred of her was too deeply seated for speculation on a possible change in his attitude. Any call to his presence meant trouble. As Anna returned home she revolved the matter in her mind, and the more she thought about it the more puzzled and filled with forebodings she became.

The next morning on her way to school she took the street on which Son Klin lived. Again she saw Krita sitting in the window, in the same attitude, his eyes bent anxiously in the same direction. Anna had the startled thought that he must have been sitting there all night. "Is your mother home yet, dear?" Anna asked.

The child answered without looking down, "No, Mem, she hasn't come yet." This was really very alarming!

As Anna entered the porch of the temple the favorite, Lady Talap, was waiting there for her. She seized Anna's hand and pulled her aside, saying, "Mem *cha,* Son Klin is in trouble."

"What's happened?" Anna asked. "Do you know?"

Lady Talap drew Anna closer and whispered in her ear, "She's in prison!" Then looking around to be sure that none of the old duennas who acted as spies was near, she went on quickly, "She isn't prudent, you know—not like you and me." In her tone were commiseration, fear, and self-righteousness.

"What did she do?"

"Ssh! Don't ask! I dare not tell you!"

"Can I see her myself?"

"Yes, if you bribe the jailers. Give them one tical each. They will demand two. And go quickly—right now!" She almost shoved Anna through the door.

In the pavilion which was the private chapel of the ladies of the harem as well as the school, priests had already begun to read prayers and recite homilies from the sacred book of Buddha called *Sasana Thai,* the Religion of the Free. The ladies of the harem had gathered and were sitting on their velvet cushions with their hands folded, a vase of flowers and a pair of fragrant candles in front of each.

Anna tiptoed out of the temple hurriedly. At the door lounged the Amazons and the two eunuchs with swords and clubs who escorted the priests in and out of the Palace and watched them during the services. A young mother with a sleeping baby was sitting nearby. Some slave girls were engrossed in a game of *saba,* a kind of marbles that they played with their knees as well as their fingers. Anna met two princesses, almost grown, in the arms of their slaves.

She quickened her pace. At the door of the prison a group of slaves idled. It was guarded by two Amazons who seemed to be deep in conversation with them. They grew silent as Anna approached. Were they talking about Son Klin? Anna caught no names. It was more difficult than Lady Talap had led her to believe to get in. She was not admitted until she paid two ticals to each guard. Inside the door a third Amazon, who also had to be bribed, led her through a long corridor. Off this were secret apartments in which prisoners condemned to death by the Supreme Court or the supreme will of the King spent their last days.

Anna breathed deeply as they passed without pausing. The prison was an irregular, rambling building encircling two enclosures which opened from the corridor, and which stood one behind the other. Here the prisoners were allowed to walk at stated times. The hall that served as court formed one complete side of the enclosures. Three vaulted banks of cells occupied the other sides. A woman confined in one of these peeped out at Anna from behind a screen, but it was not Lady Son Klin. These cells were used for the reception of women convicted of petty crimes, such as gambling, stealing, or immodest language. Lady Son Klin was in none of them.

The Amazon stopped and pulled up a trapdoor that led to one of the dungeons. Anna was horrified! Of what crime had her friend been convicted to be incarcerated here? She descended a flight of broken stone steps. They were so slippery that she could scarcely keep her feet, and so dark that she had to grope her way. She reached out to steady herself against the wall, but it was slimy under her hand. She heard the slithering sound of a lizard or snake and recoiled with loathing. No floor received her feet when she reached the bottom. A few planks, loosely laid, were soft as the mud they were meant to cover. The ooze from the nearby river had rotted them through and through.

The cell was lighted by one small window, so heavily grated on the outer side that it barred all ingress of air. It was laced with cobwebs. Only a glimmer of light came through. Overhead, the roof was black with filth and mold. The walls were rough stone covered with moss, fungi, and reptiles. As Anna's eyes gradually adjusted themselves to the darkness she saw that rude designs had been scrawled on them. Whoever had painted them—perhaps some half-mad prisoner—had exhausted a nightmare fancy on hideous personifications of Hunger, Terror, Old Age, Despair, Disease, and Death, tormented by furies and avengers, with hair of snakes and whips of scorpions.

A pair of wooden trestles on the far side of the cell supported some rough boards that formed a makeshift bedstead. Over it was spread a mat. The Lady Son Klin lay still as death on this crude bed. Her feet were covered with a silk mantle, and her head was supported by a pillow of glazed leather. Her face was turned toward the clammy wall and she did not try to see who had come so stumblingly down the stairs. At her head a little higher than the pillow were a vase of flowers, half faded, a pair of candles burning in gold candlesticks, and a small image of the Buddha.

She had brought her god with her. "Well," Anna thought with a shudder, "she needs him!"

Anna moved cautiously across the mud of the floor, trying to keep her footing on the rotten planks, and stood beside the motionless figure. She was so shocked that when she tried to speak her voice was scarcely audible. "Son Klin . . ."

The woman turned with difficulty. A slight sound of clanking explained the covering on her feet. She was chained to the trestle. Sitting up, she made room for Anna beside her. No tears were in her eyes. Only the habitual melancholy of her face was deepened. Anna thought savagely that before her was the perfect work of cruelty and injustice upon meekness and patience. It was utterly impossible to believe that the gentle woman on the bed could have committed a crime worthy of such mistreatment.

Son Klin was evidently astonished to see Anna. She reached out to touch her friend, doubting her own eyes. When she saw that Anna was indeed flesh and blood she folded her hands in the attitude of supplication and bent her head forward upon them. "Mem, Mem," she moaned. "Help me. Mem, help your poor pupil!"

Anna took the Mon woman's hands in her own and said, "I'll try, Son Klin. I'll surely try. But you must tell me why you're here. What has happened?"

When Son Klin spoke it was without expression, as if agony had bled her of all feeling. "You are aware, Mem, that we are allowed to petition His Majesty through our children." Anna nodded. She did know this. She had seen her little pupils, groomed and shining in their best clothes, carrying on golden salvers some request or other on behalf of their mothers' families.

"My family wished me to petition the King for my oldest brother. They hoped that His Majesty would grant the appointment held by my late uncle to him, not knowing that His Majesty had already chosen another noble for the post. Nor did I know it, Mem." She passed one hand over her eyes as if to banish something she seemed to see, and continued tonelessly:

"Yesterday morning I dressed Krita in his best and sent him in to the King at breakfast with the petition. The child was afraid to go, for as you know we are not in favor, but when I explained to him the reason he was willing. I waited for him at home. But when he came home he was in tears. After the King had read the petition he had flown into a rage and dashed it back into the face of my trembling little boy kneeling there before him. He accused me of plotting to undermine his power, saying that he knew me to be a Mon rebel at heart. He screamed that I hated him and all his dynasty because my ancestors were Peguans and the natural enemies of the Siamese. And the more he talked the angrier he became. So he sent one of the judges for me to summon me to trial for rebellion. I went at once leaving Krita at home, but before I could reach the Palace another judge met us with His Majesty's order to chain and imprison me without trial, since His Majesty had decided that my guilt was proved. After they had chained me here and gone away, a third judge came with an order to flog me until I confessed my treacherous plot, and the names of my accomplices."

"Son Klin! No! They didn't flog you, did they? Oh, my dear!"

The woman smiled wanly at the pain in Anna's voice. "They did, yes, for indeed they must, but without energy, so that it hurt little, for they knew that I was innocent."

"And what did you confess?"

"That I am His Majesty's meanest slave and ready to give my life for his pleasure."

"And then what?"

"Then His Majesty roared that I was to be beaten on the mouth with a slipper for lying!"

"No!" Anna exclaimed. "No!" For a Siamese this was the supreme insult, since the head was too sacred even to touch while the feet and what went on the feet too low to be mentioned in polite society.

Son Klin sat with her head hanging, no spirit left in her. "I am degraded forever," she said.

There was little that Anna could do. She comforted Lady Son Klin as best she could, told her that she had seen Prince Krita and that he was at home with the slaves, and was surely being taken care of, and promised that she would lay the matter before the Kralahome that very evening.

The Kralahome received her privately, but when she had explained the purpose of her visit he rebuked her sharply. "It is not your place, Mem, to interfere between His Majesty and His Majesty's wives!"

"She is my pupil," Anna replied stubbornly. "And besides, I have not interfered. I have only come to you privately for justice. No one knows of this outside of the Palace as yet, but if you will not help her, I shall carry the news to her family at once." The premier looked at Anna sharply, for he knew as well as she that Son Klin's family, though they were out of favor, were a large and powerful clan and would find some means of repaying the insults that had been heaped upon her. And it was an open secret that the French were on the lookout for disaffected officials who might serve their imperialistic plans. The premier stirred uneasily and asked, "Of what exactly is she accused?"

"Of seeking an appointment for her brother that had already been granted to someone else. His Majesty accuses her of plotting with her family to rebel against him. This is obviously ridiculous since they did not even know that the appointment had been made, nor did she when she sent Prince Krita to the King with the petition. And to punish one woman for what is permitted and encouraged in another is gross injustice. It can't enhance His Majesty's reputation with his foreign friends."

The Kralahome listened gravely, frowning a little at the implied threat in her last sentence. Then he sent for his secretary, and having satisfied himself that the appointment had not been published, he promised that he would explain the matter to the King at the evening audience.

"I shall tell His Majesty that there has been a delay in making known to the court the royal pleasure in this matter," he said. But he spoke with indifference, as if the treatment of Son Klin were after all of no consequence.

Anna felt chilled by his failure to respond as she had thought he would with some sign of indignation. She was more anxious than ever when she remembered the weary eyes of the boy watching for his mother's return. None of the slaves had dared to tell him the truth. What after all had she to expect from the premier's apathetic promise, if indeed he bothered to keep it?

There was nothing more that she could do. She went home lonely and sad. She had counted on the premier more than she had realized, for she had come slowly to believe that there was good moral fiber in him. He was cold, shrewd, ruthless, but she had thought just; never quixotic and unreliable, or swayed by prejudice and favor as was the King. The King's brutality and the premier's callousness weighed down upon her like a load of stones. It seemed to her as she listlessly ate a little dinner that with leaders like these the Siamese could never achieve a society where justice and mercy were a reality. She wondered again, as she did each time she grew discouraged, why she had come where her sensibilities were continually bruised by that lack of concern for human values which underlay all the evils she saw round her—injustice, favoritism, slavery, and concubinage. The King regarded his women as nothing more than stalled animals kept by his bounty for his pleasure, to be destroyed at his whim. The idea filled her with loathing and with a sense of the hopelessness of the task she had set herself. But she would not give up her determination to help Son Klin. If she was not free when next Anna entered the Palace her family at least could be informed.

Monday morning Anna approached the temple school with bated breath, hardly daring to hope, but unable to repress the swift beating of her heart. Several of the women, who had evidently been waiting for her, rushed forward with the good news. Son Klin was home with her child.

Anna decided that this was one morning when she would omit the religious service, whatever it did to school attendance, and hurried off to see her friend.

As she came down the street Son Klin rushed out to meet her and embraced her ardently. "Mem, Mem! I'm free, see! I am free! All due to your gracious goodness and kindness and to your merciful intercession on my behalf." She glorified Anna with grateful epithets from the extravagant vocabulary of her people until Anna stemmed her in embarrassment.

It seemed that the very night that Anna had called on the Kralahome he had gone to the Grand Palace and explained to the King, without appearing to be aware of the concubine's punishment, that there had been a delay in publishing the last list of appointments, but that it would be taken care of at once.

Anna felt a swift glow of gratitude for the premier. He had been more troubled than he had let her see at the mistake Son Klin had made.

"So then what?"

"So then on Sunday morning the Amazons came with the news that the King had ordered my release. And so here I am!"

Gravely she drew from her finger a treasured ring set with an emerald. Taking Anna's hand in hers she slipped the ring on one of the fingers saying, "By this you will remember the thankful friend whom you have freed."

On the following day she sent Anna a small purse of gold thread netted, in which were a few Siamese coins. This was the sort of gift which royalty was accustomed to bestow. And in the purse with the coins was a scrap of paper inscribed with cabalistic characters, an infallible charm against poverty and distress.

19

## THE KING'S BREAKFAST

BY THE time Anna's first year in Siam was drawing to a close the dim life of the Palace had come into focus. The framework, at least, was now clear. What had seemed in the beginning a chaos of color had assumed meaning. Objects and then groups fell into their proper relation.

The world within the Palace walls was a universe with a single sun and many moons. The King was the disk of light around which everything revolved. What he did day by day determined what the women of the harem did. Even the English school had to be adjusted to the orbit of the King's life. He rose at five. So, therefore, did most of the members of his household. After a scanty meal served by the women who had been in attendance through the night, he descended to the courtyard and took his place on a strip of matting, laid from one gate of the Inside through all the avenues to another. His children were seated on his right in the order of their rank, then the princesses, his concubines, his maids of honor, and their slaves. Before each person was placed a large silver tray containing offerings of boiled rice, fruit, cakes, and siri leaf, which some of the women had arisen hours earlier to prepare. There were occasionally cigars also.

A little after five the gate called the "Gate of Merit" was thrown open and a hundred and ninety-nine priests entered, escorted on the right and left by eunuchs armed with swords and clubs. As the priests came toward the royal family they chanted, "Take thy meat, but think it dust! Eat but to live, and but to know thyself, and what thou art below! And say unto thy heart, 'It is the earth I eat, that to the earth I may new life impart.' "

The chief priest led the procession. He advanced with downcast eyes and presented his bowl, which was slung from his neck by a cord and had been hidden under the yellow folds of his robe until that moment. If anyone before whom a bowl was placed was not ready, no priest stopped. All continued to advance slowly, taking what was offered without thanks or even a look of acknowledgment until the end of the long row had been reached. Then the procession retired, chanting as before, at the gate called the "Gate of Earth."

After this the King withdrew to his private temple, which was dedicated to the memory of his mother. This was a unique building decorated with beautiful frescoes representing the numerous metempsychoses of Buddha, which had been painted by Japanese artists imported for the purpose. The King ascended alone the steps to the altar and rang the bell that announced the hour of devotions. He lighted consecrated tapers and offered the white roses and lotus that he had brought. Then he spent an hour in prayer and meditation.

This service over, he retired for a nap, attended by a fresh detail of ladies-in-waiting. Those who had been on duty through the night were dismissed, not to be recalled for two weeks or a month unless as a mark of special favor. Most of them, however, waited on him voluntarily every day.

When he woke his breakfast was served with intricate formality. After he had inspected the gifts on the pavement before the Palace he entered an antechamber of the women's audience hall where a large number of the harem ladies waited. He seated himself at a long table, frequently with the little Princess Chanthara Monthon on his lap. Twelve women knelt nearby before great silver trays filled with twelve varieties of food— soups, meats, game, poultry, fish, vegetables, cakes, jellies, preserves, sauces, fruits, and teas. Each tray in its order was passed by three ladies to the head wife, Lady Thiang, who removed the silver cover, and at least seemed to taste the contents of the dish. Then advancing on her knees she set the dishes one by one on the table before the King.

Actually the King ate very little of the lavish food, although he often spent much time urging it on the princess. He was notably temperate in his diet. During the long seclusion in the Buddhist cloister he had acquired habits of abstemiousness which he never abandoned. It was amusing to watch him solemnly eating with gold chopsticks a modest bowl of boiled rice such as might have made a coolie's meal.

At these leisurely breakfasts it was his custom to hold Anna in conversation. Sometimes they discussed the news of the day. The issue of the Civil War was still in doubt. Lincoln had announced the emancipation of the slaves. England and Spain had withdrawn from Napoleon's expedition to Mexico. China was still racked by the long agony of the Taiping Rebellion. A new and interesting figure had emerged there, "Chinese" Gordon, who had assumed command of the Ever-Victorious Army organized a few years earlier by a daring American adventurer, recently dead, Frederick Townsend Ward.

At other times they discussed some topic of interest out of the King's studies or reading, or out of Anna's own studies in Sanskrit. It was at this hour that Anna came to know the King well, to admire and respect his intellectual attainments. She believed him to be the most systematically educated, the most capacious devourer of books and news, of any crowned head of that day, either Oriental or European. But she was often repelled by the extreme skepticism of his mind where people were concerned. He had no faith whatever in the integrity of any human being. He believed that every man strove to encompass his ends by good means or bad. He could not be convinced that anyone acted out of principle.

On occasion Anna would try to refute his scornful analysis of the actions of a friend, only to discover in mortification that he saw in her magnanimity some seeking for personal advantage. It was simply "to your peculiar interest to say so," he would say, adding sourly, "Money, money, money! It will buy anything," as if her friends had bribed her to uphold their cause before the King.

He passed his mornings in study or correspondence. Anna was usually free to carry on the business of her school during this time, except on mail days, which came at least twice a month. If the King was tired, he took another nap at noon. If not, he continued to study until two o'clock when he put aside his books and letters, and sent a golden candlestick to the Temple of the Emerald Buddha.

As Anna had seen on her first visit to the Palace this was the signal that the King had begun to prepare for his public appearance. Immediately all the narrow, crooked streets and lanes which intersected and crossed each other in such bewildering irregularity were thronged with women and children of every age, from the tottering dame of eighty to the two-year-old just beginning to feel the earth under his feet. This motley stream of humanity, some in silks and some in rags, some pale and downcast, some laughing and fresh, moved rapidly and wordlessly toward the audience hall of the women.

Those of lesser rank knelt on the pavement outside, while all around the hall itself in the alcoves and shadowy recesses formed by the kincob curtains hundreds of the princesses, concubines, and ladies-in-waiting prostrated themselves to await the King's appearance. In the meantime His Majesty had bathed and anointed his body with the help of his women. Then he descended to the dining salon where he was served the most substantial meal of the day. After he had finished, he entered the audience hall and chatted with his favorites among the wives and children.

The love of children was his one constant virtue. They appealed to him by their beauty and their trustfulness. They amused him with the bold innocence of their ways. He would take them in his arms and embrace them, making droll faces at the babies. He would ask the older children puzzling questions and laugh at their serious attempts to reply.

One of the strange contradictions of Siamese character, which never failed to surprise Anna, was that in spite of the King's presence and the enormous fear the women seemed to feel for him, it took the Amazons to keep discipline. If there was too much giggling and whispering behind a curtain, one of the female police would start up and lay a whip lightly on the shoulders of the more noisy. The whip was administered as often as three times during an audience. And the moment the King retired, the women scattered like a flock of geese, rushing away to their homes as if they had just escaped from an unpleasant duty.

This curious mixture of subservience and complete lack of discipline also complicated the smooth running of the little English school. Most of the time the children's manners were perfect, their attention to Anna's orders admirable. On the other hand, she could never be sure when her control would break suddenly and for no apparent reason, and the royal pupils would throw all regulations to the wind and become unmanageable. One morning she entered the temple to find every child in place. Something distracted her for two or three minutes, and when she returned to start the day's lessons the children had vanished, for no reason that she could discover. Nor could she reassemble her school until the next day. It was bewildering.

Almost every afternoon the whole school was disrupted when a company of priests, closely guarded, entered the harem city to purify it with consecrated water. As they passed from one gate to another along the streets sprinkling the water right and left, the children would make a frantic rush to prostrate themselves on the pavement within reach of the cleansing showers. Books, pencils, slates, were strewn in every direction. It was useless to try to reorganize the lesson when the priests had passed, for the children were refractory and inattentive. Anna would sigh and send them home, and they would disappear on the backs of their slaves to prepare for the afternoon audience with their father.

When the King had dismissed the women and children, he passed to the outside Hall of Audience to consider official matters with the members of his government. Twice a week at sunset he appeared at one of the gates of the Palace to hear the petitions of the people, who could not reach his ear at any other time or place. It was pitiful to see the awe-stricken subjects of the Lord of Life prostrate and abject, often too overwhelmed to submit the precious petitions they had brought.

At nine he retired to his upper chambers. Immediately there issued from them a series of domestic bulletins, orders regulating life on the Inside, assignments of special tasks to designated officers, names of the women whose presence he desired, and the list of those who were to wait upon him during the night.

About twelve or one he woke from his first sleep, and devoted several hours to study or letter-writing. If he found a word in his reading that baffled him, he would send a dozen or more slave women for Anna. Usually these words were technical or scientific terms not found in the dictionary, and not in Anna's head, either. Her inability to define them never failed to infuriate the King. He would look at her indignantly and say, "Why for do you not know? It's clear that you aren't scientific!" Then, not having demolished her to his satisfaction even with this the most damning censure he knew, he would search for words to poison the shaft of his disdain. "Well, you're only a woman after all," he would add, and being unable to think of anything worse at the moment he would add scornfully, "You can go now."

Twice a week at midnight he held a secret council of the San Luang (the Royal Inquisition). Anna never obtained any clear knowledge of the dark and terrifying sittings of this secret inquisition, for she never attended, nor would anyone talk about them with her. Certain things she learned, however, as time passed. The San Luang was silent, insidious, secretive. It was an inquisition, not overt and audacious like that of Rome, but nocturnal, unseen, ubiquitous like that of Spain. It proceeded without witnesses or warning; kidnaping a subject, not arresting him; and then incarcerating, chaining, and torturing him to extort a confession or denunciation.

The laws of the country were not intolerable, but no one not in the good graces of the San Luang could depend upon them or the regular courts for justice. The San Luang was so feared and dreaded that no man would consent to appear before it even as a witness except for a large reward. The wise citizen was careful to find a protector in some formidable friend who was a member. Spies in the employ of the San Luang penetrated every family of wealth and influence. Every citizen suspected and feared his neighbor and his servants always, sometimes even his wife.

On several occasions when Anna was more than usually annoyed by some act of the King, she gave vent to her feelings in word or look. She soon observed that if this happened in the presence of certain officers and courtiers they rapped in a peculiar and stealthy manner. This tapping, she discovered, was one of the secret signs of those in the employ of the San Luang. The warning signal was addressed to her because they imagined that she was also a member of the Inquisition, so great was her influence with the King considered to be. When this happened it was clear evidence that she had ceased to be merely a pawn on the vast and dimly seen chessboard. She had become a player in the game.

The work of the school itself was progressing rapidly and this delighted the King. As early as the fall of 1862, after only a few months of instruction, the royal pupils had begun writing little notes in English to their teacher's daughter, Avis. These were addressed in care of the Misses King, to whose school at Fulham Avis had been sent. Some of them were written on paper embossed with the royal seal, some on lace-bordered sheets like old-fashioned valentines, and some on mere scraps from notebooks. They conveyed little sense but much love, with an occasional Siamese word inserted where English had failed. It seemed infinitely sad to the royal children that Avis should have to be sent so far away from her mother. A few of them brought little gifts such as rings to be forwarded to Avis. The small donors thought that these might help comfort her in her loneliness.

As the year drew to a close Prince Chulalongkorn continued to be outstanding among the children. He was methodical in his work and very serious. He moved ahead with a steady even progress that was gratifying to his teacher and doubly so to his father. He was more self-disciplined than the rest of the children, and often helped keep his small brothers and sisters under control by example or word.

Other children to whom Anna was especially attracted were the two little sons of Lady Talap, the exquisite doll-like wife to whom the King had presented her at her first audience; Son Klin's son, Prince Krita; the oldest daughter of Lady Thiang, Princess Somawadi; and the Princess Chanthara Monthon or the Fa-ying, as the sister of Prince Chulalongkorn was called. She was an exceptionally lovely child, besides being the favorite of the King among all his sixty-odd children. She had soft dark eyes filled with a trustfulness that was very winning. Her skin was a clear and beautiful olive with a delicate flush that heightened its transparency.

Shortly before her death the late queen consort had entrusted her four children to their royal father with a pitiful tenderness and anxiety. He had been deeply moved by her pleading. As he had loved the mother, so now he loved the children. And among the four of them the Fa-ying was closest to him. She was almost always with him at meals. During state processions about the city by dragon boat or palanquin she sat beside him. In a fumbling sort of way he lavished on her a love intended to take the place of her mother's. When she was hardly more than a baby he had assigned to her the best of the tutors among the women of the harem. Thus she had started her studies in Siamese and Sanskrit at the age of three. When she came to Anna at seven she was already surprisingly proficient in both.

The pictures in her English books delighted her. She grew especially fond of the pictures of the Christ Child. Whenever she was tired of study, she would jump up into Anna's lap and settling down comfortably would demand, "Tell me a story! Tell me all about your beautiful Jesus!"

145

And after Anna had told her story the Fa-ying would smile and pat Anna's cheeks and say, "I, too, little Fa-ying, I love your sacred Jesus very much. Do He love me a little, very little? I no got mother, poor little Fa-ying! Could He love her too?"

Consciously Anna tried to shape the little princess to a pattern of kindness. She knew that she had in this the encouragement of the old great-aunt, Princess Lamom. If in the years to come the Fa-ying chose to use her enormous power over her father unselfishly, there was much she might be able to do to alleviate the cruelty of the life around her. And like her brother, Prince Chulalongkorn, she had an innate sympathy for those who suffered.

It seemed to Anna that both of these children were less like their father than their uncle, the Second King. Even as a small boy he had been known for his generous spirit. An elderly priest had told Anna how at twelve the young prince was being carried through the eastern gate of the city on the way to his mother's lotus gardens when he noticed an old man, half blind, resting by the roadside. He had commanded his bearers to halt, and had alighted from his sedan to speak to the poor creature. Finding him destitute and helpless, a stranger in Bangkok, he had had him seated in his own sedan and carried to the gardens while he himself followed on foot. There he had had the old man bathed and dressed in fresh clothes and fed with a substantial meal. And afterward he had taken his astonished client into his service as a keeper of cattle.

From stories that Anna heard on every side it appeared that this incident was not unusual. Later in life the prince had continued no less generous and romantic, a sort of Harun-al-Raschid, visiting the poor in disguise, listening to the recital of their sufferings and wrongs, and relieving them where he could. The populace idolized him and would have liked to see him king, a fact which drove a wedge of misunderstanding between the brothers. King Mongkut, whose temperament was essentially cold except when heated by rage, regarded his warm-hearted brother with suspicion and contrived to limit the Second King's activities until he became in effect a state prisoner.

It seemed unlikely, however, that the King would feel the same distrust of the warm impulses of his favorite children. They were not even aware of the fact that their father wore armor against the world. In their hands he was completely malleable. What they asked for they received. Anna looked back over the year and felt strongly that it had not been wasted if it had done nothing more than reinforce the natural idealism of Prince Chulalongkorn and the Fa-ying.

"Will you teach me to draw, Mem *cha?* I want to make some pretty pictures." A small bell-like voice interrupted Anna as she worked alone one afternoon while her pupils attended their Sanskrit class. It was the

Fa-ying, leaning confident and smiling close to her. "It's more fun to sit here by you than go to Sanskrit class. My Sanskrit teacher isn't like my English teacher at all." The little princess leaned even closer and opened her dark eyes wide as if she were about to share a solemn confidence. "Do you know what she does? She bends my hands back when I make mistakes and it hurts. I don't like her and I don't like Sanskrit either." The engaging prattler twisted her face into a deep frown. Then the frown vanished and she looked up archly into Anna's face. "But I like my English teacher and I like English. There are so many pretty pictures in my English books. And I want to draw some myself. So will you teach me to draw, Mem *cha?*"

The Fa-ying climbed up into Anna's lap and curled up like a kitten. Anna put down her pen to make room. Although the princess was almost eight, she was no larger than a four-year-old English child. Her flower-like charm was not the result of delicate physical perfection, however, but came more from a sunny spirit, which remained unspoiled even by the attention heaped upon her.

"I'll be glad to teach you to draw and paint, if His Majesty doesn't object," Anna promised. The Fa-ying slipped her arms around the Englishwoman's neck and gave her a delighted hug that stirred in Anna a homesickness for Avis.

"And when you go far away to England, Mem *cha,* will you take me along with you and Louis on the big, big boat?"

"Well, that's a little different," Anna objected. "I'm afraid His Majesty would never let you go that far away from him, even with me. After all, how could he get along without you?" She smiled down into the soft eyes that watched every expression of her face with quick intelligence.

"Oh, yes, he'll let me go!" contradicted the Fa-ying with complete assurance. "He lets me do anything I want to do. I'm the Somdet Chao-fa-ying, you know, and he loves me the best of all. So he'll surely let me go, if that's what I want to do."

"I'm delighted to hear it," Anna said, amused by the child's matter-of-fact assumption of power over her autocratic father. "And I'm also glad that you like English and drawing. Let's go and ask His Majesty if you may study drawing instead of Sanskrit, shall we?"

The Fa-ying sprang to the floor and seized Anna's hand. "Oh, yes, let's go right now!"

So they went and laid their request before the King in his upstairs study. His face softened as he looked at the little girl. And he smiled at Anna, gratified by her interest in his favorite child. He made no objection to his daughter's request, and day after day she came to Anna while her brothers and sisters attended their Sanskrit class. It was a pleasant interlude in the school routine.

Sometimes the child drew or painted. Sometimes she sat quietly and watched Anna draw. If she grew tired she climbed into Anna's lap and demanded a Bible story. She had her favorites, which she insisted upon hearing over and over. Anna marveled at the spiritual perception of her alert small mind and at her ability to grasp the meaning of these stories. There was more in her rapt attention than the natural interest of any child in a good story well told. There was a nascent humanitarianism that fed on their inner significance. The other children, even the brightest, were lovable, earth-bound mortals. This child was different. The Welsh in Anna responded to this difference, which was like a spring welling up from some source within the child's depth of spirit. If the little princess and her brother, given all the latent power that was theirs by birth and position, fulfilled their seeming promise, the Siam of the next generation would be a better place than the Siam of 1863.

Pleased as the King was with the progress of his children, it never seemed to occur to him that it would have been even more rapid if he had refrained from summoning their teacher from her schoolroom whenever he needed an English letter written. There were other breaks in the regular schedule. The children would be summoned in the middle of a class to attend some ceremony. The frequent royal cremations were especially time-consuming, but the children loved them for the elaborate theatricals and fireworks. The festivals of the Buddhist year also took their toll of school days.

Occasionally the interruption in school routine was interesting enough to compensate for the loss of time. On a certain cool morning in that first year a number of her pupils rushed up to Anna crying excitedly, "Mem, Mem, he has come! The great prince has come! Isn't it wonderful?"

"What prince has come?" she asked, thinking it was strange that she had not heard in advance of the visiting royalty.

"The white elephant! The white elephant! Our guardian angel prince!" they shouted together. As the news spread over the city, King and peasant, master and slave, young and old congratulated each other in jubilation. Prayers and offerings were made immediately in all the temples. The town crier who shouted the news along the streets was showered with gifts of money, cloth, rice, and bottles of perfumed oil.

Seventy-five royal barges and a hundred boats were ordered prepared at once and provisioned with a week's supplies to take the King and his family, the Amazons, and court officers to the place where the white elephant had been found. Anna asked permission to go with the cortege to the old capital of Ayuthia. The auspicious animal had been sighted there during the annual round-up of elephants in the forest.

Before sunset the procession was off to the firing of guns and the shouts of the thousands of people who lined the river banks. The boats reached

Ayuthia the next morning. The court transferred at once to horses and rode for miles through beautiful country to the stockade or kraal where the round-up was to take place. As soon as they arrived at the King's palace on the north side of the kraal they climbed a steep flight of stairs to an open tower with a magnificent view of the countryside. The kraal itself lay before them, made of heavy piles driven into the ground very closely to form a circle three or four miles in extent.

Beside the tower was a chamber that held an immense drum, around which twelve men were stationed ready to sound the moment for the beginning of the chase. A hundred and fifty trained elephants were ranged before the palace. There were two men on each, one at the back with a forked goad to urge the beast to the onslaught, and one in the front armed with lances, spears, and a quiver of arrows. The moment the royal party appeared the elephants wheeled and formed a semicircle. Each hunter raised his spear in salute. There was a shouted command and the great beasts sank to their knees and raised their trunks into the air, bringing them down in a mass salaam.

As soon as this was finished the colossal drum thundered the signal for the hunt. The company of elephants divided and spread out through the countryside where the wild elephants were grazing, having been cautiously moved up toward the stockade from their feeding grounds during the previous weeks. The royal party could see the hunting elephants appear and disappear through the trees for many miles. Round and round they went, each time decreasing the circle of their movements and hemming the wild beasts into a smaller and smaller compass. Sometimes they could be seen distinctly; sometimes they were lost for a while in the clumps of forest. Then came a terrific succession of wild trumpetings from the trapped elephants and shouts from the hunters, "Don't let them escape!" and a deafening peal of bugles, horns, and trumpets.

As the wild elephants moved nearer the shouts grew shriller, until at last the court could see the animals plunging madly, caught in a perfect circle formed by the hunters on their mounts. All at once a tremendous black creature thought he saw an opening close by and made a bound head foremost through the entrance to the kraal. In charged the whole herd, screaming with anger and fright, their trunks thrown high in the air. It was almost noon and the hunt was successfully over. To the hysterical joy of the royal party one great salmon-colored beast heaved and trumpeted in the sea of gray and black ones.

For hours the trapped animals ran back and forth, lashing the solid posts with their trunks, twisting them and trying to uproot them, throwing their weight against the barrier of piles. All in vain. The sun set and the weary beasts finally huddled close together with the white elephant in their midst.

The next morning they tried again to free themselves. It was afternoon before they became so faint from hunger that they gave up and tore branches from trees growing in the stockade to eat. This was a sign for the hunters on their tame elephants to enter the kraal. About sixty men with fine grass, cut and prepared, and heaps of sugar cane followed the hunters into the kraal. The tame beasts were turned loose while the newly trapped elephants were tempted with the grass and cane. In a few moments they all flocked around the men and began to feed. If any showed impatience or snatched the food too greedily, the hunters withheld it and struck the animal fierce blows. In less than half an hour the wild elephants took what was given them without snatching and even fondled with their long trunks the hands of the men that fed them. Meanwhile other men fastened chains to their legs and bound them to the tame elephants.

The white elephant alone was not bound to another of its kind. Several long silken cords were fastened about his neck and these were tied to one of the posts of the kraal. Moreover, cakes were given to him in addition to the grass and sugar cane. Immediately a wide path was begun for him through the country he must traverse to the river on his royal progress to Bangkok. A day or so later when it was complete a gold cloth was laid on his back and the triumphal return to the capital was begun. Even the King played second fiddle to the new "prince." In front of the elephant young girls danced and sang and played musical instruments; a number of men performed feats of strength and skill, tumbling, and wrestling, and knocking each other down for his amusement. Other men fanned him and fed him. Priests prayed for him. When he reached the river he was put on board a floating palace of wood, surmounted by a gorgeous roof and hung with crimson curtains. This he seemed to dislike in spite of the fact that the roof was literally thatched with flowers, ingeniously arranged to form symbols and mottoes, which the learned beast was supposed to be able to decipher with ease.

The floor of the barge was covered with a gilt matting woven in curious patterns. The elephant was installed in the middle of this. Around him were stationed attendants who bathed and perfumed him, sang lullabies to him, fanned him and praised him all the way to the capital. The royal barges were carefully disposed near his float with silken cords passed between so that the King and nobles might aid in floating him down the river.

News of his imminent arrival had preceded him to Bangkok, and he was greeted with shouts of joy, the beating of drums, the sounding of trumpets, and the boom of cannon. A great company was waiting to meet him on the river bank and to follow him to the temporary pavilion where the custodians of the Palace and the principal personages of the royal household welcomed him with imposing ceremonies. The King, the courtiers, and the chief priests gathered around him for a thanksgiving service.

Then the lordly beast was knighted, after the ancient manner of the Siamese, as a conch shell of holy water was poured over his head. The title by which he was ennobled was Phya Sri Wongsi Decha Saralai Krasat, which meant "Handsome Lord of Powerful Family." Gold rings were fastened around his tusks, a gold chain was hung around his neck, and a purple velvet cloak, fringed with scarlet and gold, was thrown over him.

For seven days he was pampered and petted while the whole city engaged in a carnival of celebration because such a token of favor from on high had appeared. Anna discovered that, contrary to the idea widely held abroad, the Siamese did not worship the albino as a deity. They did believe, however, that each successive Buddha in passing through a series of transmigrations necessarily occupied in turn the forms of white animals of certain classes, particularly the swan, the stork, the white sparrow, the dove, the monkey, and the elephant. They thought that the forms of these creatures were reserved for the souls of the good and great. Thus almost all white animals were held in reverence, because they had once been superior human beings. The white elephant, in particular, was supposed to be animated by the spirit of some king or hero. Since he had once been a great man, he was thought to be familiar with the dangers that surround the great, and to know what was best and safest for those whose condition had once been his own. So he was supposed to avert national calamity and bring prosperity and peace to the people.

A magnificent new stable had been commenced at once for the "prince." He was assiduously fed with the finest herbs, the tenderest grass, the sweetest sugar cane, the mellowest bananas, and the most delicious cakes, served on huge trays of gold and silver. His water was perfumed with jessamine. It was all too much for him. He was taken with a severe attack of indigestion during the seventh night, and although the King's own doctor was summoned to prescribe for him he died in a few hours.

No man dared to carry the catastrophic tidings to the King. But the Kralahome, always a man of prompt expedients and unfailing presence of mind, called up thousands of slaves and pulled down the new stables. They worked in nervous haste, terrified by fear that the King might come before they were through. It was not until the cool of the late afternoon that he appeared, to see for himself the progress of the building which had been nearly completed the night before. He stood rooted to the ground when his gaze met nothing but vacancy and a large patch of bare earth. The truth flashed upon him at once and with a cry of pain he sank down upon a stone and wept bitterly. The little Fa-ying, who had been judiciously coached in her part, crept close to him and kneeling before him said, "Weep not, O my father. Perhaps the stranger lord has left us but for a time." But the King could hardly control his grief.

It was some time before he could rally himself to give the necessary orders for the obsequies. The whole nation went immediately into mourning. But although the stranger lord was counted royal he was not cremated. Only his brain and his heart were thought worthy of this last and highest honor. His carcass was shrouded in fine white linen and laid on a bier. It was then floated down the river with much wailing and many dirges to be deposited at last in the Gulf of Siam.

The King memorialized the "stranger lord" in a proclamation that he caused to be issued by the royal press. He read it to Anna later when normal life had once more begun after the paralyzing interval of sorrow. Part of it described the dead animal: "His eyes were light blue, surrounded by a beautiful salmon color; his hair was fine, soft and long; his complexion pinkish white; his tusks like long white pearls; his ears like silver shields; his trunk like a comet's tail; his legs like the feet of the sky; his tread like the sound of thunder; his looks full of meditation; his expression full of tenderness; his cry like the voice of a mighty warrior; and his whole bearing like that of an illustrious monarch."

It reminded Anna forcibly of the description of Queen Victoria written by the King's ambassador on his return from her court some years before. He had said of her: "One cannot but be struck with the aspect of the august Queen of England, or fail to observe that she must be of pure descent from a race of goodly and warlike kings and rulers of the earth, in that her eyes, complexion, and above all her bearing, are those of a beautiful and majestic white elephant."

20

## THE MANSION OF THE BRASS DOOR

IN MARCH, while the King and court went to Petchaburi, Anna and Louis took a vacation in Singapore. Louis wrote to Avis when it was over that he "enjoyed it very much and had no lessons to learn and we have come back to Siam where they all love us well." Avis was in school at last. The *Ranu* had taken six months to reach England instead of three so that she had missed the entire fall term. It was a relief to Anna to have a letter from the Misses King saying that her small daughter had arrived at their school shortly after the beginning of the year. Before the end of April Anna returned to Bangkok and again took up her dual role of teacher and secretary.

May 2, 1863, was a day that she would never forget. She could divide her life into many segments. There was the old time in Wales, a dreamlike time, when she had been a child. Then the gaudy pageant of India, the brief interim in England, the Singapore years, and her life in Siam.

153

But always afterward the Siam life fell apart across that morning in May.

She had gone as usual to her temple schoolroom just as the great clock on the tower struck nine. Louis had not come with her that day because he had had a slight touch of fever. The Temple of the Mothers of the Free was empty. Her pupils were absent at a ceremony in the Maha Prasat on the other side of the Palace, and word had been left that she, too, was to attend. It was the Wisakha Bucha, Festival of the Birth, Enlightenment, and Death of Buddha. King Mongkut had revived the ancient observance and made it one of the most important religious occasions of the year.

Anna set off at once. She was careful to attend every ceremony to which she was invited, for she was trying to comprehend more intelligently the alien life about her. Every time she thought with satisfaction that she understood the intricacies of the physical and mental world in which the women and children who were her pupils lived, something happened to show her that the Inside was as unknowable and confusing as ever. In the long galleries and corridors she was still bewildered by the twilight of eye and mind, the unexpected shafts of dazzling sunlight or Stygian blackness. The smile on a baby's face; a sister bearing without sound or tears a brother's beating; a mother singing to her "sacred infant"; a slave sobbing prostrate before an impassive Buddha; a concubine with her back laid open by scourging, ministered to by silent, furtive slaves—these sights filled her with a deep sense of pity. She felt to new levels within herself the utter loneliness of the human spirit in sorrow and pain; the hopelessness of those without rights and therefore without redress.

Whenever she passed within the massive gates of the harem the oppressive feeling settled upon her that here was a jail in which women and children innocent of crime were imprisoned for life. It seemed impossible that beyond the walls of the Palace fields were green and bright with flowers, or that the children of the poor played there naked and neglected, but rich in the freedom of earth and air. Down the close and gloomy lanes of the city within a city lovely women came and went softly, the feet of many little children pattered, and infant royalties were carried in the arms of their slaves. To Anna they all seemed to move under a cloud—endlessly, sadly, hopelessly beating their wings against the bars of their cage.

Sometimes she tried to comfort herself, and so gain respite from the smothering sense of obligation which this denial of human values produced in her, by remembering that since few of them had known anything better they were not unhappy, and that she was attributing to them her own passionate love of freedom. Then she would talk with a quiet woman, catch a word or look, and feel her heart wrung again with pity. She would be forced to admit that the love of freedom was born in human hearts and was not the product of environment. Once she missed a pretty girl who had attended her classes occasionally. The girl was the mother of two children, and when Anna saw them besieging their aunt with the question, "When will mother come back?" and getting no answer, she herself inquired of one of her pupils. The woman whom she had asked looked at her without a word. Then she placed her forefinger significantly on her lips and drew it slowly across her throat to intimate that the children's mother had been executed. Anna was revolted once more by the knowledge that the women around her had no more control over their lives than the beasts of the field. Many of them entered the Palace unwillingly, knowing that they would not go forth alive. And yet there were some who accepted their fate with a repose of manner that told her even better than the discontented faces of the others how dead must be the hearts under those still exteriors. She wrote rebelliously to Francis Cobb in Singapore:

> Only twenty minutes between bondage and freedom, such freedom at least as may be found in Siam! Only twenty minutes between these gloomy, hateful cells and the fair fields and radiant skies! Only twenty minutes between the cramping and the suffocation and the fear, and the full, deep, glorious inspirations of freedom and safety!
>
> I never beheld misery until I found it here; I never looked upon the sickening hideousness of slavery until I encountered its features here; nor, above all, had I comprehended the perfection of the life, light, blessedness and beauty, the all-suffering fulness of the love of God as it is in Jesus, until I felt the contrast here,—pain, deformity, darkness, death and eternal emptiness, a darkness to which there is neither beginning nor end, a living which is neither of this world nor of the next. The misery which checks the pulse and thrills the heart with pity in one's common walks about the great cities of Europe is hardly so saddening as the nameless, mocking wretchedness of these women, to whom poverty were a luxury, and houselessness as a draught of pure, free air.

On that morning in May, however, the Inside seemed to have been emptied of its inhabitants. Anna had started to find the Maha Prasat rather hesitantly, without any clear idea of which street to take. After some random wandering she met a flower-girl who gave her directions. Following these she entered a long dark alley, passed into another, and then another. The alleys brought her in about ten minutes to a gloomy street. No sunlight penetrated between the blank house walls that lined it. The farther end was veiled in mist and darkness.

Stone benches, black with moss and fungi, stood at intervals along this road, and a sort of colorless night-grass carpeted the pathway. Anna walked on more slowly, convinced that she had lost her way. She looked first on one side and then on the other for a cross street, but there was none. Nor did she meet anyone along the entire length of it. There was something about it that gave her the uneasy feeling it was not intended for public use. Suddenly she reached the end, and faced a high brick wall.

She paused and looked about. Behind her stretched the dim unpeopled road. Before her in the wall was a door of polished brass. Above it towered a grotesque façade that threw over the deserted street a shadow like a black pall. The din and roar of palace life were not fifteen minutes away, and yet the solitude of the place was strangely hushed. Its soundlessness had an eerie quality. As Anna stood uncertainly, a wind rattled some dry grass on top of the wall with a low, mournful soughing. Goose-flesh prickled along her arms. "Here, now! None of that!" she scolded herself, and, ashamed of her feeling of panic, attacked her fear directly.

She threw her weight against the ponderous door and pushed. With well-oiled ease it swung open—slowly, noiselessly. She stepped across a high sill into a paved courtyard. There was a garden on the right, a building on the left. The wall ran all around and enclosed both. The walks of the garden were bordered with small Chinese trees planted in straight rows. Grass covered half of them and moss the rest. The façade of the mansion was even more decayed and gloomy than the one on the wall. To the Englishwoman, still holding the door open, half afraid that she was trespassing in some forbidden place, it had a sinister appearance. The windows were closed, and those on the upper story had heavy shutters like a prison.

A slight movement drew her eyes from the house to an animate figure she had not at first seen. In the middle of the garden near a small pond of water a woman was sitting on the ground. She was nursing a naked child about four years old. At that moment she discovered Anna also and raised her head with a convulsive movement. She clasped her bare arms around her child and stared at Anna with fixed, truculent eyes. She was large, strongly made, and swarthy. She looked more like a gargoyle carved from dark stone and set there to frighten intruders than a human being. Her features were gaunt, and long matted hair hung around her shoulders.

Anna let the door go. It swung back with an ominous thud. She stood trembling a little, looking at the black, defiant woman. She had made up her mind to ask for help in finding the temple, and she had no intention of prying into the secrets of the deserted house, whether they were innocent or as gory as Bluebeard's.

The moment Anna approached the woman and child she forgot her fear in a choking surge of pity. The woman was naked to the waist, and chained by one leg to a post driven into the ground, without the least shelter under the burning sky. The chain was of cast iron and heavy, seven long double links, attached to a ring and fitted closely to the post by a rivet. Under her lay a tattered fragment of matting, and farther on were a block of wood for a pillow and several broken Chinese umbrellas.

The woman made no sound, only kept her eyes warily on the white stranger. Anna sat down on the rim of the pool and looked at her helplessly. Once more she was confronted with the apathy and callousness of harem life. Even a dangerous criminal should not have been left unprotected beneath the lurid tropical sun. But here sat this slave, almost without clothes, her filthy hair in dense masses around her face. The mat, the pillow, the broken umbrellas, all testified to the fact that she had been there a long time. Unrelenting heat pulsed around her. Rain no doubt buffeted her. She had been degraded to a level where no vestige of decency could be expected of her, and yet there was something in her concern for the child that was very fine. What sort of person was responsible for this outrage, this sadistic brutality?

Indignant questions churned to the surface of Anna's mind. She could have wept from the tumult of anger that pounded in her breast. But she was silent for several minutes, unable to command her voice. At last she asked the woman her name.

"*Pai sia!*" (Go away!) was the savage reply.

Undisturbed, Anna tried again. "Why are you chained here? Won't you tell me? You don't need to be afraid of me."

"*Pai! Pai! Pai!*" screamed the woman, snatching her breast impatiently from the sucking child, and turning her back on Anna. The child set up a howling which echoed and re-echoed from the walls. The woman turned and took him in her arms, and he was quiet in an instant. He was a sturdy little fellow, begrimed with dirt but healthy. She rocked him to and fro with her face resting against his unwashed cheek. Anna looked at her more closely, and, as she observed the clean line of the bones under the rough skin, thought, "Why, she may have been very pretty once!"

A little puff of wind shook the hot blanket of air. A coconut loosened by the nibbling of a squirrel dropped with a loud report in a far corner of the garden. Anna rose from the wall of the pond and sat down respectfully on the blistering pavement beside the woman and child. Very gently she asked the child's age.

The slave looked at her with mistrust, but did not hitch away. "He is four," she replied curtly.

Anna persisted. "And what is his name?"

"His name is Thuk (Sorrow)," the slave answered reluctantly, turning away her face.

"And why did you give him such a name?"

Again the woman looked toward Anna. Something blazed in her eyes, but was gone before it could be interpreted. "What is it to you, woman?"

After this she relapsed into grim silence, gazing intently at the empty air. They sat that way, the three of them, for several minutes, but Anna refused to accept the impasse as final. The slave was obviously entitled to misgivings about the motives of other human beings. Nevertheless, there was some key to the locked door of her heart. The Englishwoman revolved first one tentative approach and then another. Before she had

157

reached a decision she heard a strangled sob torn from the woman's throat. The hard face was shattered. Slowly the slave passed her bare arms across her eyes where a flood of tears had sprung. This acted as a signal for the little boy to scream lustily. The woman quieted him and then, to Anna's great surprise, began to talk of her own accord.

"Did you come here to the garden looking for me, gracious lady? Were you sent to find me by the Naikodah, my husband? Tell me, is he well? Have you come to buy me?" With a quick shift of her body she prostrated herself before Anna. "O gracious lady, merciful lady, buy me! Buy me! Help me to get my pardon!"

Anna pushed back the brown curls from her hot cheeks and tried to discern the meaning of the woman's incoherent jumble of words. Hesitantly she asked, "Why are you chained here? What sort of crime did you commit?"

This seemed a terrible question to the woman. Her face became a mask of anguish. Her black lips moved, but no sound came from them. With a convulsive movement she threw her arms over her head and began to weep. Her body wove back and forth, racked with passionate sobbing, while Anna looked on alarmed and helpless. After a while she became quiet, and turning her face to Anna, said bitterly, "Do you want to know my crime? It was loving my husband."

Anna was more puzzled than ever. "Why did you leave him, then, and become a slave?"

"Gracious lady, I was born a slave. It was the will of Allah."

The use of the word "Allah" gave Anna a clue. "Are you a Mohammedan?"

"My parents were Mohammedans, slaves of the father of my mistress, Chao Chom Manda Ung. When we were very young my brother and I were sent as slaves to her daughter, Princess Butri."

"If you can prove that your parents were Mohammedans, I think I may be able to help you. All the Mohammedans here are under British protection and no subject of Britain can be made a slave."

"But, gracious lady, my parents sold themselves to my mistress' grandfather!"

"That was their debt, which they have paid over and over again by their faithful service. You can insist that your mistress accept your purchase money."

"Insist!" the slave's eyes blazed into fury. "Do you know who my mistress is? Do you know she is the Chao Chom Manda Ung? Do you realize that she is the daughter of Chao Phya Nikon Badinton, the Minister of the North, and the most powerful man in the kingdom next to the Kralahome? I insist?" she laughed contemptuously. "Do you know that she was the consort of King Phra Nang Klao? And that the Lord of Life himself is her son-in-law? And do you know that her daughter, Princess

Butri, was his favorite for a long time, and is still high in his graces? *Insist?* I, who was born a slave!" The fire that had lighted the woman's eyes while she talked faded away. "No, my only chance of freedom is a pardon from my mistress herself, and that she will never give me."

"But what about your friends outside the Palace?" Anna suggested. "Maybe there's something they could do. Have you sent them word of your captivity here?"

"No. I was taken too suddenly. Perhaps they think I'm dead. I have no chance to talk to anyone here, not even to the slave who brings me my food. And her life is so hard already that she would never run the risk of carrying a message outside the Palace for me. My disappearance is still a mystery after four years. No one comes here but the Chao Chom Manda Ung, and she only visits the place once in a while with the most trusted of her slaves. Now that she is old the King lets her go in and out of the Palace as she likes. Every few weeks some of her slaves come to trim the trees in the garden or clean the house, but they have nothing to do with me except to ridicule me. If one of them showed any interest in me, the others would report it to their mistress." There was despair in her voice. "There is no one to help me. I shall be chained here until I die. No one cares any more but my husband—if he is alive. And he doesn't know where I am."

The eleven o'clock bell boomed through the solitude. Anna had forgotten about the festival she was to attend. The woman lay down beside the sleeping boy to rest, apparently worn out by the emotional effort of talking. She did not appeal a second time for help, accepting as a matter of course the impotence of the stranger against one so powerfully entrenched in privilege as her mistress. Anna placed her own small umbrella over the head of the slave in such a way as to shield her eyes and those of the boy. This simple act of kindness so touched the slave that she started up suddenly and, before Anna could prevent it, kissed the soiled and dusty shoes of the white woman. Anna's eyes filled with tears.

"Little sister," she said with sudden determination, using the gentle Siamese term, "tell me your whole story from beginning to end and I'll lay it before the King."

The woman sat up swiftly and adjusted the umbrella over her sleeping child. Her eyes kindled as she began: "My name, gracious lady, is L'Ore. My brother and I were born slaves. We were both so faithful that we became favorites with the Chao Chom Manda Ung. My brother was put in charge of one of her rice plantations at Ayuthia, and I was made the chief attendant of Princess Butri.

"One day the Chao Chom entrusted me with a bag of money and sent me to purchase some Bombay silk from the Naikodah Ibrahim. It was the first time in many years that I had been outside the Palace. I felt as if I had been born into the world anew, and as if my past life had been nothing but a troubled dream. It seemed to me that the river splashed and rippled more enchantingly than it ever had done before. It was broader and more beautiful than I remembered. The leaves and buds on the trees had burst forth as if to greet me. How green the grass was! And how clearly and joyously the birds on the bushes and in the trees poured forth their song, purposely for me, while from the distant plain across the river floated the aromatic breath of new-blown flowers, filling me with inexpressible delight! I was silent with a feeling of supreme happiness! On that day a new light rose in the east, a light that was to brighten and to darken all my coming life."

She paused for a moment, half smiling. Anna was amazed at the way the slave expressed herself. She had the rare ability, much coveted by Palace women, of extemporizing in poetry. Her story had fallen into it naturally. The graceful words were strange coming from her wild face and matted tangle of hair. Anna remembered then that the princesses of Siam made it a special point to educate children born in their households. Such slaves were often among the most cultivated women in the kingdom. No doubt either the Chao Chom Manda Ung or the Princess Butri had trained L'Ore as a minstrel. Anna could see her as she must have been, seated on the floor with a lute, while her mistresses relaxed on low couches nearby. Other slaves would have knelt in front of the great ladies moving fans with languid persistence, while L'Ore chanted the plaintive story of some long-dead love.

The slave spoke again. "We moored our boat by the bank of the river, and made our way to the shop of the Naikodah. My companions entered while I sat outside on the steps. They could not come to terms with the merchant, so I went in hoping that he would sell the cloth for the price they offered when he saw the money. But I was dazzled instead. I drew my tattered scarf tightly around myself and sat down. My friends continued to bargain while I wondered where I had seen him before, and why he had such an effect on me.

"After a great deal of bargaining about the silk, we came away without it, but the next day we went again and bought it at the merchant's price. I was surprised to see that he left five ticals in my hands when I paid him. 'That is our *kamrai* (perquisite),' the other women said snatching it. Time after time the Chao Chom sent us back to the same shop. The merchant was always respectful in his manner toward me. He invariably left five ticals for us, but I refused to share in this kind of profit.

"The merchant began to watch me closely, and one day after we had bought some boxes of fragrant candles and wax tapers, and I had paid him the full price, he left twenty ticals on the floor beside me. My companions pointed to the money, but I wouldn't touch it. When the merchant saw that I was unwilling to take it he picked up fifteen ticals and left five as usual.

"We returned by the river as was our custom. Every moment of freedom was sweet to us and we paddled our canoe very slowly. I hated to go back to the Palace. I was even tempted to plunge into the water and escape, but the responsibility of the money made me hesitate. Still almost unconsciously I had begun to indulge the hope of obtaining my freedom. I didn't know how or when."

She paused again. Anna was leaning forward listening. In a moment the musical voice took up the tale, but with a kind of wistful sadness. "Gracious lady, we all love Allah and we are loved of him. And yet he has made some masters and some slaves. Strange as it may seem to you, the more impossible my hope of freedom, the more I longed for it. Then one day a slave woman came to my mistress with some new goods from the Naikodah. When she saw me she asked for a drink of water. As I handed it to her, she said in a low tone, 'You are a Moslem. Free yourself from bondage to this unbelieving race! Take the price of your redemption from my master! Come out of the *Nai Wang* (Inner Palace) and be restored to the true people of God!'

"I listened in astonishment, afraid to break the spell of her words by questioning her. She left me suddenly, as if she were afraid of having said too much or of having aroused the suspicions of my mistress. I was in a more disturbed state of mind than I had ever been before. My thoughts flew hither and thither like birds during a storm, flapping their silent and despairing wings against the closed and barred gates of their prison. I found comfort only in trusting to the Great Heart above, and with the instinct of all sufferers I turned at once to him.

"When I saw the woman a second time I asked her, 'How shall I get my purchase money? Tell me quickly! Won't your master hold me as his slave?' She answered, 'He will give you the money, and never repent having freed a Moslem and the daughter of a believer from slavery.' I threw my arms around her, shaking with joy, but she freed herself quickly and, taking some money from her scarf, tied it into mine. Then she left me without another word. I was terrified for fear I would be caught with the money in my possession, so I came here that night and hid it under the pavement on which we are sitting.

"Several weeks later we were sent again to the Naikodah to buy sandalwood tapers and flowers for the cremation of young Princess Adung. I had never been so conscious of the shabbiness of my clothes as I was that day. We made our purchases and paid the money. When I stood up to go my friend the slave woman, whose name was Damni, beckoned to me. Her master followed us into an inner chamber and said—I remember every word—'L'Ore, you are so guileless and so beautiful that you have aroused my pity. See! Here is the money you have just paid me, double the price of your freedom. Take it, and forget not your deliverer!'

" 'May Allah prosper you!' Damni said in awe. But I could say nothing. All I could do was burst into tears. The merchant smiled as if he understood, and went back into the shop, while Damni found a handkerchief and dried my eyes. From that time on I lived from day to day, waiting and hoping. Physical freedom seemed to be almost within my grasp, but there was a new kind of bondage in my heart. 'I am more a slave than ever,' I thought, 'for who can ransom me from the sweet feverish servitude of love? I am the good merchant's slave forever.'

"I bided my time like a mother watching for the return of an only child. I knew that I could not persuade the Chao Chom to grant me my freedom unless she was in the mood for it, since she was proud and haughty and I was useful to her. So I waited long and anxiously, praying to God every day, calling him Buddha! Father! Goodness! Compassion! Praying passionately only for freedom.

"One day the Chao Chom was so kind to me that I thought my opportunity had come at last. I threw myself at her feet, and said, 'Gracious lady, be merciful to your child and hear her prayer. As the thirsty traveler beholds afar the everlasting springs of water, or as the dying man has foretastes of immortality, even so your slave L'Ore has tasted freedom through your goodness and would more fully drink of the cup. It is the only desire of her heart, the dream of her slave's life. Here is the price of my freedom, gracious lady. Be merciful! Set me free!'

"I didn't dare to look at her face, but when she spoke I knew that she was angry. She reviled me for ingratitude in wanting to leave her. She reviewed all her kindnesses to me, all the care and teaching that had been lavished upon me, and accused me of selfishness. I begged and implored and wept. 'You were born my slave,' she said coldly, 'and I will not take money for you. You are much more valuable to me than money.'

"But I only begged harder. I laid the money before her three times, as is the custom, and pleaded with her to accept it. 'Take double, most honored and gracious lady, only let me go!'

" 'Never!' she screamed in a terrible voice. 'Be still at once! I'll never set you free!' And then as if she had guessed half of my thought she asked suddenly, 'Do you wish to be married? Is that it? Very well, I'll find you a good husband, and you shall bear me children as your mother did before you. Pick up your money and go, or I'll order you flogged!'

"So it was all in vain. I gathered up my silver and returned to my slave's life, hopelessly defeated. I soon recovered from my disappointment, though, because I had made up my mind to escape. The Chao Chom was suspicious of me for more than a year. My companions saw that I had fallen into disgrace, and they pitied me, but I paid no attention to them and wouldn't answer their questions. I did my best to appear obedient and cheerful. After two years the Chao Chom gradually took me into her confidence again, although she never let me go out of the Palace. Finally she arranged a marriage for me with Nai Thim, one of her favorite men slaves. I didn't object. I even pretended that I was happy at the prospect of being free to spend six months of every year with my husband.

"The day before my marriage I was sent to see Nai Thim's mother with a small present from my mistress. Two strong women accompanied me. I had hidden my purchase money in my panung. As soon as we entered my future mother-in-law's house, I asked permission to speak to her in private. She thought that I had some communication from the Chao Chom and took me to the back part of the house. I sat down on the edge of the bamboo raft, which kept her house afloat. Without giving her time to ask any questions, I told her my whole story. Then I took the money from my panung and shoved it into her hands. And before she could refuse it I plunged into the river. I heard one startled scream above me as I disappeared under the water.

"I am a good swimmer, and I swam desperately for my life. The current took me rapidly downstream. I came to the surface from time to time for air, and then dived back under. The old lady's house was far below the Palace and there were no boats there as there are here in the heart of the city. When I found my strength failing I made for the opposite bank and climbed its steep side. I dried my clothes in the breezes that came upon me as if let free from heaven. There were no houses about and I was sure that no one had seen me from the moment I sank below the water. The old lady would think that I had drowned myself and the slaves would go back to the Chao Chom with her story. She, too, would count me dead. I had accomplished what had been the beginning and end of all my thoughts for two years. It seemed to me at first that perhaps it was a dream. Then I knew that it was not, and my joy was so great that I laughed out loud, and danced, and sang.

"From day to day my soul had been slowly withering away. Now it blossomed forth afresh as if it had never known a moment of sorrow. My laughter came back to me, and in very truth, gracious lady, I shall never again rejoice and sing in the desert places of my heart, or in the solitary places of my native land, as I did on that day. In the extremity of my emotion I forgot that night was a possibility. I could do nothing but rejoice. I do not know how many hours I sat there, but they were as minutes. Suddenly the sun set. The night descended. Darkness covered the earth as with a mantle. The wind began to blow in fitful gusts. I heard strange sounds, which seemed to come not from the earth but from some hideous realm beyond. But I knew that there were angels who heard the cries of human distress. So I prayed to them to come and hover near me, and as I prayed a deep sleep came upon me.

"When I awoke the stars were in the sky, but the strange noises disturbed me so that I fell on my knees and cried, 'O God! where art thou? Bring, oh, bring the day! Come with thy swift chariot and bring the light! Come and help thy unworthy handmaiden!' 'To believe,' says the

Prophet, 'is to have the world renewed every day.' So in answer to my prayer came the Angel Gibhrayeel and snatched away the dark mantle of Phra Kham, god of the night, and swift came Phra Athit, god of the day, scattering the shadow monsters of the world of darkness and making his glory fill my heart with praise, even as it filled my glad eyes with light."

She paused again musing. "I had been dazzled with the idea of liberty. But now I was faced with the question: Where shall I go? Who will employ me? There was no one in all this vast city to whom I could turn but the merchant and his slave woman. It was evening when I entered the hut of Damni, footsore and weary. Damni was overjoyed to see me. She gave me food and shelter and her best robe.

"Some days after this the merchant came to visit me. I felt dimly that the hardness of my heart would be complete if I resisted his kindness, and yet I could not believe that a rich merchant would marry an outcast slave like me. But one morning I found a white sari in my humble shed. After Damni had dressed me in it she led me to a room where the Mullah, the merchant, and a few of the merchant's friends were waiting.

"The Mullah put down his hookah and stood up. He put his hands before his face and uttered a short prayer. After that he took the end of my sari and bound it securely to the end of the merchant's *angrakah*, gave us water in which myrtle and jessamine flowers had been dipped, and placed a gold ring on my finger. Then he blessed us and went away. That was our marriage ceremony.

"During the days that followed I was as one drunk with new wine. I thanked Allah for the sun, for the beautiful summer days, the radiant yellow sky. I thanked him for the freshness of dawn and for the dew of evening. The glory of God shone upon me and filled my soul with intense delight. It blossomed like a garden of flowers in the perfect pattern of happiness.

"One day, about three or four months after my marriage, as I was sitting on the steps of my home, I thought I heard a voice in my ear. I had hardly time to turn when I was seized, gagged, bound hand and foot, and brought back to this place. When I was taken into the presence of my mistress, she ordered me chained to this post. Here I was chained until my time came and my child was born. A month after his birth I was chained here again, and my child was brought to me to nurse. This was done until he could come to me alone. But they are not unkind. When it is very wet the slave woman takes him to sleep under the shelter of her little shed."

L'Ore's voice had become feeble and almost inarticulate. "I could free myself from these chains if I would promise never to quit the Palace. That I will never do," she said in an exhausted whisper. Her head drooped on her breast. Then she fell forward on the stones, her hands clasped, her face buried in the dust. Anna knelt quickly beside her, but it was not a faint. She had fallen into a sort of stupor.

164

Anna sat back again on the stone coping of the pond to stretch her cramped legs and think. She looked at the woman lying inert on the pavement before her and marveled. The rudeness of her appearance, the sun-parched skin, the unkempt hair! But four years of unremitting cruelty, of exposure to sun and wind and rain, had not dimmed her courage or broken her spirit. Surely the slave's body could not endure much more, nor could her mind. Anna had a little awe-struck feeling that she herself was the answer to L'Ore's impassioned prayers. Else how had she come to the brass door? In the labyrinth of the Palace her seemingly aimless wanderings had had direction.

Anna reached down and touched L'Ore softly on the shoulder. The slave turned up a haggard face and asked if she had been dreaming. Her mind seemed to be in a daze so that she sometimes imagined her life only a nightmare which would pass, and not reality. Anna, looking deeply into that gutted face, gave up any attempt to comfort L'Ore with words of promise. Action alone would serve, and it was impossible to tell what could be done.

She left the slave face down on the burning pavement once again and passed through the silent door. The wind still soughed through the grass in the crevices of the old wall, but there were no shadows. The long dark street was empty as before. Anna moved soundlessly over the pale grass that covered it.

After twenty minutes of straying in and out of the harem streets she found one that was familiar. When she reached the schoolroom it was twelve o'clock and her pupils were all in their places waiting for her. In the ordered bustle of the temple that strange scene in the far corner of the Inside seemed completely unreal.

Margaret Ayer

21

## A SLAVE IS FREED

WHEN SCHOOL was over that afternoon Anna went to find the shop of the Naikodah Ibrahim. She had little difficulty, for it was in the section of the city where Indian cloth merchants had congregated, called Mussulman Square. It was a prosperous shop full of rich silks, perfumes, altar candles, scented tapers. The Naikodah himself was a tall Indian with kind eyes. Anna asked to speak to him privately and was taken into the apartment back of the shop. When she told him that she had come from his wife and child in the Palace, he was at first overjoyed to know that both his wife and the son about whose existence he had never heard were alive, and then moved to tears by their distress.

That night a deputation of Mohammedans, headed by the Mullah Hadjee Baba, called on Anna. Together they drew up a petition addressed to the King, which Anna agreed to deliver the next morning. The same invisible power that had drawn her to L'Ore seemed to be working still, for she was summoned early to the King's presence. She carried the petition with her and a gift, a small book entitled *Curiosities of Science*.

The King was very much pleased with the book and very gracious as she handed him the petition. He read it carefully, and then gave it back to her saying, "Inquiry shall be made by me into this case."

On the next day she received a note from him:

LADY LEONOWENS:—I have liberty to do an inquiry for the matter complained, to hear from the Princess Phra Ong Butri, the daughter of the Chao Chom Manda Ung, who is now absent from hence. The princess said that she knows nothing about the wife of Naikodah, but that certain children were sent her from her grandfather maternal, that they are offspring of his maid-servant, and that these children shall be in her employment. So I ought to see the Chao Chom Manda Ung, and inquire from herself.

S.S.P.P. Maha Mongkut, Rx.

His Majesty was as good as his word. As soon as Chao Chom Manda Ung returned, he ordered the chief of the female judges of the Palace, her ladyship Khun Thao Ap, to make an investigation. This turn of events pleased Anna, for she counted the judge a friend, and knew her to be scrupulously just.

By the King's order Anna carried to Khun Thao Ap the petition that the Mohammedans had signed. She found her in the open sala that formed one side of the prison and was the court. As Anna entered the judge raised her eyes from the scroll of the law that she had been studying.

"Ah, it is you, Mem," she said, taking off her spectacles. "I wish to speak to you."

"And for my part," Anna said, with more boldness than she felt—for she was almost as much in awe of the stern woman before her as were the ladies of the harem—"I have something I should like to lay before you."

"Yes, I know. You have a communication to make that has already been presented to His Majesty. Well, your petition is granted."

"Granted! How?" Anna asked in astonishment. "Is L'Ore already free to leave the Palace?"

"Oh, no! But His Majesty's letter gives us authority to proceed against the Chao Chom Manda Ung."

"But I thought your authority extended to all the women in the Palace."

"Yes, in a way it does. We are said to have the right to compel any woman in the Palace to come before us, but these great ladies will not appear personally unless they are summoned by a royal letter such as this one," she explained. "They merely send a frivolous excuse and do not come."

Seeing that Anna was still puzzled she explained what L'Ore had already explained in part—that the Chao Chom Manda Ung (Mother of a Royal Child Ung) was the daughter of one of the great families of Bangkok in addition to having been a consort of the late King. Her family's influence at court and her own position were such that in practice she was immune to any but the King's specific orders, which of course were law for everyone. Furthermore, her only daughter, Princess Butri, had been a consort of the King and was believed to be high in his favor. She had been the teacher of the late queen, mother of Prince Chulalongkorn. She was thus a privi-

167

leged person, and in addition she was much admired and respected as an authority on palace etiquette and as a fine poet.

Anna smiled fleetingly at the last words. She had been correct, then, in her guess that L'Ore's manner of speech was not an accident, but the result of her education.

Khun Thao Ap turned to one of the female sheriffs, and sent her for the Chao Chom Manda Ung, the Princess Butri, and the slave woman L'Ore. It was nearly two hours before the dowager consort and the princess appeared. They were accompanied by an immense retinue of female slaves bearing luxurious appointments for their royal mistresses' comfort during the trial. There were fans and cushions, betel sets and trays of refreshments. The sheriff, bending very low, followed the procession at a respectful distance.

The great ladies took their places on embroidered velvet cushions obsequiously placed for them by their slaves. Anna looked at them curiously. They were both small and finely boned, much alike except for the difference in age. They had unusually well-shaped noses for Siamese, disdainfully arched; heavy-lidded eyes; and thin tight-lipped mouths. There was an air of authority about them, and a subdued insolence in their manner toward the judge.

But Khun Thao Ap was unimpressed. The soft eyes in her heavy face did not alter their aloof expression. Only her graceful hands adjusted her spectacles as if better to see the women before her. She looked at the great ladies for a moment and asked, "Where is the slave woman, L'Ore?"

The dowager cast a malicious glance at the judge, but did not answer. She busied herself with tucking a pinch of tobacco under her lower lip before beginning to chew the fresh cud of betel which a prostrate slave held out to her. In the silence of the court her unspoken defiance echoed more loudly than words.

Around the open *sala* a rabble of slave women and children had collected, crouching on their heels in all sorts of attitudes and all sorts of rags. Anna, looking out over the stubbled heads, was deeply moved by the expressions on their faces. One of their humble number had challenged the great ladies of the Palace, and they hardly dared to believe that she could succeed in gaining her freedom. They all knew her story.

They saw the superciliousness and contempt on the faces of the queen dowager and her daughter. They looked from them to the austere face of the judge with anxious concentration, evidently astonished at her temerity, trying to fathom her enigmatic expression. The queen dowager had openly defied the judge. Would Khun Thao Ap really dare . . . ? Hope burned in unblinking eyes. For not one of them, lowly and half-clad, but knew that in the heart of the dark stern woman before them there was as great respect for the rights of the meanest as for those of the queen dowager herself.

With deliberation the judge read aloud in a clear voice the letter she had received from the King. When it was finished the dowager and her daughter saluted the letter by prostrating themselves three times before it.

Then the judge asked the ladies, "Can you advance any reason why the slave woman L'Ore should not be emancipated when she has offered to pay the full price of her freedom?"

Every eye in the crouching throng outside the pavilion left the face of the judge and fastened on the face of the queen dowager. She spoke with difficulty, struggling to control the rage that shook her. From head to foot her whole person mocked the judge. "The slave L'Ore was born in bondage. We do not choose to free It, since It has been useful to our daughter."

Khun Thao Ap's face looked sterner, more impassive. She ignored the calculated discourtesy of the other woman and spoke in a slow, measured voice: "It is the law and custom of this country that bond-servants have the right to redeem themselves." And taking from a casket a dark scroll of the Law she read:

> In the one thousand five hundred and fifty-seventh Year of the Buddha (A.D. 1013), in the sixth lunar month, during the waxing of the moon, the day being Sunday, His Majesty Baroma Bapit, being seated on his throne, gave command to his four chief Ministers that they should write an Appendix to the Law of Servitude. The sixth clause of this Appendix reads, "A bond-servant who is not pleased to abide with his master and who has secured the price of his redemption is hereby empowered to offer such redemption money to his master with a view to redeeming himself thereby. Any refusal on the part of the master to accept the redemption money and thus free the bond-servant is contrary to law, and punishable by fine."

The queen dowager cried in a ringing voice, "And what if every slave in my service should bring me the price of her freedom?"

All eyes turned again to the judge, sitting calmly on her little strip of matting. Every ear strained to catch her reply. "Then, lady," she said with quick emphasis, "you would be bound to free every one of them. That is the law."

"And serve myself?" screamed the dowager, her rage no longer controlled.

The voice of the judge was as cool as a lake. "Even so, my august mistress," she said, bowing low.

A sigh escaped the squatting crowd outside the pavilion. The Chao Chom Manda Ung turned very pale and trembled slightly.

Khun Thao Ap went on in her measured tones, ignoring both the mounting excitement of the rabble and the blazing anger of the royal ladies. "The bond-servant L'Ore desires to be free. It is the wish of the Kru Yai to redeem her, and His Majesty's pleasure that this shall be done in accordance with the Law of Servitude. I therefore declare and decree that the bond-servant L'Ore is no longer the slave of the Chao Chom Manda Ung, but the property of the Kru Yai. I do further decree that the price of her redemption shall be set at forty ticals."

The dowager looked at Anna spitefully. "Let her purchase money be paid down now, and she is freed from my service forever."

Anna was distressed. She had not brought that much money with her. But the judge spoke directly to her as if the pettiness of the dowager were a small matter not worth her attention. "You are now the mistress of L'Ore. I will have the *dika* papers made out. Bring the money to me to-morrow and all will be arranged."

"Thank you! Thank you very much," Anna said in a low voice. She rose from the floor, her knees stiff and shaky. She bowed coldly to the great ladies but they ignored her. This troubled her not at all, for her heart was full, and she returned home for once radiantly happy.

The next day she presented herself at the court again. Only three of the female judges were present with several of the sheriffs or *pa-kums*. Khun Thao Ap handed her the *dika* that freed L'Ore and ordered one of the *pa-kums* to go with her to see the money paid, and L'Ore liberated.

Once more Anna went through the tortuous alleys and came into the mysterious street that ended at the brass door. Her heart was beating rapidly as she pushed it open and stepped within. There was the slave, chained as before. But the piazza of the deserted house was full of people. Anna's heart leaped in triumph. The Princess Butri and the Chao Chom Manda Ung sat there, surrounded by their sympathizing women. They pretended to be unaware of Anna's presence, but they had not dared to absent themselves, as she had been afraid they would.

The *pa-kum* was timid and hesitant, so obviously afraid of the consequences to herself even of the discharge of her official duty, that Anna finally advanced alone. She opened her reticule and took out forty pieces of silver money. She had hardly laid them before the dowager when the angry woman dashed them away with her foot in token of her contempt. They went rolling hither and thither on the pavement. Anna ignored this childishness and kept her eyes fixed on the woman's face. Grudgingly the dowager gave the order that L'Ore was to be released and allowed to go.

A female blacksmith, a dark and ponderous woman, moved to the side of the slave and filed the rivet asunder. L'Ore was free at last! To Anna's amazement she did not move. When her chains fell off she merely sank to the pavement and lay inert with her hands folded in supplication before her royal persecutors. Anna stepped forward and spoke to her, but she made no sound. It was as if the chains had fallen from her leg and not from her mind, leaving her as helpless as before.

The thought had come to Anna when she had first talked to the slave that her long ordeal might have affected her mind, so that even physical freedom would not restore her. She could not drag L'Ore away by force, yet to leave her there would be a terrible humiliation as well as a serious defeat of justice, and the death of hope in many hearts. She whispered to the *pa-kum*, "What is the matter? What has gone wrong?" But the timid sheriff cast down her eyes and did not answer.

Anna was profoundly troubled. Currents and cross-currents flowed about her, and their meaning eluded her. She felt, as she often did in the harem, that she was walking uneasily over treacherous quicksands. The royal women on the piazza were chattering busily without looking at the prostrate slave or Anna. L'Ore lay like one dead. Her brown back was burned almost to ebony by the sun. Her matted hair had fallen forward over her outstretched arms. As Anna stood determined not to be driven away or outwitted a woman with a child in her arms passed behind her and said in a barely audible voice, "They have taken away her child."

So that was it! She had not foreseen this maneuver. The royal ladies had planned cleverly and maliciously. Free the slave they must, since the King had ordered it. But nothing had been said about the child. The faces of the crowd, which had been growing every minute as person after person seeped through the door, were marked with sympathy and sadness, as if the miracle of L'Ore's freeing had been too much to hope for after all. They exchanged glances. Anna caught faint half-whispered sighs. Then the same woman said in her ear, "Go back! Demand to buy the child!"

There was nothing else to do. She went back, alone and sad, more than half afraid that the case was lost. L'Ore would not leave her son, and Anna did not know whether there was any hope for him in the law or not.

Khun Thao Ap was still sitting on her strip of matting in the court when Anna reached it and stated her case. She said nothing, but opened a casket, drew out a roll and started toward the house of the brass door. When they reached the mansion the scene was just as Anna had left it. There sat the royal ladies, holding small jeweled hand mirrors and creaming their lips with a sublime air of indifference. There lay L'Ore still prostrate before them, her face hidden on the pavement. As Anna and the judge appeared, the crowd of women pressed anxiously in, and all eyes were strained to see what the judge was about to do.

She bowed courteously to the ladies and opened the dark scroll to read the law: "If any woman have children during her bondage, they shall be slaves also, and she is bound to pay for their freedom as well as for her own. The price of an infant in arms is one tical, and for every year of his life shall be paid one tical."

The precise terms of this declaration produced a strong effect on the crowd, and none whatever on the royal ladies. Ever so many betel-boxes were opened and the price of the child pressed upon Anna. She took the first offered and laid four ticals down before the women on the piazza. They only preened themselves the more in their mirrors. The judge, seeing that they intended to do nothing about restoring the child to his mother, sent one of the *pa-kums* for the boy.

In half an hour he was in his mother's arms. She did not start with surprise or joy, but turned up to heaven a face that was joy itself. Both mother and child bowed ceremoniously before the great ladies, who disdained to notice them. Then L'Ore tried to stand up and walk, and failing at first, laughed at her own awkwardness. Eager hands pulled her to her feet and she limped and hobbled away, borne along by the exulting crowd, at whose head marched the judge. Her weakness and difficulty in walking did not lessen her radiance. With her face pressed close to her boy's, she talked to herself and to him: "How happy we shall be! We, too, have a little garden in your father's house. My Thuk will play in the garden. He will chase butterflies in the grass, and I will watch him all day long."

The keepers of the gate handed flowers to the boy as L'Ore and Anna passed through, saying, *"Phutho di chai nak na! di chai nak na!"* (Merciful Buddha, we are very glad indeed! very, very glad indeed!)

In some mysterious way the news had spread outside the Palace. Before Anna, L'Ore, and Thuk had more than stepped through the gates on their way to the river they were surrounded by a host of Malays, Indians, Siamese, and some few Chinese, who had loosened their cummerbunds and converted them into flags.

So with an army of many-colored banners flying, the men, women, and children running and shouting along the banks of the Chow Phya, spectators crowding to the front of their floating houses, L'Ore and her son were put into a boat that took them down the river to their home.

The next day the Naikodah Ibrahim called on Anna to repay the money she had advanced for his wife and child, and to tell her that his son's name of Thuk, or "Sorrow," had been changed to "Free."

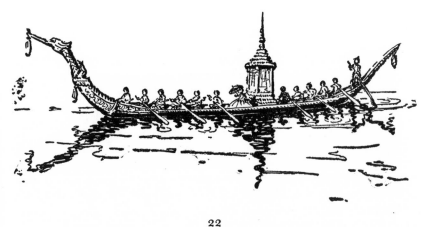

## 22

## THE DEATH OF THE FA-YING

THE EFFECT of L'Ore's almost miraculous return to her husband was far-reaching. Anna found herself famous overnight. Slaves going into the city from the Palace on business told the story to shopkeepers, who passed it on to their customers. Some of the great ladies of the Inside complained bitterly to their families outside. What, after all, was to happen to society if a slave could demand and get freedom merely because the price of it was available? From that time forward Anna had powerful enemies among the nobility who suspected her of revolutionary ideas.

That knowledge was for the future. In the spring of 1863 she was more aware of the common people. They fell on their faces as she passed. They crawled to her with their petitions as she sat on her piazza in the evening. When she entered the temple schoolroom she found at her place and on her chair flowers plucked by slave hands and woven into garlands. It was as if the humble people of Palace and city, the almost nameless—for they had only their given names like "Red" or "Black" or "Fat" or "Lotus"— had heard a long way off a bell intoning a new day, and had lifted their heads in hope of something better than they had known.

This new fame was to prove onerous, even dangerous, before the end. Anna's heart was to be wrung again and again with helpless pity. She was to give and give out of her small salary, even to dip into her principal in an effort to alleviate the daily parade of suffering which came to her. "The White Angel" they called her in awe. "Go to the house of the White Angel and she will help you," became a message of hope whispered in the ears of the distressed. They never knew her name, these people who came to her in simple faith. It is said that fifty years later when one of her grandsons tried to find the house in which she had lived by asking for

"Mem Leonowens' house" he met blank stares. But when he asked to be shown the "House of the White Angel" they took him to it gladly.

Only a week after L'Ore's freeing, the attention of the court swung away from Anna to other things, and she felt relieved. The King and all those about him were much occupied with the cremation of Prince Witsanunat, His Majesty's second son. He was not in the line of succession because he had been born before the King went into the priesthood. He was one of the two sons of the King's first wife. The Prince had been thirty-seven when he died the previous December, leaving eleven children, some of whom were older than his young step-sisters and brothers. He had been very close to his royal father and had handled His Majesty's private prop-erty for some years. His cremation, therefore, was on a grand scale. School was dismissed for a week in order that the royal children might attend the ceremonies and the ensuing festivities.

Anna was glad of a little respite. It gave her time to catch up on her personal correspondence and to teach Boy, as well as to attend to many household tasks. It so happened, then, that both she and Louis were on their piazza that afternoon of May 14 when he called out, "Look, Mama, look!" and pointed excitedly up the river toward the Palace. One of the royal barges, long and filled with rowers, had shot out into the midst of the river traffic and was coming toward them with tremendous speed. The boats of the market people, the launches shoving importantly among them with flags flying and boatmen in livery, gave way hurriedly for the barge.

The moment it had come alongside the quay a slave ran to Anna with a letter bearing the King's seal. She broke it open and read:

My dear Mam,—
    Our well-beloved daughter, your favorite pupil, is attacked with cholera, and has earnest desire to see you, and is heard much to make frequent repetition of your name. I beg that you will favor her wish. I fear her illness is mortal, as there has been three deaths since morn-ing. She is best beloved of my children.
                    I am your afflicted friend,
                        S.S.P.P. MAHA MONGKUT.

And the slave added an entreaty. "My lady," she cried, "three slaves are lying dead in the princess' court. And the Fa-ying was seized this morning. She keeps crying out for you. Please come to her quickly!"

Anna paused only long enough to tell Louis that he could not come with her, that he must stay with Beebe, and go nowhere, nowhere at all, and eat nothing except what Beebe cooked. Then she was in the barge. There was a coldness around her heart and her hands were wet with sweat. The boat seemed to crawl across the river. She learned that the little princess had gone with several other of the royal children to the theatricals and fireworks, which were part of the cremation festivities, on the evening before. She had seemed perfectly well. There had been cholera in the city for some weeks past, as there was every year, but no one had thought much about it, for the epidemic was not serious.

Anna urged the rowers on, but they were already exerting themselves to the utmost. The current shoved against them. And when she reached the heavy gates, how slowly they opened! She was breathless when she arrived at the little princess' room. Dr. Campbell from the British Consulate was standing near the door. He shook his head at Anna. His mouth formed words soundlessly, "She is dying."

The Fa-ying lay on a mattress in the middle of a carpet. Over her hung a canopy on which mosquito bars were draped. Around her bed relatives and slaves were chanting in anxious urgency, *"Phra Arahan! Phra Arahan!"* the most sacred of the titles of Buddha, which is repeated in the ears of the dying until life is extinct to remind the soul to go to heaven and not to lose its way. Old Princess Lamom, who had raised the child, was prostrate on the floor at her feet, apparently too overcome to do more than whisper the sacred syllables.

Anna crept close to the bed, her heart breaking and her eyes overflowing. Not this child! Of all the children in the Palace surely not this one child. The Fa-ying opened her eyes. Recognition stirred. She held out her arms. Anna clasped the little girl to her breast, the Fa-ying nestled close with a faint sigh, and lay still. Anna closed her own eyes in a vain effort to press back the tears. When she looked down again the Fa-ying was dead.

Anna kissed the delicate face, thinking with a spasm of grief that there was no more need for the chant since this little one would never lose her way again. She laid the tiny body on the mattress and straightened up. The significance of what she had done reached those in the room. The death chant was succeeded by a sudden burst of wailing. The sound rose thinly through the afternoon air and was caught up by others of the harem who were kneeling on the pavement outside. Anna could hear the shrill lament echo and re-echo faintly through the streets of the Inside as word was passed along.

"Dr. Bradley and I did everything there was to do," Dr. Campbell said heavily, picking up his bag. "It was already too late when we were called. Her pulse was imperceptible and her skin cold. Too bad, too bad."

Anna was stunned by the swiftness of the cholera. Only yesterday the Fa-ying had been alive and happy. Just a few short hours before she had embodied all that was dear to her royal father and many of her English teacher's hopes for the future. And now incredibly with all her promise and charm she was gone.

One of the women in charge implored Anna to go to the King and tell him what had happened. None of them dared to carry the terrible news that his favorite child was dead. Anna demurred, but finally responded to the real panic of the women.

Attendants conducted her to him. He was sitting apart in his study, still dressed in the white garments he had worn to the cremation of his son. He had just returned from igniting the pyre. As Anna entered the room she searched her mind for words with which to break the news to him gently. She could find none, but she did not need any. He read her face and, covering his own with his hands, wept passionately. Strange and terrible tears welled from a heart that sometimes seemed desiccated and shriveled to the point where it held nothing but an engrossing conceit of self.

What could she say? She sat helpless and yet unwilling to go, leaving the King alone with his grief. No one else had ventured to enter the room with her. It was late afternoon and the last of the sunlight slanted through the windows. The great clock on the nearby tower tolled six. The King sat with his head sunk in his hands, mourning for his child, calling her by tender names as if she were on his knee to hear them. Tears streamed down Anna's cheeks as she listened.

So for an hour they sat almost without speaking, but close in spirit. During that little time they were not an English school teacher and an imperious Eastern monarch, but a man and a woman weeping together for a beautiful child they had both loved. Then Anna stole quietly away.

It was morning before the King had sufficiently recovered his control to go to the hall where the Fa-ying's body lay on a white satin cushion, fringed with heavy gold. Princess Lamom was still prostrate at the feet of the child, and would not be comforted. As the King entered silently she moved to him across the carpet and mutely laid her head on his feet, moaning *"Phutho! Phutho!"* In the silent room all were weeping. Speechless, with trembling lips, the royal father took the little body in his arms and bathed it in the ceremonial manner by pouring cold water over it.

In this he was followed by other members of the royal family, by relatives, and the ladies of the harem in waiting upon him. Each advanced in the order of her rank and poured water from a silver bowl over the slender body. Two sisters of the King then shrouded it in a sitting posture, wrapping it tightly in long strips of waxed cloth, overlaid it with perfume, frankincense and myrrh, and swaddled it in a fine winding sheet. All the things necessary for this last office to the dead child had appeared silently in the hands of those whose duty it was to prepare the royal dead for the lying-in-state.

When these preparations were complete each person crept to the body and took a formal leave of it by repeating, *"Pai sawan na! Chao-fa-ying cha."* (Go now to heaven, Chao-fa-ying.) After the leave-taking was over, three young girls dressed in white brought two golden urns. The body was gently deposited in the first and this in turn was placed in the second, which was of finer gold and richly adorned with precious stones. The inner urn had an iron grating at the bottom, and the outer an orifice at the most pendant point through which the fluids of the body could be drawn off daily by means of a stop-cock.

These preparations were all harrowing to Anna, who had never seen them before, but she solaced herself by thinking that they could in no way disturb the rest and tranquillity of the little girl who had gone.

The double urn was placed on a gilt sedan and borne under a royal umbrella to the temple of the Maha Prasat where it was mounted on a graduated platform six feet high and surrounded with lighted tapers, tall candles, and fragrant oil lamps which hung from the ceiling. These lights would burn night and day for the six months that would pass before the cremation.

The King had followed the body of his favorite child from the palace to the temple with anguish in his face. During the ceremony he sat apart, his head buried in his hands, while the trumpeters and blowers of conch shells performed their lugubrious tasks. Insignia pertaining to the rank of the little princess were placed in formal order below the urn, as though at her feet. Then the musicians struck up a lamentation, ending in a plaintive and solemn dirge. When this had been completed His Majesty and all the princely company retired, leaving what was mortal of the lovely Fa-ying in the peaceful beauty of the Maha Prasat.

But she was not entirely alone. For three times daily, at early dawn, at noon, and at twilight, the musicians came to perform their requiem for the soul of the dead "that it might soar on high from the flaming, fragrant pyre for which it was reserved and return to its foster parents, Ocean, Earth, Air, and Sky." Mourning women joined the musicians in bewailing the early death of the child, extolling her beauty, her graces, and her virtues. Between the services four priests, who were relieved every fourth hour, chanted the praises of Buddha, bidding the spirit of the child "Pass on! Pass on!" and boldly sped it through the labyrinth before it, "through high, deep, and famous things, through good and evil things, through truth and error, through wisdom and folly, through sorrow, suffering, hope, life, joy, love, death, through endless mutability, into immutability!"

Three days later the King issued a proclamation to his foreign friends telling of the death of his little daughter:

The moreover very sad & mournful Circular from His Gracious Majesty Somdetch P'hra Paramendr Maha Mongkut, the reigning Supreme King of Siam, intimating the recent death of Her Celestial Royal Highness, Princess Somdetch Chowfa Chandrmondol Sobhon Baghiawati, who was His Majesty's most affectionate & well beloved 9th Royal daughter or 16th offspring, and the second Royal child by His Majesty's late Queen consort Rambery Bhamarabhiramy who deceased in the year 1861. Both mother and daughter have been known to many foreign friends of His Majesty.

To all the foreign friends of His Majesty, residing or trading in Siam, or in Singapore, Malacca, Pinang, Ceylon, Batavia, Saigon, Macao, Hong-kong, & various regions in China, Europe, America, &c. &c. . . .

Her Celestial Royal Highness, having been born on the 24th April, 1855, grew up in happy condition of her royal valued life, under the care of her Royal parents, as well as her elder and younger three full brothers; and on the demise of her royal mother on the forementioned date, she was almost always with her Royal father everywhere day & night. All things which belonged to her late mother suitable for female use were transferred to her as the most lawful inheritor of her late royal mother; She grew up to the age of 8 years & 20 days. On the ceremony of the funeral service of her elder late royal half brother forenamed, She accompanied her royal esteemed father & her royal brothers and sisters in customary service, cheerfully during three days of the ceremony, from the 11th to 13th May. On the night of the latter day, when she was returning from the royal funeral place to the royal residence in the same sedan with her Royal father at 10 o'clock P.M. she yet appeared happy, but alas! on her arrival at the royal residence, she was attacked by most violent & awful cholera, and sunk rapidly before the arrival of the physicians who were called on that night for treatment. Her disease or illness of cholera increased so strong that it did not give way to the treatment of any one, or even to the Chlorodine administered to her by Doctor James Campbell the Surgeon of the British Consulate. She expired at 4 o'clock P.M., on the 14th May, when her elder royal half brother's remains were burning at the funeral hall outside of the royal palace, according to the determined time for the assembling of the great congregation of the whole of the royalty & nobility, and native & foreign friends, before the occurrence of the unforeseen sudden misfortune or mournful event.

The sudden death of the said most affectionate and lamented royal daughter has caused greater regret and sorrow to her Royal father than several losses sustained by him before, as this beloved Royal amiable daughter was brought up almost by the hands of His Majesty himself, since she was aged only 4 to 5 months, His Majesty has carried her to and fro by his hand and on the lap and placed her by his side in every one of the Royal seats, where ever he went; whatever could be done in the way of nursing His Majesty has done himself, by feeding her with milk obtained from her nurse, and sometimes with the milk of the cow, goat &c. poured in a teacup from which His Majesty fed her by means of a spoon, so this Royal daughter was as familiar with her father in her infancy, as with her nurses.

On her being only aged six months, His Majesty took this Princess with him and went to Ayudia on affairs there; after that time when she became grown up His Majesty had the princess seated on his lap when he was in his chair at the breakfast, dinner & supper table, and fed her at the same time of breakfast &c. almost every day, except when she became sick of colds &c. until the last days of her life she always eat at same table with her father. Where ever His Majesty went, this princess always accompanied her father upon the same, sedan, carriage, Royal boat, yacht &c. and on her being grown up she became more prudent than other children of the same age, she paid every affectionate attention to her affectionate and esteemed father in every thing where her ability allowed; she was well educated in the vernacular Siamese literature which she commenced to study when she was 3 years old, and in last year she commenced to study in the English School where the schoolmistress, Lady Leonowens has observed that she was more skillful than the other royal Children, she pronounced & spoke English in articulate & clever manner which pleased the schoolmistress exceedingly, so that the schoolmistress on the loss of this her beloved pupil, was in great sorrow and wept much.

. . . But alas! her life was very short. She was only aged 8 years & 20 days, reckoning from her birth day & hour, she lived in this world 2942 days & 18 hours. But it is known that the nature of human lives is like the flames of candles lighted in open air without any protection above & every side, so it is certain that this path ought to be followed by every one of human beings in a short or long while which cannot be ascertained by prediction, Alas!

Dated Royal Grand Palace, Bangkok, 16th May, Anno Christi 1863.

A few days later the same royal barge that had come to summon Anna to the deathbed of the Fa-ying, bearing the same female slaves, came again in haste to her house. His Majesty commanded her presence at once.

"Is someone else ill with the cholera?" she asked in alarm. But they would not say. They seemed to be full of a suppressed and almost pleasurable excitement.

When she arrived at the school pavilion she found it decorated with flowers. Her chair had been painted red, and around the back and arms and legs fresh flowers had been twined. The books of the Fa-ying were laid out in order on the table in front of Anna's accustomed place. Across them had been placed a sheaf of roses and lilies.

Mystified and interested, Anna tried to get a hint of what the proceedings meant from the women of the harem who were bustling about. Some of them whispered to her that an extraordinary honor was about to be bestowed on her. Puzzled and apprehensive, she submitted quietly to being enthroned in the gorgeous chair. The paint was hardly dry, and she groaned inwardly at the thought of the damage to her dress. Boy, with the conservatism of childhood, protested nervously.

In a little while a messenger came from the King to ask whether Anna had arrived. As soon as he knew that she was in her place, he descended from his chambers, accompanied by the great ladies of the harem, the dowagers, his sisters, cousins, and aunts, paternal and maternal.

When he had shaken hands with Anna and Louis he explained the nature of the occasion. He was about to confer on Anna a distinction that had never been given to any foreigner. It was in consideration of her devoted interest in his daughter, and for her "courage and conduct," as he expressed it, at the deathbed of his well beloved royal child, the Somdet Chao-fa-ying. Then bidding Anna remain seated he carefully took seven threads of unspun cotton and passed them over her head and over the dead child's books and then placed the end of each single strand in the palm of each of seven of his elder sisters. This done he solemnly waved in rhythmic and formal motion a few gold coins, and dropped twenty-one drops of water from a jeweled conch shell. Finally he chanted a passage of Sanskrit in a low tone, and then placed in Anna's hand a small silk bag and commanded her to rise *Chao Khun Kru Yai* (Lord Most Excellent Teacher).

Later, she found the bag contained a patent of nobility and the title to many roods of land which pertained to it. The estate was in the district of Lopburi. Inquiry revealed that to reach it she would have to make a journey overland through dense jungle on the back of an elephant. She decided to leave it to its inhabitants—tigers, elephants, rhinoceroses, wild boars, armadillos and monkeys—to enjoy unmolested and untaxed, while she went on the even tenor of her way. In fact, she and Boy decided not to mention the matter at all. She had become so much more accustomed to hard work and opposition than to adulation that the only emotion she had felt during the ceremony had been one of acute discomfort, and fear that she was being made ridiculous. The solemnity of the occasion, the importance that the Siamese attached to her title, had only increased her discomfort.

"How did I look, Boy," she asked Louis on their way home, "with my head in string like a grocer's parcel?"

"Silly, Mama!" he giggled.

## 23

## THE KING'S SPECTACLES

THE ROUTINE of school was broken again in July when the King decided that his family should accompany him to Ayuthia. Anna was required to go with them. Louis enjoyed the change immensely and wrote to Avis: "We had a pleasant trip to Ayuthia in the King's beautiful yacht called *Royal Sovereign*. I saw some oh such large idols and I carried off one of the little ones." Anna enjoyed it, too, but was sick when she returned home to discover that her house had been ransacked by thieves and plundered of all its valuable contents. There was no doubt in her mind that her old enemy, the Kralahome's half-brother and interpreter, was responsible. The antagonism which had sprung up between them on the first meeting had never diminished—and he lived next door. She was able to buy back a few things at the pawnshops, but others were gone forever.

As the school grew it had been necessary to divide the classes. Some of the children made more rapid progress than others and this entailed further subdivision. Anna had been looking at her older pupils speculatively for months, hoping to find among them one or two who could help teach the younger children.

Lady Son Klin was far enough advanced, but because of her unfortunate position in the harem Anna hesitated to employ her assistance. Furthermore, the Mon princess was deep in a project of her own with which Anna was helping her twice a week. In the course of her reading she had discovered *Uncle Tom's Cabin* and was entranced. She read the book over and over until she talked about the characters as if she had known them intimately for years. Her grief over the early death of Little Eva was as real as if the child had been her own. Every time she read that part of the book she wept, and for days afterward went about with the saddened face of one in deep mourning. Suddenly the idea of translating it had come to her. Excited and happy, she worked with unflagging enthusiasm, turning the beloved story into Siamese.

Her admiration for the author of *Uncle Tom's Cabin* was extravagant. She told Anna one afternoon that she had decided to adopt the name of Harriet Beecher Stowe as part of her own, in token of her veneration for the American woman. From that time on she signed her frequent little notes to Anna "Harriet Beecher Stowe Son Klin," although she pronounced it "Stow-a."

The next most promising candidate for assistant teacher was one of the King's ladies-in-waiting named Prang. She was a girl of about sixteen, always dressed in the gayest colors. She was tall and slender with a dark complexion, waving jet black hair, and laughing eyes. Anna had noticed her at once on the first day she came to the temple. There was a vivid look of high spirits about her. Then, too, her hair was conspicuous. Unlike the other women she wore it long, in a heavy knot, fastened either with jeweled hairpins or a garland of fresh flowers. The frank smile with which she approached Anna that first afternoon was different, also, from the cringing and timid air that was generally affected by girls on their entrance into the school.

The minute Anna started to teach Prang a thrill of excitement went through her. The girl had a quick and brilliant mind. In a few weeks Anna was sure that she had found someone who could help her with the teaching. Prang rapidly overtook and passed the other pupils. Anna began to devote an hour a day to helping her and was delighted to see that she progressed with a speed impossible to the rest of the school. The girl explored the world of English books with enthusiasm as fast as she was able to read them. She committed long passages to memory for the sheer joy of learning.

Then after months of advancement quite unparalleled in Anna's experience, Prang's attitude changed. She was as vivacious as ever, but apathetic about her lessons. This was a disappointment to Anna, who had been planning to turn some of the classes over to her in a few months.

Any number of the women of the harem had shown a brief flare of interest in the school, only to grow bored a few months later, as Mrs. Mattoon had warned her they would. Intellectual discipline was foreign to them. Once the novelty of learning English had palled they returned to their own less exacting pursuits. But Prang had seemed different. She had ability and she had tasted the pleasure of study for the sake of knowledge. Her mind was too good to be abandoned without an effort to vacuity. Anna was sure of this. Therefore she tried in many little ways to revive Prang's interest, thinking that the girl had reached one of those plateaus where some stimulus from her teacher was needed to rally her interest.

One day Prang would be in her chair, working over hard sentences, spelling out words, writing and translating for hours on end. Even when the other pupils had gone home she would sit poring over her books, smiling to herself as the meaning of what she had read dawned on her. But the next day she would be listless and indifferent, or worse. She would spend her time impishly kicking the children under the table, hiding their books, or making faces at them. If Anna remonstrated with her, she would be absent from school for days or even weeks. On the other hand, if Anna ignored her pranks, she would take advantage of this seeming indulgence to wreck the ordered activity of the school. Yet she had a shrewd understanding of just how far she could go. Every time Anna had decided to be severe Prang would show such industry that Anna would begin to hope again that the girl's interest in her studies was firmly rooted at last.

If Prang had not been so capable of development, Anna could have handled her drastically without compunction, even if it meant that she left school permanently. But Anna could not put away the secret thought that in this girl she had the material of a good teacher. The problem was to find some way of controlling Prang's erratic ambition, and of curbing her puckish inclination to mischief. The girl was like a highly bred colt kicking its heels in the sun, determined not to be mastered. Anna thought ruefully that she herself seemed to have been cast more in the role of trainer than teacher. Nor could she make up her mind whether it was the part of wisdom to persist with kindness or to use an occasional flick of the whip.

Then one morning Prang arrived at the schoolroom very late. Anna looked up in annoyance from her little class to see the girl walking slowly across the floor. Her pretty face had a contrite look that stopped the sharp words of rebuke on Anna's lips. "She knows how I dislike having people come in late," Anna thought, mollified a little by the appeasing glance Prang sent her. "I won't scold her in front of the children."

Prang had hardly taken her seat before Anna heard titters and little shrieks from the children. So far as Anna could see, however, the girl had done nothing out of the way. Anna reproved the children quietly and turned back to her class, gathered around her at the head of the table. Every now and then a half-suppressed giggle told her that something was going on which amused the school. She looked at Prang suspiciously, but the girl was sitting near the far end of the table studiously reading a book.

When the disorder continued Anna dismissed the five children in her class and stood up to enforce attention. Then she saw the reason for the excitement. Seated on Prang's shoulder was a little black monkey, dressed in tiny crimson trousers, a crimson fez, and a blue shirt. He was holding one of Prang's books upside down, and seemingly was as much absorbed in study as his mistress. The sight was so funny that Anna could not help laughing. This was a signal for the children to give vent to the merriment they had been trying to smother.

The monkey accepted the compliment. He dropped his book and planted himself on Prang's head. He began to take the jeweled pins out of her hair, one by one, grinning and chattering at the children all the time. Prang took no notice of him and pretended to be completely engrossed in her book. He pulled her hair and scratched her head as if he were looking for fleas, and climbed all over her, but she did not look up. Then he darted at the other children as far as the string by which he was tied permitted. The children shrieked with delight, but still Prang acted as though she were unaware of the commotion.

Anna sighed. If the girl had deliberately set out to create a situation in which her teacher would have to resort to authority, she could not have found a better way. "Prang," Anna said, "your monkey is disturbing the other children. Take him outside, please!"

The girl darted a quick appraising look at Anna. "Oh, please let him stay, Mem *cha*," she pleaded. "He'll be good. Mentu, come back here and be quiet or the Mem will send you away!"

Anna shook her head firmly. "I'd like to let him stay, Prang. He's really very clever. But no one will be able to study as long as he's here. So tie him outside until school is over and then we can all watch him do his tricks."

The girl began to pout. "If you won't let Mentu stay, I won't come to school any more." Then she flashed her most winning smile at Anna. "Just try him once more, Mem *cha*. I promise you that he'll sit perfectly still and not bother anyone."

She ordered Mentu to take his book and go on with his lessons. Instantly he stopped pulling her hair and jumped to the table. He seated himself demurely as at first on her left shoulder, and pretended to study, peering at the other pupils over his book. As he did this he rolled his eyes with the oddest human expression as if to say, "Teacher's an old crosspatch, isn't she?" It was too much for the children. They let out an uproarious shout of delight. They hopped up and down in their seats laughing and pointing.

184

Anna was sorry that Prang had forced the issue which she herself had carefully avoided, but since the girl's challenge was now in the open it was impossible to evade it any longer. For if Anna ignored it, that subtle revolt every teacher fears would spread through the school with Prang its focal center. Some perversity in the girl had resisted Anna's kindness and had galloped headlong to this crisis. It was hard to imagine why it should give Prang satisfaction, but quite obviously it did. "Prang," Anna called peremptorily above the noise, "take Mentu out at once!"

Instantly the children were quiet. The girl stood up in her place, eyes blazing with anger. One by one she took her books and threw them to the floor, then her pencil, her notebook, and finally her slate, which shattered in an explosion of sound. Only after the last of the objects connected with her school work lay at her feet did she take the monkey in her arms and stalk out.

Day after day and week after week passed and she did not come back. Anna went to see her and to remonstrate with her, but it was useless. She even took Prang little presents, but the girl sulked and refused to return. So in the end Anna dismissed Prang from her mind and began to look around for someone else who could be trained to help her.

The matter would have rested there—much as Anna hated to admit defeat where a human problem as interesting as Prang was concerned— if it had not been for the disappearance of the King's spectacles. He had several pairs, but one pair in particular that he liked. He had taken them off and left them in the study while he went upstairs for a nap. When he came down they were gone. He flew into a rage that lasted not for hours but for days. Everyone around him suffered. Nothing anyone did was right. Dozens of women were thrown into prison. Many more were whipped for the slightest offense or for none at all. The food set before him was not fit to eat.

The women whose duty it was to wait upon the King searched every nook and crevice of the various residences in which the King lived, but without success. The Amazons started methodically through the houses of the women, and when they, too, failed to find the spectacles a kind of helpless panic descended on the harem. Life on the Inside was reduced to a frantic effort on the part of everyone to escape from the King's vindictiveness.

Then it occurred to him to offer a reward. This produced results. An old woman returned the spectacles to the King within twenty-four hours, saying that they had been brought to her secretly the night before by one of his maids-in-waiting. A little pressure extracted the name from her. And when Anna entered the Palace next morning, the first thing she saw was fifteen of the younger ladies-in-waiting being publicly whipped by Amazons for having participated in a conspiracy to steal the King's spectacles.

After the scourging they were carried off to prison weeping loudly to serve a term of several weeks. Prang was among them.

As soon as school was over Anna went to the prison, which was becoming a familiar place to her, and discovered from the Amazon guards that, as she had more than half surmised, Prang had been the leader in the reckless escapade. Was the girl mad? She would lose her head before she was twenty! She could torment her English teacher with impunity, but not the King! Anna sympathized with her Siamese friends who believed that *phi*, mysterious devils or spirits, often took possession of otherwise normal human beings and made them do all sorts of unaccountable things. There were *phi pluai* who would not tolerate the wearing of clothes; *phi pop* who were sent by sorcerers to devour the livers of their enemies; *phi pakkalong* who could locate stolen property, and many other kinds of *phi*. Since Anna was asking herself, "What gets into the girl to make her do these insane things?" she could not feel superior about the simple and not illogical explanation that satisfied the women of the harem. It was hard to understand the willfulness of Prang, although it was easy to see the highly dangerous direction that it was taking.

When Anna entered the court of the prison the girls had dried their tears and were playing *saba* on the pavement. Mentu was seated on a bench nearby, cracking peanuts and stuffing himself in a sly and furtive manner. Anna called Prang to her, and the girl came smiling as openly as if she had not just been caught and punished. "What made you steal the King's spectacles?" Anna asked her reproachfully.

"What made me?" the girl repeated airily with a toss of her head. "Why, nothing made me. I did it because I wanted to, for the fun of it, for a change, because it was something new. We were all bored with the stupidity of our lives here and we were looking around for something interesting to do. So I suggested that we ought to get together and do something really desperate this time, just to see if we couldn't stir up a little excitement in this dull old place. We talked over everything that we could think of, and we agreed that it would be fun to hide the King's favorite spectacles and see what would happen.

"Well, then we made our plans. And when it was my turn to wait upon His Majesty, I slipped them off the table and hid them in my vest while he was upstairs taking a nap. After a little while he came downstairs and missed them and began to rave, and of course we were all enchanted. It was much better than we had expected. We could hardly keep our faces straight. You should have seen him! He roared and danced around like a puppet, and stamped his feet up and down, and thundered like a wild beast."

She threw back her head and laughed heartily. "I thought I was going to burst out laughing right there. As soon as we were off duty we ran to my room and shrieked with laughter because our trick had turned out even better than we had hoped. And it was funny to see the King so upset day after day over a trifle. He kept shouting that he couldn't study nights until his spectacles were found.

"But after a while we began to be afraid because the King didn't forget about the spectacles and didn't stop being angry. We weren't sure what we ought to do next. We had planned to return the spectacles so that it would look as if the King had misplaced them himself and then forgotten where he had put them. That would have made it seem as if he had made all the fuss about nothing. But no one dared to try it, after all. We were afraid we'd be caught. The Amazons were looking everywhere for the spectacles and searching the houses, too. None of the other girls would keep them in their rooms, so I had to take them myself, and I knew that when the Amazons got to me they'd find them in my box of clothes. Then when the King offered a reward I began to be afraid that one of the girls would tell on me and claim the money. So I went and sold them to an old woman who lives around the corner from me, and I made her promise that she would say that she had found them lying on the ground and didn't know where they came from. But the wicked old thing took them back to the King and got the reward, and then she told on me and so here we all are in prison. But I'll tell you one thing, when we get out of here we'll lead her such a life that she'll think all the devils in hell have descended on her for breaking her promise. Believe me, she'll be sorry!"

"You're the one who ought to be sorry, Prang," Anna said. "Your prank wouldn't have been funny if you were six, and at sixteen it is inexcusable. Look at the number of women who had to suffer from the King's anger because of your stupid joke. Nothing is funny that causes other people pain." Then her voice softened. Of course this girl found the walls of the harem unendurable. Ennui drove some of the women to the illicit excitement of gambling. It drove this girl to practical jokes. Anna wished fiercely as she had so many times before that she had the power to throw open the gates and let such fettered creatures as this go free. But all she could hope to do was to help a few of them find escape into a new world of ideas and mental activity. "I suppose it is dull, Prang," she said, "but if you came to school every day, you'd have something to think about and you wouldn't get bored. So when you're released I want you to come back to school and really study. That will be your way of telling me you're sorry for throwing your books on the floor the way you did, and for playing a childish trick on the King."

The girl looked up at Anna impishly. "But I'm not sorry," she objected. "I'm not sorry even a little bit. It was fun. I never enjoyed anything more in my life. If you could have seen the King bouncing around like a shuttlecock with his face all purple, and shrieking like a parrot . . ." She went off into gales of laughter. "And even being whipped is a sort of change in this tiresome old place," she concluded defiantly.

Anna left her. The girl was surely like a colt. "All right," Anna thought, "I'll be persistent and I'll be kind, but I won't give up until I break her to the saddle." The analogy did not satisfy her. "What I mean," she reflected on the way home in her boat, "is that I must help her get the saddle on herself before she destroys herself. As she is now, she's a menace to her own future."

Anna remembered herself at sixteen and realized how horrible Prang's narrow existence would have seemed to her then. This beautiful, slender, high-spirited girl should never have been forced into so plodding a life. Anna felt a warm impulse of sympathy for Prang's futile explosions of rebellion. Nevertheless the harem life was now the only one that Prang would ever have. School and books would make it less monotonous.

When Prang was free again, Anna waited to see if she would reappear at the school. Several days passed and she did not come. Anna called on her. Again and again she went to Prang's house, pitting her will against the girl's. She talked no more about school. She didn't cajole, she didn't upbraid. She listened to Prang's stories of life as a lady-in-waiting. She talked about Avis in England, or about India, or Singapore, or England. At first she felt that Prang was braced against her. Even when the girl's antagonism melted Anna said nothing about school. But she kept visiting the girl's house, week by week, always pleasant, always interested. Then suddenly one day Prang burst into tears and threw her arms around Anna's neck, pouring out a torrent of words—her unhappiness and boredom in the Palace; a flood of accusations against herself for her ingratitude to Anna, the only person who cared about her, incoherent promises.

The saddle was on. From that day forward as long as Anna stayed in Siam, Prang was her loyal assistant in the school.

## 24

## THE KING'S BIRTHDAY

IT WAS a rainy afternoon in the middle of October. School was in full swing when a small page came to the Temple of the Mothers of the Free for Anna. "His Majesty orders the Mem to come at once to the Audience Hall. Something has happened."

Anna was annoyed at having to drop her school books in the middle of a lesson, but there was no choice. She snatched her umbrella and hurried off through the storm. When she reached the Audience Hall she was half drenched. The King seemed to be abnormally excited and incoherent. He was marching up and down with rapid angry steps, shrieking in a shrill and exasperated voice, "Eighteenth of October, eighteen hundred and sixty-three! Eighteen hundred and sixty-three!"

When he reached the far end of the hall he would about-face in a sudden bound and come leaping toward Anna with the same cry. She stood bewildered. Had he taken leave of his senses at last as she had feared that he some day must from the excess of rage that shook him so frequently? He paid no attention to her entry, but continued his curious march for almost half an hour, leaping and bounding up and down the hall, and shrieking again and again, "Eighteenth of October, eighteen hundred and sixty-three! Eighteenth of October, eighteen hundred and sixty-three!" She was perplexed and half afraid of the seeming lunatic before her, uncertain whether to run or to wait his pleasure. To her further confusion he then sprang close to her and screamed, "Mem, do you understand the meaning of the word 'agility'?"

She replied coolly, "Your Majesty has been giving me a very practical illustration of the word."

"Aye, aye!" laughed the King. "It is true, very true. You understand the English word 'agility.'" Then with a return to his previous mood of wrath, "On the eighteenth of October, eighteen hundred and sixty-three, I shall be fifty-nine years old. And you can see that I am as young and as strong as ever!" He waved a newspaper clipping under her astonished nose. "But certain American missionaries have published a statement about me in an English newspaper, and have said that I am a 'spare man.' How can I be a spare man? A King cannot be a spare man. How can I be spared from my kingdom? Who can fill my place? I ask you that? Who can fill my place?" And he resumed his infuriated march.

Anna shook with silent laughter. "But, Your Majesty," she protested to his retreating back, "the word 'spare' has two meanings. One of them is 'extra,' but the other one is 'thin.' All the missionaries meant to say was that you are a thin man, and not that you are superannuated and unnecessary, as you have interpreted it." Anger had stopped his ears to reason, and no matter how much she tried to explain he refused to be cajoled into listening.

"I will prove it I am not a spare man," he shouted, drowning out her explanations. "I'll show them I'm as young as ever."

Then he ordered her to sit down at once and write invitations to a birthday dinner to be given on the eighteenth, only three days off. Every European and American in Bangkok was to be included. Furthermore, she was to set the table herself in the Audience Hall so that everything would be done in the best European style and according to European etiquette. Everything must be perfect to the last detail! His slaves would cook the dinner and serve it and provide her with all she needed. But she must supervise them and be responsible for all arrangements.

"But, Your Majesty," she protested, "your birthday comes on Sunday this year. The missionaries will surely decline."

"Very well, make it on Monday then. They shall come. They shall see I'm not a spare man!"

Anna sighed at this new stretching of her duties. It was useless to remind the King that her little school was in session. There was nothing that she could do but dismiss it and begin on the invitations. She went home through the rain and got out her copy of Dr. Bradley's *Bangkok Calendar*. Turning to the list of foreign residents she began to write. Since there were more than fifty invitations to be issued, it was a tedious business. English, French, American, Spanish, German, and Portuguese residents of the city were all asked.

When the task was finished and the invitations delivered to the King's chief messenger, she began to inquire about table arrangements. She would place the British Consul, Sir Robert Schomburgk, who was the King's own age and the senior member of the small diplomatic corps, at the head of the table, and would herself take the foot.

Eighty-two were expected and on the morning of the nineteenth the tables were arranged and handsome carved chairs brought. Women appeared with a length of perfect heavy white silk, richly brocaded, that went from head to foot of the board and was to serve as a table cloth. But there were no table napkins. While Anna hurried some of the women off to look for napkins, others arrived with a magnificent dinner service of pure gold in an antique pattern. She had never seen anything so superb even in a museum. There were plates, dishes, goblets, vases, stands, candelabra and ornaments of every form, shape, and size, all most exquisitely worked and inlaid with precious stones.

Anna enjoyed setting the table with the beautiful service. It was worthy of a king when she had finished. But as yet there were no knives and forks or other silver. When she demanded these, the woman brought her instead a basket of chopsticks, also of gold. "No, no!" she said. "These will never do. You must find me some knives and forks and spoons. We Europeans couldn't eat soup or anything else with chopsticks."

The women shook their heads in amazement and started off dubiously. A long search failed to reveal any knives, forks, and spoons worthy of the table. All they could find was a box of old ones of the commonest kind, rusty from long disuse, and these had to suffice, for there seemed to be no others. When Anna left in the late afternoon to dress for dinner the napkins had not yet arrived, but everything else was ready. The hall was brilliantly decorated with flags and burnished armor, garlands of flowers, and innumerable gold and silver lamps. The dinner table which reached from end to end of the great room was resplendent, seeming actually to bend under the weight of gold and silver on it. Incense and perfume filled the chamber. There was nothing further Anna could do except urge the importance of napkins upon the sluggish servants, who seemed unable to comprehend her concern.

When the guests began to arrive the King himself received the men in one of the drawing rooms. Everyone exclaimed over the flowers arranged with the unrivaled skill of the ladies of the Inside. There was a roll of pleasant conversation. While Anna led the women to a room prepared for them, the King entertained the men by firing with his own hands a twenty-one-gun salute in honor of his birthday.

Among the guests, most of whom knew each other from long acquaintance, were two strangers—Sir Richard McCausland, Recorder of Singapore, and his sister. They were traveling through Siam and Burma, and had arrived in Bangkok opportunely on the sixteenth of October by the *Chow Phya.* Sir Richard was a long-time correspondent of the King. He was, moreover, in especial favor with His Majesty as a result of his opposition to the extreme policies of Colonel Orfeur Cavenagh, Governor of Singapore, Malacca, and Penang. Sir Richard had often given the King sound and cautious advice on affairs of state, which His Majesty interpreted as the intervention of a friend designed to checkmate somewhat the rapacious Cavenagh. The King was delighted, therefore, that Sir Richard and his sister could be present at the banquet.

The Honorable Miss McCausland was in full evening dress of the very latest fashion with low neck and short sleeves. The other ladies looked dowdy beside her, the more so because her arms and neck were dazzlingly white and of exquisite proportions. Anna introduced her to a few of the guests and then started the movement toward the dining hall, hoping fervently that the napkins had arrived. When all the guests were assembled about the table and ready to sit down the King himself entered with a bottle of rose-water in each hand to sprinkle them, as was the pleasant Siamese custom. He was smiling affably as he came in holding the bottles.

Then he stopped suddenly. He had known that Sir Richard was bringing his sister with him, but he had not yet seen her. The unexpected vision of the beautiful Irish girl dumbfounded him. The few white women in Bangkok had long since lost all bloom and acquired the pallor of people who live many years in the tropics. But Miss McCausland, newly arrived from England, bloomed like a rose fresh from a country garden. Everyone in the room was discreetly enjoying her charm. The King, however, seemed completely overwhelmed. He stopped short with his mouth slightly ajar. When he could move, he said to her, "Wherefore have you decorated yourself more than all the rest? Shall it be for my observation?"

Miss McCausland blushed a deep crimson, and was at a loss to know what to answer. But the King, unconscious that he was breaking the rules of English etiquette, trotted round and round the embarrassed girl, chuckling and ejaculating, "She is very fine! She is very fine indeed!" Suddenly he halted his circling promenade and asked, "Are you an anecdote?"

The girl's embarrassed eyes took on an expression of alarm. Anna, who had started for her own place at the foot of the table, turned and hurried back. Miss McCausland threw her a beseeching look. Anna was afraid that she knew all too well what was going on in the King's mind. If she were right, she must intervene quickly, not only for Miss McCausland's sake but for the King's. Nothing but trouble would come from a public rebuff such as Sir Richard might feel obliged to administer to his old friend.

After the death of the Fa-ying, Anna herself had been showered with the King's attentions. The underlying antagonism that had existed between them from the second meeting when she had refused to live within the harem walls had been dissolved in a warm tide of favor. It had begun with the conferring of her title and ended only recently with the gift of a valuable diamond ring. She had been wary of accepting even the title, and troubled by the stream of gifts. She had been afraid of being placed in a false position, sensing uneasily a current whose direction she could not determine. An increase in salary would not have affected her in this way, but it was not offered. And because it was the King's custom to bestow favors generously on those with whom he was pleased, she was reluctant to disrupt the new and pleasant atmosphere by any seeming discourtesy. So she had accepted even the ring.

There had been something a little odd in the King's manner when he gave it to her, but although she puzzled about it the rest of the day she could not define it. Then the next mail had brought a letter to the King from a Frenchwoman suggesting that she would be happy to become a member of his harem. During the period that Anna was to serve as the King's secretary she was to handle not less than twenty of these genuine offers from French demoiselles. The letters usually enclosed pictures of very pretty girls and were more enterprising than any other "proposals" that she had to translate. His Majesty rejected them all emphatically. He entertained a lively horror of being beguiled into fathering a Franco-Siamese heir to the throne.

On this particular occasion Anna handed him the letter with a little laugh. He read it and returned it to her.

"No, no," he said hurriedly, "write her and say 'No.'" Then he gave Anna again the curious look that he had given her with the ring. It was a long look, speculative, and a little more. "If she were English. . . . But no, no, not a Frenchwoman. . . ." He hesitated, looking at Anna meaningfully. Then he seemed to change his mind and turned away without saying more. And in that instant she knew what the diamond ring had been intended to say. She remembered with sudden clarity the enormous sums offered year after year through solicitors at Bangkok and Singapore for an English girl of good family. And here she was herself, not a girl, since she was twenty-eight, but English, and of good family, and so useful!

The next day she had quietly returned the diamond ring. "Your Majesty," she explained, "I hesitated to accept so valuable a present, and now that I have had a week to think it over I have decided that I shouldn't have taken it in the first place. Of course, any time that you feel my services deserve an increase in salary—well, I should be very grateful for that instead." The King had accepted the ring without a word. They had looked at each other, both faces masked by outward formality, but with perfect understanding. And from that day on Anna found herself again on the old basis with her employer.

All this flashed through her mind in the few seconds it took her to reach Miss McCausland. The King never gave up easily. Here was a beautiful girl fresh from England, and furthermore the sister of a friend! Anna felt that she must interpose herself between the impulsiveness of the King, who might not realize how preposterous it would seem to a man like Sir Richard that his sister be invited to join a harem, and the amused derision of the guests who were watching the drama with too much avidity to please

Anna. But before she could come to the rescue the King continued, "I mean are you an unmarried woman?"

"Your Majesty," said Anna, taking the situation firmly in hand, "an anecdote and an unmarried woman are not the same thing in English. In fact, the two words mean surprisingly different things."

The King looked extremely annoyed. "No they don't!" he retorted. "An anecdote is something that is not yet told, and an unmarried woman is something that is not yet given forth, and they are the same! There is no difference, I say!" He cast Anna a baleful look designed to put her in her place, but she refused to see it.

Then, as if to settle the argument, he took his two bottles of rose-water and with a swift motion deluged the pretty girl before him from top to toe —hair, shoulders, gorgeous dress—with the entire contents of both bottles. "There!" he said with satisfaction. "Now sit down, everyone!" And smiling triumphantly he turned away to someone else.

Anna did what little there was to do for Miss McCausland, who was close to tears. Sir Robert Schomburgk seated her gallantly at his right. "Well, Miss McCausland," he said, "now you know what an anecdote is. And I have an idea that your friends in England will enjoy this one even if you didn't." She smiled a little tremulously, and the alarm faded from her eyes.

Anna thought, as she hurried down to her place, that the dinner had begun like a nightmare. Bangkok would rock for days with descriptions of Miss McCausland's unexpected shower bath of rose-water. Someone would probably write a letter to the Singapore papers, perhaps even to the London papers, and the King would be furious. Still, the faces of the guests seemed to indicate that at least they were highly diverted. The napkins had not arrived either!

Before the guests had finished chuckling discreetly over the plight of Miss McCausland, the King's dwarf appeared with the obvious intent of entertaining them. Anna's heart sank again. She had not been told that Nai Lek (Master Little) was to be a part of the program or she would have objected vigorously that he would be abhorrent to many of the diners.

Anna had seen the dwarf for the first time a year before in a procession. She had observed what looked like an ostrich riding a horse. It was full-feathered, with a long neck, curious head and beak, and enormous tail and wings, which kept flapping up and down. The more she looked and asked and wondered the more the people near her had screamed and shouted and clapped their hands with delight at her bewilderment.

Since she and Boy had been mounted also, she rode close to examine the extraordinary bird. But the mystery remained. The creature had the head, body, wings, and tail of a huge ostrich. Anna had never seen wilder eyes or a more idiotic grin. The creature's hands and feet were as large as a man's. Before she could analyze the oddity the procession ended, and she and Boy had had to turn their ponies over to the grooms in attendance, and take their places beside the royal children in the King's pavilion to watch the fête.

A roar of laughter from the crowd brought them to the front again to see what was going on below. There was the half-human, half-bird monster performing grotesque somersaults. Every new leap, every turn of the bird's head over its human heels brought explosions of merriment from the crowd. Now the ostrich stood on its tail, now on its hard beak, fluttering its wings and two short dumpy legs in the air. Now it thrust its arms out of sight, and its two short legs into the ostrich legs that were dangling on its breast, and was transformed wholly into a bird, except for those two dark human eyes.

Twice streams of blood issued from the nose and mouth, but this seemed to disturb no one, and least of all the ostrich. Apparently the joy of making the King and royal family laugh until tears ran down their cheeks more than compensated for the bleeding nose and battered teeth. When all the antics were finished the King threw the bird a sack of money. Two men came out leading his horse and lifted him once more astride the beast. The ostrich raised his beak three times in the air, flapped his wings violently by way of saluting the King and royal family, and rode away amid cheers.

The next day Anna found that the ostrich was in fact a dwarf, a Lao from the north, who had been born to a peasant couple some years before. The parents were sure that the child was a trick of the devil or an impersonation of the devil himself. From the beginning he had looked like a freak, and as he grew older it became apparent that he was half-witted. Some of the neighbors suggested leaving him in the woods to die. The parents would not do this, partly because he was their child, and partly because they were afraid that his spirit would return to haunt them in some more dreadful form. So they took care of him, although they were convinced that he was not a human child but a hobgoblin from some other realm.

He was discovered by one of the King's half-brothers on a hunting trip into the north and brought to Bangkok to be trained in athletic and gymnastic tricks. When he had learned these, he was presented to the King as a comedian and buffoon.

Anna had been eager to see him out of costume but he was not allowed to enter the harem except on special occasions because he frightened some of the royal children. When she did see him she found him revolting in the extreme. His head was covered with woolly hair, his forehead was low and receding, his eyes were set close, like those of an ape, and were wild and rolling. From his enormous mouth two great teeth protruded. His ears were large, his chin sharp and pointed. He was only a few inches more than three feet tall, and his legs were so short that except for the immense flat feet they seemed hardly strong enough to support his huge head and square shoulders. As if to strengthen the resemblance to the ape his hands almost reached his feet. The mere sight of him was enough to ruin any appetite.

It was this creature who now approached the beautifully appointed table and picked up a tureen of soup, which he began to juggle audaciously to the breathless amazement of the guests. Everyone stopped talking and watched. He placed it on the tip of one forefinger and whirled it over his head, but nothing spilled! Then he returned it to the table and vanished. The next instant he was back with another dish to continue his performance. Every few minutes he would reappear and the process would be repeated, to the delight of the guests and to Anna's acute anguish. She had done everything in her power to make the dinner arrangements correct and dignified. What could she do? She was all too well aware that, if one word of ridicule or criticism reached the King after the banquet was over, it would be herself who would be blamed.

Just then a page crept in and summoned her with the news that the napkins had arrived. She hurried out, wondering how to distribute them tactfully. In the corridor she met Prince Chulalongkorn and behind him the King bustling toward her with great speed, and in their arms bales and bales of table napkins. The King thrust those he was carrying unceremoniously into her hands and rushed back to his guests. He had remembered the original purpose of the banquet, which had been driven from his mind temporarily by the loveliness of Miss McCausland. Anna heard him exclaim dramatically, "Who can say that I am a spare man?" He cast a dark look at the group of missionaries at the foot of the table, but they were serenely unaware of their fault and missed its significance.

Anna was struggling with the napkins. They had been brought from the warehouse just as they had arrived from Europe, in long strips of twelve. And there were no scissors to cut them apart. Finally, in despair at this new complication, Anna distributed a roll to each guest, and left to each the problem of how to manage them.

After that everything went smoothly. The food was delicious, European and Siamese dishes alike. Salads of vegetables daintily carved in the perfect likenesses of flowers came on golden platters with a tart sauce. There were ducks, roasted and boneless, delicate little cakes, and pastries of a dozen kinds. The dwarf wearied of his game and disappeared. The rest of the servants behaved extremely well.

It had rained in the late afternoon and the fresh air that came through the high open window was scented with the spicy odor of some flower. The guests laughed and talked and seemed to enjoy themselves thoroughly, forgetting for the time being the endless quarrels that separated them. Even Miss McCausland regained her composure and began to eat.

Once again at the end of the dinner the King made his appearance. The guests rose to drink his health. The British Consul, who had held a whispered colloquy with Anna regarding the King's strange pronouncement, and who had thus learned the story of the occasion for the dinner, proposed the toast:

"To His Gracious Majesty, the King of Siam, our host. It would be a sad day for the country if her King ever became a spare man."

A look of surprise flitted across the faces of some of the guests. Had Sir Robert, who was known as a heavy drinker, had perhaps—well, one too many?

But the King's smile was that of a pleased child. He looked triumphantly at the missionaries, still innocent of their fault and unaware of his displeasure. Ha! He had proved his point, he had!

25

## A BABY IS AUCTIONED

FOR A FEW months Anna had stood so high in the King's favor that she had been immune from some of the vexations which made her ordinary life difficult. But the peaceful interlude after the death of the little princess was short. She had not been entirely free from annoyance even then, for the vengefulness of the interpreter, who lived next door to her, never abated. She had been robbed in July, almost surely at his instance. Now in October he upset her little household again.

She was startled one morning soon after the dinner party to hear a great outcry in the alley that ran beside her compound. Through the uproar she caught an occasional coherent phrase indicating that Moonshee was in trouble. She rushed downstairs to see what was happening. The noise had ceased by the time she reached the gate, except for a low moaning. On the ground lay Moonshee, hardly more than half conscious. His clothes were torn and stained with blood, his turban lying beside him. There were welts on his head and one eye was badly swollen. Beebe came running, as did some of the neighbors, and between them they managed to carry the old man to his room.

"What happened to him?" Anna asked the neighbors. "Who beat him? Did any of you see?"

One of them explained that Moonshee had been standing by the gate when the interpreter and his servants approached on their way from the river. The interpreter had stopped and commanded the dignified Moonshee to bow. Moonshee had refused. The interpreter had then given orders to his servants to beat the old man until he prostrated himself "as is proper before one of my rank," and they had set upon him with clubs. Moonshee moaned on his bed and asked over and over, "Am I a beast that I should grovel before these infidel princes? Am I an unbelieving dog that I should lick the dust over which they pass? O son of Jaffur Khan, how hast thou fallen!"

This was too much! Minor irritations could be ignored, but not this insult, Anna thought angrily. The proud old Persian was not a Siamese. She had no intention of letting anyone enforce the custom of prostration upon her household. She had rejected it for herself from the beginning and she rejected it for Moonshee and Beebe. It was not their way any more than it was hers. Old Moonshee was always courteous according to the manner of his own country, and that was enough. Besides, she hated prostration, seeing in it a mirror of slavery. Each man must grovel before his superior, while he demanded the same gesture of submission from his inferior. One American who asked a Siamese friend somewhat petulantly why the alleys and walks of Bangkok were so narrow that two could not proceed abreast, had been answered incredulously: "But you have been here a long time! You know the Siamese! Have you ever seen two Siamese of exactly equal rank? But of course not. So why should the walks be broad enough for two, since there are no two in the kingdom who could walk together? One must go ahead and one must follow. Or if they meet, one must get off the walk and prostrate himself until the other has passed."

As soon as Moonshee's wounds had been washed and dressed, Anna put on her bonnet and went to the Kralahome's palace to enter her complaint. During the eighteen months that she had been in Siam she had gone often to ask for assistance. She had come to have a genuine respect for the prime minister's sense of justice. He was not cheerful and friendly like fat Prince Wongsa, the King's half-brother and physician, who was the most popular Siamese in Bangkok with the European and American community. He was not suave and accomplished and genuinely kind as was the Second King. But he had great power balanced by keen intelligence. Anna had taken many cases to him, usually in someone's else behalf, and had found him fair; never really cordial, never really concerned for the abstract principles of right and wrong, but fair. In a country still governed according to the ancient pattern that was a great deal, since the average court decision went to the person who could pay the highest bribe. Government was only nominally by law; actually it was by the will of the King and of the feudal lords. Each great noble maintained a court with judges, where his own brand of justice was dispensed. Even the nascent police force under Mr. Ames had jurisdiction only in the area of the great bazaar. Its authority did not extend to this side of the river. Anna had a choice, then, of taking Moonshee's case to the Kralahome or of taking it to the British Consul. And so far she had been chary of appealing to the consul.

"Your Excellency," she began without preamble as soon as she had been admitted to his study, "the servants of your brother have beaten Moonshee in front of my house for refusing to prostrate himself. He is a Persian, and not accustomed to prostrating himself before anyone. I strongly object to this insult to an old servant and myself, and I have come to you for justice."

The Kralahome stared at her with his habitual coldness. She could not read his look, but she waited confidently. Ever since the time he had helped her in the matter of Lady Son Klin's imprisonment she had been content to ignore his appearance of indifference, confident that it cloaked a stern morality. But today he refused to be concerned about his brother's lawlessness.

"The old man is a fool," he said with emphasis. "What happens to him is of no concern to me. Keep him out of my brother's way if you don't want him beaten again. Or command him to prostrate himself before his superiors like everyone else. If he refuses to follow the customs of the country, why should I protect him? Furthermore, I have no time to waste on affairs of such a trifling nature as what happens to an old Persian servant of yours. And in the future you mustn't trouble me with things of this sort. You meddle too much in matters of no moment. They do not interest me! Kindly remember that from now on! You may go."

"No," retorted Anna, thoroughly aroused, "I'm not going yet. Not until I've said what I have to say. I came to you for justice because the people in this part of the city are under your jurisdiction. You are the supreme law here, and it is your duty to decide such cases as this. You are respected everywhere in Bangkok and even all over the country because you are supposed to be a man of honor. I don't take much of your time. I come to you only once in a while when some poor human being is unable to get a fair hearing from one of your own judges, who can be bribed, even if you can't. Believe me, I don't do this to annoy you. I do it because I trust your integrity. And so far I haven't been disappointed. But I am disappointed today. You say that what happens to my old Moonshee isn't important to you, but I think that it is. It's important because what happened to him was something that your own brother did. Your reputation for justice will suffer if you allow members of your family to take the law into their own hands. You say that a matter like this is a trifle. And I say that it is a big thing when a man in your position overlooks the ruffianly behavior of his brother and condones brutality by refusing to right the wrong done, or even to reprimand the offender."

She turned and went toward the door. "Just one other thing," she added. "I came to you because I preferred to honor the government of this country by expressing in action my belief that it is capable of administering justice. You have shown me how wrong I am. Very well! Unless you do something to prevent a repetition of this morning's outrage, I'll go where the word justice is respected as something more than an empty sound to be ignored when it conflicts with vested privilege. I shan't need to trouble you again with complaints. I can always take them directly to Sir Robert Schomburgk. Good morning."

And she swept from the room without giving the Kralahome a chance to say anything more. As she was leaving the palace she met the inter-preter coming in, but she ignored him.

That same evening she sat on her piazza where the air was cooler than in the house, embroidering a coat for Boy's approaching birthday. She was planning to invite the few children living in Bangkok for a small celebration. Beside her on a table stood a heavy Argand lamp. She heard nothing, not the sound of the gate opening or closing, nor a footfall. But all at once she felt a heavy blow on the head. As she pitched sideways she overturned the table and the lamp.

She did not know how long she was unconscious, although it was probably only a matter of seconds. But when she awoke it was to blackness. The light had gone out, and so fortunately had not set fire to anything. Boy was beside her trying with all his strength to lift her from the floor, and crying at the top of his voice, "Beebe, *maree!* Beebe, *maree!*" (Come here), reverting in his excitement to Malay. In a moment there was the sound of Beebe's feet running from the river where she had been bathing. Anna tried to get up, but was too sick and dizzy to move. "Quiet, Louis! I'm all right," she said weakly, and put her arms around him to reassure him.

When Beebe came with a lamp there was blood on the floor from a deep gash in Anna's head. Beside her lay a jagged stone four inches long and two inches wide. Beebe set down the lamp and began to cry, wringing her hands, and wailing, "First my husband, and then my mistress! It will be my turn next, and then what will become of the *chota baba sahib?*"

"Beebe, stop it!" Anna ordered feebly. "Help me to bed, and get some bandages."

Together Beebe and Boy supported Anna into the house. The blood continued to gush from her wound. Beebe hurried for clean rags and water while Louis leaned over his mother with tears streaming down his frightened face. Beebe was very deft and quick and in a few minutes the wound was washed and bandaged. Anna was so weak that she sank into an exhausted sleep. When she awoke in the morning Louis was in a chair beside her, his head resting on her pillow. Although she was still quite shaky from loss of blood, Anna felt better. Her head was badly swollen, but things could have been worse. The stone had been thrown with great force at close range, and if it had hit her temple might have resulted in a fatal injury.

When Beebe came in her face was wet with tears. "Moonshee is dying," she said between sobs. Anna struggled to her feet at once and, supporting herself on Beebe's arm and Louis' shoulder, went to see her teacher. She was relieved to find that he was not dying, although he was still very ill. The shame and outrage of his beating evidently troubled him as much as the physical wounds. "Mem sahib," he said in a whisper, "we must go back to Singapore on the next boat. They will murder us in this land of *Kafirs*. First me and then you!"

Anna tried in vain to convince the terrified old man that such a catastrophe could hardly happen again, since she was going to appeal to the British Consul for protection if the Kralahome failed to act. He would not be beguiled. "Such barbarians! Such infidels!" he wept. "They will creep into the house and slit our throats as we lie sleeping in our beds if we stay here another day. We must go by the first boat, Mem sahib, before they have time to kill us!"

Anna assured him that her wound was only skin deep, and that she was certain there would be no further violence. Trying to convince him, she convinced herself, but so far as Moonshee was concerned her words had no effect. He had no faith in the power of the British Consul to control a people so depraved as the Siamese. In the end Anna was obliged to promise Moonshee and Beebe that they could return to Singapore on the next trip of the *Chow Phya*. How she would get along without them she did not know, but she could not coax them into staying. They tried to persuade her that she ought to go with them for Boy's sake if not for her own. But she was adamant.

Before she wrote to Sir Robert, she sent for Mr. Hunter in his official capacity as secretary to the Kralahome. When she told him what had happened, he looked at her bandaged head and pale face long and seriously. Then he started for the premier's palace abruptly. The next morning he was back with several copies of a proclamation in the Siamese language signed by the Kralahome himself to the effect that persons found injuring or in any way molesting members of Mem Leonowens' household would be severely punished.

As he was leaving to post them in conspicuous places in the neighborhood, Anna remarked, "Oh, by the way, Mr. Hunter, would you be sure to leave one or two in a friendly way at the home of my neighbor on the left there?" The expression on Mr. Hunter's face as the truth slowly dawned on him was a blend of indignation, disgust, and contempt.

"The pusillanimous rascal!" he exclaimed, as he hurried off toward the interpreter's house.

It was several days before Anna was strong enough to go back to work. The King sent for her twice to help with some urgent French correspondence, but she replied that she was weak and ill and could not come.

He was upset by the first overtly aggressive move against Siamese territory on the part of the French. It had become known in Bangkok that Admiral de la Grandière, Governor of Cochin-China, had signed a treaty with King Norodom of Cambodia in August. Norodom, who like the other Cambodian princes had grown up in Siam, had been King Mongkut's personal friend and own appointee for the position of viceroy. He was at that time awaiting coronation by Siamese officials. He wrote hastily to King Mongkut to explain that he had signed the treaty under duress, and had protested unavailingly that by rights De la Grandière should have negotiated any treaty with him through Bangkok. The admiral had tried to flatter the prince by assuring him that France stood prepared to recognize Cambodia's "independence" of Siam. And under the velvet glove of cajolery lay the steel of sixty ships and their guns, stationed at the mouth of the Mekong River. So Norodom, timorous and uncertain, had signed a treaty dictated by the French, which defined the "conditions upon which His Majesty the Emperor of the French consents to transform his rights of suzerainty over the Kingdom of Cambodia to a Protectorate."

Bangkok was seething with speculation. The general view was expressed by Dr. Bradley in his *Bangkok Calendar* where he said:

> The startling news arrives that the French government has made a treaty with the Rajah of Cambodia (well known as being a dependent of Siam) not only without the least reference of the case to the Siamese government to whom it was unquestionably due, but positively in the face of the King's disapprobation of anything of the sort. By the treaty as understood here, the Rajah of Cambodia gives France the exclusive privileges of establishing a consulate at the mouth of the Cambodia River, and hence the exclusive privilege of all the trade of that noble stream. If this report be true, it remains to be seen whether Napoleon III will sanction such an act of his officials. To do so would reflect great shame upon that distinguished idea of honesty; that it was a crime, no less, to take advantage of certain circumstances of weakness in the Siamese government to filch from her a grand bit of Siamese territory, while as yet France was in unbroken treaty of friendship with Siam, without the least shadow of any provocation to commit the foul deed, but an enormous lust of empire. We will hope for better tidings.

When Anna could return to her work, the King scrutinized her thoughtfully. She was still pale, and her head was bandaged. Before they plunged into the French correspondence he remarked: "Mem, there is a house or apartment building nearby our Palace. Should you like to live in it, you may have it when it is finished. Then you can come more quickly when I shall have need of you. You may look at it and see if you like."

That was good news, almost good enough to compensate for the blow on the head. It would put her not only on the same side of the river as the Palace, but also on the same side as the British Consulate, and a long way from the interpreter. In addition she would be living in the area policed by Mr. Ames and his constables, and near the new road that the King was having constructed parallel to the river, the first modern road that Bangkok had ever seen. A few people were already talking about importing carriages, while others were riding out morning and evening to get the air. The road made it possible to reach the British Consulate by land from her new residence. She would feel much safer. In the event of illness she would be near Dr. Campbell, and in case of extreme danger, near the best refuge the city offered.

She was almost comforted for the loss of Moonshee and Beebe. Moonshee still insisted on going, so Anna made reservations on the *Chow Phya*. But at the last minute Beebe with tears in her eyes refused to accompany her husband to Singapore. She unpacked her things and prepared to stay. He did not urge her when she wept, and said: "How can I leave the Mem and the *chota baba sahib* alone in this terrible land when they have been so good to me all these many years? They cannot take care of themselves without me." So Moonshee went alone, not particularly disturbed by his wife's defection. A wife, after all, was something that a good Moslem could always replace.

Before the move across the river could be made one more calamity overtook them. Anna had a violent attack of fever. She had been late arriving at school that morning because of the sudden illness of one of her servants. When she reached the gate of the inner city and found that the clock of the observatory had already struck ten, she ran rather than walked through the streets, and arrived breathless at the long corridor leading to her temple schoolroom. Here her progress was stopped by a crowd of women, children, slaves, attendants, all hurrying in the same direction.

As it was long past the hour for morning service, and was not a fête day, she wondered, while she pushed and squeezed her way through the crowd, what was going on. When she succeeded in entering the temple she found that it was jammed with high court ladies and their maids, and a still greater crowd of slaves, who filled every inch of the vast hall down to the lowest steps. The excitement could not have been more intense if the occasion had been an execution.

Anna continued to work her way toward her schoolroom table and finally reached the inner ring of women. There on the table lay the object that had produced both the crowd and the wild interest. Lying naked, surrounded by the grinning and ejaculating women, was an extraordinarily beautiful white child, a little girl perhaps eighteen months old. A mass of golden curls clustered around her head. Her skin was pearly soft. There was a slight flush on her cheeks. She was smiling at the crowd of women. If she had had wings sprouting from her shoulders she would have looked like a cherub plucked from one of Raphael's pictures.

A dark, rather handsome woman was perched on the table near the child. She was calling: "My ladies, she is worth a great deal more than ten ticals. She is worth her weight in gold. I would not sell her for less than two hundred ticals, and I do so only because I am very poor and cannot afford to keep her myself. Look at her skin! Look at her hair! Look at her lovely hands and feet!" As she talked she pointed to the various features with her index finger. Immediately a dozen or more voices shouted:

"Fifteen ticals!"

"Seventeen!"

"Twenty!"

"Twenty-five!"

"Thirty!"

"Thirty-five ticals!"

Then came another pause. The auctioneer did not cry, "Going, going, gone!" as in an Occidental auction, but again described enticingly the charms of the little girl, ending with, "You cannot have her for thirty-five ticals. I'll keep her myself, even if I have to starve!"

Then came another rush of bids for the child, who was still smiling, as though she were half asleep. Her fists dug into her eyes and she yawned, showing tiny white teeth as perfect as everything else about her. The bidding shot up to fifty-five ticals.

"No one shall have her for that price," shouted the woman. "Look at her hair, like sunbeams, or like the gold that you wear around your necks, my ladies. Look at her skin, like the inside of a conch shell for satin. See, she is plump and well! See, she is happy and laughing all day long! What a jewel of a child! And you offer me only fifty-five ticals. Wa! It is nothing!"

"Sixty!"

"Sixty-five!"

"Seventy!"

"Seventy-five ticals!"

The final bidder was Lady Piam, not the Kralahome's sister, who had first brought Anna to the Palace, but one of the royal consorts. She was not among Anna's personal friends in the harem, although she had two sons in the school. She belonged to the small coterie of powerful court ladies who dominated the Inside, and was the only woman who ever managed the King with acknowledged success. She was not pretty, but she had a good figure. She was totally uneducated and of barely respectable birth, being Chinese on her father's side, but she had succeeded where others had failed because she had tact and a nice intuitive appreciation of character. Once she had sensed her growing influence over the King, she had contrived to foster it with only a slight rebuff now and then. She had been in the Palace eight years, and during that time had amassed a considerable fortune, procured good places at court for members of her family, and had introduced many merchants from the Chinese community to the King in a business way, much to her own profit. Such a swift rise to power would ordinarily have left behind a trail of enemies, but Khun Chom Piam was a diplomat. She seemed to live in continual fear. She retained in her pay most of the female executive force in the Palace. She was warily humble and conciliating toward her rivals, with the result that they pitied her rather than envied her. This pity would probably have come to an abrupt end if they could have foreseen that her three little daughters—two toddlers and a new baby—would some day be the three queens of King Chulalongkorn; and that Lady Piam's artful politics were to ensure her family's position, make her the grandmother of two kings and one queen, and the great-grandmother of a third king.

Suddenly as the auctioneer paused Anna heard her own voice. "One hundred ticals," she said in a faltering tone.

A loud burst of laughter hailed her bid. It was well known that Anna looked upon the traffic in human beings as wrong.

"What do you want with her?" asked Lady Piam. "You have a white child of your own."

When Anna made no reply, she turned and bid one hundred and ten ticals.

At once Anna cried vehemently, "One hundred and twenty ticals!"

At this there was another pause. The auctioneer tried to stimulate the crowd to a higher price, but it was no use. People around Anna began to murmur that one hundred and twenty ticals—at that time the equivalent of seventy-two American dollars—was far too high a price for a child who would probably die on one's hands. The sale was over. The crowds began to hurry home for their midday meal. Some of the great ladies gathered around Anna to ask her what she was going to do with the child, and she hardly knew how to answer, since she had no plan.

Lady Piam came up to her and said, "Mem, you are paying too much for the little girl, but I have taken such a fancy to her that I'll give you one hundred and thirty ticals for her, if you'll let me have her."

"What will you do with her?" Anna inquired.

"Why, I'd have her carefully brought up, and make her a dancing girl for the Palace."

"But you see," Anna explained, "I bought her to keep her from that kind of life. And no money can buy her into it now."

This answer infuriated the usually cautious Lady Piam, and she flounced away without bothering to hide her anger. Anna turned to the auctioneer, who was also the child's mother, and told her to wait until school was over. The baby, worn out with the heat and excitement, was fast asleep.

After school Anna took the woman and child home across the river. She had her servants prepare food and while the woman ate Anna learned her story. She said that her name was Monthani, which meant "adornment," and that she had been married to the English mate of a Chinese vessel, the *Li-Hun*. He had treated her cruelly and she had run away, taking with her his child, because, she said, she "wanted to spoil his heart for him," for he loved the child very much.

She called this English sailor only "Capitain." By much inquiring and cajoling Anna learned that his name was George Davis. After some months Monthani had found herself so poor that she had decided to sell the child. She had carried Mae Khao (Miss Fair One) to the Inside because she knew that she would get the best possible price for her there. Anna listened to the story sympathetically, and then got up to find the money she had agreed to pay. Since she was earning only a hundred dollars a month, this gesture on her part was costly, but she did not regret it. She found that she had not enough money in the house, and asked Monthani to come with her to the British Consulate where she knew she could borrow the rest. It seemed a good idea, anyway, to have the proper paper of sale made out at the Consulate so that there could be no possible future question as to her ownership of Mae Khao.

Monthani was not unwilling, but she refused to leave Mae Khao with Beebe. She said that she wanted to keep the little girl in her arms as long as she could, and she pleaded so earnestly, with tears starting in her eyes, that Anna yielded. Monthani with the baby climbed into the boat first, then Boy. The stones of the landing quay were very slimy, and as Anna started down them carefully her foot slipped. She stumbled, tried to recover her footing, and stumbled again head first into the river. She heard a scream and the water closed over her head. The tide was running out swiftly. She struggled against it vainly, but could not reach the surface. She had a sense of many thoughts chasing one another through her mind, and grew unconscious.

When she opened her eyes again, she was in her own room, lying dressed but still wet on her own bed. A light was burning beside her on the table. Standing around her were all the servants, Boy, and the boatmen. But no Monthani or Mae Khao. The boatmen had dragged Anna out of the river, but in the meantime Monthani had disappeared. Anna sent the boatmen away with the promise of a reward. Beebe took care of her through the long hours of semi-delirium that followed. Anna was troubled about the disappearance of the little white child. But by the next day she was too sick with fever to think any more.

When Beebe saw how very ill her mistress was she rushed to the Mattoons for help. They had her carried to their own home, and night after night took turns sitting up with her until the crisis was past.

During the month that she was absent from the Palace, Lady Son Klin sent her notes almost every day. They were full of love and concern, but a little short on punctuation. The Siamese language used none and it was hard for all the royal pupils to understand why it was essential in English.

My dear Mrs. Leonowens

I know you sick falls a that boat. I am very sorry not happy. I think to you often very much. Why fall down now is sick. My dear friend am writing to school night time.

Son Klin

Saturday evening

My very dearest Friend

I do not understand your note very many word if you please perhaps will you like me a little but please to come and express to me today did you my dear? If you do not come today my heart so unhappy then I think in my heart I am now like a person blind eye. You please and take me to go straight upon the Road don't let me fall down in the darkness. with mine and dear Krita best love to dear Louis and yourself.

I am dearest Friend yours affectionately

Son Klin

You must drink my medicine very good for sick that believe me my dear. S.K.

Thursday morning

My very dearest Teacher

You please to believe me truly I prayed to God tonight for you and dear Louis and I dream about you and you will to be well very soon my dear you don't to be sorry and my very dear Teacher don't forget me. And my dear truly I dream of medicine will you please to drink some or not as you please perhaps will you please to drink some you must drink one time. I am yours affectionately

Harriet Beecher Stowe Son Klin

Tuesday morning

My dearest Friend

I hearing that you very ill. I am very much sorrow and truly and can't happy for you and dear Louis perhaps will you like me and my mother a *little* more you please to drink medicine of mine and dear mother for three day. and perhaps you cannot drink medicine mine and dear mother truly. I and my mother very much sorry to you indeed and I am cannot love you a little more truly I can't send my Mama and brother and my servant to go visit you again and you can't like me and my very dear mother truly because you do not drink.

I am yours affectionately

Harriet Beecher Stowe

In some of the notes, besides urging medicine, she kept reassuring Anna that all would be well, that Anna was not to worry; that she, Lady Son Klin, was much in intercession and prayer. Furthermore, she had made a vow which would ensure Anna's recovery.

As soon as Anna was well enough she made inquiries about Monthani and Mae Khao, but she could learn nothing. She half expected to hear that the mother had taken the child once more to the Inside and offered her for sale. When she was able to resume her teaching, she learned not only that this had not happened, but also that it could not happen again.

As Anna seated herself at her schoolroom table, she saw that the Siamese women were looking at her curiously. They regarded her as one resurrected from the dead. Many of them found occasion to tell her of their wonder at her survival. Lady Talap said: "You were bewitched when you bid for that strange white child. She wasn't a child but a changeling. The devil often assumes the form of beautiful children, especially beautiful girls, in order to destroy human beings. That child was nothing more nor less than the devil, who wished to kill you because of all the good deeds you have been doing, and don't you see that he would have succeeded except for those boatmen?"

Anna did not see that Mae Khao was the devil incarnate, but she did see that it was a great advantage to have the women of the Palace go on thinking so. Nothing could have induced the guards at the gate to admit the little girl again, so, whatever dangers she was in from poverty, she was safe at least from slavery on the Inside.

Lady Son Klin took all the credit for her friend's recovery from imminent death. She put her arms around Anna and embraced her, saying, "I made you well! I made you well!"

"And how did you do it?" Anna asked, touched by her friend's affection.

Lady Son Klin's plain dark face was illuminated as she leaned toward Anna. "I made a vow in my favorite temple to save seven thousand lives if yours were granted to my prayers."

Anna did not smile. Such childlike faith inspired no mirth, but she was curious. "How can anyone save seven thousand lives?" she asked.

The Lady Son Klin was delighted to see that she had mystified her friend. "Oh, there is no trouble about that," she answered with a gay wave of her hand. "Wait a little while and you will see!" She summoned one of her slaves and whispered to her.

In an hour the slave was back with seven closely woven baskets. In each were masses of writhing small fish, a thousand to a basket. Immediately Lady Son Klin, Anna, and the slaves set off for the narrow open ditch that conducted water from the river into the harem. There with pomp and ceremony, music, singing, and beating of drums, the fish were dumped into the water, and so their seven thousand lives were saved.

26

## ROYAL LOCUSTS

THE NEW house was on the eastern side of the Palace. It was one of a row of two-story brick apartments. From her upstairs window Anna could see the Suthaisawan Palace, a long pavilion surmounting the high white walls across the street, from which the King and court watched processions. Directly in front of the house was a broad plaza of several acres called the Sanam Chai, or Field of Victory.

The long trip back and forth across the river had taken a great deal of time each day. Now she stepped out of her house in the morning, crossed the Sanam Chai and the road to one of the handsome gates that flanked the Suthaisawan Palace. Usually she entered by the northern one, called the Gate of the Guardian Angel. Either gave access to the court between the inner and outer walls, from which she passed directly into the formal garden fronting the Hall of Audience. Five minutes was time enough to allow from home to work.

There was one disadvantage. Living only a few hundred feet from the Palace made her so accessible that the King called her more and more frequently in the evening. Since she liked to spend her evenings with Boy she resented the long hours after supper spent in correspondence. Often she was aroused at one or two in the morning by a troop of shouting slaves who drummed on her door and carried her away with them to the King's presence.

At first when these summonses had come in the middle of the night, Anna's heart had pounded with the certainty that something disastrous had happened in the harem. But experience had shown her that there was no way of knowing what to expect. Once she had been awakened from heavy sleep by the King's messengers and ordered to come to the Palace with all haste. She had dressed hurriedly, thinking that another of the royal children might have been stricken with cholera. She had kissed Louis, asleep on his bed, called Beebe to stay with him, and rushed off through the tropical night with the messengers in the lead.

Sleepy Amazons had admitted them and they had threaded their way through the maze of buildings, fountains, and statues, grotesque in the dark, to the women's hall of audience, which was brilliantly lighted. In the middle of it the King lay full length on his stomach, with his chin propped on his hands, and an enormous book in front of him. When Anna approached she saw that it was an English Bible open at Genesis. She sank to the floor, as she had been instructed to do when the King was in this, his favorite position for study.

He had turned to her impatiently, "Mem, your Moses shall have been a fool!"

"But, Your Majesty—"

"I say," interrupted the King with asperity, "your Moses shall have been a fool." Tapping the Bible, he continued: "Here it stands written that God created the world in six days, and rested on the seventh. You know and I know and all scientists know it took many ages to create the world. Your Moses shall have been a fool to have written so! You may go!"

When she would have answered him, he drove her forth with a haughty gesture, refusing to allow her to utter a word. Again and again she was so aroused in the middle of the night by noisy female slaves, and dragged in haste and consternation to the hall, only to discover that the King was not at his last gasp, but simply bothered to find in Webster's *Dictionary* a word that existed nowhere except in his own fertile brain, or perhaps he was in excited chase of the classical term for some piece of scientific equipment he wanted to order from London.

Before her arrival in Bangkok it had been his not uncommon practice to send for one of the missionaries when he needed help. The poor man was beguiled or abducted from his bed and conveyed three or four miles by boat to the Palace because the King wanted to know whether it would be more elegant to write "murky" instead of "obscure," or "gloomily dark" rather than "not clearly apparent." If the sleepy missionary ventured to state a preference for the ordinary over the extraordinary form of expression, he was dismissed with irony, arrogance, or even insult, and never any apology for the rude invasion of his privacy, or thanks for his assistance.

Even Sir Robert Schomburgk had not been immune. One night a little after twelve the King, who was on the point of going to bed, had fallen to wondering how most accurately to render into English the troublesome word *phi*. Should it be ghost, spirit, soul, devil, evil angel, or what? After puzzling for more than an hour and getting himself possessed with the word as with the evil one it stood for, he ordered his second-best state barge manned and sent with speed downriver for the British Consul. The consul, thinking that some serious diplomatic crisis had arisen, dressed with unceremonious celerity. Perhaps the French had invaded the eastern provinces or blockaded the port of Bangkok to enforce their territorial demands! He hurried to the Palace, conjecturing all the way on the various possibilities of politics and diplomacy, revolution and invasion, which could have caused the King to send for him at so late an hour.

He found the King *en deshabille,* engaged with a Siamese-English vocabulary, and mentally divided between "deuce" and "devil." His Majesty gravely laid the final choice before the consul, who thought of several appropriate uses for either word. Inwardly chafing at the "confounded coolness" of His Majesty, he dared do nothing but decide, with what grace he could muster, on "devil" and go back to bed.

One of the distinct advantages of the location of her new home was that it made possible certain plans Anna had been considering. Now Louis could have his coveted pony. There was a cavalry barracks near at hand where she was able to make arrangements to have the pony stabled. The several miles of new road, which the King was opening formally with a great celebration in March, made riding in almost any season feasible. Louis named his new pet Pompey, after the little Welsh cob that his mother had had when she was a girl.

Then Anna had wanted to supplement her formal classroom teaching with other contacts, which would fulfill the King's urging that his children be taught European manners and customs. She had been thinking that this could best be done by bringing a few of the children at a time into a proper setting and teaching them both by word and example the principles of European etiquette. Their lives were so circumscribed that the introduction of any idea opposed to their own experience and Siamese training was extremely difficult.

The maps and the globes had broken down their concepts of geography and astronomy. Even that battle had to be fought over with each new child who entered the class. Recently a very beautiful little girl named Wani Ratana Kanya, a newcomer, had rejected quite firmly the modern ideas set forth by her teacher. "I believe," she had said, "that the moon is the beautiful daughter of a great king of Ayuthia, who lived many thousands of years ago, and the head wife of the sun, and not a great stupid ball of earth and rock rolling about in the sky to no purpose but for the sun to shine on!"

The children's love of pictures had helped to widen their horizon. They were able to gain some idea of the outside world from views of other countries and people, which Anna sedulously hunted and brought to class. Whenever she could find an unusual object, she brought it with her in the morning and allowed them to examine it—a lump of coal, which they could compare with charcoal such as their slaves used for cooking meals; a strip of fleece from a sheep, with pictures of a carder and spinning wheel, and of a modern mill; and samples of yarn and woolen cloth. Hand weaving the children understood, since many of the slaves wove skillfully on looms set up in a section of the Inside.

One day the steamer *Chow Phya* had brought the King a box of ice from Singapore. Anna had obtained some for an object lesson. The children examined the novelty with a great deal of interest, and as word of it spread women from the harem crowded into the temple to see it. They felt it and giggled to find it cold; then they watched it melt and turn into water. With the ice before them they found no difficulty in believing that water froze in the colder countries of the world until it was possible to walk on it. Anna showed them some pictures of boys and girls skating on the canals in Holland and they were excited and interested. But when she went on to say that rain in such countries froze as it fell and became a white substance that the people called snow, the whole school was indignant at what they considered an obvious effort to stretch truth out of all reason and impose a ridiculous fantasy on them.

Lady Son Klin laid her hand gently on Anna's arm and said in a low voice: "Please do not say that again. I believe you like my own heart in everything that you teach me, but this sounds like the tale of a little child who wishes to say something more wonderful than anything that was ever said before."

The lesson on snow proved a stumbling-block for several days. By some misfortune she could not find any pictures of snow. Her pupils' imaginations had taken alarm, and they could not be brought to believe the simplest statements. Their resistance to what she was trying to teach them proved such a handicap that she told the King about her dilemma, and he came to her aid in person. He stood at the head of the schoolroom table one morning and explained to the royal children that it was possible that there was such a thing as snow, for English books of travel, which he had read, spoke frequently of a phenomenon called snow.

Shortly after her move to the eastern bank Anna had an opportunity to start her lessons in European etiquette. Louis and she were invited to tea by her royal pupils. The tea party was at the residence of one of the late queens. This quaint old palace was enclosed by a high, half-ruined and time-stained wall, overgrown with creepers, grasses and flowers. When the female porters opened the iron gates, Anna saw in the distance an orange grove in full blossom. As she walked down the path in the evening sunlight she could see shadowy vistas on either side: flower gardens and arches;

bright fountains and marble basins where many-colored fish swam about; stone seats, groups of banana trees and graceful palms.

There was an amphitheater in front of the royal dwelling enclosed in a thick border of ilex and oleander. It had been spread with costly Indian carpets. Two slave women dressed in scarlet and white were seated on stone benches at the end of the walk. As Louis and Anna approached, one of them rose and came forward to greet the guests. She invited them to take their places on a carpet. There they waited for half an hour, while Anna reflected that in Siam as in Europe royalty is proverbially late.

At last the sound of many voices reached them. The gates of the palace were thrown open. Anna's two oldest pupils flashed into sight, the Princess Ying Yaowalak and the Princess Somawadi. They were dressed in scarlet, gold, and blue, spangled with diamonds and costly gems that sparkled in the slanting rays of the sun. A troop of female slaves followed, also dressed in their best, with gold and silver ornaments. The princesses advanced smiling down the avenue to the carpet on which Anna and Louis sat. Ying Yaowalak, the older, came first. She took both of Anna's hands into hers with reverence, and bowed until her forehead touched them. Her half-sister, Princess Somawadi, did the same. Then they dropped down one on either side of Anna, charmingly solicitous for their teacher, now also their guest.

Presently thirty more of the royal pupils streamed through the gate, each accompanied by at least a dozen slaves, mostly young girls. The children salaamed Anna in turn, and then arranged themselves comfortably at full length on the carpets, while their slaves crouched behind them. It was certainly an unusual setting for a tea party. Reclining or crouching under the open sky were about five hundred people, quiet and orderly, although pleasantly titivated with anticipation.

Almost immediately other girls came into sight through an opening in an avenue of ilex, dressed in brilliant colors and flowing draperies. They advanced in rhythmic measure carrying tambourines, flutes, cymbals and guitars. There was a barbaric beauty in the richness of their clothing and the movement of their bodies that made Anna think they were like a column of savage queens emerging from a primeval forest. As they approached the royal party they dropped to the pavement and hid their faces, nor did they rise until Princess Somawadi gave a signal. Then they formed into various groups, some the orchestra, some the chorus, and some dancers. A half hour concluded the program. Richly dressed slaves next brought teapots of at least ten different shapes, all of them gold, enameled and set in curious trays of gold and silver. Out of them the slaves poured different kinds of tea into beautiful jeweled cups.

Anna saw that she was expected to drink at least one cup of each kind of tea. There were a dozen or more—the rose-scented tea, the jessamine-flavored tea. the tea of life, the tea of friendship, the tea of mirth, the tea of wakefulness, and many others. The tea of wakefulness was strongly stimulating. The leaves had been plucked when quite young and dried in large copper pans over fires. Anna was careful not to offend her hostesses, so she went through the ceremony of tasting all the teas, and praising each one. Each did have its own peculiar flavor, some quite pleasant and some the reverse.

Various other small dishes were set in front of them. It was a delightful occasion except for one circumstance. Princess Ying Yaowalak, who had very long nails, and who wished to be polite to her teacher and Boy, would every now and then put one of these long nails into a dish of preserves, and spear a portion of the fruit on it. She would then present it to their mouths as if her nail were a fork. There was nothing for them to do but open their mouths and swallow with the best possible grace. According to Siamese etiquette this manner of feeding on the tip of the nail was an act full of kindness and poetic sentiment. But Anna almost wished during the course of the party that she had no mouth at all, since she could not overcome her revulsion.

At last the sun set and she and Boy rose to go. They invited the royal children to an English tea party on the following Saturday evening, if the King would consent. The children were wild with delight at the prospect of going to Anna's house, especially since it stood outside the walls of the Palace.

The King gave his consent willingly. It was part of his plan for his children to have them understand and know how to observe European customs. On the evening of the party Anna decorated her dining room with English flags, and put quantities of flowers on the tables, which were spread with tea, coffee, homemade cakes, English preserves, bread and butter. Anna had invited thirty of her pupils, and it was her intention to arrange them around tables and to have the tea served in the old-fashioned English way.

She had not thought to limit the number of attendants, however, and when the royal pupils arrived each was accompanied by many slaves. The children, excited by the strange new experience of an English tea party in an English home, were dressed in their brightest silks and weighted down with masses of gold and diamond ornaments. To Anna's distress the slaves insisted on coming in with their masters and mistresses. The whole motley throng streamed through the open doors of the little house. Those who could not get in by that way because of the crowd jumped through the windows, until there was hardly an inch of standing room left.

Vainly Anna tried to enforce order. She thought if she could persuade the children to sit down there was a chance that she could get the situation in hand. But her voice was lost in the din of all the attendants, who were screaming and bawling and elbowing each other for standing room in a house that had never been intended to hold four hundred people. The princes and princesses did not seem to understand that they were expected to sit in the chairs around the tables. They went to the tea tables and looked at them with interest. Some poked their fingers into the preserves to feel their consistency. Some handled the cakes and set them down again. Some looked in the teapots. Then, without having eaten anything, they spread through the house with their slaves, like a swarm of locusts, laying hands on everything that struck their fancy.

Anna was like a chip of wood in a swirling stream. Up and down and around and over her they eddied, shouting and laughing and grabbing and exclaiming. The slaves watched the flittings of their royal charges with unbounded delight. Anna had taken it for granted that the quiet and order of their own entertaining of her would come with them into her home. She was struck dumb to discover that they were rifling her drawers, her toilet table, her closets and her cupboards. On her bed was a handsome crocheted quilt lined with pink silk, which one of the smallest of the princesses, not finding anything else to her liking, was dragging off with both her little hands when Anna rushed to its rescue.

There would hardly have been a needle, a vase, a picture or a handkerchief left in the house if the boom of the clock striking from the high tower across the street had not announced the close of day. There was a sudden rush for the Palace. The slaves snatched up their royal charges loaded with booty and vanished as unceremoniously as they had come. The house was in ruins. The only thing completely untouched, as beautifully arranged as when the party began, was the row of tea tables, still set with dishes, bread and butter, preserves and cake.

Anna sat down weakly to contemplate the damage. She had seen before the unpredictable strata of discipline and complete absence of it in Siamese behavior. She even knew that royalty had the right to take anything that pleased them. One dissolute prince roamed the streets of the city helping himself to whatever potables he could find in the shops of the merchants, and no one dared to interfere because he was of royal blood. It had never occurred to her, though, that her pupils who obeyed her willingly day after day in the schoolroom would burst all bounds and become hoodlums when they stepped out of their orbit and came into her home. She hadn't a pair of scissors, a spool of cotton, a pin or a thimble left. These especially had attracted the children.

The next day, which was Sunday, brought a procession of slaves from the Palace. When the first appeared Anna hoped for a moment that she had come to return some pilfered item. The slave had been sent by the mother of one of the children, not with what the child had taken but with a chest of tea. Others came with boxes of tobacco, camphor, and snuff, compensatory offerings for the plunder of her house. Most of the gifts were of ten times the value of the things taken. The only trouble was that they were of no earthly use to her.

27

## THE SERVICE IN THE TEMPLE

ANNA'S CONTACTS with the mothers of her pupils continued to be many and varied. She was on excellent terms with all of them, but there were a select few to whom she was especially close. This small group were alike in that—with the exception of Lady Son Klin—they were among the most influential women of the harem. Anna had not selected them as friends for that reason, but because she had much in common with them. They all had an outreaching quality, a practical concern for those around them, that attracted her very much. Individually they were different, and their relationships with Anna reflected these differences.

Lady Son Klin gave Anna valuable assistance in her study of the Siamese language. She was always delighted to see Anna in her home, and would produce hot tea and cakes with a rush of pleased attention that was heart-warming after a tiring day in the schoolroom. Her advice was shrewd and cautious. She understood the intricate politics of the harem and steered her friend through them with diplomatic skill. Anna was saved many a blunder by her careful little warnings.

Anna's relationship with Lady Thiang, mother of Princess Somawadi, was almost as intimate, but of quite another sort. She had quickly discovered the greatness of this Siamese woman's heart. Life in the harem was supportable for many of the women of the Inside only because the head wife was a person of broad sympathy and discretion. Lady Thiang's own sister, Choi, had very nearly been put to death five or six years previously. She had been the favorite at the time. While acting in a court play one of the young nobles had fallen in love with her. His wife in a passion of selfless devotion had sold herself to the concubine as slave and go-between. Before the noble's plan to abduct Choi from the Palace could be carried out, one of her notes to him was intercepted. The plot was discovered. The noble and his wife were horribly tortured and then executed, and Choi herself was saved only because Sir Robert Schomburgk intervened.

Perhaps this incident as much as anything else had ploughed and harrowed Lady Thiang's heart. Anna had often carried some story of distress to her and had invariably been reassured if Lady Thiang said quickly, "Don't worry any more, Mem *cha,* I'll attend to it myself."

The head wife had devised a little court drama of her own in which she cast Anna for the leading part and used her again and again, with marked success. Whenever Lady Thiang thought that the King was dangerously angry and ready to loose the whip on one of the women of the harem, she would quickly summon Anna. It was Anna's role to go immediately to the room in which His Majesty was, book in hand, to consult him about a translation from the Sanskrit or Siamese. She kept a store of such questions ready against the need. Transparent as the device was, or perhaps because of its simplicity, it usually worked.

There was no possible way, so far as the King could have guessed, for Anna to learn that a woman was about to suffer from his wrath. He would see her standing hesitantly at the door with her book and would motion her to come in. Then he would turn with comical abruptness from curses and abuse to absorbed interest in the question she raised. The scholar would triumph over the man. Often he would motion the culprit, still kneeling before him, out of the room with an absent-minded wave of his hand, the better to devote himself to the attractive problem that Anna had brought him. Again and again as she approached his study and heard his voice shrill with anger, she would feel her heart sink and her steps slow down. This time he would guess! But he never did.

Princess Lamom was the third woman whom Anna especially liked. The princess continued to seek advice about Prince Chulalongkorn and his brothers. Without her co-operation it would hardly have been possible to plant the principles of humanitarianism in Chulalongkorn's mind. Anna made it a point to tell him of her efforts to help this or that unfortunate person. He listened gravely, his eyes alert and interested. She was convinced that she was having an effect—by example if not by words—when he deplored the cruelty with which the slaves were treated in the Palace. It was something, she felt, to have opened his eyes to this.

She herself, to use the King's phrase, was "a candle flame blowing in the wind." If she could light one lamp that would some day illuminate every corner of the kingdom, her work in Siam would have been more than the trivial round it often seemed. None of her friends knew the utter loneliness of her life, the sense of futility that overwhelmed her. The load of duties, the provocations, and the fears accumulated month by month, and there was almost no release. The society of Bangkok was narrow and ingrown. Companionship was harder to find there than in any place she had ever lived. Fresh arrivals came seldom to the stagnant community. Even new books were rare and there was no theater, no music. Singapore had been alive, exciting, a crossroads of the world. Bangkok was a dead end.

What compensation there was had to be found in her private studies and in her work. Perhaps nuns felt like this, she thought, when they passed within convent walls and left the glitter of the world behind. But their renunciation was of the will, while circumstances beyond her control had stripped her of the people who meant everything to her. And yet was it not possible that they had endured the same impoverishment, so that when the glory that was life had become husks they found it good to exchange those dead things for service and whatever vicarious happiness could be salvaged? Maybe selflessness was only selfishness on another level.

Sometimes Anna knew a thrill of accomplishment when she had succeeded in helping one of the many who came to her for assistance. But it was always tempered the next day by the reflection that while she had remedied a single injustice ten had grown. It was not in her power to change the system that bore the malodorous fruit of sorrow around her. There was always the exciting chance, though, that Prince Chulalongkorn could. And this thought sustained her more than once when she grew discouraged or impatient.

So it seemed a far better reward for her efforts than the paltry sum the King gave her when she noticed that the young prince was trying to teach kindness toward the slaves by his own example. He had his slaves carefully dressed and well fed, and he treated them with consideration. He insisted that his younger brothers and attendants do as much. One day he startled Anna by saying thoughtfully: "I don't think they ought to be called slaves. They have more right to be called noble than we have, because they have learned how to endure. We princes are the ones who haven't learned that there is nothing noble in oppressing our fellow men."

Khun Thao Ap and Lady Talap completed the circle of Anna's particular friends on the Inside. At the beginning of 1864 Lady Talap's position had been greatly enhanced by the elevation in rank of her father. Her older half-brother had long been chief judge of the Palace court. Numerous others of her family held important positions. In January of that year the Minister of the North, father of Chao Chom Manda Ung, who had owned L'Ore, died. Partly through Lady Talap's influence as favorite her father had succeeded to the position. He had formerly been Lord Mayor of Bangkok. Now he was equal in rank to the Kralahome and thus one of the two most highly placed nobles in the kingdom.

Lady Talap was a zealous Buddhist. She was eager to make her English friend understand her religion and frequently invited Anna to one or another of the religious services in the harem. "Come, Mem," she would say with a wave of her hand, "today is our day for going to the temple. You must come, too. I will explain for you." It was still hard for Anna to believe that she was not a young girl, for she was so full of gaiety, so childlike and unsullied in appearance.

On one such occasion they set off together through the freshness of the morning for Wat Phra Kaeo. The bells on the pagoda made breezy gushes of music. A page asked Anna her destination, and when she answered inquired further, "To see or to hear?" She replied, "Both."

The women of the harem were already seated on the floor of polished brass diamonds when she and Lady Talap entered. They were dressed in white panungs with white silk scarfs drawn from their left shoulders in careful folds across their breasts and back, and thrown over their right shoulders. Their slaves sat a little apart. They were dressed in the same manner except not in silk. As a matter of fact, many of the slaves were half-sisters of their mistresses, children of the same father by a slave mother.

The women were sitting in circles. Each had a vase of flowers and a lighted candle in front of her. Slightly in advance of the women was a circle of Anna's pupils, who were, of course, higher in rank than their mothers. Close to the altar sat the priest, Chao Khun Sa. In his hand was a concave fan, richly embroidered, jeweled and gilded, and lined with pale green silk. It was an emblem of his rank and was held in front of his face according to the Buddhist custom. His yellow robe was open from throat to girdle, and closed below the waist. It suggested the Roman toga. From his shoulders hung two narrow strips, also yellow, resembling the scapular worn by certain orders of the Roman Catholic clergy. At his side was an open watch of gold, the gift of his sovereign. Seventeen disciples sat at his feet, protecting their faces with fans less richly adorned.

Anna and Louis put off their shoes like the rest. There was no need to hush Boy. The reverence of the worshipers had already done that. The abbot sat motionless with his face covered in order that his eyes should not tempt his thoughts to stray. Anna was very curious about this priest for a number of reasons. She shifted her position to get a glimpse of his expression. He caught her movement and sent her a quick half-glance of remonstrance, and moved his fan so that his face was screened again. Then he began the opening chant.

At once the whole congregation raised themselves on their knees and all together prostrated themselves three times profoundly. With heads still bowed, palms folded and eyes closed, they delivered the responses, much in the manner of the English liturgy, first the priest, then the people, and finally all together. There was no singing, and no standing up and sitting down. There was no changing of robes or places, no turning the face to the altar, or north, south, east, or west. People and clergy knelt still, with hands folded straight before them, and eyes strictly closed. Anna lost some of the responses in the simultaneous repetition, and when the exhortation began she could follow it only imperfectly. She did understand enough to know that the priest was urging his listeners to practice principles of charity. Chao Khun Sa was an eloquent speaker, one of the new school that prepared sermons on vital subjects and was not content to mumble old homilies from memory.

While he talked the Amazonian guards lounged in the porches and vestibules of the temple. The reverent attention of the worshipers did not reach to them. They were engrossed in amusing themselves. Some were gambling, some flirting with the custodians of the temple. It was another of the endless contrasts in Siamese life that puzzled and interested Anna. Her mind wandered from the sermon to the preacher. With his unwillingness to have her look on his face, she could not help but compare fleetingly the antics of a young priest named Maha Rot. She had noticed the rich diapason of his voice during a service, and had commented on it to the King. His Majesty had passed on her praise to the priest, a hulking young man, who was chanting the responses with a deep and musical rhythm. When the King turned away, the priest had winked at Anna mischievously from behind his fan. She had been amazed, but was even more so when he called on her a few days later.

It happened that Annie Elliot, the young dressmaker who had helped with the court dresses for the harem ladies on the occasion of their reception of Lord John Hay, was sewing for her that afternoon. The priest had fallen in love on the spot with the pretty English girl. The next day he brought her a rose plant in bloom in a costly Chinese vase. When Anna teased him by asking whether he thought Miss Elliot prettier than the Siamese women he knew, he answered, "Oh, yes! Our women are yellow, but she is red and white and blue and every color!"

In spite of the fact that such open admiration of a woman was contrary to the rules of his order, he was shocked when Annie Elliot jumped up and rushed over to shake hands with him to show her appreciation of the gift. He drew back quickly. The spirit of the rule he could break, but not the letter. When he saw that she was offended, he tried to find a solution compatible with his scruples. First he extended his old Chinese umbrella to her and suggested that she shake it. When she refused, he covered his hand with a dirty handkerchief and offered that, only to be refused again. Finally in desperation he suggested that she go behind a pillar where no one could see him and then he would be willing to shake her hand. He could not understand her even more emphatic refusal. The incident had ended with a proposal of marriage by the priest, who said that he would be willing to leave the priesthood for such a "blue-eyed-lotus beauty." When he was rejected, he had calmly asked for his gifts back and gone his way.

There was none of this casuistry in Chao Khun Sa, Anna knew. He had entered the priesthood as a young boy and stayed in it until he attained high rank. Then he had left it for six years. The ladies of the harem had whispered to Anna that he had re-entered it only because of a bitter disappointment. They said that Chao Khun Sa and the young girl who became queen consort had been very much in love, but that her family did not approve of the match. When she was presented to the King, Chao Khun Sa had entered the priesthood again. Anna looked at the quiet scholarly man preaching from the gilded chair at the front of the temple. He was speaking in a calm but forceful voice and the women all around her were listening intently. He had earned the profound respect of everyone in the city and the Palace for the probity of his life.

Anna wondered as she looked at him sitting cross-legged with the fan before his face whether the old romantic tale were indeed true. If so, it had not separated him from the King. His Majesty was even then building a new temple to be called "Wat Rachapradit Sathit Maha Simaram," which meant, "The Temple Erected by the King." The abbot was to be transferred to it as soon as it was complete so that he could come to the King on short notice. The location that the King had selected was close to the Palace itself, on the eastern side, not far from Anna's house, in what had been an old coffee garden. Anna had attended some of the ceremonies. She was to remember them long after for what had seemed at the time a trivial event.

The laying of the foundation had been the occasion of unusual festivities—theatrical performances, a carnival of dancing, mass at every corner-stone, banquets to priests, and distribution of clothing, food, and money to the poor. The King had presided morning and evening under a silken canopy. The favorites of the harem had also been present in specially erected tents, where they could witness the shows and participate in the fun with which the work of merit-making went on.

After the corner-stones had been consecrated by the pouring on of oil and water, seven tall lamps were lighted to burn above them seven days and nights. Seventy priests in groups of seven, forming a perfect circle, prayed holding in their hands the mystic web of seven threads. Pretty girls had brought offerings of grain and wine, honey and flowers to place on the consecrated stones. After that pottery of all kinds had been brought—vases, cups, bowls, ewers, goglets, and urns. These were flung into the foundations and then pounded to bits by the girls, while other people brought similar donations. It was a gala occasion. Musical instruments and the voices of the court singers kept time to the measured crash of the wooden clubs. The King tossed coins and ingots of gold and silver into the foundation.

To the obbligato of the priest's ringing voice Anna's mind recalled the scene. She and the King had been discussing the new French Consul, who had arrived on April 8. Monsieur G. Aubaret was hot-tempered, overbearing, haughty. He had been a commandant in the French Navy and he had carried his quarter-deck manner with him into diplomatic life. On this afternoon the King, whose fear and hatred of the French had been stirred to the boiling point by the new consul, was raving about the rudeness of M. Aubaret, the cupidity of the French who were gobbling up his eastern territories, the apathy of the English who should have intervened, and the fatuity of all geographers in calling the form of government in Siam an "absolute monarchy."

"Am I an absolute monarch? For I have no power over French. Siam is like a mouse before an elephant! Am I an absolute monarch then? What shall *you* consider me?"

Since Anna considered him a particularly absolute and despotic king, she held her peace. And he did not wait for an answer. "I have no power," he scolded. "I am not absolute! If I point the end of my walking-stick at a man, whom being my enemy, I wish to die, he does not die, but lives on, in spite of my 'absolute' will to the contrary. What does geographies mean? How can I be an absolute monarchy?" And he reproached the fate that made him powerless to point the end of his walking-stick at M. Aubaret with absolute power, while he vacantly flung gold and silver among the girls who were preparing the foundation of the temple.

Anna chuckled soundlessly at the memory of the King's regretful expression. But the trivial event which took place next held no laughter for her. The King's manner had suddenly changed. Anna saw that he had forgotten the French Consul and the imbecilities of geographers. He was looking at one of the girls. She was very pretty with a fresh and unusual beauty, and a piquant expression. She was having a good time pounding up the urns and vases and dishes. The instant she realized that she had attracted the notice of the King, she sank down and hid her face in the earth, disregarding the falling pottery. Anna watched the King sharply, but he merely inquired her name, which was Tuptim, and the name of her parents and turned away.

The service at Wat Phra Kaeo was over. Anna gathered her straying thoughts and prepared to go back with Lady Talap to the harem.

"Did you understand the reverend abbot's sermon, Mem *cha?*" she asked.

"Some of it," Anna said, "enough to know that he was urging all of you to practice charity."

"Yes, that's right," Lady Talap agreed, gratified. "And next week, Mem, I shall do what the good priest says. I am having a special ceremony in my home, which I have every year on the occasion of the Wisakha Bucha. You must come and see it, so do not forget!"

A number of well-dressed slaves came for Anna on Saturday the twenty-first of May. The year before, the celebration of the Birth, Enlightenment, and Death of the Buddha had brought Anna the deeply moving encounter with L'Ore. She was thinking of this as she walked through the cool morning air to the home of Lady Talap. Her residence was in the most aristocratic suburb of the Inside. It was a brick building with a low wall running around it, which enclosed some acres of ground, divided between the gardens and the residences of her numerous slaves and attendants. Anna was the first guest to pass between the two brick and mortar lions that guarded the entrance.

Lady Talap, looking sixteen instead of twenty-six, stood in the entrance hall dressed in white silk. Her sons stood one on either side of her, Prince Thawi Thawanya Lap who was eight, and Prince Kap Kanaka Ratana who was six. After Anna had been received she took her place at the inner end of the antechamber which gave access to the residence proper. Lady Talap stood beside a small marble fountain. All around it were huge Chinese vases containing plants covered with flowers, and between them were silver water-jars, each large enough to hold two people, and each containing a great silver dipper. Thirty young slave girls were filling them with water drawn from a well in the garden.

The hall was furnished with striped floor-matting, and with cushioned seats for a hundred guests. In the garden opposite the doors of the hall was a circular thatched roof supported on a mast, like a tent with a center pole, the theater erected for the occasion. In one part was an elevated stage for marionettes. Both stages were gracefully decorated.

Fifty or more women porters came from an inner court as Anna watched, carrying on their heads massive silver dishes of sweetmeats and choice food, which they placed along the hall. They were followed by girls in white who arranged flowers in gold vases beside each seat. When this was done they took their places behind their mistress. They were girls of good family, some relatives, some not, who were entrusted to her as maids-in-waiting. Anna, mystified, watched the preparations with growing interest, wondering who the guests were to be. It was just seven o'clock, but the women of this household had evidently been up for hours. The grounds and house were immaculate. The vases of roses were reflected in the sides of the silver jars. Everything was ready.

The gate was thrown open and into the fairy-like scene of flowers and sunshine and fragrance the guests were ushered, one by one. A hundred decrepit and unsightly beggar-women! They were covered with filth and rags and the vilest uncleanliness. Lady Talap advanced to meet her guests with courtesy and a delicate graciousness that was charming for its lack of any appearance of being patronizing. She led them to seats on the low stools beside the fountain. Then with her maids-in-waiting she removed their tatters and began to wash them with sweet-smelling soap, and water from the silver jars. Their hair was washed and dried and combed, parted and arranged with flowers. They were dressed in new white clothes.

Then they were seated on the cushions before the silver trays. Lady Talap and her maids knelt and served them with food that had been prepared for them. After breakfast the music struck up and the actors and puppets appeared on the stages. The royal female bands were assembled for the occasion and relieved each other in succession. The acting was interspersed with plaintive songs.

Anna had liked Siamese music from the start. She thought she traced a similarity in the scale used to that of the Welsh songs of her childhood. She felt that the words showed poetic genius and pleasing measure. There were no harsh, disagreeable sounds, and no abrupt transitions. The movement of both music and words was soft, lively, and harmonious. This morning the musicians seemed to outdo themselves for their strange audience.

After several hours the curtain dropped on the last act. The cadence of the voices and instruments died away, and a loud buzz of pleasure broke from the old women. As they prepared to go Lady Talap gave each a present of money. Anna's last glimpse of the crones was as they jostled each other happily on their way out of the gate.

Anna arose to go also. Lady Talap took her two hands and said, "This I do every year as a symbol of my love and obedience to my teacher, the Buddha."

28

## THE AFFAIR OF THE GAMBLING CONCUBINE

THE SCREAMS were horrible, not quite human and yet not animal. Anna and Boy, who were walking toward the river, looked quickly around. Behind them came two stout men dragging Nai Lek, Master Little, the Palace dwarf. His hands were chained and there was a rope around his neck. At every unwilling step he howled in protest.

Anna paused and waited for the men to catch up with her. The dwarf was half nude, and his face was contorted into a hideous mask. He chattered like a monkey, then, lifting his head, bayed out his anguish in long crescendo wails in which the animal sound obliterated the human. As the men approached her Anna had to raise her own voice to be heard at all.

"What's the matter with Nai Lek?" she asked them.

They stopped and the yowling stopped. Nai Lek blinked his eyes at Anna and twisted his face into a grimace.

"He's always doing something he shouldn't," one of the men answered. "He stones the dogs and frightens the children and chases the calves and worries the kittens. We've driven him away from the stables a hundred times, but we can't keep him out. Now he has cut off the beautiful long tail of the King's favorite mare, so we're going to hang him and be done with his tricks."

At this a yell broke from the dwarf. He threw himself on the ground and struggled so violently with the rope around his neck that it looked as if he might strangle himself and save his captors the trouble.

Anna spoke quietly to the men. "You know that you can't do that without the King's permission. And if you keep on tormenting him like this I'll go right now and complain to the King."

As soon as he heard Anna's promise Nai Lek gave a bound and stood erect. He grinned at her with a wide senseless gaze, and shook his huge fists, bound together as they were, at his captors.

"Well," one of the men said abashed, "what we're really going to do is take him to prison and lodge our complaint with the judge."

So instead of going for the sail on the river that she had planned, Anna and Louis followed the men and the dwarf. As they emerged from the covered way in which they had met and entered the great square, every person far and near ran toward them to see what was happening to the dwarf. They were followed by a motley crowd to the long low building of the prison where he was cast, howling and screaming, and grinding his wolf-like teeth with rage.

As Anna stood, half in pity, half in repugnance, the strange little figure appeared at a grated window. Tears rolled down his soiled, grimy face. He wailed, "Let me out! Let me out!" Boys in the crowd picked up bits of clay and pelted him, and others snatched sticks and tried to poke the ugly head away from the window, jeering and mocking him as he continued to cry, "Let me out! Let me out!"

Anna hurried to the jailer and complained, and the mocking crowds were dispersed. Night came with the swiftness of the tropics, but she stood for some time in the darkness by the window trying to quiet the dwarf, who screamed and shook the gratings of his prison cell. She moved up closer and said loudly: "Don't cry any more. I'll tell the King what has happened to you and he will let you out. Now go to sleep quietly, and you'll be out tomorrow!"

The words seemed to enter the dim intelligence and the screams ceased. As Anna turned away to start home the dwarf put out his huge hand and grasped hers, blubbering like a loathsome sort of child, as in fact he was, for he was not more than fourteen years old. He put her hand close to his heart, then raised it to his nose and smelled it, saying, *"Hom, hom, hom!"* (Fragrant, fragrant!)

Early the next morning Anna went by the prison on her way to the King's study. Nai Lek was at the same window peering out, and the moment he saw her he began to howl. The jailer told her that he had screamed throughout the night and had refused food. Anna tried to comfort him by pointing to the Palace and telling him that she was on her way there and that he must be patient. But it seemed in vain.

She was disappointed to find that the King was occupied elsewhere for the day, and that no one would interfere to set Nai Lek free. When she was ready to return home she did not have the courage to pass near the prison for fear her failure to keep her promise would upset Nai Lek. She sent her servant to inquire about him instead, and learned that the dwarf continued to cry, "Let me out!" and to shake the prison bars, and that he would eat nothing.

On the second morning Anna was able to see the King. She told him that Nai Lek had cut off Mae Duna's tail, and added, "now he is in prison for it." The King went off into gales of laughter at this latest prank of his favorite, which was only increased when Anna said that the stablemen were furious and were complaining to the judge. "Poor Nai Lek just stands at the window and howls," she said. "He can't understand why he is in prison, and he won't eat. He hasn't taken a bite of food and I'm afraid he'll starve before he ever comes to trial."

The King sobered immediately, realizing that the strange half-wild thing could no more comprehend the right and wrong of ordinary human morality than the ape he resembled. Without her asking it, he wrote a royal order setting Nai Lek free.

When Anna presented this to the jailer, the prison doors opened to her. She found Nai Lek lying on the bare floor of his cell, exhausted. The moment he saw Anna he began to whine like a dog. His eyes were rolled up in their sockets, and Anna feared he was actually dying from over-exertion and the want of food and water. But when she told him that the King had given orders that he was to be set free, he sprang to his feet and rushed out of the prison. Anna saw him scamper away toward the house where he lived with an old woman whose duty it was to take care of him.

Ten or twelve days later Anna saw him again, sitting astride a wall, whipping it and making all the motions of being on horseback. As soon as he caught sight of her he jumped down and came running toward her on all fours. He crouched beside her, took her hand in his, smelled it, and said, *"Hom, hom!"*

The King gave orders that Nai Lek was never again to be molested, so that the dwarf was safe from all but the jeers of passing boys. Anna was his beloved benefactor as long as she remained in Siam. In the fog of his mind that much was clear. Once she made him a blue shirt as a gift, and he was delighted. Every little while he would appear below her window and yell to let her know that he was there. When she and Boy looked out he would perform somersaults and acrobatic stunts for their amusement. Each new set of tumbles he learned he brought to them as a kind of offering, and Louis would laugh and clap with pleasure. Anna was touched by the persistence of Nai Lek's memory of her small act of kindness, especially since in higher quarters, where she had every right to expect it, she had less appreciation.

By the end of 1864, when Anna had been almost three years in the Palace, she decided to ask the King for the increase in salary which had been promised her when her work grew. There was no doubt that her work had doubled and trebled. She was busy with her school all day and had to translate in the evening until ten o'clock. Even these long hours did not free her from the possibility of being called during the night. Her royal pupils showed progress and the King often expressed his gratification with it. It cost sixty pounds a year to keep Avis in school in England. Living in Bangkok was not cheap. There were servants to pay, food to buy, Louis and herself to clothe. And there were the claims upon her of the distressed who came in an ever-increasing stream.

But when she broached the matter of her salary to the King, confident that he needed only to be reminded, to her astonishment he turned on her angrily. He said that "she had not given satisfaction," and added that she was "difficult and unmanageable, more careful about what was right and what was wrong than for the obedience and submission. And as to salary," he continued, "why you should be poor? You come into my presence every day with some petition, some case of hardship or injustice, and you demand, 'Your Majesty shall kindly investigate, and cause redress to be made'; and I have granted to you because you are important to me for translation, and so forth. And now you declare you must have increase of salary! Must you have everything in this world? Why you do not make *them* pay you? If I grant you all your petition for the poor, you ought to be rich, or you have no wisdom."

That ended the argument. The King refused to discuss the matter further. Anna was almost deprived of words, anyway, by the discovery that the King actually thought she would batten off the procession of misery that crawled to her for help. She turned quietly away, feeling as if she had been hit with a bludgeon.

There was little consolation in the thought that her influence had grown to the point where even the women and children of the Inside looked to her for help. Many of them, seeing that she was not afraid to oppose the King, imagined that she had more than human powers. So not only the poor, but the highly placed ladies of the harem came to her secretly with their grievances. Without intent she found herself set up between the oppressor and the oppressed. Day after day she was called upon to resist the cruelty of the judges. In cases of torture, imprisonment, extortion, she tried again and again to excuse herself from interfering, but still the mothers or sisters implored her until she had no choice left but to try to help them. Sometimes she sent Boy to the judges with her "clients," sometimes she went herself. Boy had become a great favorite with the King.

He had written Avis: "I like the King. He gave me some gold leaf for you which I send you with all my love." Anna had to admit honestly to herself that justice was granted not from a sense of right, but either through fear of her influence with the King or through Boy's known popularity.

When her Siamese and European acquaintances began to whisper that she was amassing a fortune, it was almost more than she could bear. Yet she was too proud to defend herself. She had not had enough experience to know that this was merely the usual suspicion of the comfortably self-centered for the incomprehensible few who set out to help their fellow men or to reform ancient and accepted evils. Besides, an honest survey of her own motives had convinced her that perhaps there was some reason for people to think that her rescues were not disinterested. In one sense they were not. She suffered so acutely from the sight of suffering that she was driven to action in pity for herself as much as for the sake of the in-jured. She was like the unjust magistrate in the Bible, she thought, who avenged the wrongs of the persistent widow "lest by her continual coming she weary me."

In addition to the outsiders there were always some among her pupils who needed special help. One of these was a little princess as beautiful as the Fa-ying had been. She had not been among the royal children brought to Anna at the beginning of the school, in 1862. She had come a year or more later, accompanied by a slave, and had entered the schoolroom timidly, as if she half expected to be rebuffed. She was a delicately formed little girl of about six when Anna first knew her, with large soft eyes that looked pleadingly from under thick lashes. Her low voice and subdued manner were not natural in a young child. They suggested a premature experience of sorrow or unkindness.

Her name was charming—Wani Ratana Kanya, which meant "Maiden of Jeweled Speech." She caught Anna's interest from the first by her shy loveliness and by her patience, and Anna made every effort to win her confidence. Wani smiled wistfully at her teacher, but maintained an air of reserve. She came to school regularly, however. Anna went to more than ordinary pains to encourage her, until one day when Lady Thiang, the head wife, called and took Anna aside in deep concern. She begged Anna to be less demonstrative. "Surely," she said dramatically, "you wouldn't bring more trouble on that wounded lamb, would you?"

"But of course not!" Anna exclaimed in alarm. "I only want to help her. She seems so forlorn!"

She tried to find out the reason back of Lady Thiang's warning. Why should it be dangerous to Wani to have her teacher show an interest in her? But Lady Thiang merely reiterated the warning and would not be drawn out on the subject of Wani's past, nor would any of the other women with whom Anna was intimate. Here apparently was a child who had fallen under a shadow so black that the whole Inside shunned her. The look on Wani's face reminded Anna of Lady Son Klin's expression when she had first known the Mon princess.

After that she was careful to avoid any appearance of favoritism in the classroom. But she would not give up her purpose of encouraging the little princess, and merely transferred her campaign to the little girl's home. It was a long one-story house with a wide verandah around it. A high wall enclosed the garden, which was planted with rare trees and flowers. On the first afternoon that Anna called there a carpet had been spread under a tamarind tree and Wani was sitting on it poring over her books. Surprised and pleased to see her teacher, she patted the carpet, saying, "Here, teacher, sit close to me!"

Anna stayed an hour and Wani soon lost her shyness and prattled happily like any normal child. She was very fond of animals, she said, and had several cats, some pet rabbits and squirrels. Sparrows had built their nests in the eaves of her house and there were parrots and Java sparrows in the garden trees. They flew in and out of the house as freely as they flew about in the garden because no one ever frightened them. Wani pointed to the nest of a bulbul in the beautiful acacia tree that stood at the center of the garden. The bird came every year to that tree, she said, and was now so tame that it would hop to the threshold and beg for the worms which fell from the mulberry trees. Wani would gather the dead worms, and the bulbul would take them from her hand, fly away with them to the young in the nest, and come back quickly for more.

After that Anna often visited Wani. She hoped to meet the princess' mother on one of these visits, thinking that she could learn something about the little girl's history, but she never did. There were always a few slaves about, but no one else, and Wani never mentioned her mother, although Anna knew that Khun Chom Kaeo was still alive. When she questioned the slaves they answered vaguely that the "Chao Chom was away." Wani apparently had no friends except the animals who were her pets. With them she had a kind of magic and there were always some of them frisking about her. Her nurse had bought her a tame turtle-dove, which perched on her shoulder and took seed from her open palm. Sometimes the bird would put its bill caressingly against Wani's mouth as if it were comforting the child.

In spite of the gulf that separated Wani from the favored life of the other royal children she was neither thin nor pale, and in her own home she seemed happy. The translucent olive of her cheeks was touched with a rose-petal flush which came and went if anything pleased or excited her. Her mother might be neglecting her, or might be unable to care for her, but she was healthy. This seemed to be the result of the care given her by one of the few slaves she possessed. While most of the royal pupils owned many slaves, Wani had no more than five or six. One of them, Mae

Noi, who was about twenty-five years old, seemed as devoted to Wani as if the little girl had been her own. It was comforting to Anna, who was troubled by the extreme isolation of the child, to see the attachment between this slave and the princess. Mae Noi carried Wani in her arms to and from school, fed her, fanned her during naps, bathed and perfumed her every night, and then rocked her to sleep. Wani's face would kindle at the sound of Mae Noi's step, her big eyes would shine, and the color would come and go in her cheeks. She would be for that moment as lovely as the petted Fa-ying had ever been.

Mae Noi studied with Wani, sitting at her feet at the schoolroom table. On some days Mae Noi apparently could not come, and then what Wani had learned at school during the day she taught to Mae Noi in the nursery at night. Anna was surprised when she first discovered that the slave kept pace steadily and read and translated as correctly as her mistress.

It was obvious that Mae Noi and Wani's other slaves went to some pains to keep the little girl out of the King's way. Apparently she was not in favor with her royal father, although the child herself did not seem to be aware of this and adored him with an unquestioning love. She liked to fold her hands and bow before the chamber where he was sleeping, and she spoke of him as a kind of god. She would say to Anna, "How glad my father will be when I can read English." One of the other children would giggle and nudge his neighbor as if the idea that anything Wani did might please the King was preposterous. Anna would look at the hopefulness in the princess' eyes, and marvel at the faith of a child which can be deceived without being discouraged. She could find no words in which to prepare the little girl for disappointment.

Wani's story, when Anna succeeded in getting it, was simple enough. She was the only daughter of Khun Chom Kaeo, who had once been the King's favorite. The concubine had fallen into disgrace because of her inveterate gambling. When the King discovered she had squandered the entire patrimony of her daughter, with the exception of half a dozen slaves, he had thrown her into prison. Wani was caught in the net of her mother's degradation. The King seemed to feel no pity for her, only intense dislike. The offense of the mother had made the child offensive to him.

When at last Wani's mother was released from prison, her term completed, Anna called one day and met her. She was a sullen unhappy woman with traces of the same beauty that made her daughter so lovely. Wani, in her innocence, appeared at the next afternoon audience with the other children. Perhaps Mae Noi had relaxed her vigilance, perhaps Wani's mother had permitted it. The minute the King caught sight of the little girl prostrate with the other children he became enraged. He taunted her about the misdemeanors of her mother with a coarseness that was revolting. It would have been cruel enough if she had been responsible for them and the gainer thereby. It was doubly cruel in that she was innocent of them and injured by them. Then he drove the little girl roughly from his presence.

The child was thoughtful and depressed for days. Anna's heart ached for her, and she felt an almost uncontrollable detestation of the King. His ridiculous prejudice not only wounded its victim, it cheated him of the only little princess among the seventy or more royal children who, both in physical beauty and intellectual brilliance, was like the beloved Fa-ying. Wani's memory was extraordinary and her progress swift. She had learned to spell, to read and write, and to translate almost intuitively. This was due partly to her mental keenness and partly to the fact that there was the same novelty and inspiration for her in the new world that her English books opened up as there had been for Lady Son Klin. Often on fête days she was Anna's only pupil, unwilling to miss a single hour of the new life she had found. No doubt Mae Noi had had something to do with this, since it was probable that the slave used the inducement of long hours alone with the Mem to dissuade her small charge from appearing where the King might see her. To her teacher she brought gifts out of the riches of her poverty, sometimes fruit, sometimes flowers from her garden. With them she offered a love that warmed the Englishwoman, even as it stirred her pity for this exquisite child, so full of affection and so unloved.

A little incident, curiously pathetic, showed that Wani had felt the snub from her father. Like an oyster she had carefully hidden the alien matter in pearl. In a book they came to a verse from the Bible—"Whom the Lord loveth He chasteneth." Anna had promised the King not to evangelize the harem, but she did not interpret this to mean that she could not explain verses that occurred in the readers she used, nor tell her pupils stories from the Bible. Once when the King remonstrated with her she asked whether he could teach the Siamese language without mention of Buddhism. When he replied that he could not, she said, "No more can I teach English and omit references to Christianity."

Wani read the verse thoughtfully. "Whom the Lord loveth He chasteneth." When she had translated it she looked up at Anna with a troubled expression. "Does your God do that?" she asked. "Oh, Mem *cha*, are *all* the gods angry and cruel? Hasn't he any pity even for little children who love him?" And then she added with a precocious sadness, "He must be like my father. He loves us, so he has to be *rai* (cruel) in order to teach us to fear evil and avoid it." There were tears in her eyes but also complete acceptance.

Then something happened. The change was nebulous at first. The little princess came to school as usual, but a strange woman attended her. Mae Noi no longer appeared. After a few days it was obvious that the child was not well groomed and cared for as she had been. Finally she seemed so listless and thin that Anna was forced to abandon the carefully disin-

233

terested attitude she had adopted to protect Wani from the jealousy of the harem. "Where is Mae Noi, Wani?" she asked her. The little girl burst into a storm of tears, but would not answer. When Anna inquired of the strange woman who had brought the child to school, she shrugged her shoulders and replied, *"Mai ru."* (I don't know.) Mystified and troubled Anna gave up the questioning for the time being.

She did not have to wait long for her answer, however. Three weeks after the disappearance of Mae Noi, Anna entered her schoolroom one morning and knew instantly that something unusual was taking place. All the female judges of the Palace were present, and a great crowd of mothers and royal children. On the steps innumerable slave women, old and young, crouched and hid their faces. As Anna worked her way toward the schoolroom table, she stopped, holding her breath. There was the King, furiously striding up and down.

But the most conspicuous object was little Wani's mother, manacled and prostrate on the polished marble pavement. The princess knelt beside her, hands clasped helplessly, eyes tearless and downcast, trembling. Anna was shocked to see how terror and sorrow had transformed the child. As well as Anna could understand from the King's angry torrent of words as he strode up and down, and from the spectacle itself—for no one dared to explain anything to her—Wani's mother had been gambling again, and had staked and lost her daughter's slaves, her one remaining possession. Anna knew finally the reason for Wani's tears and silence when she had been asked about Mae Noi. By some means, probably spies, the matter had come to the King's ears. His rage was insane, not because he loved the child, but because he hated the mother.

He shouted an order to lash the concubine. Two Amazons with heavy thongs advanced to execute the sentence. The first blow, delivered with savage skill, raised a long and bloody welt across the back of the woman on the floor. Before the thong could descend again Wani sprang forward and flung herself on the bare, quivering body of her mother. She clasped her arms around her mother's neck and called in a voice shrill with pain, "Strike me, O my father! Strike me instead!"

Into the deathly silence that followed came an anguished cry from Boy, who was seeing for the first time in his short life an act of insensate cruelty. His piercing threne of horror hung suspended in the air like the whips of the Amazons. Then its agonized and wordless protest shivered through every heart and was still. Louis, sick with loathing, buried his face in the folds of Anna's skirt.

For a moment nothing stirred—the prostrate concubine, the motionless lashes, the women and children on their knees, nor the King, his face livid with rage, lips drawn back from teeth, veins distended. The pleading of the Siamese child, the revulsion of the English boy echoed through the hall. And from the deep pulse of maternity on the pavement rose a soundless tide of prayer that beat wave on wave against the heart of the King, entreating his pity.

For a moment Anna thought that it might prevail. The King's sagacity was not blinded by his passion. He measured instantly the danger in that challenge. He, the accuser, now stood accused by the instinctive protest of two children. If the thong fell again, it would strike deep into the sensitivities of every woman at his feet. Then anger surged up in him and he rejected reason and mercy. In a thick voice he shouted, "Remove the child and bind her!"

It took the united strength of the two Amazons and a third woman to loosen Wani's arms from her mother's neck. She made no further sound. They dumped her down on the pavement and bound her hands and feet. Anna was close enough to see her face. The child looked steadily at the monster who lived in the form of her father, and all her faith in him and love for him were shattered. Her god was dead. Anna thought for a moment she had actually heard the thin sharp crack of the child's heart breaking.

Then there was no sound at all but the thud of the lash.

It was weeks before Anna could persuade the little girl to come back to school. Anna tried a thousand ways to divert the princess from the depressed state into which she had withdrawn, but the child looked at her vacantly and did not respond. The more Anna thought about it the more important it seemed to her to find Mae Noi if possible. Wani had nothing to hope from her father, nor from her mother, who was again in prison.

One aspect of the affair had puzzled Anna as soon as she began to think about it. Obviously, if Wani's mother had been gambling, she had not been gambling alone. Furthermore, she had lost Wani's slaves to someone, who was as guilty as she. But Khun Chom Kaeo alone had been publicly whipped. Why? There could be only one reason. The other party to the disreputable transaction was not to be punished. Then she was some woman high enough in the King's favor to have her peccadilloes overlooked. In all probability she was not a concubine, unless she was a recent favorite. The most likely possibility was that she was a princess, perhaps a sister of the King, or a niece.

No one would tell Anna who had won Mae Noi, and this confirmed her suspicion that Mae Noi's present owner was a great lady. The whole transaction and everyone concerned in it except Wani's mother was being kept a profound secret. This could be only because some important person was to be shielded at all cost. Then, by a happy accident, she overheard a scrap of conversation, hardly more than the name of Mae Noi and the name of one of the princesses in the same sentence.

Acting on the chance that she had discovered Mae Noi's new owner, Anna called on the princess immediately, and asked her to restore Mae

Noi to Wani. The princess did not deny her ownership of the slave. After a great deal of argument, coaxing, threatening, and pleading, Anna reached an agreement with her. She was to buy Mae Noi, and to pay for her freedom by a monthly installment of ten ticals, at that time six American dollars. At the end of one year the debt would be paid off. The princess agreed to free Mae Noi on that very day, however, and to bind Anna debtor in the slave's place. The paper was drawn and Anna signed it gladly. Mae Noi was now her property. There was humor in the thought that she, who hated the whole institution of slavery, owned a slave. And she intended to keep on owning her, for if she were to give the papers of transfer to little Wani it was likely that Khun Chom Kaeo would once more gamble the slave away.

Mae Noi was summoned by the princess and handed over to Anna. She threw up her arms and invoked the blessings of heaven on the English-woman. She kissed Anna's hands and feet passionately, and wept tears of joy. Then the two set off for Wani's house. The joy in the child's unbelieving eyes, the wordless rush with which she threw herself into the arms of the only person on earth who could be depended upon to love her, stayed with Anna as long as she lived.

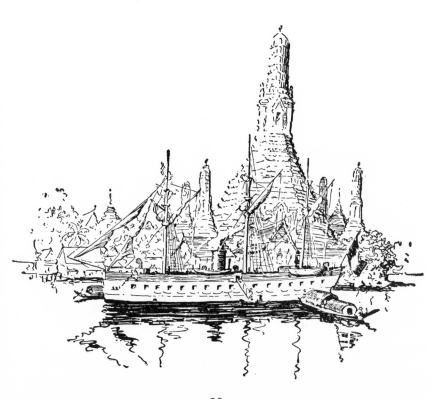

29

## L'AFFAIRE FRANÇAISE

ALL OVER the world 1864 and 1865 were troubled and uncertain years. In the United States the tide of the Civil War turned when Grant took over the Armies of the North in March of 1864. But ahead lay the final effort for victory, and still to come were the assassination of Lincoln and the long misery of reconstruction.

In May of 1864 Maximilian and Carlotta arrived in a sullen Mexico where Juarez's guerrillas would organize to bleed the French cause to death. Resentment against Napoleon was very deep in the United States. All through the years until 1867, when Maximilian was killed, there was talk of war with France. Napoleon was rumored to have solicited England's help in the event that war came.

Prussia had taken advantage of French involvement in Mexico to consolidate her position in central Europe by the Austro-Prussian and the Danish wars.

In the East, China was only beginning to recover from the agony of the Taiping Rebellion, which had taken millions of lives and destroyed an incalculable amount of property. "Chinese" Gordon had finally dissolved his army in June, 1864.

Repercussions from all these events were felt in Bangkok. French expansionism, particularly, was a constant worry to the King. The French were working swiftly to acquire colonies before the British could assume control of every weak nation in the Orient. India was lost to them, and Burma. Hongkong was already British and with it the cream of the south China trade. Malaya was fast being absorbed into the empire. But there remained 'Annam, as well as Siam and its tributaries.

In 1843 M. Guizot, Minister of Foreign Affairs, had ordered Vice-Admiral Jean Cécille and M. Théodose de Lagrené to search in the East for a place where French commerce and, if necessary, the French Navy could find refuge. His instructions were specific: "It is not for France to be wanting in that part of the world, where already the other Nations of Europe are established. In case of shipwreck our vessels ought not to be without a place to repair, and ought not to be obliged to go to the Portuguese Colony of Macao, the English port of Hongkong, or the arsenal of Cavieto in the Spanish island of Luson." The instructions gave preference to an island in a favorable situation away from hostile neighbors, where health conditions were good and revictualing possible. Admiral Cécille and M. de Lagrené followed their instructions with elementary simplicity. They looked around carefully and selected the Isle of Basilan, near Mindanao, at the southern end of the Sulu Archipelago. They landed a force and occupied it, and then obtained cession of it from the Sultan of Sulu. The Governor of the Philippines protested, arguing that it was Spanish territory, and he was backed up by the cabinet in Madrid. M. Guizot, who was engaged at the time with the delicate negotiations of the Spanish marriage, decided to drop the lesser question for the greater.

Fifteen years later, in 1858, Admiral Rigault de Genouilly, who commanded the French naval station in China, was instructed to proceed to Annam and force King Tu-duc to desist from his persecution of French and Spanish priests and native Christians. The particular occasion was the death of Mgr. Diaz, Bishop of Tonkin, as the result of imprisonment and torture. There had been many Catholic priests in Siam and the countries of Indo-China for two centuries. In Siam their activities had been curtailed sharply by the government after the Siamese became convinced that they were the political agents of the French in the abortive effort of Louis XIV to acquire Siam by diplomacy near the end of the seventeenth century. Some few priests had remained throughout the eighteenth century, but they had been closely watched under constant suspicion of being spies. None of them had acquired political influence.

But in Annam and Cambodia their activities had been less restricted. One of them, Pigneau de Béhaine, Bishop of Adran, had been instrumental in placing Tu-duc's grandfather, the Emperor Gia Long, on the throne of Annam in 1790 in return for substantial promises to the French. Admiral de Genouilly's advisers were Jesuit priests familiar with Indo-China from long residence. In Cambodia Mgr. Miche, Bishop of Dunsara, was involved in intrigues aimed at bringing that country under French control.

Ostensibly Admiral de Genouilly's expedition against Annam was punitive only. But several years later when it had been completed by one of his successors, the *Revue des deux mondes* of Paris commented: "By the force of circumstances (it is said in an official report) the end first proposed has been singularly overpast, and we have become conquerors when we only went to redress grievances." The booty which the French secured from their treaty with Tu-duc in 1862 was three of the richest provinces of Annam and one island, taken by the force of French arms against a weak state in no way equipped to resist cannon and gunboats. These provinces were in the southern part of the peninsula around the city of Saigon, called by Europeans generally Cochin-China. They had belonged to the ancient kingdom of the Chams, which the Annamese had conquered less than two hundred years before.

The American Consul at Bangkok had already informed the Secretary of State—"At Saigon the French have and are still collecting large quantities of naval and military stores. They have a fleet of about sixty vessels in and near that point, the magnitude of the force and preparations excite rumor everywhere in the East." In July a private correspondent wrote: "You have doubtless heard that the French have recently made a treaty with Cochin-China by which the Cochin-Chinese have ceded three large rich provinces bordering on the Gulf of Siam and the China Sea to the French, and are to pay twelve millions of dollars as an indemnity for the expenses of the war. The indemnity goes to Spain for troops sent from Manila, and punishments inflicted by the Cochin-Chinese on Catholic priests. The French are making toward Bangkok, and many are of the opinion that in a few years all Siam will be under the French government."

Saigon appeared to be a very promising port to the French who had just taken it, but it would be even more so if the hinterland were also in French hands. The next plum was obviously Cambodia. What did it matter that in 1856 the French Ambassador who negotiated the treaty with Siam, M. Charles Louis Nicholas Maximillien de Montigny, had told King Mongkut that the Emperor recognized Siam's suzerainty over Cambodia, and had instructed M. de Montigny to request King Mongkut's permission to make a commercial treaty with the vassal?

Cambodia lay just north of the three new provinces, on the Mekong River, which the French confidently expected to develop as a rival to the Pearl River that emptied into the China Sea at Hongkong. Furthermore, there existed one of those situations which have made the paths of imperialism easy. The King of Cambodia had died in 1860, leaving several sons. For more than a century no one had thought to dispute the right of Siam to decide the succession. Several of the Cambodian kings had come to Bangkok for their coronation. It was true that Annam, aggressive and acquisitive, had pushed farther and farther south and west, and had demanded and secured tribute from Cambodia. But even the kings of Annam, some of whom had been refugees in Bangkok themselves, had not questioned the King of Siam's right to regulate the succession. The late King of Cambodia had spent half his life in Bangkok, and his sons had all been raised there. King Mongkut appointed the oldest of them to succeed his father as King Norodom, but one of the younger sons rebelled against his brother. When King Norodom was compelled to flee from his capital, the Siamese sent an expedition which defeated the pretender and restored Norodom to the throne.

The French, once they had decided to control Cambodia, used both guile and force. They suggested to Norodom that they would be willing to recognize him as independent of Siam, if he would request them to do so, and to ensure him against the encroachments of his brothers. All that they required in return was that he place himself under their protection and grant them certain trifling commercial privileges. It was comparatively easy to plant in Norodom's mind the suspicion that, if he refused, the wily Europeans would throw the weight of their gunboats and army back of one of his more tractable brothers. Vice-Admiral Pierre de la Grandière, Governor and Commander-in-Chief of Cochin-China, prepared a secret treaty and took it with him on a visit to King Norodom in 1863. With the help of Mgr. Miche the treaty was signed on August 11. Norodom immediately wrote King Mongkut:

> I requested a postponement in order to report to Bangkok, but he would not agree to it. If I had refused to sign the treaty, hostilities would have ensued. Your Majesty had told me that the French would conclude any such treaty at Bangkok, but on this occasion Admiral de la Grandière, Commander-in-Chief of the French fleet at Saigon, compelled me to conclude the treaty in Cambodia . . . However, I am as loyal to Your Majesty as before. I should prefer to remain Your Majesty's subject to the end of my life. My feelings in this matter have not changed.

But the camel's nose was in the tent. The French had acquired a protectorate over Cambodia, which instead of making Norodom independent was to make him a puppet. Under the Siamese he had been free to do as he liked so long as he fulfilled his feudal obligations. Under the French he was more and more restricted. The treaty specified that the consuls of no other countries were to be admitted to Cambodia without French consent, French goods were to be free of export and import duties, and the French Resident at the capital was to have the rank of Grand Mandarin.

But before the extent of French determination and ambition had become clear King Norodom had signed a treaty with King Mongkut on December 1, 1863. Actually there was little that was new in the treaty. It merely defined what had been the relationship between Cambodia and Siam for centuries. It stated flatly that "Cambodia is a tributary State of Siam": and that "the Cambodian rulers have been accustomed to receive their appointments from Bangkok." It arranged for the extradition of criminals, the regular payment of tribute, and other matters relating to trade and government procedure. Not surprisingly the French took violent exception to it when it was published for the first time in the *Straits Times* of Singapore on August 20, 1864.

M. Aubaret had arrived in Bangkok in April of that year and undertook at once to secure the annulling of the treaty. He was irascible, unpleasant, ill-mannered. One of the local papers said of him:

> We fear from all accounts that M. Aubaret is a very unfit man in point of temperament to hold the post he has; and the French foreign minister could not have been aware of the discourtesies and almost bullying manner with which he discharged his function towards the government of Siam. French consuls and diplomats generally understand how to combine the SUAVITER IN MODO with the FORTITER IN RE, and had M. Aubaret been trained in the work in the proper school no doubt he could do so. The training of a man of war is certainly not suited to acquiring the necessary qualifications.

In the course of a few months he was detested by everyone in Bangkok except a few of his compatriots who were as eager as he was to see the extension of French power in the East. His relations with the Siamese government were one long succession of quarrels. Sometimes when the King was more than ordinarily perturbed by the aggressive notes of M. Aubaret, he would send for Anna. He took for granted, since she was English, her sympathy for him and her hatred of the French. He would whisper to her that he wanted her to "consult Mr. Thomas George Knox." He was too afraid of the French to write directly to London himself, even though he secretly longed for the intervention and protection of the English. When Anna would protest that Mr. Knox was too honorable to engage in an intrigue against a colleague even for the protection of British interests, he would rail at her indifference. He knew better than she did that Mr. Knox was constantly engaged with intrigues of one sort and another which concerned both Siam's foreign and domestic relations.

But he was not on the same friendly footing with Mr. Knox as he had been with Sir Robert Schomburgk, who had retired the year before. The King had not been pleased by the appointment of Mr. Knox as British Consul. Mr. Knox was too closely identified with the King's brother, the Second King, to be acceptable to Mongkut. As in the case of M. Aubaret and the French government, so in the case of Mr. Knox and the British

government the King had not had the temerity to go so far as to ex‧
plain that he was *persona non grata*. He had written a letter to Queen
Victoria, however, commending Sir Robert Schomburgk, the retiring
consul, very highly. He had also had a suggestion:

> We would beg your Majesty will be graciously pleased to direct
> Your Ministers to select a person of rank and possessing the like good
> qualities as Sir Robert Schomburgk to be appointed in the place of
> Sir Robert Schomburgk without delay. We also beg that the new
> Consul at Siam may be a person of intelligence and well acquainted
> with his duties. We would prefer a person sent direct from England,
> and whose good qualities and abilities the British Government is
> aware of from personal acquaintance.

The British government had not seen fit to comply with these sug-
gestions, and the King was without the support he believed he would
have had from Sir Robert in the long quarrel with the French.

Aubaret's primary concern was to force the Siamese to recognize openly
the *de facto* hold Admiral de la Grandière had established over Cambodia.
He tried argument, threats, and intimidation, and at last on April 9, 1865,
the French man-of-war *Mitraille* appeared in the port of Bangkok. It was
the final effective argument. On April 14 under its frowning guns the
Cambodian treaty with Siam was formally annulled by the Siamese
government. On the same day a treaty was signed with France in which
Siam renounced her rights in Cambodia and agreed to acknowledge the
protectorate of the French there. Siam had lost the first of many large
tracts of territory to France. In the end she succeeded in maintaining her
sovereignty—although there were not many foreign residents of Bangkok
in 1865 who would have thought that possible—but at the expense of more
than 290,000 square miles of her territory.

M. Aubaret was exultant. He immediately began another quarrel with
the government, this time on behalf of a French priest, the Rev. John
Martin, pastor of Conception Church in Bangkok. Fr. Martin had differed
with one of his parishioners, a Siamese nobleman of venerable years but
positive spirit, whose name was Phya Wiset. He was a high official in the
military department of the government, and in addition he was the chief
man among the Cambodian Catholics in Bangkok. M. Aubaret wrote to
the King asking His Majesty to depose Phya Wiset and to replace him
with a French officer, M. E. Lamache, who had been acting as drill master
to the King's troops, and who had the Siamese title of Luang Upathet
Thuiyahan. The reasons that M. Aubaret advanced for the change were
that Phya Wiset was known to be of bad character, and that the Emperor
of France would be extremely gratified by the promotion of M. Lamache.
The petition ended with the suggestion that the matter be consummated
before the consul left for France at the beginning of September. It was not

hard for the King to believe that both the consul and the Emperor would be glad to see a Frenchman in high military position in Siam. In time of crisis it might be of less benefit to His Majesty, however. He could hardly afford to place persons of doubtful loyalty in such strategically important posts. The request was presumptuous and the King decided to ignore it, since it was hardly likely that M. Aubaret would back up so relatively small a matter with a gunboat.

Fr. Martin and Phya Wiset took their differences to court on August 23, 1865. They appeared before Mom Rachothai in the Royal Court of Equity, commonly called the International Court. Mom Rachothai, the judge, was a man of unexceptionable character, universally admired by both Europeans and Siamese. He had been one of the ambassadors to Queen Victoria and had written a poetic account of the trip to England that was exceedingly popular with the Siamese. He was a prince and a cousin of the King. It was a tribute to his ability as well as to his integrity that in his position of chief justice of the court which adjudicated cases between Europeans and Siamese his judgments were widely accepted as fair and impartial.

As soon as Fr. Martin and Phya Wiset met in the courtroom they fell into a loud and angry altercation. The priest called Phya Wiset a liar and Phya Wiset replied in kind. Fr. Martin immediately hurried off to the French Consulate to make a complaint on the ground that Phya Wiset had dishonored his cloth by the use of the word liar. He insisted that not only he but his religion had been insulted.

It was evening when the matter was laid before M. Aubaret. His quick temper flared immediately and he penned a note to the King demanding in a peremptory manner that Phya Wiset be removed from office without further investigation. He added that, if the demand were not complied with at once, he would take it as an insult to Christianity as well as to the French government, and as an infraction of the treaty. The note was committed to M. Lamache, who set out with it for the Palace.

It was two o'clock in the morning before M. Lamache arrived at the Palace gates, having fortified himself heavily on the way. M. Aubaret had told him to present the note summarily, and as an officer commanding the King's troops he was admitted to the penetralia. His Majesty had been feeling ill for some days, but was that night a little better. He had called some Buddhist priests for the purpose of holding special devotional services. The King was irritated by the sudden unceremonious appearance of M. Lamache in his quarters and demanded the business of the intruder, pointing out the lateness of the hour.

M. Lamache presented the consul's letter without apology. When the King had read it he said that he would have the matter attended to "to-morrow," and that he would order a suitable investigation.

"No investigation is necessary, Your Majesty," replied M. Lamache with an impertinence born of the assurance that the French Consul could be counted on to second him. "I myself heard the offensive language that Phya Wiset used to Father Martin. M. Aubaret insists that Phya Wiset must be shown that he cannot treat a French subject in this way with impunity."

"Yes, yes," said the King impatiently. "I will see to it tomorrow. You may tell M. Aubaret that I have promised to order an investigation. And now you may go."

But M. Lamache refused to leave. He expostulated with the King a second, third, and fourth time, demanding insolently that the nobleman be removed by the King's order that very night. The King's patience snapped. It had been held in check, in spite of M. Lamache's disregard of protocol, only by his almost superstitious fear of the French, but the effrontery of M. Lamache was beyond all reason. The hour for the Buddhist ceremony had arrived and His Majesty ordered M. Lamache to withdraw.

M. Lamache drew himself to his full height and planted his feet firmly. "I refuse to go, Your Majesty," he retorted with deliberate impudence, "until you have granted M. Aubaret's very reasonable request."

"Throw him out!" shouted the King to the guard who crouched near him. With a rush they closed in on M. Lamache and took him bodily out of the hall, out of the courtyard, through the gates, and deposited him roughly in the public road in front of the Palace.

The Frenchman picked himself up slowly and set off to report to M. Aubaret. Angry and humiliated, he embroidered his story. He said that the King had spoken disrespectfully, not only of His Imperial Majesty's consul, but of the Emperor himself, besides outrageously insulting a French messenger.

The King had intended to answer M. Aubaret's note in the morning, but when morning came he was ill again and postponed the matter. In the meantime M. Aubaret grew more and more inflamed, both by reflection on the story M. Lamache had told, and by the insult he imagined in the King's delay. Finally, unable to contain himself longer, he wrote a second note saying that in expelling Lamache from the Palace the King of Siam had been guilty of a political misdemeanor, and had rudely disturbed the friendly relations existing between France and Siam. He accused the King of antagonism toward the French and threatened to lay the implications of the King's attitude, with suitable recommendations, before the Emperor in six weeks, since he expected to be in Paris by that time. He added ominously that during his absence he would ask the admiral in command of the French fleet at Saigon to take measures to insure the "protection of French interests in Siam."

Instead of writing an answer the King sent Mom Rachothai to explain to the consul, for, as Anna wrote of this incident, "His Majesty knew how to confront the uproar of vulgarity and folly with the repose of wisdom and dignity." It was obvious to the King that M. Lamache was misrepresenting the occurrence in the Palace, and he believed that a reasonable explanation from one of the most respected men in Bangkok would satisfy the consul.

Mom Rachothai was a serene, quiet man of more than middle age. He went on his difficult assignment immediately. "Your Excellency," he began courteously, "His Majesty has asked me to call and explain that you have unfortunately an erroneous idea of what happened at the Palace when M. Lamache presented your note. He is sure that as soon as you understand the circumstances you will realize that . . ."

He got no further. The consul stood up with insane rage glowing in his eyes. He walked over to the dignified Siamese judge and picked up the insignia of his rank, which his servants had placed on the table beside him as was the custom. These were all gifts from the King and were an official's most precious possessions. They were carried behind him wherever he went by slaves specially selected for that purpose. With deliberation and malice the Frenchman threw the insignia one by one to the ground from his verandah, which was raised many feet above it. The betel-box broke into pieces in front of the prince's slaves who crouched waiting for their master.

Then the consul turned to the judge, in whose face horror and incredulity were mixed. Before the Siamese could guess what the barbarian from Europe contemplated M. Aubaret's hand shot out toward Mom Rachothai's head. Among a people who regarded the head as sacred and untouchable the gesture itself was insulting. But M. Aubaret did not stop there. He grasped the prince by his hair and with all his strength swung the slight Siamese up and threw him down the stairs to the ground after his insignia.

For seventy-five years this unthinkable, incredible, unendurable insult to the Siamese nation was to rankle in Siamese minds and keep alive their hatred of the French. M. Aubaret left almost immediately for France. After he had gone—everyone hoped for good—the Bangkok *Recorder* said:

> It is evident from what has been transpiring ever since M. Aubaret has been here that he is not the man to get along with the Siamese, and we doubt if he could get along smoothly anywhere. If he return to Siam he must return with sufficient force to make Siam virtually a French province, and himself the chief man in it.

Most of the Europeans in Bangkok as well as many of the Siamese were convinced that this was exactly what M. Aubaret wanted to do. They could only hope that his Imperial Master was too heavily involved in Europe and Mexico to make it possible.

30

## THE SLAVE TUPTIM

ONE DAY in the fall of 1865 when Anna was dismissing school she heard a little prince say to another in Siamese, "Come on, let's go hunt for Tuptim." Tuptim! The name rang ominously in Anna's mind. She had not thought of the girl in months, perhaps a year. The last time she had seen the young concubine she had vaguely resolved to talk to her and get better acquainted. But Tuptim had not come to the schoolroom again and the determination had died unborn.

"Why are you going to hunt for Tuptim?" Anna asked the little prince in surprise. "Where has she gone?"

Before the child could answer Princess Ying Yaowalak, the oldest of the royal children, angrily seized him by the arm and hurried him away. Anna had no wish to inquire further. She had had more than enough of the troubles of the Palace, and she did not want to involve herself in another stormy contretemps with the King. Sometimes it seemed to her that their association had been one long struggle in which the incidents were mere variations on the theme of their different points of view. The King was too accustomed to sycophancy not to try to enforce at least outward submission on all those close to him. Anna was too conscious of the dignity that she regarded as the natural right of human beings not to resist the implication of his attitude both for herself and for others. No amount of familiarity and adjustment could resolve completely the latent friction between them.

She was tired of the Palace, tired of wrongs she could not right, tired of the callousness of those around her, and the irresponsible cruelty of the King. Nevertheless, as she walked home that day she could not free herself from anxiety for Tuptim, suddenly called to remembrance by the words of the little prince. The scene at Wat Rachapradit when the King had been talking about M. Aubaret and the geographers who perversely called Siam an absolute monarchy had come back to Anna many times. In her mind's eye she could still see Tuptim sink to her knees in the midst of the falling pottery, as if the King's gaze were a withering blight. Well, M. Aubaret was on his way to France and there was a lull in his offensive aggressions. But Tuptim—what could have happened to her?

Anna might have forgotten the trivial incident if it had not been for what followed. A week after the ceremonies at Wat Rachapradit she had been walking through one of the long corridors within the Palace on her way to work when she saw the girl lying on the marble pavement among the offerings placed there for the King, which he would inspect on his leisurely progress toward his breakfast hall. She lay in the midst of bales of silk, supplies of perfumed candles, boxes of spices, and the many other gifts that were always to be found there. Two women were crouching on either side of her, waiting to make the presentation.

Anna had grown accustomed to such sights, but she was surprised at the unusual interest this girl appeared to excite in the other women of the harem. Several of them were standing nearby, whispering and talking together, expressing their admiration of her beauty in the most extravagant language. She was certainly very lovely. Those who had sent her had used all the resources of art to enhance her natural charms. Her lips were dyed a deep crimson, and her eyebrows were continued in indigo until they met on her brow. Her eyelashes were stained with kohl, the tips of her fingers and nails with henna. Enormous gold chains and rings adorned her neck and hands. No wonder the girl had been frightened that day when she saw she had attracted the attention of the King. Apparently she had foreseen what his interest would mean! She had looked so happy and free then! Anna stopped a moment in sadness, and went on.

Among the hundreds of women of the harem who had been presented to the King in the same way Anna would hardly have given much thought to this particular girl except that first one thing and then another distinguished her. Three months or so after her presentation to the King, Anna saw her for the third time. She was standing in the same courtyard exhibiting to several other young girls like herself a pomegranate. It was the largest and finest fruit of its kind that Anna had seen and she stopped to get a closer view. The girl showed it to her happily. It was not a real fruit at all, but a casket of gold, exquisitely molded. It had been enameled to resemble the fruit and was inlaid with rubies, which looked exactly like the seeds of the pomegranate. It was made to open and shut at the touch of a small spring and was intended for a betel-box.

"Where did you get it?" Anna asked, for it was an enormously costly trinket.

The girl turned to Anna with a child's smile and pointed to the lofty chamber of the King. "My name, you know, is Tuptim," she explained.

Then Anna understood the gift, for Tuptim meant "pomegranate" or "ruby," and the little box combined the two meanings. The King had a new favorite!

Again, weeks later, on a day when Anna went to Lady Thiang's house to request fresh supplies of paper and ink, she came upon Tuptim weeping bitterly. The head wife was reproving her with unusual warmth. Lady Thiang paid no attention to Anna's entrance, and this was unusual also. When she had finished her scolding she turned to Anna with a kind of despair and asked, "What shall I do with this Tuptim? Shall I whip her or starve her until she minds me?"

"Forgive her whatever she's done, and be good to her as you are to everyone," Anna whispered.

"Why should I forgive her?" Lady Thiang asked, in an offended tone, evidently thinking that Anna was making light of a serious situation. "She makes me more trouble than any girl in the Palace. Do you know what she's been doing? Why, when she's been told to stay upstairs with HIM, she runs away and hides in the rooms of her friends. You've seen her with Maprang and Simla? They're her most intimate friends and they seem to think that it's funny to help her, and then we older women are accused of being jealous of her and mistreating her. And we have to search all the houses of the Choms until we find her, usually sound asleep, and bring her to HIM. And the minute she comes into HIS presence she goes down on her knees and looks so innocent that HE's enchanted, and declares that she is the most perfect and fascinating woman in the harem. But as soon as she can get away, she does it all over again, only finding some new place to hide.

"Mem *cha,* I'm in despair. I honestly don't know what to do with her. Why will she act like a child? Now she says she's ill and can't wait on the King. But the physicians who have examined her say that there's nothing at all wrong with her. I don't know what to do next. I can't tell HIM the truth. You know what would happen to her if HE ever found out what she's been doing. She won't listen to my advice, or to anyone else's, either. And I'm terribly afraid that she'll find herself in real trouble if she doesn't. I've told her that she might just as well make up her mind to bear her life here more patiently, because if she doesn't it can get much much worse. But will she listen to me?" Lady Thiang was wringing her hands in genuine distress. Tuptim knelt before her, head hanging.

"How old is she?" Anna inquired.

"Oh, fifteen perhaps," Lady Thiang answered.

Anna looked at the girl with a new stab of pity. She did appear either ill or very unhappy. But for all her childlike appearance there was a great deal of poise about her. Tuptim's eyes brimmed with tears and she protested passionately that she was sick at heart, and that she could not go upstairs any more. Anna was sure that Lady Thiang's condemnation did not indicate any real anger, but rather concern, so she put her arms around the head wife and succeeded at last in obtaining permission for Tuptim to be absent from duty for a few days until she felt better. A smile of gratitude lighted the girl's tear-stained face and she crept away.

"She's too unsophisticated!" Lady Thiang complained as soon as Tuptim was out of sight. "She won't even try to get used to the life here. She says that she didn't want to come, and she doesn't like it. I pity her from my heart, Mem *cha*, but I mustn't let her know it. She would take advantage of me and keep away from HIM altogether. And you know what would happen then. She isn't the only girl who has been brought here against her will. Why can't she try to like it, or at least pretend to until she gets used to it? Lots of the other women would be glad to be the favorite, goodness knows. Look at the gifts she receives! But no, not Tuptim! She mopes in her room, and cries, and avoids HIM if she can." Lady Thiang sighed deeply. "And we head wives get the blame. She doesn't! HE thinks that we're jealous and intriguing and afraid of our younger rivals, and that we try to keep Tuptim away from HIM with one excuse or another so that she can't supplant us in HIS affections, when the holy Buddha in heaven knows that there's nothing but kindness and sympathy in our hearts for her. Look how we shield her from HIM!"

Not long after this Tuptim began to come to school. She wanted to learn to write her name in English, she said, and she came once or twice a week. Usually Maprang and Simla came with her. They were listless and idle, but she was absorbed in the lessons. She would sit on the marble floor for hours listening to the simple exercises of translating English into Siamese and Siamese into English. Anna began to hope that Tuptim might find the same outlet for her pent-up emotions that Prang had found. Prang who had been wild and restless and full of hazardous mischief was now steady, quiet and seemingly happy.

One day when Anna was alone in the schoolroom, Tuptim asked her to write the name "Khun Phra Palat" in English. Anna wrote it without even wondering whose name it was. Tuptim immediately began to trace the letters for herself. Anna saw tenderness in her large dreamy eyes as she copied and recopied the name, and thought briefly without curiosity that the owner of the name must mean a great deal to the girl.

Perhaps it was because Tuptim rarely came alone, perhaps because she seemed guileless and younger even than her years, that Anna never tried to learn anything about her background, or what she was thinking and feeling. Lady Thiang said nothing more, and Anna took it for granted that Tuptim was reconciling herself to the new life that had been thrust upon her. There was only once that Anna almost attempted to gain Tuptim's confidence. In later years she wished a thousand times that she had. Tuptim had come running to her one day after school. She had taken a scrap of paper from her vest and held it up silently before Anna's eyes. On it was written the name "Khun Phra Palat" in an excellent round hand. Anna praised the improvement in her caligraphy and then asked her for the first time, "But whose name is it, Tuptim?"

The girl cast down her eyes and hesitated, then raised them. "It's the name of the favorite disciple of the abbot, Chao Khun Sa," she answered. "He lives at the temple of Rachapradit, and sometimes he comes and preaches to us in the Palace."

There was deep reverence on her face such as Anna had seen on the faces of many of the women at any mention of the great priest. Anna looked at her sharply but saw nothing else. A dozen half-formed questions rose in her mind, but she did not ask them. She had not known before that Tuptim had an interest in religious things. Or was Tuptim finding some release from the stifling pressure of life in a new devotion to religion? This was not uncommon in the harem, although Anna would not have expected it of Tuptim, who had seemed rebellious and freedom-loving in her attitude. It was then that she vaguely resolved to try to talk to Tuptim and help her if possible. There was some indefinable need about her, some nameless hunger that made her seem restless and unsatisfied. But that was the last time Tuptim came to the school, and Anna, busy with other things, let her impulse drop to the bottom of her mind and lie there forgotten.

The remark of the little prince about hunting for Tuptim troubled Anna, sensitive as she now was to the moods of the Palace. She thought about the young concubine off and on during the next day, which was Sunday. Would she have continued to come to school if she had been encouraged? Had she needed help or guidance? Would she have accepted advice from an Englishwoman when she had flouted Lady Thiang's? Where was she? Was she still playing her dangerous game of hide-and-seek with the King?

As if in answer to Anna's troubled self-questioning her little Siamese maid told her that evening that a slave from the Palace wished to speak to her in private. There was something familiar about the slave but Anna could not remember where she had seen her. The woman had a broad plain face and a low forehead. She crawled close to Anna's chair and whispered, "I am Phim. My mistress, Khun Chao Tuptim, has sent me to you." She looked around apprehensively. "You know that my mistress has been found?"

"Found?" Anna exclaimed. She was alarmed by the slave's furtive manner. Tuptim had been found many times before in some corner of the Inside without any particular harm coming from it. "Explain what you mean! Where was she found? How long has she been lost this time?"

The slave repeated the question in evident astonishment. "Why, Mem *kha*," she asked, "didn't you know that my mistress had disappeared from the Palace, and that His Majesty had offered a reward of twenty catties to anyone who brought information about her? And that no one could discover any trace of her at all, even though everyone has been searching?"

"No," Anna said, "I hadn't heard a word of it." She was deeply perturbed. "How long has she been missing?"

"A long time," the slave girl replied vaguely. "Many, many months until everyone thought that she had drowned herself."

"But how could she possibly get out of the Palace through three rows of gates, guarded and bolted, too? The Amazons would have seen her. And I don't believe she could have bribed them to do anything so dangerous to themselves."

"I know, Mem *kha,* what you say is true. It is impossible to get out. But she did get out, anyway." The girl's brow under the low-growing brush of hair was wrinkled as if in pain, and her cheeks were wet with tears. She had evidently been weeping for a long time and was close to hysteria. Anna was convinced that however Tuptim had managed her escape Phim had been involved.

She had been right, then, in her intuition. She realized now that her subconscious mind had known that the girl was unwilling or unable to bend herself to harem discipline. Tuptim had revolted openly when the strain became more than she could bear. Anna was not really surprised even at the form of that revolt. It was what, if she had thought about it carefully, might have been expected. Tuptim had run away from the environment she hated, with the heedless disregard of consequences that was part of her immaturity. Phim, her parents if they had sheltered her, Tuptim herself, everyone in any way involved was going to suffer severely— perhaps horribly! Anna shut her eyes against the picture of the King's rage at being so scorned by one upon whom he had lavished his favor. Poor Lady Thiang! Her worst fears had come to pass.

"Where was she found?" Anna asked sorrowfully.

Phim's whisper was barely audible. "Two priests discovered her this morning in the monastery at Wat Rachapradit. They brought the information to the King, and he ordered her arrested and imprisoned in one of the Palace dungeons." The slave placed her palms together and raising them high over her head prostrated herself before Anna in the most abject supplication. "So I've come to you for help, Mem *chao kha.*"

Anna was appalled. This was infinitely worse than anything she could have imagined. No woman was allowed to defile a monastery by her presence. "It means death," she thought hopelessly.

"But what could I or anyone else possibly do?" she asked aloud.

"Oh, gracious lady, if you won't help her she's lost!" the slave cried, forgetting to whisper, and burst into tears. "She'll be executed!" Phim clasped her hands around Anna's feet and laid her face upon them in frantic humility. "Mem *chao kha,* I implore you to go to the King and ask her life! He'll forgive her for your sake. Everyone knows that he will grant even life to you. I'm sure he will, I know he will! Everyone says that he will do anything you ask. Only ask him, then, Mem *chao kha,* or he will order my little mistress killed!" She writhed in an agony of fear, babbling almost incoherently. "What shall I do? Where can I go? I've no place to go but to the Mem. If she won't help then nobody will. No one can help her but you, gracious lady. You must go to her! You must beg the King for her life!"

Her terror made its impression on Anna's quick sympathies, even though she was convinced that this time there was nothing she could do. She leaned down and tried to soothe the slave. "Tell me, Phim," she urged, "why did your mistress leave the Palace, and who helped her get away? I know that she couldn't have done it alone."

But the girl would not answer her. "Please, come and see her for yourself," she kept repeating. "Come and talk with her. You can go to the Palace now that it's dark, and the gate-keepers will let you in. No one will guess that you're going to see my mistress. You must come! Nobody else can help her! Please, gracious lady, say that you will come!"

The more Anna said that it was impossible, that there was nothing she could do, the more hysterical the girl became. At last, to quiet her, Anna promised she would go to the Palace and talk to Tuptim. She was convinced that Phim had helped Tuptim in her escape, and that the slave was as much afraid of the disclosure it was in the power of her mistress to make as she was of the punishment that awaited Tuptim.

After the slave had left, Anna sat at her window and watched the stars come out. They shone with unusual splendor in the cloudless sky. As a little girl she had always thought that Sunday was different from other days—that the sun shone more brightly and that the rain fell less often, that there was a special hush in the air. Now, far from her native Wales, she felt the peace of Sunday creep into her heart. In spite of her promise to Phim she felt a deep reluctance to go into the Palace. She longed to keep on sitting in her chair in the dark, watching the far and quiet stars, and dreaming a little of Avis at school. Surely tomorrow would do as well. But the thought of Tuptim alone in one of the slimy underground dungeons kept obtruding. The Palace! She looked across at its white walls gleaming in the starlight and hated it and its endless woes. Couldn't they leave her alone even on Sunday, her one free day? She shuddered at the thought of entering the grisly prison world after nightfall, and put the thought away from her. At least until morning. What could she accomplish by going? So she sat in torpid uncertainty until a warm hand was laid on hers. She turned her gaze from the sky and saw at her feet Phim's distressed face.

"Mem *kha,* the gates have been opened for the Kralahome," she said in a low pleading voice. "You could get in now without difficulty." Then she melted into the night.

Anna sighed. It seemed impossible to convince the simple people who brought their problems to her as to a deity that she had no superhuman power. Most of them were sincerely convinced that she was not only a member of the dread San Luang, but so close to the King that he would grant her any petition. This was ironic in view of the antagonism that so often existed between them. Yet when she had failed in some mission of mercy, she had seen more than once in the sad eyes of the disappointed petitioner a numbed acceptance of finality and the conviction that had she wanted to succeed she could have done so. The legend of her omnipotence had grown to be a weary weight.

With another sigh for the cool quiet evening she got up resolutely from her chair by the window. She told Boy where she was going, put twenty ticals in her purse, wrapped a black cloak about her and slipped out of the house. The distance to the Palace was only a few hundred feet. She hurried across the commons eager to get her errand over. The guards knew her and admitted her without question. She dropped two ticals into the hands of the Amazon at the gate of the Inside saying that she had come on business, and begging her to keep the gate open for an hour or two.

"You must be back before it strikes eleven," the Amazon warned her good-naturedly, and asked nothing more.

As soon as Anna entered the main street within the walls, Phim joined her, crouching and running along the deep shadows of the houses, until they reached the doors of the prison. Then she disappeared into the darkness.

Anna knocked and was admitted to the central hall. It was an immense room with innumerable pillars, and a floor in which were set the many trapdoors to the dungeons, double-barred and locked. The few lanterns that lighted it were hung so high that they looked like stars and gave the dimmest of light. There were about a dozen Amazons in the guard, some already stretched in sleep on their mats and leather pillows, with their weapons lying nearby. The eyes of those who were still awake turned toward Anna. They knew her well, and her visits of mercy.

They made a courteous return to her salutation. Mae Ying Thahan, chief of the guard, inquired pleasantly why she had come so late at night.

"I have just learned that one of my former pupils, Lady Tuptim, is in some sort of trouble—I don't know exactly what—and I have hurried over to see if I can be of any help to her."

"The child is in trouble indeed," answered Mae Ying Thahan gravely. "She's not only got herself into prison, but her two friends, Maprang and Simla."

"Can I help them?"

"No, Mem," said the Amazon, and the gentleness of her voice modified the flatness of her refusal. "You can't help her, either. No one can. This time her guilt is too great."

"Can you tell me exactly what she has done?"

But to this Anna could get no answer. She tried vainly to persuade Mae Ying Thahan, and grew more alarmed at the immediate seriousness of the situation as the Amazon steadfastly refused to tell her. Admitting failure, Anna tried to induce her to admit her to Tuptim.

"*Mai dai!*" (It is impossible!) was the persistent reply. "We can't let you see her without an order from the King. If you bring us one, we'll be glad to let you in, but without it we can't." "*Mai dai!*" was the only answer Anna could get to her urgent entreaties. It was useless, as she had feared. She sat hopelessly looking at the Amazons, who seemed in the dim light of the lanterns to have been transformed from the good-hearted women Anna knew them to be into fierce, vindictive executioners. She looked at the trapdoors at her feet. Beneath one of them the three "children"—the Amazons were right to call them that—were imprisoned. No sound, no cry, no indication of life escaped from any of them. Tired and despondent, Anna rose and left the prison without another word.

As she went back toward the gate she saw Phim crouching in the shadows on the opposite side of the narrow street, and keeping pace with her. When Anna turned into the next street Phim joined her. The slave had hidden under the portico of the prison, and had heard all Anna's conversation with the Amazons. There was no need to tell her anything. Anna would have hurried on, but Phim threw herself in front of her on the ground and implored her not to forsake Tuptim.

"But Phim, there's nothing I can do!"

The slave would not give up. "She will be brought to trial before the court in the outside hall of justice tomorrow morning very early," she said. "Please, Mem *kha,* come! Come very early! Perhaps you can persuade Khun Thao Ap to be merciful to her."

With a sickening sense of her powerlessness, Anna promised to be at the trial.

## 31

## THE KING'S VENGEANCE

AT SEVEN o'clock on the following morning Anna was in the San Shuang, the court in the second enclosure of the Palace. The building was of one story only, and totally unlike the rambling combination court and prison in which Anna had tried to see Tuptim the night before. The main entrance was through a long corridor, on both sides of which were apartments so dilapidated as to be scarcely usable. They looked out over the barracks, the magazine, and the fantastic grounds of the Palace gardens.

The floor of the main hall was nothing but worm-eaten boards roughly nailed together. The windows were lofty like those of the royal residences, but the doors were narrow and mean. And everywhere there were big black spiders, which seemed to have been in undisturbed possession of the walls and ceilings for a century.

Several of the judges, both men and women, were already present, exchanging greetings and the contents of their betel-boxes. Phya Phrom Borirak, half-brother of Lady Talap and chief of the men judges, sat apart, as did also Khun Thao Ap, chief of the women judges. The latter had her head bowed in an attitude of reflection and sadness. Before them were low tables on which lay rolls of the law, Siamese paper for recording testimony, pen and ink. By custom there was no prosecuting attorney, no lawyer for the defense, no jury. All the functions were performed by the judges themselves. Some lesser judges and clerks crouched nearby. The whole group examined Anna with curiosity as she took a seat near the end of the hall, but no one made any objection to her staying. Two priests, evidently the men who had found Tuptim in the temple, sat a little distance from Anna.

She had not been there long when a file of Amazons appeared bringing Tuptim and her intimate friends, Maprang and Simla, whom Anna had often seen with her when she came to the schoolroom. Anna was stupefied by the transformation in the pretty girl. Her hair was cut close to her head, and her eyebrows had been shaved off. Her cheeks were hollow and sunken, her eyes cast down. Her hands were manacled, and her little bare feet could hardly drag the heavy chains fastened to her ankles. Her scarf was tied tightly over her bosom, and under it her close-fitting vest was buttoned to the throat. Her whole form was as childlike as before, but she held herself erect and her manner was self-possessed.

The Amazons laid before the judges some priests' garments and a small amulet on a yellow cord. These had been taken from Tuptim when she was found. Anna understood at once the device that Tuptim had used to escape unnoticed from the Palace—the reason for the shaved head and eyebrows. "Oh, Tuptim, Tuptim!" she thought in horror. The vestments were the sort used by *nens,* or novices, and the amulet was such as was worn by all Siamese of the time.

The trial began. When the yellow silk that formed the envelope of the amulet had been opened, a piece of paper was found stitched inside with English letters written on it. It was passed to Khun Thao Ap, who was sufficiently versed in English to read aloud the name "Khun Phra Palat." Anna's heart thundered in her breast as she began to discern the pattern of the young concubine's act. She herself had taught the girl to write those words! If she had only inquired then, talked to the girl, won her confidence . . .

Tuptim was ordered to come forward. She dragged herself along as well as she could, and took her place in the center of the hall. She made no obeisance, no humble prostrations, but neither was there any discourtesy in her manner. Anna caught her eye and smiled encouragingly. The girl's eyes were dark and sad. An almost imperceptible smile flitted across her face in return to the greeting. Her expression was aloof, controlled. But it was more. She had left her childishness behind. As she sat there before her judges she was a woman, and there was about her something strong, something heroic. Whatever she had done, right or wrong, had brought her to a new level of herself, far above anything she had formerly been. The calmness and purity of her face might have been chiseled by a sculptor carving his ideal of womanhood.

Simla and Maprang were examined first, and without any apparent compunction or reserve told the court all that Tuptim had ever confided in them, and a great many irrelevant matters as well—her unwillingness to come to the Palace in the first place; her dissatisfaction with the life; her interest in the young priest at Wat Rachapradit named Phra Palat; her shirking of attendance on the King. But when Simla spoke of Tuptim's escape from the Palace as being connected with Phra Palat's coming in for alms on a particular morning, Tuptim interrupted her and motioned her to stop. "That isn't true at all!" she exclaimed. "You're wrong about that, Simla. You're only guessing and you know it. It wasn't that time and he had nothing to do with it!" Then, as if recollecting where she was, she added proudly, "But after all, it doesn't matter. Go on and say whatever you like."

"Well, well, how interesting!" said Phya Phrom Borirak, leaning forward with a sardonic expression. "If your friends know nothing about your escape, perhaps you'll tell us exactly what did happen."

Tuptim looked at him with a direct simplicity that ignored his tone. "And if I tell you the truth, will you believe me and judge me accordingly?"

The judge scowled. "I'll order the bastinado applied to your back, if you don't confess your crime right away," he retorted with savage emphasis.

Tuptim did not speak immediately. By the expression in her eyes and the alternate flushing and paling of her face it was evident to Anna that she was debating whether to make a full confession or not. Was there any use? Anna could almost read her thoughts. Phya Phrom's cynical face seemed to defy her to convince him of the most elementary truth. Why try at all? What was there to be gained? Finally, with an air of decision, she turned toward Khun Thao Ap and addressed her.

"My lady, Khun Phra Palat had nothing to do with my escape from the Palace. It's true, as Simla says, that I admired him very much, but it's also true that he didn't know it. I had never spoken to him or communicated with him in any way while I was in the Palace. He didn't know anything about my escape from the Palace until I was found in the monastery yesterday morning. Whatever I have done, he hasn't sinned against his vows in any way, gracious lady. He is completely innocent! All the guilt is my own, as I shall tell you. I planned and carried out my escape myself without any help from people outside the walls because I was unhappy in the Palace and wanted to be free again. That was all.

"I've always loved to be free. I hated to be locked behind these high walls and told to do this and go there and come here and do that. And sometimes in the night I couldn't sleep for the misery of it. I would get up from my bed and begin to pray. When I prostrated myself before my image of Somdet Phra Buddh, the Chao, in the stillness of the night, thoughts of escaping from the Palace would come to my mind and distract me from my devotions. In the end I thought they were the voice of the holy Buddha himself, and they took complete possession of me. I couldn't think of anything else. I came to believe that all I had to do was obey, and after that I began to plan ways of getting out. I didn't talk about it with anybody, not even Maprang and Simla. And one night I thought the holy Buddha himself showed me how I could get away. So a few mornings later I dressed myself as a novice, and shaved off my hair and eyebrows—"

"Now we're getting somewhere!" interrupted Phya Phrom with satisfaction. "That's what we want to hear. Tell us who bought the priest's robes for you and smuggled them into the Palace! Was it your mother, or one of your servants, or your sister? And who shaved your hair and eyebrows? Speak a little louder, too!"

Tuptim turned to look at the venal face of the judge, disdain coloring her dignity. "My lord," she replied firmly, "I'm telling you what I did myself and not what anyone else did. I'm speaking the entire truth so far as it relates to myself. Beyond that I cannot and will not go!" A sudden flush spread over her face, making it very lovely.

A little gasp ran through the courtroom. The judge shrugged his shoulders. "Go on, go on," he urged. "Tell your story in your own way, then. We'll find a means of making you tell us all we want to know in plenty of time."

"*Dek nak!*" (She is very young!) Khun Thao Ap spoke. Her tone was mild, but there was reproof in the words. It was obvious that the other judge had decided the case so far as Tuptim was concerned; without the evidence, he had found her guilty, and wanted to get on with the discovery of her accomplices.

The sunlight streaming across the hall fell just behind Tuptim, revealing the exquisite transparency of her olive skin. With a look even more thoughtful and serene than before she continued: "At five o'clock that morning when the priests were admitted to the Palace, I crawled out of my room and joined the procession as it passed near my street on its way to receive the royal alms. No one saw me but Simla, and even she didn't recognize me. She only looked wonderingly at me as if to ask why a priest came so near the houses of the Choms."

"That's true," Simla broke in eagerly. "I never even knew that Tuptim had run away until Khun Yai sent to ask why she was absent from duty so long, and then I began to think about the young priest I'd seen that morning near her house, and I began to wonder if he had something to do with her disappearance, but I didn't guess that it was Tuptim herself. I saw her plainly, too, but without her hair she didn't look at all like herself. So I don't see how you can blame me for not knowing that it was she. I don't think anyone could possibly have guessed. And when the women searched our houses for Tuptim I was afraid to say anything about the priest I had seen near her house for fear we'd be accused of knowing something about her escape, or maybe of helping her get away."

Tuptim waited patiently for Simla to be through speaking and then continued: "In a few minutes I was outside the Palace gates. It was so easy that I was more sure than ever the holy Buddha himself was guiding me. But after I was out and on the public road I didn't know what to do. I couldn't go home because I knew that my home would be watched. I hadn't planned anything except how to get out of the Palace. I stood a few minutes thinking until I was afraid that people would stare at me and suspect something, and then I went straight to Wat Rachapradit and sat down at the gate. I sat there all day trying to decide what to do next. People came and went but no one paid any attention to me. Toward evening the great Chao Khun Sa came out and saw me. He asked me who I was and what I was doing. I didn't know what to say and so I begged him to let me become his disciple and live in the monastery and wait upon him. 'Whose disciple are you now, child?' he asked kindly. And I began to cry because I couldn't think how to answer. I didn't want to deceive the holy man and of course I couldn't tell him the truth. He turned to the priests who were following him and told Phra Palat to take me under his charge and instruct me faithfully in all the doctrines of Buddha. I hadn't planned it. I hadn't planned anything. How could I?"

Her look asked Khun Thao Ap to believe this one incredible coincidence. "If you will ask his lordship, Chao Khun Sa," she continued, "he will tell you that I didn't ask to become a disciple of Khun Phra Palat, but only to become *his* servant and wait upon him. I don't know why he assigned me to Phra Palat, except that Phra Palat is one of his favorite pupils. It seemed so very strange. But I only thought that the holy Buddha's voice that seemed to tell me how to escape, had guided the great abbot in this also, and I was all the more sure that what I had done was right."

Her voice was very low, and there was a catch in it. "Then Phra Palat took me to the cell in the monastery," she went on, "where he lived with several other *nens* whom he was teaching. But he didn't recognize me. Not then or ever." She hesitated briefly, and continued: "Not even though he had known me since he was a boy. His name used to be Daeng, and I had been betrothed to him by my family before I was brought to the Palace. But still he didn't know me with my hair shaved off and in the yellow robes. He had put me out of his mind completely, anyway, when I was presented to the King. If he ever thought of me at all, he thought of me as gone forever beyond the wall of the Inside. After I was sent to the King, he entered the priesthood, and he studied so faithfully that he became the favorite disciple of Chao Khun Sa."

At the unexpected revelation of Tuptim's former connection with the priest several of the women judges threw up their hands in astonishment, and the men grinned maliciously, displaying gums red with betel juice. Anna wondered briefly if Tuptim had not made a tactical error in being so frank. To her the story became more plausible by this admission, rather than less so, but apparently not to those who were to determine the girl's fate. Tuptim saw instantly the line their thoughts had taken. Her lips, already pale, quivered.

"Phra Palat," she continued with simple earnestness, "whom you have condemned to torture and death, hasn't sinned. He is innocent of the sin you are accusing him of in your minds and innocent of complicity in my escape. I have told you, and I tell you again, that the sin was mine, and mine alone! I knew that I was a woman, but he never knew! If I had known all the things he taught me since I became his disciple, I couldn't have done what I did. I wouldn't have run away from the Palace. I know now it was wrong and that it was my own heart that whispered to me to escape and not the voice of the Buddha. I would have tried, O gracious lady, believe me, I would have really tried to learn to endure my life. I grew quiet and happy because I was near him, and he taught us every day. I can say the whole of the Divine Law by heart. Ask his other disciples who were with me and they will tell you that I was always modest and humble, and that he paid no more attention to me than to any of them. We slept at his feet at night. They didn't know that I was a woman, and do you think I could have deceived them, living there in the same room with them, if I hadn't deceived him also? Call them and let them testify to his innocence of the crime of which he is accused! Believe me, gracious lady, I no longer wanted to be his wife, or to be anything to him at all, but only to be near him where he could teach me.

"Then on Sunday morning those men," she pointed to the two priests who still sat apart, "came to the cell to see Phra Palat, and it happened that I had overslept. The other novices had all gone out with the priest when I awoke. I got up thinking I was alone and began to arrange my robes when I heard a low, chuckling laugh. I turned and faced them, and instantly I felt that I was degraded forever.

"Believe me, most honored lady," continued Tuptim, growing more eloquent as she became more earnest, "I was guilty when I fled from my master, the King. That is true. I confess it freely. I am ready to suffer for it. But I never even contemplated the sin that I am accused of by those men. I knew that I was innocent of it and I begged them to let me leave the temple and hide myself, anywhere, anywhere, if they would only keep my secret. I told them that Khun Phra Palat had no idea who I was, or that I was a woman and that the other novices didn't know either. But they only laughed and jeered at me. I fell on my knees at their feet and implored them, in the name of all that is holy and sacred, to keep my secret and let me go before the priest and the novices came back, so that none of them would be involved in what was my sin alone. But they only laughed louder than ever and mocked me more coarsely. They call themselves disciples of the Merciful One, but they would not be merciful. Not even for the sake of their friend." Here she gasped for breath, while two large tears coursed down her cheeks. She gritted her teeth. "And then I defied them, and I still defy them for their foul thoughts and their cruel hearts!" She shook her manacled hands at the two priests.

They looked at her unmoved, chewing their betel like cattle incapable of emotion. The judges listened in silence, an air of amused incredulity on the faces of several. Only Khun Thao Ap's face retained its habitual sadness. She seemed to listen without scorn or prejudice, as if weighing Tuptim's words in the scale of her mind. The court scribes were writing rapidly, to keep up with the flow of words.

The girl was pale as she went on in a low tone: "Just then Phra Palat and his other disciples came back from their morning ablutions. I crawled to his feet and confessed that I was Tuptim. He recoiled from me to the end of the cell as if the earth had quaked beneath him. Anyone could have seen that he hadn't the faintest idea who I was. I lay prostrate on the floor of the cell, overwhelmed with horror at the thought of what I had done to him. In a moment he came back close to me. He was weeping bitterly himself, but he begged me not to cry any more. The sight of his tears made me feel as if I were being swallowed up in a great black abyss. It was my selfishness that had brought him to this. Because I hadn't thought, because I had done what I had done, had run away from the Palace and stayed on in the monastery when I could easily have gone somewhere else, I had ruined the life he had built for himself. He tried to comfort me as I lay there weeping. He said, 'Tuptim, what you did was wrong. But don't be afraid any more. We're innocent. And for the sake of your love for me I'm willing to suffer even death for you.'" The room was hushed as the girl ended simply, "That is the whole truth."

Phya Phrom spat, a long stream of betel juice, red as blood. He spoke derisively. "Well, well, well. A pretty story, and you told it beautifully! Only nobody believes you, of course." He spat again. "Now let's go back to the beginning. Suppose you tell us who shaved off your hair and eyebrows, and brought that priest's robe into the Palace for you."

The grandeur of the fragile childlike woman as she folded her chained hands across her breast to still it and replied, "I will not!" took Anna's breath away. She had drawn near to Tuptim when she began her narrative, in order not to miss any of it. She had been so absorbed in it, and in admiration of Tuptim's fearlessness, that she had been rooted to the spot, standing there mechanically. But the effect of Tuptim's answer was startling. It went through the courtroom like a trumpet call, and it brought Anna suddenly to a full appreciation of the scene before her.

Here was a girl of sixteen hurling defiance at the judges, knowingly, at her own risk, in an effort to save the man she loved and, no doubt, to shield Phim, her slave. Anna was never to think of the verse in the Bible, "Greater love hath no man than this, that a man lay down his life for his friends," without seeing Tuptim so before her accusers. For they were her accusers, and not her judges. To make such a reply was to accept death. And not only death, but all the agonies of cunning and merciless torture. Tuptim knew it. Her refusal so startled the assembly that for a moment there was profound silence. The beauty and majesty of her slight figure facing the sensual men, the cold-faced women, were awe-inspiring.

Then anger flamed in Phya Phrom's face. "Strip her and give her thirty blows with the lash," he shouted in a voice hoarse with fury. And to Anna's shocked surprise Khun Thao Ap looked calmly on, not dissenting. Could she possibly be convinced of Tuptim's guilt, or was she silent out of deference to Phya Phrom? Wouldn't she insist that other witnesses be called, the novices who had lived in the cell with Tuptim, Chao Khun Sa, priests from adjoining cells? Surely she couldn't shut her mind to the possibility that Tuptim was telling the truth!

Before the Amazons could carry out the order there was an interruption. The crowd that had gathered thick about the windows and doors opened, and a litter borne by two men was brought into the hall. On it lay the mutilated form of the priest, Palat, who had just undergone torture in order to make him confess his guilt and that of Tuptim. But as the records of the ecclesiastical court stated, "It was not possible to elicit from him even an indication that he had anything to confess." His priestly robes had been taken from him, and he was dressed like an ordinary layman, except that his hair and eyebrows were closely shaven. They laid him down beside Tuptim, hoping that the sight of her under torture would induce him to make some damaging admission.

The next moment Tuptim was stripped of her scarf and vest, and bound to a stake. The executioners lifted their flexible cudgels of bamboo. The first blow laid open the girl's thin back and delicate shoulders. Anna had told herself repeatedly that this was a case in which she could not interfere, since religious prejudice was involved. But it seemed to her later, when she thought back to the day, that she had lost all control over her actions. She had forgotten that she was a stranger and a foreigner, and as powerless as the weakest of the oppressed around her. She had known only that she must do something. She sprang forward. And she heard her own voice as if from a great distance commanding the executioners to desist if they valued their lives!

The Amazons at once dropped their uplifted bamboos. "Why so?" asked the judge, who knew her well from previous encounters.

262

"At least until I can plead for Tuptim before His Majesty," Anna replied.

"So be it," said the judge, leaning back and helping himself to a fresh cud of betel. "Go your way. We'll wait for your return before proceeding further."

Anna forced a path through the curious crowd standing on tiptoe with necks outstretched trying to catch a glimpse of the accused. As she left the court she met the slave girl Phim, who followed her into the Palace, wringing her hands and sobbing bitterly.

The King was in his breakfast hall. The smell of food made Anna sick and dizzy as she toiled up the lofty staircase, for she had not stopped to eat that morning before hurrying to the court. In spite of her faintness she walked quickly across the room toward the King, fearing that she might lose courage if she deliberated for a moment.

"Your Majesty," she began, and again her voice was not her own and the words seemed to come from a long way off, "I have just come from the trial of Tuptim, and I am convinced that she is innocent of the crime of which she is accused. She admits that she was wrong to run away from the Palace. But even in that there is one mitigating circumstance. She has just told the judges that she was already betrothed before she was brought to the Palace. If Your Majesty had known that, I am sure you would never have allowed her family to present her to you. She insists that Khun Phra Palat, the man to whom her family had betrothed her and in whose cell she was found yesterday, knew nothing about her escape or even who she was. I know that it sounds improbable. But Your Majesty is too intelligent to rule out the possibility that what is improbable may be true. I believe if you had heard her tell her story just now as I did that you would have been convinced that she was telling the truth. She says that it is sheer coincidence that Chao Khun Sa assigned her to Khun Phra Palat. If that is true, Chao Khun Sa will know. It's the sort of statement that can be tested. And she says that she and Phra Palat are innocent of any relation except that of teacher and pupil. And there, again, her statement is capable of outside proof, since she was only one of several novices living in the same cell with the priest. Phya Phrom Borirak has ordered her put to the torture, but surely the truth can be found in other ways. Won't Your Majesty order the court to forgo the torture until more witnesses have been examined? Or better still, considering the strange circumstances, won't Your Majesty pardon both the girl and the priest? I am so convinced of their innocence that I feel justified in pleading with Your Majesty to prevent a miscarriage of justice, since Phya Phrom is prejudiced and a fair trial is impossible." The effort had been too much. Her voice faded away, as did her strength. She sank to the floor near the King's chair in a half faint. "I beg Your Majesty's pardon . . ."

The King looked at her out of the glittering narrow eyes that reminded her so often of a bird's.

"You're mad!" he said. He regarded her with a cold stare, full of suspicion, and then leaned over and laughed in her face. She started to her feet as if he had slapped her. Rallying her strength she faltered to a pillar and leaned against it, looking at him. As her face was stripped of its ordinary patina of polite social intercourse by the sudden impact of his laugh, so also was his by the emotions rampant behind it. She saw something indescribably revolting in him, something fiendish that she had never seen before. He was not interested in the merits of Tuptim's case, nor even in the possible innocence of the priest who had become enmeshed in it. His sense of decency and justice was gone, swallowed in a bestial need to sate in blood the injured pride of the scorned male. Anna was seized with an inexpressible horror of him. She was stupefied and amazed, as much to find herself still trembling against the pillar as at the naked evil she had seen within the King's heart. Thought and speech had left her. She turned to go.

But the King had read and known what her face said. Her disgust had shocked him back to normal and instantly he made one of his characteristic about-faces. "Madam," he ordered, "come back! I grant your petition. The woman will be condemned to work in the rice mill for the rest of her life. The man will be set free. I will send my decision to the court in a few minutes. You do not need to return there. You had better go to school now."

Anna could not thank him. Her revulsion was too great. Her head throbbed and she felt dizzy. She went away without a word. At the head of the stairs she passed one of the women judges bringing the records of the trial to the King. Instead of going to the schoolroom Anna went home. She felt too ill to do anything but go to bed.

It was two o'clock when she awoke, heavy and unrefreshed. The house was quiet. Beebe had taken Louis downriver to spend the day with the Bradley children and they would not be back until bedtime. Anna's little maid brought her some lunch on a tray, but she scarcely touched it.

The sound of a crowd milling around drew her to the window. She was startled to see two scaffolds being set up on the plaza close to her house. Workmen were driving stakes and bringing up strange machines under the instruction of high officials. A vast throng of men, women, and children had collected to see the spectacle, whatever it might be. There was appearance of great excitement among the crowd.

Anna summoned her maid and asked the reason for all the preparation and commotion. The maid reported that a *Parachik* (a guilty priest) and a *Nang Ham* were to be exposed and tortured for the improvement of public morals that afternoon. The King had reversed his decision! Anna thought frantically of what she could do, but she had exhausted the resources of the Palace. Mr. Knox, the British Consul, might have helped, but he had gone to Moulmein to settle a lumber claim. The American Vice-Consul was a local merchant and without influence, and the French Consul, the hated Aubaret, was on the high seas.

The scaffolds were about five feet tall. To each were attached long levers, which could be fastened to the neck of the victim to prevent his falling off. They were so arranged as to strangle him if that were the sentence. On the Palace wall across the square was the long pavilion from which the King and his court watched public ceremonies and processions. As Anna stood at the window she saw the shutters thrown open. Slaves rushed about preparing the pavilion for the King, the princes and princesses, and such of the great ladies of the court as were to see the torture of their former associate and the priest.

Anna looked on in helpless despair. What had gone wrong? She did not know until months later that she had hardly left the King before the proceedings of both trials had been laid before him. When he read them he flew into a violent rage that included Anna as well as the concubine and the priest. He ordered the two Siamese tortured publicly and then executed, but he could think of no way of punishing the Englishwoman except by having the scaffolds set up directly under her windows. And he swore vengeance against any person who dared in the future to oppose his royal will and pleasure. Anna considered escaping down the river and taking refuge with the missionaries. It would have been difficult, but not impossible, although the crowd was already dense. But much as she longed to run away, she felt that to desert Tuptim was unthinkable. There was nothing she could do but sympathize and pray for her, and yet she could not leave the girl to suffer alone.

A little before three o'clock the instruments of torture were brought and arranged beside the scaffolds. Soon a loud flourish of trumpets announced the royal party, and the King and all his court were visible at the open windows of the pavilion. Amazons dressed in scarlet and gold took up their posts in the turrets to guard the ladies of the harem. Suddenly the crowd sent up a cry. Guards had come from the Palace enclosure with the two prisoners. The priest, apparently too weak to walk alone, was hoisted upon the scaffold to the right, while Tuptim tranquilly ascended the one to the left without assistance. This was the nearer of the two to Anna's windows. They were closed, but she could see clearly through the latticed blinds. She saw the priest turn his face toward Tuptim, with an expression of love and grief.

The girl's hands, no longer chained, were folded on her breast. She looked down calmly at the rabble who flocked close to gloat over the spectacle. They would greet with ferocious animal howls the cries of the victims. But something in the girl's attitude stilled them. Anna felt that a kind of unwilling awe was being drawn out of them by Tuptim's quiet steadiness. And a few, evidently believers in her innocence, prostrated themselves before her as if she were a martyr. Anna could not take her eyes from the tiny figure whose scarf fluttered like a brave red flag in the breeze. Fascination and horror kept her leaning against the shutters.

Two trumpeters, right and left, blared forth the crime of which the pair were accused. Ten thousand eyes were fixed on Tuptim and Palat, but the crowd was mute, not to lose a single word of the sentence. Again the trumpets sounded, and the conviction, with the judgment that had been passed, was announced. The spell was broken. A great shout went up from the crowd. Foul abuse was rained on the girl standing calmly on the shaking wooden posts. Nothing could have surpassed the dignity with which she endured the storm. Anna could see the color coming and going in her face, first crimson and then deadly pale, as anger flashed from her eyes, but that was all. The fear she must have felt was not revealed either in her face or in her attitude. She did not bow her head or quail.

The trumpets sounded for the third time. The multitude was quiet again as the executioner mounted a raised platform to apply the torture to Tuptim. The blows began to fall. Now her back was crimson with more than the fluttering of her scarf. For the first few moments it seemed as if the agony would prove too much for her powers of endurance. She half turned from the royal spectator at the window. Her body writhed involuntarily and she tried to hide her face in her hands. But almost immediately, by a supreme effort of will, she stood erect again, and her voice rang out across the square like a deep-toned silver bell: "I have not sinned! Khun Phra Palat has not sinned! We are innocent! The holy Buddha in heaven knows all!"

She just managed to finish speaking before she pitched forward upon the two levers of the scaffold, with a piercing cry which went through Anna like a sword. The girl lay insensible until physicians restored her to consciousness, and then the torture was resumed. Once again her voice rang out, more musical than before: "I have not sinned! Khun Phra Palat has not sinned! The holy Buddha knows all!"

One by one every excruciating device that would agonize but not kill was used to wring a confession from Tuptim. But every torture, every pang, failed to bring forth anything but her incomparable courage. She confessed nothing, she asked for no mercy. With sublime stamina she confronted her persecutors, her judges, and the King with her innocence. The honor of the priest seemed more precious to her than her life. The last words Anna heard her cry were: "All the guilt was mine. I knew that I was a woman, but he did not!"

After this Anna neither heard nor saw anything more. She was not aware of her own exhaustion, that she had no strength left to endure the sight below her window. Consciousness simply left her and she knew no more.

The house was very still when she awoke. Lying on the floor, crumpled and weak, she saw that the room was full of shadows. Outside there was no sound. It was minutes before she could recollect why she was there. Then fearfully she pulled herself to her knees and looked through the window blinds. The scaffolds were gone and there was no one in the square. The sun had set. She strained her eyes to see across the great common before the house. There was a thick mist loaded with vapors, a terrifying silence, an absolute quiet as of the tomb.

At last she saw a figure slipping through the darkness toward her. Her maid was nowhere about so she tottered downstairs herself, and unbolted the door to admit Phim. The slave had come in secret to tell Anna of Tuptim's and Palat's end. They had been condemned to death by fire at the King's command. Neither had confessed anything under torture, and at last torture had been abandoned for fear it would extinguish life before the flames could be applied. They had been dragged through the streets to Wat Saket, and there burned publicly outside the wall of the cemetery. The common people who followed had been terribly affected by the sight of the priest's invincible courage and Tuptim's fortitude.

Phim's whole soul was in her face as she told how the awe of the people had increased until there were no scoffers left. Gradually a muttering had begun to grow against the two priests who had been the informers. Under her low and massive brow the slave's glistening eyes were wild as she described the final glimpse of her mistress, enveloped in flames, holding up her mutilated hands, and crying feebly but clearly, so that all could hear: "I am pure! And the priest, my lord Palat, is pure also! See! These fingers have not made my lips to lie. The holy Buddha in heaven judge between me and my accusers!"

The people had been so overcome, so convinced of the blamelessness of the concubine and the priest, that they would have lynched the two informers if they could have found them, but the men had prudently fled to another town.

Phim's grief was deep and lasting. She owed her life to the resolute bravery of her mistress. To the end Tuptim had refused to implicate anyone in her escape. Every seventh day the slave offered fresh flowers and perfumed tapers on the spot where Tuptim and the priest had suffered, believing that their disembodied souls still hovered about it at twilight. When she met Anna she would assure her that she could hear their voices moaning through the mellow evening air, growing deeper and gathering strength as she listened. She said that she could hear them, now weeping together, now exulting, until they became indistinct, and finally died away into the regions of the blessed and the pure.

Anna did not see the King for a month after Tuptim's death. He had gone almost immediately to Ayuthia where the citizens were erecting a temple to which he had subscribed. By the time he returned his brother, the Second King, was very ill, and he was often at his brother's palace a mile up the river. The rest of the time he was occupied with preparations for the tonsure of his son Chulalongkorn, which was to be celebrated in magnificent style.

At last one day he summoned Anna to his presence. She had never felt so cold, so hard, so unforgiving as that day in December when she once more entered the breakfast hall. He took no notice of her manner, but as soon as he saw her continued their previous conversation as if no interval had occurred.

"I have much sorrow for Tuptim," he said, and Anna saw that with his usual quixotic change of attitude it was true. His face was genuinely sad. "I shall now believe that she is innocent. I have had a dream, and I had clear observation in my vision of Tuptim and Palat floating together in a great wide space, and she has bent down and touched me on the shoulder, and said to me, 'We are guiltless. We were ever pure and guiltless on earth, and look, we are happy now.' After discoursing thus, she has mounted on high and vanished from my further observation. I have much sorrow, Mem, much sorrow, and respect for your judgment; but our laws are severe for such crimes. But now I shall cause monument to be erected to the memory of Palat and Tuptim."

And he did. At Wat Saket on the spot where they had died two tall and slender *chedis* were erected by the King's order. Each bore the inscription—"Suns may set and rise again, but the pure and brave Palat and Tuptim will never more return to earth." Believing as he did in the endless cycle of birth and rebirth that ended only in the attainment of Nirvana, *Nipphan,* his words were a testimony to his conviction that Tuptim and Palat had escaped by their purity from the wheel of reincarnation.

Margaret Ayer

32

## THE DEATH OF THE HIGH PRIEST

ONE EVENING as the lingering sun trailed shadows through the columns
of the temple a group of pages came hurrying to where Anna worked alone
in the cool depths of the schoolroom. The King wanted to see her at once.
Long association with him had taught her not to pause even to collect her
papers and books. She put on her bonnet and cloak and prepared to obey
—reluctantly, because so many of these sudden interviews had been pain-
ful. She followed the pages out through the gates to Wat Rachapradit,
which was only forty yards from the eastern wall.

Anna had watched this temple in the building and felt a peculiar interest in it. Here Tuptim had lived and studied, and from here she and Khun
Phra Palat had been taken to their death. The sculptures and carvings on
the pillars and façades were of half-fabulous, half-historical figures, conveying allegories of the triumph of virtue over passion. They were the
King's tribute to the great Abbot Chao Khun Sa, who lived there.

Usually at evening contemplative priests in saffron robes could be seen walking slowly back and forth along the graveled paths between the trees and shrubs, but tonight there was no one. The pages hurried through the temple grounds and led Anna to the monastery. It had been built in medieval style, and like the temple was substantial and elaborate. The sun was setting below a red horizon as she reached the monastic buildings. Wide tracts of corn and avenues of oleander screened from view the distant city with its pagodas and palaces. The air was fresh and balmy. It sighed among the betel and coco palms that skirted the temple confines.

The pages led her to the steps of the principal building and told her to wait while they announced her to the King.

"What is it?" she asked, astonished to be brought to this part of the temple, ordinarily forbidden to women. "What does the King want of me here?"

The pages all raised their joined palms in salute toward the building and one of them said, "The High Priest is dying."

Anna sat down on the stone steps to wait. The sanded yard of the monastery was very peaceful. Lacy shadows from palms shifted across the ground.

Behind her in the building she could hear the evening chant of the monks:

*Thou Excellence of Perfection, I take refuge in thee.*
*Thou who art called the Enlightened One, I take refuge in thee.*

As she sat quietly listening to the solemn cadences starting low and gradually rising, the cares of the day melted into the gathering darkness. Long after the moon had come out, clear and cool, Anna sat thinking of other moons in happier days—of India and the good years, of little Avis in Fulham, and of the priest who lay dying within.

The King had told her about him many times. More than a year ago on a day when she had been working in his library with some French correspondence he had asked her, "Do you understand the word 'charity'?" He had been sitting at a desk reading the *First Epistle to the Corinthians*. "I hate the Bible mostly," he had said once to his friend and teacher of long ago, the American missionary Jesse Caswell. Still it fascinated him, as Luther fascinated him, as the missionaries themselves fascinated him— for some quality, dimly perceived, that he could not grasp.

"Do I understand 'charity'?" Anna had inquired, looking up. "Is that what Your Majesty asked?"

"Yes. Tell me, do you understand *maitri*, or 'charity' as your apostle Paul explains it in the thirteenth chapter of his *First Epistle to the Corinthians?*"

"I believe I do," she answered slowly. She was puzzled, for off and on during the morning they had been discussing the religion of the Buddha.

"Then tell me, what does St. Paul really mean, what custom does he allude to when he says, '. . . though I give my body to be burned, and have not charity, it profiteth me nothing'?"

"Custom?" she asked. "I don't know of any *custom*. He considered the giving of the body to be burned as the highest act of devotion and purest sacrifice that man could make for man."

"Exactly!" said the King, beginning to pace up and down. "You have well said! It is the highest act of devotion that can be made, or performed, by man for man, the giving of the body to be burned. But if it be accomplished from a spirit of opposition, for fame or popular applause, is it still regarded by him as the highest act of sacrifice?"

"Of course not. That's just what St. Paul means—the motive consecrates the deed."

"But all men are not fortified with self-control which shall fit them for great exemplars, and of many who have appeared in this character, if strict inquiry be made, their virtue would be found to proceed from other than a true and pure spirit. Sometimes it is indolence, sometimes restlessness, sometimes vanity impatient for gratification, and rushing to assume the part of humility by purpose of self-delusion. .

"No," the King continued, taking several long strides and warming to his subject. "St. Paul in this chapter," he declaimed as from a pulpit, "evidently and strongly applies the Buddhist word *maitri*—or *maikree,* as pronounced by some Sanskrit scholars—and explains it through Buddhist's custom of giving the body to be burned, which was practiced centuries before Christian era, and is found unchanged in parts of China, Ceylon, and Siam to this day. Giving the body to be burned has ever been considered by devout Buddhists the most exalted act of self-abnegation. To give all one's goods to feed the poor is common in this country with princes and people, who often keep nothing back, not even one cowrie shell to provide for themselves a handful of rice. But then, fear of starvation or death by hunger is unknown in Buddhist country."

He fell to musing as he paced. "I know a man of royal descent, and once possessed of untold riches. In his youth he felt such pity for poor and old and sick, and such as were troubled and sorrowful, that he became melancholy, and after spending several years by the continual relief of the needy and helpless, he, in a moment, gave all his good, in a word ALL, 'to feed the poor.' This man had never heard of St. Paul or his writing, but he knows and tried to comprehend in its fullness the Buddhist word *maitri*.

"At thirty he became a priest. For five years he toiled as a gardener. For that was occupation he preferred, because in pursuit of it he learned much useful knowledge of medicinal properties of plant, and became a ready physician to who could not pay for healing. But he could not rest content with so imperfect a life, while the way to perfect knowledge of excellence, truth, and charity remained open to him, so he became a priest. This happened before I was born, sixty-five years ago. Now he is ninety-five years old, and I fear has not yet found the truth and excellence he has been in search thereof so long."

The King's face was infinitely sad. "But I know no greater man than he," he went on. "He is great in the Christian sense, loving, pitiful, forbearing, pure. Once when he was a gardener, he was robbed of his few and poor tools by one who had been befriended by him in multiple ways. Some time after that the King met him and inquired of his necessities. He said he needed tools for his gardening. A great abundance of such was sent him, and immediately he shared all with neighbors, taking care to send the most and best to the man who had robbed him.

"Of what little remained to him, he gave freely to whoever lacked. Not his own but another's want, were his sole argument in asking or bestowing —not loving life, nor fearing death, desiring nothing the world can give, beyond the peace of a beautiful spirit. This man is now a high priest. He would, without so much as a thought of shrinking, give his body to be burned, alive or dead, if by so doing he might obtain one glimpse of eternal truth or save one soul from death or sorrow."

The conversation came back to Anna vividly as she sat in the temple yard. It was this man, then, who was dying. His life had spanned almost a century. Three years before he was born, Siam had fallen to Burma and all the treasure and beauty of Ayuthia had been burned. He had seen the city of Thonburi rise, seen the Chao Tak go mad and die, seen the Chakri kings build the new capital at Bangkok, seen four of the kings of that dynasty rule, seen the coming of the Europeans whose influence was growing stronger and stronger. What were his thoughts this last day of his life?

At length a young man appeared in the door above her and beckoned. He was robed in white and he bore in one hand a lighted taper and in the other a lily. She followed him through the long, low passages that separated cells of priests. The sound of many voices chanting the hymns of the Buddhist liturgy fell on her ear. The darkness, the loneliness, the measured monotone, all combined to produce in her—matter-of-fact person that she prided herself on being—an excitement close to awe.

As the page came to the threshold of one of the cells he whispered to her in a tone of entreaty to take off her shoes. This she did quickly. At the same moment he prostrated himself with abject humility before a low doorway. Anna slipped past him and stooped to scan curiously the scene within the cell. There sat the King, cross-legged on the floor. At a sign from him she bent and entered to take a place beside him.

On a rude pallet, about six and a half feet long and not more than three feet wide, with a bare block of wood for a pillow, lay the dying priest. A simple garment of faded yellow covered him. His hands were folded on his breast. His head was bald, and the few blanched hairs that might have remained to fringe his sunken temples had been carefully shorn. His eye-

272

brows, too, were closely shaven. His feet were bare and exposed. His eyes were fixed, not in the vacant stare of death, but with solemn contemplation upward. No sign of disquiet was there, no suggestion of pain or trouble. Anna was startled and puzzled. Was he then really dying?

Her entrance and approach made no change in him. In his attitude and expression she saw only sublime reverence, repose, absorption. He seemed to be communing with a spiritual presence. At his right was a dim taper in a golden candlestick, and on his left a golden vase filled with white lilies, freshly gathered. These were the offerings of the King. One of the lilies had been laid on his breast, and contrasted with the faded yellow of his robe. Just over his heart lay a coil of unspun cotton thread, divided into seventy-seven filaments, and distributed to the hands of the priests. Closely seated, they filled the cell so that none could have moved without difficulty. From time to time one or another of the solemn company raised his voice in a chant and all the rest responded in unison.

"*Sang-khang sara nang gach cha mi.*" (Thou Excellence of Perfection, I take refuge in thee.)

And the choir responded, "*Nama Pootho sang-khang sara nang gach cha mi.*" (Thou who art called Buddha, I take refuge in thee.)

"*Tuti ampi sang-khang sara nang gach cha mi.*" (Thou Holy One, I take refuge in thee.)

And again the response, "*Te satiya sang-khang sara nang gach cha mi.*" (Thou Truth, I take refuge in thee.)

As the familiar words reached him a flickering smile lighted the sallow face of the dying priest with a mild visible radiance. The rapture of that look, which seemed to overtake the infinite, was almost too holy to gaze on. Anna shut her eyes in awe. Riches, station, honor, kindred—he had resigned them all more than half a century since, in his love for the poor and his longing for truth. Here was none of the vagueness or incoherence of a wandering, delirious death. He was going to his clear eternal calm With a smile of perfect peace he spoke: "To Your Majesty, I commend the poor. And this that remains of me I give to be burned." That, his last gift, was his all.

Gradually his breathing became more laborious, and turning with infinite effort toward the King he said tranquilly, "*Athamaphap cha pai diau-ni.*" (I am going now.)

Instantly the priests took up a loud chant, "*Phra Arahan sang-khang sara nang gach cha mi.*" (Thou Sacred One, I take refuge in thee.)

A few minutes more and the spirit of the high priest had breathed itself away. The eyes were opened and fixed, the hands clasped, the expression sweetly content. Anna's eyes and heart were full of tears, but she was strangely comforted, strangely at peace, as she had not been for months in the tumult of the Palace.

On the afternoon of the next day she went, at the King's command, to the temple of Wat Saket, where the high priest's will was to be carried out. Anna followed the King's order with much reluctance. There was no place to which she had less inclination to go. It was here that Tuptim and Phra Palat had been burned alive, and here that the King's memorial to them had been erected. The temple was outside the city wall. The buildings and grounds were extensive, for it was the national burning-ground of the dead. Within the mysterious precincts were performed the Buddhist rite of cremation, under circumstances that were horrible to the Western mind. A broad canal surrounded the temple and yards. Not only the dead, but also the living had often been burned here. Into the canal at the dark of the moon unfortunate wretches who had dared to oppose the San Luang, the secret inquisition, had been thrown.

None but the initiated dared to approach these grounds after sunset, so universal and profound was the horror the place inspired. It was frightful and offensive to Anna's eyes as she entered it, for the vows of the dead, however ghoulish and monstrous, were faithfully consummated here. The walls were hung with human skeletons, the ground strewn with skulls. Here were scraped together the horrible fragments of those who had bequeathed their carcasses to the hungry curs and vultures that hovered and snarled and tore at the rotting human flesh. The half-picked bones were gathered and burned by the outcast keepers of the temple, who were not rated so high as priests. They received from relatives of the dead a small fee for this final service. In the midst of the foul incense of burning flesh and bones, which never left the place, the priests watched and prayed night and day for the regeneration of mankind. So the Buddhist vow was fulfilled, and the Buddhist deed of merit accomplished.

Fortified with smelling salts and many handkerchiefs and dressed carefully in mourning white, Anna arrived. The men hired to do the dreadful offices upon the dead had already cut off all the flesh and flung it to the dogs that haunted the monstrous human garbage-field. She was thankful to have been spared that much. The bones and adhering flesh had been placed in an urn upon the funeral pyre. This was a broad platform with four high posts, crowned by a canopy not unlike the umbrellas which were placed above the King's throne and carried over him in procession.

One by one the vast throng that had gathered lighted tapers and joss sticks and set them against the pyre. Then the great fire of wood was ignited and several priests stood at hand to sprinkle it with water as it roared skyward. It was fully three hours before the burning was finished. When at last the ashes were gathered into an earthen pot to be scattered in the little gardens of peasants too poor to afford manure, Anna was faint from the nauseous odor and the hideous sights around her. All that was left now of the great man was the remembrance of a look.

"This," said the King, who had come close to her, "is to give one's body to be burned. This is what your St. Paul had in mind, this custom of our Buddhist ancestors, this complete self-abnegation in life and death, when he said, '. . . though I give my body to be burned, and have not *maitri,* it profiteth me nothing.' "

Sickened and sorrowful, she turned away.

## 33

## THE PRINCE'S TONSURE

ANNA WAS very conscious during the last months of 1865 that Prince Chulalongkorn was growing up. His wrists hung out of his jacket. The roundness of his face had disappeared, and the childish droop of his mouth was gone. He was much taller than he had been and more slender. The little boy she had begun to teach in 1862 was turning into a man.

The whole Palace was seething with preparations for his coming tonsure. The prince was now thirteen and would soon enter the novitiate of the priesthood, since this event must take place before a boy was fourteen. At that time his hair and eyebrows would be shaved in accordance with Buddhist custom. It was therefore important that the long lock of hair which had been reserved uncut on the top of his head since infancy should be removed according to the Brahmin rite of *Sokan* before it was less ceremoniously shaved.

From the day the Prince was born, King Mongkut had been eager to settle the succession upon him. According to the laws of the country the final choice of each new monarch rested with the Senabodi. King Mongkut had always been afraid that the council would choose his younger brother, the Second King, to succeed him rather than Prince Chulalongkorn, since there was a strong prejudice against boy kings, few of whom survived the Palace intrigues that surrounded them. He could proceed to his goal only by indirection. He knew very well that his own elevation to the throne had thwarted the ambitions of the Usurper, who also had wanted a favorite son to succeed him. Mongkut was afraid for Chulalongkorn, afraid that his own ambitions might be thwarted in the same way. Therefore he did what he could to elevate the prince in the estimation of the nobility and the people. He even talked with the Kralahome about abdicating in favor of Chulalongkorn when the boy was a little older, and of directing his first steps in the kingship from a palace he planned to build adjacent to the Royal Palace.

Now he arranged the most elaborate tonsure he could devise, knowing that ceremonies of this sort enhanced the importance of the prince in the eyes of the whole nation. For the first time in recorded Siamese history he himself, the King, prepared to play the role of Siva, from whose tonsure of his son Ganesa the rite of *Sokan* was supposed to have been derived. This alone would greatly increase the significance of the ceremony and would proclaim to the kingdom as nothing else could the King's desire for his son.

The King had explored the records of Siam and Cambodia and had compiled a detailed description of a curious procession that had attended a certain prince of Siam centuries before on the occasion of his tonsure. His Majesty had decided to conduct Chulalongkorn's tonsure with the same display, only more elaborate and costly. There would be a pageant, borrowed partly from the *Ramayana* and partly from the ritual of the kings of Cambodia. The King had had the ancient narrative poem *Kailasa* adapted for the occasion.

The whole royal establishment had been set in motion. About nine thousand young women, among them the most beautiful of the concubines, were cast for parts. Boys and girls of good family were brought from all quarters of the kingdom to assist in the mammoth spectacle. So intricate were the preparations that school suffered. Regular studies had to be abandoned and in their place were rehearsals of singing, dancing, recitation, and pantomime.

An artificial hill called Mount Kailasa was erected in the center of the Palace gardens. It was fifty feet high and had a circumference at the base of not less than three hundred feet. The framework was teakwood, shaped to describe peaks, valleys, clefts, and caves, covered with bamboo wattling.

Over this was laid paper of metallic appearance, so that parts of the mountain seemed made of iron, other parts of copper, brass, tin, silver, or gold. On the summit a golden temple was erected and richly hung with tapestries, its spire reaching another thirty feet into the air. Two revolving silver wheels attached to mirrors were over the doors of the temple on the east and west, representing the sun and the moon.

The cardinal points of the hill were guarded by a white elephant, a sacred bull, a horse, and a lion. These figures were mechanized so that they turned on pivots. At a certain point in the rite they were to be brought together and a rain of sacred water from the Brahmaputra was to be showered from their mouths on the prince as he stood in a marble basin. Summonses were sent to the high officials in each province and feudal state to attend the ceremonies. Priests from all over the kingdom were invited to participate. Every nation was to be represented in the grand procession.

On New Year's Eve—December 31, 1865—selected monks assembled in the Dusit Maha Prasat to chant appropriate texts, while the Brahmans performed their own peculiar rites in a specially erected chapel. On each of the three preliminary days the procedure was the same. The mornings were devoted to religious services by the two sets of priests. In the afternoon the prince was carried on a palanquin by a long and roundabout route through the Palace grounds to the Dusit Maha Prasat. Here the King awaited him and together they made offerings of tapers and incense before the images. Then in the same palanquin both King and prince returned over the same route.

The procession was exactly as the King had directed. First came the bearers of gold umbrellas, fans, and great golden sunshades; then four hundred Amazons arrayed in green and gold with their armor. Behind these walked twelve girls in cloth of gold, with fantastic headgear adorned with precious stones, who danced to the gentle monotonous movement of tabors. In the center of this group moved the three loveliest girls, one of whom held a peacock's tail, and the others carried two branches of gold and silver, sparkling with leaves and rare flowers. The girls were guarded by two duennas on either side.

After them stalked a dignified group of court Brahmans, bearing golden bowls filled with roasted rice, which they scattered on either side as emblems of plenty. Another group of Brahmans followed with tabors which they rattled as they moved along. Then came two young nobles, splendidly robed, who bore golden cages, lotus-shaped, in which were birds of paradise, the sweetness of whose song is supposed to entrance even beasts of prey. After them marched the sons of the nobles, burdened down with the gold ornaments they wore. Next was the King's Japanese bodyguard in terrifying horned masks, painted armor, and striped pantaloons; then another line of boys representing the natives of India in costume, Malayan boys in typical dress, Chinese and Siamese boys in English dress; and finally the King's infantry, headed by a company in European uniforms.

Outside the line of this long procession marched five thousand men in rose-colored robes with tapering caps, reminiscent of dunce caps. They represented guardian angels attending upon the different nations of the world. Then came bands of musicians dressed in scarlet, imitating the cries of birds, the sound of falling fruit, and the murmur of distant waters in the imaginary forest they were supposed to traverse on their way to the sacred mountain.

At this point came the prince himself, borne in the gold palanquin of state, very serious of face and dignified of bearing. He was dressed in handsome robes of white, richly embroidered with gold. On his head was a small jeweled coronet, a miniature of the crown worn by his father on state occasions. His arms and legs were weighted with heavy gold bracelets.

Immediately behind him came four young girls of the highest birth, bearing his betel-box, spittoon, fan, and sword, the emblems of his rank. After them were seventy others carrying reverently in both hands the vessels of gold and all the other accoutrements proper to a prince of the blood royal. And behind them were yet more girls holding over their right shoulders golden fans.

A great troop of children came skipping along, the sons and daughters of the nobility, dressed in the most costly garments their families could afford and hung with heavy gold jewelry. Then the maids of honor, personal attendants, and concubines of the King, less conspicuously dressed than the children, but crowned with gold coronets and also wearing gold chains and rings of great value and beauty. After them came a crowd of Siamese women, painted and rouged, in European costume, troops of children, ladies in Chinese costume, Japanese ladies in rich robes, women of Hindustan, Karens. And last of all were the slaves and dependents of the prince.

On the fourth of January excitement reached fever pitch, for this was the great day of the actual tonsure. The route to the Maha Prasat was somewhat shortened and the procession started earlier. Near the temple the prince was met by a group of girls who held before him tufts of palm and branches of gold and silver. They escorted him to the inner chamber of the temple, where he was seated on a carpet heavily fringed with gold, placed before an altar on which were lighted tapers and offerings of many kinds. A strip of palmyra leaf was put into his hand, inscribed with the mystic words:

> Even I was, even from the first, and not any other thing: that which existed unperceived, supreme. Afterwards, I am that which is, and He that was, and He who must remain am I. Know that except Me, who am the First Cause, nothing that appears or does not appear in the mind can be trusted; it is the mind's Maya or delusion, —as Light is to Darkness.

On the reverse side was inscribed this sentence:

Keep me still meditating on Thy infinite greatness and my own nothingness, so that all the questions of my life may be answered and my mind abundantly instructed in the path of *Nipphan!*

All the princes, nobles, and high officers of government, with the Brahman priests who were to officiate, and a company of Buddhist priests, musicians, trumpeters, and conch-blowers were assembled. As the priests took up their chant a Brahman placed a ball of unspun thread in the hands of the prince. The ends of it were carried around the sacred mountain and then around the temple itself and finally into the inner chamber where it was bound around the head of the young prince. From there nine strands were passed around the altar and into the hands of the officiating priest. These latter threads, forming circles within circles, symbolized the mystic word *Om,* which may not escape the lips even of the purest, but must be meditated upon in silence.

The King poured a few drops of lustral water from a conch shell on the prince's head, the favorable moment was proclaimed by trumpeters, conch-blowers, and other musicians, and the supreme climax of the ceremony had arrived. The royal sire handed to the Brahman priests first the golden shears and then a gilded razor. The long lock that had been growing on the prince's head since babyhood was clipped, and then his head was shaved.

The King emerged first from the temple and was carried away in his gold palanquin, borne on the shoulders of eight men. A golden umbrella, eighteen feet in circumference, was carried over him on his way to Mount Kailasa where he would wait for the young prince. There the curious drama so carefully prepared was to take place. The principal parts were assumed by His Majesty, the Kralahome, and the Phra Klang, or Minister of Foreign Affairs. The King was dressed as *Phra Isuan,* or Siva. The Kralahome impersonated the architect and artificer of the gods, whom the Siamese called *Wisawakam,* and the Phra Klang was Indra's charioteer, *Matali.* The imperial elephant followed in the part of *Airavata.* It was caparisoned in velvet and gold, and bore the supernatural weapons, the *vajra* or thunderbolts, and was led by allegorical characters representing winds and showers, lightning and thunder.

Once the royal party had passed into the enclosure around the mountain a number of hideous monsters riding on gigantic eagles appeared on the east. Their heads reached almost to their knees, and their hands grasped indescribable weapons. They were Yaks, the mythological giants of the *Ramayana,* and were appointed to guard the Sacred Mountain from all vulgar approach. A little distance from them, around a pair of stuffed peacocks, were a number of young men in the attire of warriors representing the viceroys, governors, and chiefs of the several dependencies of Siam.

They cautiously approached the Yaks, performing a ceremonial dance while chanting in chorus, "Come, let us go to the Sacred Mountain!"

The Yaks, pointing their weapons at the intruders, and dancing and chanting in the same rhythm, replied, "Come, let us slay them all!"

The drama continued with the Yaks dancing, striking and thrusting until the princes, rajahs, and governors dropped one by one as if wounded or dead. This play stopped when the young prince arrived in his palanquin. Near the foot of the mountain was a cave and in it a pool representing Anotatta Lake on the real Mount Kailasa. To this the young prince was led where he was seated on a rock beside the King. The white elephant, the bull, the horse, and the lion were brought together and from their mouths baptized him with the sacred waters. The King then poured over him the contents of a great conch shell, as did his royal uncles, the prime ministers of the North and South, and finally the chief of the Brahmans.

The prince was then led to a pavilion where women of rank changed his white bathing garments for others, still white but of the richest silk, and a jeweled crown.

In the meantime the King retired to the pavilion on the top of the mountain, which represented Siva's palace. When the little prince was ready the King commanded his two celestial attendants to descend and conduct him to the top of the mountain. They led him up by the western approach to where the King waited to bestow his blessing on his heir. The King presented the prince to the people and they all did him homage by prostrating themselves three times. Then the two of them entered the pagoda and the King solemnly uttered in Pali his royal benediction:

"Thou who art come out of the pure waters, be thy offenses washed away! Be thou relieved from other births! Bear thou in thy bosom the brightness of that light which shall lead thee, even as it led the sublime Buddha, to *Nipphan,* at once and forever!"

The King presented the prince with a jeweled coronet larger than the one he had formerly worn, and other insignia of high station. His Majesty then withdrew, and the prince was led down to his palanquin. Two lines of young men fancifully dressed as guardian spirits, holding purple cords and standing ten feet apart, surrounded the mountain. The prince's palanquin and a part of the procession that had originally accompanied him moved in stately order between these lines, circumambulating the mountain three times within the enclosure, and without it twice more. Then the whole procession withdrew. With the end of the rites the priests were served with a princely banquet, and the nobility and the common people were also feasted.

About noon two standards, called *baisri,* were set up within a circle formed of princes and nobles. These were about eight feet high. The central staff was fixed in a wooden pedestal and supported five circular, deep-rimmed trays, each smaller than the one below. The different stories of the trays were made of plantain leaves decorated with gilt and silvered paper. In them had been placed a little cooked rice, a few cakes, some sweet-scented oil, a handful of fragrant flour, and some young coconuts and plantains. Other edibles of many kinds were brought and arranged about the *baisri*. A bouquet adorned the top of each standard.

A golden throne surmounted by a three-tiered umbrella had been erected between the *baisri* for the prince, and his insignia were arranged on side tables near him. When he was seated a curious ancient rite was performed, a kind of ceremony of blessing, called *Wien-thien*, or "the rotation of the candles." Selected nobles and princes moved around the throne, keeping their right shoulders always toward the prince, and as they moved they passed seven golden candlesticks with the candles lighted from one to the other. As often as they came in front of the prince they performed three circles on a vertical plane with the candles and wafted the smoke toward him with the free hand. Nine times they moved solemnly around the young prince, revolving the candles.

Then the chief of the Brahman priests stepped forward to offer food to the spirit of the prince, which after a period of wandering during early childhood, was supposed to rest finally in the body of the boy on whom the tonsure had been performed. The priest took a portion of the rice from the *baisri* and mixed it with coconut water before presenting it to the prince to eat as food for the spirit or *khwan*. Then he tied around his ankles protective threads. Last of all, dipping his finger first in the scented oil and then in the fragrant flour, he anointed the right foot of the prince by making upon it a *unnalom* scroll, the sign of Siva, it being forbidden to touch the head of a prince. The prince himself completed his own unction by passing his right forefinger over the sign and then marking his forehead between his eyebrows with the *unnalom*. The last step in the anointing was the pouring of a few drops of water from the great conch shell on the prince's head by the King.

The main ceremonies for which the whole Palace had been preparing for many months were over. Now presents of silver and gold were laid at the feet of the boy. Every prince not of the immediate family, and every noble and high officer in the kingdom, were expected to appear with gifts. It was said that the gifts on this occasion amounted to a million ticals. The King had commanded, however, that careful note be kept of all sums of money presented by officers of the government in order that the full amount might be refunded with the next semi-annual payment of salary.

On the two succeeding days the ceremonies connected with the *baisri* and the presentation of gifts were continued. And on the last day of the rites the hair that had been cut from the prince's head was carried in state procession to the river and ceremoniously cast into the water.

34

## THE DEATH OF THE SECOND KING

THE FOLLOWING Sunday morning—January 7, 1866—Anna slept late. She was tired after the six days of festivities, although her own responsibilities had been small. About ten o'clock Louis came running in to tell her that the Second King was dead. The news was not unexpected, for the Second King had been ill for months. Early in December he had been rushed to Bangkok from his retreat at Saraburi, and since then the end had been expected at any time. It had been a source of much anxiety—if he died before or during the tonsure ceremony the nation would be plunged into mourning and the festivities would cease. With the consideration that had marked his whole life he had waited to die until the rite was complete.

Anna lay back on her pillow and thought with compassion, "Well, he has escaped at last!" The prince, whom every European had regarded for thirty years as the most enlightened member of the royal family, had been in effect a prisoner of state for two reigns. In many ways his life had been easier during the first reign, from 1824 to 1851, when his half-brother, the Usurper, Phra Nang Klao, was king. Prince Mongkut had taken refuge in the priesthood, but Prince Chuthamani had decided to go on as before. Watched constantly by spies, but outwardly serene, he had led a busy life. He had learned English from Mr. Robert Hunter, and had used it with a grace and correctness that Mongkut was never to attain. The King had appointed him Superintendent of Artillery and Malayan Infantry, as well as Secretary for English Correspondence, and raised him in rank and title to Krom Khun Isaret Rangsan.

Early in the reign he had been sent to superintend the construction of important works of defense near the mouth of the Mekong River. In 1842 he had commanded a successful expedition against Cochin-China. Then he was commissioned by the King to reconstruct the ancient fortifications at Paknam after Western models. He had engaged a corps of European engineers and artisans and eagerly seized the opportunity to improve his knowledge of Western science, navigation, naval construction, armament, coast and inland defense, engineering, transportation, telegraphy, the working and casting of iron, and whatever else his quick mind could extract from the men in his employ.

The Europeans whom he met admired his liberal spirit and his wise comprehension of world events. He was the embodiment of the hopeful qualities of his nation and of its most progressive tendencies. His talents as a statesman commanded the respect of the embassies that came to negotiate treaties during Mongkut's reign. George Bacon, one of the Americans present at the exchange of ratifications of the treaty with the United States in 1857, wrote that he found him "one of the most remarkable men in the world."

He was handsome, proficient in all sports, and so popular with his own people that at the death of the Usurper in 1851 it was widely hoped that he would be chosen king. If Mongkut had decided to stay in the priesthood, Prince Chuthamani's succession would have been sure. But Mongkut chose the throne, and so relegated his more able brother to the powerless position of Second King.

Since Mongkut had been in the priesthood for almost thirty years, his decision to leave it must have been a shock to the younger prince, who had prepared himself in every way to assume the throne, but he bore his disappointment in silence. His great talents were turned to modest works of construction within his palace grounds. Rather grudgingly the older brother wrote of the younger after his death:

> He made everything new and beautiful, and of curious appearance, and of a good style of architecture, and much stronger than they had formerly been constructed by his three predecessors, the second kings of the last three reigns, for the space of time that he was second king.

284

He had introduced and collected many and many things, being articles of great curiosity, and things useful for various purposes of military acts and affairs, from Europe and America, China, and other states, and placed them in various departments and rooms or buildings suitable for those articles, and placed officers for maintaining and preserving the various things neatly and carefully. He has constructed several buildings in European fashion and Chinese fashion, and ornamented them with various useful ornaments for his pleasure, and has constructed two steamers, in manner of men-of-war, and two steam-yachts, and several rowing state-boats in Siamese and Cochin-Chinese fashion, for his pleasure at sea and rivers of Siam; and caused several articles of gold and silver being vessels and various wares and weapons to be made up by the Siamese and Malayan goldsmiths, for employ and dress of himself and his family, by his direction and skilful contrivance and ability. He became celebrated and spread out more and more to various regions of the Siamese kingdom, adjacent States around, and far-famed to foreign countries, even at far distance, as he became acquainted with many and many foreigners, who came from various quarters of the world where his name became known to most as a very clever and bravest Prince of Siam. . . .

As he pleased mostly with firing of cannon and acts of Marine power and seamen, which he has imitated to his steamers which were made in manner of the man-of-war, after he has seen various things curious and useful, and learned Marine customs on board the foreign vessels of war, his steamers conveyed him to sea, where he has enjoyed playing of firing in cannon very often. . . .

He pleased very much in and was playful of almost everything, some important and some unimportant, as riding on Elephants and Horses and Ponies, racing of them and racing of rowing boats, firing on birds and beasts of prey, dancing and singing in various ways pleasantly, and various curiosity of almost everything, and music of every description, and in taming of dogs, monkeys, &c., &c., that is to say briefly that he has tested almost everything eatable except entirely testing of Opium and play.

Also he has visited regions of Northeastern Province of Sarapury and Gorath very often for enjoyment of pleasant riding on Elephants and Horses, at forests in chasing animals of prey, fowling, and playing music and singing with Laos people of that region.

When Mongkut was raised to the throne, he had insisted that his brother be given a title higher than that of any previous second king, Phrabat Somdet Phra Pin Klao Chao Yu Hua, and other honors to enhance the empty position. Before long, however, jealousy between the brothers began to be apparent. No one knew how it started. Some whispered that the Second King chafed under the knowledge that the woman he loved best was forbidden to marry him because she was a princess of the first rank and might be offered only to the Supreme King. Others said that each king was traduced by the corrupt tongues of his own courtiers—those of the First King whispering that the Second King's popularity was a constant threat to the throne, and those of the Second King pointing out how unworthily the older brother suspected the younger brother of rebellious intentions.

Perhaps the seeds of this feeling had been sown in childhood. An old priest named Phra Net, who had been one of Prince Chuthamani's tutors, told Anna many stories about the prince's youth. He told her sadly that the astrologer who cast the prince's horoscope at his birth had foretold for him an unnatural death. Because of this prophecy his mother had watched over him with such devotion and imprudent partiality that her older son must have found himself almost excluded from the warm circle of affection. If that were so, the feeling between the brothers was probably not new, but arose from their mother's favoritism. During the years of exile it was latent, united as they were by their common exclusion from their heritage.

After the birth of Prince Chulalongkorn, the First King was known to be eager to settle the succession on his own line, and very much afraid that premature death would deprive his son of the throne. Instead of employing his brother's abilities, he excluded him more and more from active participation in the government, until at last the Second King became nothing but a captive in his narrow domain. More than once it was in the power of the Second King to overthrow his brother and seize the throne, but he never made a move to do so. It was said that many disaffected groups would have united to accomplish this even without his consent if the Kralahome had not intervened, and if the Second King had not sided with the Kralahome immediately. Yet Mongkut, incapable of trusting anyone, continued to be suspicious of his brother's motives.

Among the many small discourtesies endured by the Second King was the continual presence with him of a certain doctor. He knew, as did everyone else, that the man was a spy placed close to his person by King Mongkut. The doctor was in a position to poison the younger brother if and when it suited the older one's plans to order it. In spite of the rift between the brothers there was no open break for many years. Then one day the Second King sent a request to the Royal Treasury for a large sum of money. By the express command of the First King the order was not honored. On the next day King Phra Pin Klao left Bangkok with his most trusted courtiers for the North. He went directly to Chiengmai, the most powerful of the tributary Lao provinces. The Prince of Chiengmai was a spirited ruler who had more than once confronted the King of Siam with a haughty and intrepid resistance. King Mongkut had never dared push him too far, fearing open revolt which might throw the Lao provinces into the hands of the British.

As soon as the prince knew of the insult to the Second King, the money he had required was brought and laid at his feet without ostentation. This gesture of sympathy was the beginning of a solid friendship. The prince declined to accept the entire sum, but did take part of it. Instead of returning to the capital he went to Saraburi, a hundred miles northwest of Bangkok on the Pasak River, and erected a fortified palace, which he named Ban Sita (The Home of the Goddess Sita). After that he rarely went to Bangkok except when business demanded it, or when he was required to go for the semi-annual oath of allegiance.

King Mongkut, alarmed by the possibilities in the friendship of the Prince of Chiengmai and his brother, ordered the Lao Prince to send his son to Bangkok as a hostage. When the summons was repeated more peremptorily, the son of the prince fled to Ban Sita for a time. Nor did he ever appear at the Grand Palace. His stout old father came down the river in state and brought his own hostage to Bangkok. Although King Mongkut chafed at this flouting of his authority, he accepted it with a show of graciousness. To do otherwise was fraught with danger.

The friendship of the Prince of Chiengmai for the Second King resulted in the marriage of his beautiful niece, the Princess Sunatda Wismita, to Phra Pin Klao only a little more than a year before his death. She was a celebrated and much coveted beauty, whom King Mongkut would have liked to add to his own harem, but had been unable to secure. Etiquette forbade the royal brothers to pry into each other's *serail*, but King Mongkut knew very soon of the marriage of his brother and the princess. He grumbled that when he traveled no one came around with pretty girls for him, but that wherever his brother went the chiefs threw their loveliest daughters at his head until it was a disgrace.

The Second King had been at Ban Sita when his final illness began. The King's physician, fearing that he might die there, took hurried steps to get him back to the capital. He was rushed downriver to the palace of Krom Luang Wongsa, physician to King Mongkut, and half-brother of both, who was a member of the Academy of Medicine of New York. Prince Wongsa saw at once that there was nothing he could do. Death was only a matter of time.

So the Second King was taken to his own palace, and laid in a chamber looking to the east. That was on December 6, 1865. The same night he asked to see his brother. King Mongkut and the Kralahome hurried to his bedside. No words were spoken. The brothers embraced each other, and the older wept bitterly. The younger was, as he had been all his life, the greater: he had sent for his brother to make clear to him before he died that all that had lain between them was forgiven.

Something else happened at that interview, however. The First King, suspicious as always, and more than ordinarily well versed in the medical science of the time, was puzzled by the nature of his brother's illness. Some of the symptoms were strange.

When Anna went to the Palace after the Second King's death, the tonsure had been almost forgotten in the excitement that surrounded the beginning of national mourning. The King had already issued an order to stop work on the Nantha Uthayan Palace. When his oldest children had been about five he had begun the construction of a large palace and series of mansions directly across the river from the Grand Palace. He had arranged that his wives and children should be transferred there if he died before his brother and if his brother succeeded to the throne. Now that brother was dead and the reason for the palace, which had been under construction nine years, had ceased to exist.

All the royal artisans were transferred to the Second King's palace to complete a building in which the First King might live temporarily. It would not have been suitable for him to stay in one of the already occupied mansions. But his brother had almost finished a handsome structure in the Chinese style just north of the main palace. Here the First King took up his residence within a week.

Ostensibly this was so that he might act as administrator of his brother's estate, and at his brother's request. Living in the harem of the Second King's palace were daughters of the Second Kings of all four reigns, and these, so it was said, had been entrusted by the younger to the older brother as a solemn responsibility. In the circular which King Mongkut issued he himself explained:

The Second King, on his being worse, has said to his eldest and second daughters, the half-sisters of the eldest son, distempered so as he cannot be in the presence of his father without difficulty, that he (the Second King) forenamed on that time was hopeless and that he could not live more than a few days. He did not wish to do his last will regarding his family and property, particularly as he was strengthened to speak much, and consider anything deeply and accurately: he beg'd to entreat all his sons, daughters, and wives that none should be sorry for his death, which comes by natural course, and should not fear for misery of difficulty after his demise. All should throw themselves under their faithful and affectionate uncle, the Supreme King of Siam, for protection, in whom he had heartfelt confidence that he will do well to his family after his death, as such the action or good protection to several families of other princes and princesses in the royalty, who deceased before. He beg'd only to recommend his sons and daughters, that they should be always honest and faithful to his elder full brother, the Supreme King of Siam, by the same affection as to himself, and that they should have much more affection and respect toward Paternal relative persons in royalty, than toward their maternal relative persons, who are not royal descendants of his ancestors. . . .

In the afternoon, the Second King invited His Majesty the Supreme King, his elder full brother, and his Excellency Chow Phya Sri

Surywongse Samuha P'hra-Kralahome, the Prime Minister, who is the principal head of the Government and royal cousin, to seat themselves near to his side on his bedstead where he lay, and other principals of royalty and nobility, to seat themselves in that room where he was lying, that they might be able to ascertain his speech by hearing. Then he delivered his family and followers and the whole of his property to His Majesty and His Excellency for protection and good decision, according to consequences which they would well observe.

When day after day passed and the King did not return, the harem became restless. Some of the bolder spirits abandoned themselves to gaiety, while many of the women sent their confidential slaves to consult the astrologers and soothsayers. Gossip was rife. Little groups could be seen whispering together any hour of the day. Feminine telegraphy and secret service were working full time. It was believed that the King had been bewitched by some enchantress in his brother's palace and was no longer a free agent.

It had long been bruited about Bangkok that the ladies of Phra Pin Klao's harem were the most beautiful from among the women of Laos, Pegu, Burma, and Cambodia. The women of the First King's harem were reported to be much inferior. The famous Princess of Chiengmai was supposed to be the loveliest woman in either harem, although not many people had ever seen her. There were rumors, too, that she was talented musically, very graceful and charming.

Then one day Lady Son Klin whispered to Anna that the most attractive and accomplished women from the Second King's harem had been quietly transferred during the previous night to King Mongkut's. It was contrary to all precedent. The whole Inside was indignant and scandalized. There was more open murmuring against the King than Anna had ever heard before. The following day she saw some of these women for herself. She was particularly impressed with the Lao women. They were taller and fairer than the Siamese, and much handsomer. Their hair grew long and luxuriantly black, and was gathered into a knot at the nape of their necks. Their dress, too, was different. Instead of the panung, which was pulled up between the legs like an inverted diaper, they wore graceful skirts called *pasins*, which reached to their feet. Some of the skirts were of heavy silk woven with gold.

The jealousy and rage of the Inside against the "interlopers" united for the moment the entire city of women. They could not express their resentment against the King for taking his brother's wives, so with one accord they turned on the wives. They found a thousand ways of showing their contempt and of ignoring the existence of the new arrivals.

"Is the Princess of Chiengmai with them?" Anna asked Son Klin.

She shook her head. "No," she said, scarcely moving her lips. "No, she isn't here—at least not yet."

"And the King? Has he come back?"

Again Lady Son Klin shook her head.

Even the royal children were infected with the uneasiness that stirred the inner city. They whispered among themselves, and giggled. Anna could scarcely hold their attention. She finally gave up, dismissed them an hour early, and went home with Princess Somawadi to call on Lady Thiang. The King's absence had relieved her of the responsibility of the royal kitchen. She was playing with her youngest child, a little girl named Khae, who was about two. A son, Lady Thiang's ninth child, had died the year before only a few days after his birth.

"Mem," she said with pleasure when she saw Anna. "Come in, come in! You see I have nothing to do."

"Yes, I see. You're having a real vacation."

They talked of the children and the school, but inevitably their conversation swung around to the topic uppermost in every mind. Had Anna seen the Lao women? She had! Lady Thiang sniffed.

"If HE isn't careful," she said with an ominous shake of her head, "HE'll find himself poisoned."

Anna looked at her quickly, sensing a meaning deeper than the words. "Why do you say that?" she asked, half expecting an evasive answer.

Lady Thiang shot Anna a glance out of her clear intelligent eyes, closed her lips firmly, thought a moment, and then said: "I mean that HE'll come to the same end as his brother. Someone 'up there' will put poison in HIS food. HE'd do better to stay here with me for his meals. After all, I've guarded HIM for years from such a fate."

The implication was appalling. "Do you mean," Anna said slowly, feeling her way, "that the Second King died of poison?" She did not wish to ask more than Lady Thiang cared to answer.

The latter nodded. "But he didn't know it," she whispered. "They have just found it out, HE and the Kralahome. HE suspected something when HE first saw HIS brother after they brought him down from Ban Sita." And she went on to tell Anna the whole story.

Among the Second King's concubines there was a woman named Klip. She was the mother of many of his children, the oldest of whom was more than twenty. Like Lady Thiang in the First King's palace she had been appointed to control the royal cuisine. But she was envious of the other women, suspicious of their designs upon her position, intriguing and ambitious. Years before, when she found that she could not have the influence she coveted over the King's affections, she had gone to an old and infamous sorcerer, named Khun Het Na (Lord of the Future). He was an adept of the black arts, much consulted by women of rank from all over the country.

For enormous fees he had prepared a variety of charms, philters, and incantations for her. She had mixed his nostrums in the Second King's food, not just once, but many times over a long period. The poisons had done their work slowly, and had gradually undermined the sturdy physique of the Second King. Then they had affected his mind, so that near the end of his life he was despondent and excitable, the prey of nebulous fears. He had consulted many physicians, none of whom could diagnose his illness. At last he had been carried home to die, still unaware that he had been poisoned by his own wife. Anna remembered the story of the horoscope that had been told her by the old priest, Phra Net. The dire prediction had come to pass after all!

"And I think," Lady Thiang concluded, "that HE is going to punish Klip and Khun Het Na publicly."

"You mean proclaim their crime and then torture and execute them?"

"No, no, no, no!" exclaimed Lady Thiang in horror. "Of course, HE'll never proclaim it! No one knows that the Second King died of poison, and if they did there would always be idle tongues to whisper that HE was really to blame and that Klip was just an accomplice, or even that she didn't have anything to do with it."

Anna conceded the wisdom of this. The Lao and Peguans as well as the Cochin-Chinese and Cambodians living in Bangkok were all passionately devoted to the Second King. Add to that his popularity with his own people, and the situation was full of explosive possibilities. If it became known that the Second King had died of poison, the jealousy of the First King for his younger brother would arouse suspicions—all the more because of the constant presence with the Second King of the physician who was known to be the First King's spy. There would be some to say that the physician had actually given the poison and that Lady Klip was merely a scapegoat. These suspicions might even result in action, if the Prince of Chiengmai, say, were to put himself at the head of a group of insurgents, or solicit the all-too-willing French to help him with their large military force from Saigon.

"Has anything been decided?" Anna ventured, seeing Lady Thiang was still communicative.

"Yes," she said in a low voice, "yes, it has. The royal physicians and the San Luang are all sworn to secrecy. But the sentence will be carried out tomorrow. If you look out your window, you will see the procession go by."

And so it proved. The concubine Lady Klip, the fortune-teller Khun Het Na, and nine female slaves were tortured and publicly paraded through Bangkok. Their crime was not named to the curious crowds that gathered to watch them. Afterward they were thrown into an open boat, towed out to the Gulf of Siam, and abandoned there. Among the women of the Palace it was whispered that celestial avengers had slain them with arrows of lightning and spears of fire.

Two weeks after the King had left his own palace to take up residence at his brother's he returned suddenly and without warning. He was in a villainous mood that baffled everyone. The most tactful measures failed to placate him. Lady Thiang summoned Anna hurriedly one day to play her old part in their little drama. For the first time it failed to work. Anna walked into the King's presence diffidently with her Sanskrit book. He ordered her out, and told her that she was not to come back until he sent for her. Daily after that women suffered from his tyranny, cruelty, and spite. It became a common experience to pass along the streets of the Inside and hear women and children sobbing in house after house. There were sullen complaints on every side, and there was not a woman in the harem who did not think the King was a victim of black magic.

Anna had her own private theory. The Princess of Chiengmai had not appeared in the harem. If she were as strong-willed as her uncle, it was quite possible that she had resisted His Majesty's overtures. She was known to have been deeply attached to the Second King. The First King, however, was tenacious. He had been openly envious when the famous beauty became his brother's wife. Since all the women seemed to agree that it was not his brother's financial affairs that had kept His Majesty so long, perhaps there was room to believe that he had tried a second time to win the princess for himself. If she had scorned him, his ill-temper was easy to understand.

Margaret Ayer

## 35

### THE MYSTERIOUS PRINCESS

ANNA WAS too weary to care much about the King's ill-temper. She was even glad that she could be relieved for a little while from struggling with his correspondence, although she pitied the women whose life was fast becoming almost unbearable. Her thoughts were much with young Prince Chulalongkorn, who was to enter the priesthood in July for three months. Anna's influence over him would end at that time temporarily, perhaps permanently.

He was dreamy-eyed and thoughtful during this period. The tonsure ceremony had impressed him deeply. From his studies both in English and Pali he had evolved an exalted ideal of life, and precocious, inexpressible yearnings. Anna wished helplessly that she could spare him the shock of his first contacts outside the Palace but that was impossible. She could only hope that he would not jettison all his lofty aspirations when reality first impinged on him.

Anna had wondered if the tonsure, which had cost hundreds of thousands of ticals, and had employed the energies of many thousands of people, would fill him with self-importance. He had been the principal figure in a drama that would hardly be equaled in his lifetime. It would not have been strange if the effect had been to inflate his ego, but apparently this was not the case. He had said to her recently in a burst of self-abnegation that he envied the death of the venerable priest, his uncle. He would rather be poor and have to earn his living than be king. "It's true," he said thoughtfully, "a poor man has to work hard for his daily bread, but then he is free. And his food is all he has to win or lose." He seemed to be examining his own motives and desires. "He can possess everything that is important in possessing the First Cause who pervades all things, the earth, the sky, the stars, the flowers, and little children." He paused in his effort to frame thoughts almost too deep for his thirteen-year-old mind. "I can understand that I am great, since I am part of the Infinite. But great in that one thing alone. And that all I see is mine, and that I am in it and of it. If I could only be a poor boy, I could be perfectly happy, I think."

Anna thought how little the child knew of poverty and its different but no less urgent problems. She respected his sincerity and intelligence too much, however, to point out what his own powers of observation would show him later—that the lot of a poor boy in a country like Siam where he was at the beck and call of some noble was far from idyllic. The poor boy of whom Prince Chulalongkorn was dreaming would have to be branded on the wrist to show to whom he owed allegiance. He would be subject to not less than three months' service every year, and if he made the mistake of showing great ability, his term of service would be lengthened. Anna was convinced that the low level of literature and art in Siam was due to the fear that every talented person felt of being impounded into royal service if it became known that he had more than ordinary gifts.

As the terrible heat of March and April approached Anna grew more listless and weary. She had written Tom Wilkinson, her husband's cousin, asking him to try to find a school for Louis. She had determined to send him home as soon as possible. Her friends were urging her to return with him, and there were days when she wanted nothing else. Francis Cobb, who was leaving Singapore, had written begging her to use him in any way she cared to, if she decided to go to Europe. He had ended the letter in the usual devoted way—"Put your foot upon me, dear, and step upwards."

Before she had reached a decision her health broke completely. She was taken violently ill with a return of the fever, and Beebe hurried for Dr. Campbell from the British Consulate. Day by day he attended her as Anna's fever remained high and her strength diminished. One afternoon he told her gently that she might not be strong enough to survive and that she had better appoint a guardian for her children. The British Consulate would, of course, carry out her wishes. The effect of the warning was to release her from the pressing weight of her troubles. She felt a sharp pang for her children, Avis in London and Louis in Bangkok. But she was so weary and sick, both in body and spirit, that the prospect of rest and of reunion with Leon, who had been dead six years now, seemed undiluted pleasure. The hard years in Siam had sapped her will to live.

In one of the lucid intervals between periods of delirium she had her red leather trunk moved out from under her bed. It had held her important papers for many years. Once while she was still living on the other side of the river it had almost been stolen. She thought it was the interpreter who was to blame. Like everyone else in Bangkok she slept under a mosquito net. Hers was large, almost like a room, and she had kept a lighted lamp on a table next to her bed so that she could see quickly if awakened. Opening her eyes one night with a start, she had felt someone in the room. Suddenly she saw the corner of her red leather trunk emerge from under the bed. She held her breath until she saw a greased arm follow the trunk, and a sinuous brown body, also greased, follow the arm. Then she snatched the lamp and flung it at the thief crying, *"Pen arai ma!"* (Who do you think you are?), and fell back fainting with fright. When she opened her eyes again the shattered lamp and the trunk were there, but the thief had gone.

She remembered this incident now and had the trunk opened. She sorted out the few papers that would be important to Louis and Avis. Then she called Beebe and had her burn the rest, her little keepsakes, and all the personal letters, even her prized letters from Leon. She was determined they should not fall into the hands of her enemies or even the idly curious. Her will was already made. She turned it over to Dr. Campbell. She was ready for the end.

Still her life hung on by a slender thread. She seemed to have no will to fight, yet death did not come. Then one day Dr. Campbell brought her a message from the King, saying that she might die in peace, for he would adopt her son. The shock was a stimulant. She drew Dr. Campbell down and whispered weakly, "He means it well, I know, but I'd rather live a thousand years in any kind of torment than let him adopt my son!" From that moment she began to rally.

In April she had a long friendly letter from the King. It closed with what he called a "Very private post script," which took her mind back to the Palace:

Will you have remembered? once before some several months ago where you have said to me that I should dignify my first son or Prince Chaufa Chulalongkorn as my heir apparent like the Prince of Wales of England? I have refused and denied your word and have stated unto you that our general people do not have more pleased on me and my descendant, I am very sorry even many foreigners are so as our native general people. Although I have been doing nothing unfavorable to right of general people they considered me as unpopular! then you have denied to me that you have learnt such from none, some-time since your arrival to Siam until that very day. Why! how will you have learnt such the word! as almost every one of our native people and foreigners as ascertainedly knowing that you are really my partisan even may be my spy! Who would say such before your audience!

Now I can have witness or testimony of that statement which had been said to you by me before.

There is a newspaper of Singapore entitled *Daily News* just pub-lished after last arrival of the Steamer *Chow Phya* at Singapore, in which paper, a correspondence from an Individual resident at Bangkok dated 16th March 1866 was shown. but I have none of that paper in my possession. Mr. Jan Kim Ching did not sent to me for my perusal. I have read one in hand of an individual here I did not notice the number and date to state to you now. but I trust that the paper must be in hand of several foreigners in Bangkok, may you have read it perhaps otherwise you can obtain the same from any one or by order to obtain from Singapore after perusal thereof you will not be able to deny my statement forementioned moreover as general people both native and foreigners here seem to have less pleasure on me and my descendants than their pleasure and hope on other amiable family to them until present day. What was said there in for a princess considered by the speaker or writer as proper or suitable to be head of my harem (a room for confinement of women of Eastern monarch) there is no least intention occurred to me even once or in my dream indeed I think if I do so I will die soon perhaps!

The said correspondence date 16th March 1866 I conject must from one of the British consulate but not from the Consul himself or must from the consul of D. no doubt, not from American journalists or Mr. Chandler the idea of whom may be otherwise.

This my handwriting or content hereof shall be kept secretly.

I beg to remain
Your faithful and well wisher
S.P.P.M. Mongkut R. S.
on 5441st day of reign
the writer hereof beg to place his confidence on you always.

The reference to the "other amiable family" seemed to show that the King's jealousy of his brother's popularity had not ended even with his brother's death. Anna looked up the objectionable reference in the Singa-pore paper. It read: "The King has his eye upon another princess of the highest rank, with a view to constituting her a queen consort." This in itself would not have been so bad if the context had not made it clear that the writer had been led to believe that the princess in question was Princess Duang Prapha, familiarly called Princess "Tui" (Tubby). She was a woman of about twenty-eight, one of the older daughters of the Second King, and therefore His Majesty's niece. Obviously the correspondent had

296

heard the rumors about the Princess of Chiengmai and had confused the persons involved.

The Bangkok *Recorder* had added salt to the wound by rebuking the King in its comment on the Singapore report:

> Now, considering that he is full threescore and three years of age, that he has already scores of concubines and about fourscore sons and daughters, with several Chowfas among them, and hence eligible to the highest posts of honor in the kingdom, this rumor seems too monstrous to be credited. But the truth is, there is scarcely anything too monstrous for the royal polygamy of Siam to bring forth.

Anna quite understood the King's resentment of this less than tactful remark, but she was a little puzzled by the King's virtuous indignation. Of course he had no designs on his niece. But was it so certain that he had not some interest in the Princess of Chiengmai? It was five years since there had been a consort who was regarded as of the rank of queen. Except for the fact that she had been his brother's wife, the Princess of Chiengmai would have been in many ways an ideal queen. Furthermore, her marriage to the King would have tied the recalcitrant Prince of Chiengmai to the throne.

By the time that Anna was well enough to return to the Palace curiosity about the Princess of Chiengmai was dead. The Inside was stirring with other gossip. Even Bangkok had grown tired of the topic that had absorbed everyone for months. The notorious M. Aubaret was returning to Bangkok in June, and speculation about the meaning of his unwelcome reappearance had the foreign community agog.

The Palace was preparing for Prince Chulalongkorn's entrance into the novitiate of the priesthood, which was set for July 19. When he emerged at the end of October he would be considered too old to live within the confines of the Inside. Preparations were under way to alter a building close to his father's palace, within the outer but not the inner wall, for his new residence. The building had been occupied by a division of the Palace treasury whose duty it was to procure and store the articles used by the King in merit-making. It was being refurbished for the prince. Henceforth it was to be called Wang Suan Kulap (Rose Garden Palace). Princess Lamom was busy getting ready to move and take over its management. There were even rumors that the King had selected his son's first wife, who would be installed in the new residence in due order. The choice would probably fall on a granddaughter of the Kralahome.

The rite of entering into the novitiate of the priesthood was more solemn than the tonsure but much simpler. The first day was devoted to the performance of the *Wien-thien,* the revolving of the candles in blessing. This took place in the Audience Hall before a select company of guests, who were later feasted.

On the second day the prince was dressed in costly white robes and ornaments similar to those he had worn at the tonsure. Earlier that morning his eyebrows and his hair, which had begun to grow in a short brush all over his head, had been shaved. He was taken in charge at his father's palace by a body of priests and conducted to the Temple of the Emerald Buddha. On the way his barefoot escort chanted hymns from the Buddhist liturgy. At the entrance to the temple another band of priests divested him of his fine robes and dressed him in simple white, as the chanting continued. Within, the monks were arranged in a double semicircle, each with a lighted taper in his folded palms. The prince advanced humbly toward the high priest in the center of the semicircle with his back to the altar, and bowed three times asking to be admitted to the Order. The high priest received him and with their hands mutually interfolded, one upon the other, the prince vowed to renounce the world with all its cares and temptations, and to observe with obedience the rules of the novitiate. This done he was dressed in the yellow robes of the Order, instructed briefly in his duties, and the ceremony was complete.

After breakfast had been served to the priests, gifts were presented to him. His father was the first to make a gift, then his brothers, uncles, aunts, and cousins; then the prime minister and other high officials; and finally the Chinese and Indian merchants. Most of these gifts were to be turned over by the prince to his associates in the priesthood. After the presentation the prince's brothers entertained the assembly on a little stage. Dressed in full state costume, loaded with gold and precious stones, they put on a performance of fencing, in the Siamese style. A Chinese nobleman took this opportunity to give each of them a gold watch, much to the delight of the children and His Majesty. When it was all over Prince Chulalongkorn was led from the Palace which had been his home for almost fourteen years, to the monastery at Wat Bawonniwet, where he was to stay for three months.

## 36

## THE RED VELVET LETTER

AUGUST 10, 1866, was another of the days Anna was never to forget. It began pleasantly enough. Beebe had found some delicious custard apples in the market, and Anna and Louis had them for breakfast. The morning was clear and sweet. There was nothing in the weather to warn of approaching storm, nor did Anna have any premonition that the curtain was going up on the last act of her drama with the King.

His Majesty sent for her early. "Mem," he said as she entered, "write a letter at once to tell Sir John Bowring I have changed my mind. I do not want him for ambassador to France in writing of new treaty. I shall send an embassy from this place with Phya Suriwong Wai Wat."

The King's changes of mind were too common to arouse her indignation any longer, although she did feel that Sir John was being treated rather shabbily. On the last day of June M. Aubaret had returned from Paris. The French in Bangkok openly rejoiced. They saw in him a Gallic Stamford Raffles who would wrest from Siam further rich territories, and might even manage the annexation of the entire kingdom to the Empire. They were well aware of the superstitious fear that the King felt for the peppery little consul with his fierce mustaches and beady black eyes.

M. Lamache, who had been discharged for his insolence toward the King the year before, had returned to the royal employ. A correspondent had written the Bangkok *Recorder* asking why it was that the King had restored M. Lamache, "the once famous Drill Master, to his former position and rank. Is such conduct as he has been guilty of a guarantee for favoritism?" Dr. Bradley printed the letter with the question, "Can any one of our readers oblige our correspondent with a solution to his query?"

One of the French merchants, M. Alloin, berated old Dr. Bradley for this. He told him bluntly that he imperiled his life by such impertinence, and that M. Lamache had it in his heart to give him a thorough thrashing, and, in fact, had threatened to kill him at the first opportunity. Dr. Bradley pulled at his gray beard and replied imperturbably: "He would then reveal himself a murderer, and worse than I had supposed him. Furthermore, he would have to pay the penalty for his act with his life."

"And why shall he care about that," shrieked M. Alloin, "if he may take yours? He may then kill himself. Why not?" Then he added, "When M. Aubaret returns he will prosecute you, anyway, for publishing in your *Bangkok Calendar* that he caused a hubbub at the Palace last August."

"And do you deny that it was true?"

The merchant had no reply, only more imprecations for the American who dared to publish unpleasant references to the acts of the French Consul.

M. Aubaret brought an autographed letter from the French Emperor, and a magnificent sword for the King, as well as a sword from the Prince Imperial of France to Prince Chulalongkorn. These were presented in formal audience. All this looked friendly, but as everyone in Bangkok was confidentially informing everyone else, behind lay a grand plot to transform Siam into a French protectorate. M. Aubaret added fuel to these suspicions by immediately opening negotiations for revision of the treaty in relation to Cambodia that he had forcibly extracted from the Siamese the year before. One article of that treaty had not been satisfactory to his superiors in Paris. It read:

> Article IV. The boundary lines of the province of Battambang, Nakon Siemreap, together with the Laos provinces belonging to Siam, bordering on the kingdom of Cambodia, the French agree shall remain as they are at the present time supposed to be fixed.

Battambang and Siemreap had been governed directly from Bangkok since 1794, while the rest of Cambodia had been governed feudally through its own king. Since these two provinces had once been a part of Cambodia proper the French regarded them as the next step toward domination of the area they had marked out for conquest. Thus they did not want to acknowledge that they were Siamese, even temporarily.

The King was stubborn. The most that M. Aubaret could get from him was a reluctant promise to send an ambassador to Paris to negotiate, and a secondary promise that the Siamese would send a delegate and suitable display to the great exhibition to be held in 1867. Anna had been ordered to write to Sir John Bowring requesting his services as plenipotentiary to the Court of France. This letter had hardly had time to reach its destination, and now the King had changed his mind and planned to send the son of the Kralahome instead. She sighed and set to work.

Before she had anything written the King added a further injunction. She was to explain the countermanding of the appointment in such a way as to attribute His Majesty's change of mind to the advice of Mr. Thomas George Knox, the British Consul, whom she well knew the King disliked so heartily that he was quite ready to embarrass him with his influential countryman. Or, if she had scruples on that point, to say anything else she liked as long as she justified the King's course without antagonizing Sir John. Why not say that the advice was her own?

Anna started up from her chair. "Your Majesty," she exclaimed, "I'll consent to do nothing of the kind." Then, warned by the rage gathering in the King's face, she added that she would express to Sir John His Majesty's regrets, but that she would not attribute his change of mind to Mr. Knox or to herself, since neither of them had had anything to do with it. She had expected that he would be angry, but not that his anger would reach the proportions it did. His fury was so vast as to seem grotesque. His talent for invective was always formidable. He tried to beat down her resistance with vicious terms of opprobrium, and when these failed, with threats. She stood up, and without replying, walked out of the Palace, across the commons, and into her home.

The pleasant coolness of the morning had been replaced by gathering heat. The atmosphere became sultry, and every now and then a rumble of distant thunder reached Anna's ears as she sat at home trying to work on her own correspondence, which was much in arrears. No breeze stirred the heavy air. The parched trees and leaves drooped. Nervous and upset by her scene with the King, she began to wish more and more that she had left Siam as her friends had been urging her to do. If she had not been so deeply absorbed in her work, particularly in the education of young Prince Chulalongkorn, she would have gone long ago. She had been held by the knowledge of her influence over him. Now that he had entered the novitiate there was no assurance that she would be permitted to continue teaching him after the three months had passed. Perhaps it would be better to go to England with Louis as soon as she could arrange it, and give up the unequal battle with the King.

Then, too, there was her health. Since her illness the number of hours she could work had been sharply reduced. The King had reluctantly taken Dr. Campbell's word that it was impossible for Mrs. Leonowens to continue to do all she had been required to do previously. But even the limitation on time could not protect her from the capricious temper and extravagant demands of the King. They were more difficult to endure than long hours of work.

In the late afternoon Phra Alak, the King's private secretary, appeared with a paper. He was accompanied by a group of slaves from the Palace. On the paper were a number of accusations that she was to read, acknowledge, and sign, for him to take back to the King. She was also to admit that she was guilty of ingratitude, and atone to the King by prompt compliance with his wishes in the matter of the letter to Sir John Bowring. The accusations were many and varied:

1. She had stolen a valuable Sanskrit book from his library.
2. She had often disobeyed the King's commands.
3. She had thwarted his wishes.
4. She had presumed to scold His Majesty for certain matters of conduct, which were not her concern.
5. She had shown him disrespect, as by standing while he was seated, thinking evil of him, slandering him, and calling him wicked.
6. She had walked over the head of His Majesty.
7. She had honored and favored the British Consul, Mr. Thomas George Knox, at the expense of the American Consul, Mr. James Madison Hood. In support of this last charge—she had written the American Consul's name at the bottom of a royal circular, after carefully displaying her own and the British Consul's at the top of it.

Anna read the ridiculous accusations, her anger kindling. How tenacious was the King's memory of any slight fault! How easily he forgot faithful service! Once, long ago, before she understood palace etiquette, the King had expressed a desire for a certain book. She had remembered that it was in the room above where His Majesty had been working earlier in the day, and, supposing that she was obeying his wish, if not his command, she had hurried upstairs after it. All unthinking she had entered a room directly over the one in which the King was sitting, secured the book and come downstairs, expecting him to be pleased. But she had "walked over his head." To her surprise the attending women were shaking in terror. With trembling lips they had assured her that if she ever committed such a breach of royal etiquette again she would be cast into a dungeon.

The other charges were equally farcical. She handed the strange document back to Phra Alak without a word.

"But you haven't signed it," he demurred.

"No, and I never will," she replied curtly. "You can tell the King so."

The slaves all dropped on their knees and begged her, in the names of their various mistresses, to yield to the King's demand, and do what he required. She realized that they acted out of love for her, fearing the consequences to her. But she would not agree to do what she could not. Phra Alak, who was a man of resources, produced the other string to his bow. He offered Anna a substantial bribe. No doubt the money had been collected by the women of the Palace for just this contingency, since he could hardly have had so large a sum himself.

"Phra Alak," Anna said reproachfully, "you know perfectly well that I can't be bribed. If what the King asked me to do were right, I'd do it without money. But it's wrong, and I won't do it, and certainly not for money."

It pained her to realize that the scribe, like the King, could not be convinced of her integrity. It was four and a half years since she had begun her work in the Palace. Not once in that time had money been a consideration in any of her dealings as advocate for the suffering and oppressed. Yet this man, whom she had helped so many times, thought she could be bought! What, after all, was the use of even attempting to work with people incapable of recognizing the force of principle and the impelling guidance of conscience?

Phra Alak raised his bid. When she refused again, she saw by his face that he imagined she was merely bargaining. For two hours he argued and pleaded, slowly increasing the sum he was willing to pay for her signature to the charges, and the letter to Sir John Bowring. The slaves added their frantic pleading. Finally Anna stood up to show the interview was over. It was past tea time. She had been very patient, hoping to convince Phra Alak that she could not be bought, but without success. He departed in despair, convinced that the large sum he had offered was insufficient for the cupidity of this Englishwoman. He went with his head downcast, mourning for himself because he must return unsuccessful to the King, and might expect the most unpleasant consequences to his person.

Anna was so exhausted by the long argument that she could hardly eat her dinner. The rain had not come and the atmosphere was still oppressive. Little puffs of breeze and occasional thunder held out promise of relief, but no drops fell. After dinner she sat alone in her downstairs living room unable to stop thinking about the events of the day. Here she was once more plunged into a conflict not of her own choosing, but no easier for that. Fears crowded thick about her. They were increased by an anonymous note from the Palace telling her that the King's anger had grown by her refusal to sign the paper he had sent by Phra Alak. He had shouted to his assembled courtiers, "Will no one rid me of this woman?" Anna called her servants and had the doors locked and barred. She told them that they were to admit no Siamese, not even from the Palace, unless she ordered them to do so.

She had only once before feared for her personal safety. She had believed that as an Englishwoman she was immune from the quick death that found many of the Siamese subjects of His Majesty. She had incurred the jealousy of certain courtiers, it was true, and the enmity of much of the privileged class. If the King had actually suggested that he would be glad to have her done away with, was she being foolishly timorous? Wasn't it possible that there was at least one of them who would send a hired assassin to carry out his sovereign's will?

On a single previous occasion she had seen the King as angry at her as he was now. She had refused to write a letter to the Earl of Clarendon giving his objections to Mr. Knox. The King had been so violent then that she had thought he would do her physical harm. She had barred herself behind locked doors and windows for three days. Afterward she had laughed at herself, and in retrospect her fears had seemed imaginary. Yet had they been? Or had she sensed an actual peril that had passed when the King's anger passed?

For a long while she had believed that the Kralahome would act as a brake on the King's impetuosity. But her relations with the Kralahome had ceased to be cordial. His half-brother, the interpreter, had told her long ago that he would prejudice his brother against her. She had come to believe that he had succeeded. She no longer felt that she could depend on the Kralahome for help.

She had become aware of the change when she called with one of her "clients" to see him. A Chinese man had been murdered and robbed by a favorite slave in the household of the Kralahome's brother, leaving his wife and children in helpless poverty. The murderer had screened himself by sharing the plunder with his master. The widow sought redress in vain. The ears of the magistrates were stopped against her by the high position of the Kralahome's family, and she was too poor to pay her way. Still she went from one court to another, until she annoyed a judge so much that he had her eldest son seized and imprisoned on some pretext. She came to Anna in wild despair, wailing and praying for help. Anna secured the release of the son, but to protect him she had to take him into her own household and change his name. "Timothy," Anna called him, and "Ti" he became.

The next step was to go with the woman to see the Kralahome and try to recover some of the stolen property. The premier was sitting on the floor playing chess when they arrived. Seeing Anna enter, he sent a slave for a jacket which he put on. She remembered the time when he had not thought she rated this courtesy. He paid no further attention to her, however, until he had finished his game of chess.

When she had explained her errand he seemed vexed, but sent for his brother. They had a long talk in low tones. At the end the Kralahome frowned at the Chinese widow and warned her that if she made any more complaints to the judges he would have her flogged. Facing Anna with a grim smile he said, "Chinese too much bother. Good-by, sir."

It was the first time Anna had ever known him to be deliberately un-just. It could mean only that his brother had prevailed and that she could no longer look to him for redress. The evening of that same day as she sat alone in her drawing room, she had heard a slight noise. Looking around, she saw to her surprise the interpreter crouching by the piano.

"How dare you come into my house unannounced?" she demanded.

"Mem," he said, "your servants admitted me. They know from whom I come, and would not venture to refuse me. And now it is for you to know that I am here from His Excellency the Kralahome, to request you to send in your resignation at the end of this month."

"And by what authority does he send me this message?" she had asked.

"I know not. But it were best that you obey."

"Tell him," she had replied, "that I shall leave Siam when I please, and that no man shall set the time for me!"

The interpreter had departed cringing and excusing himself from any share in the matter. She had not slept that night. Again and again pru-dence had advised her to seek safety in flight, but in the morning she had decided to stay. She would not be driven out! Her friends in the Palace had been alarmed for her security, but she had laughed at their fears. About three weeks later when the King was going up-country and had told her that she was to accompany her pupils, the Kralahome had been required to prepare a cabin for her and Louis on his yacht, the *Volant*. Before they left the Palace Lady Son Klin had begged her to promise that she would eat no food or take anything to drink on board the steamer.

These and other incidents raced through Anna's mind now as she sat deep in thought. It had not been time to go then, but perhaps it was time now. She hated to leave her pupils just as she was seeing so much im-provement in them. Still she could not do as the King insisted she must. It was probably better to resign and go with Louis to London, or, as some of her friends had urged, especially Francis Cobb, go to the United States and build a new life.

She was suddenly recalled to her surroundings by what at first she imagined must be an apparition or some delusion of her tired mind. She realized that for hours she had been sitting like a statue staring at an open window. She started up. A pair of black eyes were watching her through the leaves of some flowering shrubs with the fixedness of a basilisk. Anna's first impulse was to scream for help, her second to choke down the panic that had risen in her. How timid she was becoming! If the person outside were an assassin, a knife could have reached her heart long since. Sum-moning all her courage she demanded, "Who's there?"

"It's only me, your ladyship," said a low voice, a woman's but not familiar. "I've been waiting for a long while, but your servants won't let me see you. They say you've forbidden them to let any Siamese person enter."

"Yes, that's true," Anna said. "I don't want to see anyone at all this evening, not even my friends. I'm ill and tired. Now go away, and if you have business with me come back in the morning."

"*Phutho!*" said the woman, still in a low tone. "I'm not a Siamese, and I don't live in Bangkok. You wouldn't have the heart to send me away if you knew that I'd rowed thirty miles against the tide to see you."

Another client, Anna thought in despair. And on what a night, of all nights! She said a little impatiently: "There isn't any use in telling me your business. I don't even want to know what it is. Now, you simply must go! It's not safe for you to walk about the city at this late hour."

"But, Mem *cha*, please let me come in for just a minute. All I want is to say one word to you in private, just one! And then I'll promise to go away. Won't you let me come in?" The woman's voice was more and more pleading, her face still in the heavy shadows.

Anna compromised. "Say what you want to tell me now, then," she answered shortly, annoyed with herself for melting even this much. "There's no one around who could overhear you. I'm not going to let you in, no matter what you want."

"*Phutho! Phutho!*" the woman said reproachfully, as if to herself. "I wouldn't have rowed all this long distance alone if I hadn't heard that she was a good woman, and a brave woman, too. Of course, some people said that she was not. Still I thought I would try her. After all, what I wanted was so little! And now she says she can't let me in! A poor fugitive and desolate slave girl like me! They said she was kind and that she had helped many people, but, no, she will not give me five minutes of her time, or listen to my request. *Phutho!*"

Even though Anna knew that it was a performance, and a very good one, she was touched, partly by the woman's genuinely despairing tone, and partly by the ruse she had employed to present her case. "I'm afraid I can't help you, whatever your trouble is," she said kindly. "The King is angry with me and the judges know it, so I have no more influence with them."

The woman seemed to recognize the change in tone. Anna had hardly finished speaking before the stranger had put her hands on the sill and vaulted through the open window. As she had said, she was not a Siamese. She was a Lao. Her hair was pulled back from her forehead in the style of the northern people. Her eyes were bright and intelligent. She held her head erect, although her hands were clasped in the attitude of supplication. She was unusually tall and strong, with handsome regular features and a look of character. Anna saw at once this was no ordinary person, and almost against her will felt her interest kindle. The Lao woman's *pasin* was held by a wide English belt, which showed off her beautiful figure to the best advantage.

The moment she stood before Anna she began to talk with a fluency and gestures that were amazing. Anna had become so accustomed to Siamese restraint that she was bewildered by the animation with which the Lao woman spoke. Tears flowed spontaneously down her face and her voice rose and fell in passionate cadences.

The whole time she was speaking, however, she watched Anna's face with a shrewdness which suggested that she would vary her approach if the effect were not satisfactory. Even while Anna realized this, her interest increased so rapidly that the Lao woman noticed her altered expression and came to the conclusion she had gained the entire sympathy of her listener.

"There," said the slave, "I knew from your face that you had a kind heart in spite of your words." She came forward with a graceful salutation and laid a thick letter in a velvet envelope at Anna's feet. It was fastened with silk cords and sealed with English sealing wax. The writing on the outside was not in Siamese, but in some characters unknown to Anna.

The woman dropped to her knees and raised her hands in supplication. "Mem *chao kha*," she said softly, "all that I ask is that you take this letter into the Palace to a woman, whose name I will tell you, if you agree." Anna tried to say that she could not undertake so dangerous an errand, but she found herself unable to speak. The woman continued to kneel before her. She was immobile, yet there was such vehement pleading in her dark eyes that it was hard to resist the impact of her will. Her joined hands implored Anna's help in a daring scheme, which Anna had neither the courage to undertake, nor the hardness of heart to refuse.

Why did people ask these impossible things of her? As gently as she could she told the Lao woman that it was as much as her life was worth to carry a letter to a woman in the Palace. The slave had said the woman was a prisoner. Well, that was a hundred times more difficult. Then she added: "It's not only for my personal safety that I am afraid. It's for my son's also. His father is dead, and if anything happened to me there would be no one to look after him."

As Anna spoke the woman's features grew rigid. Her color receded until her appearance was that of a death's head. Perspiration broke out on her forehead, and she swayed as if she were about to faint. Anna's resolution to be firm and sensible melted before the slave's utter desolation. With a kind of despair at her own vulnerability she began to chafe the woman's cold hands. "Does your letter matter so much?" she asked. But the woman was past the power of speech. She looked at Anna dumbly. With a last stab of remorse for her own weakness Anna cried, "Oh, for goodness' sake, tell me what your trouble is, and I'll do my best to help you."

The effect of the promise was immediate. A look of life came into the slave's eyes and her color slowly returned. She laid her hand on the Englishwoman's arm, gasped and spoke hurriedly, as if she feared that Anna might change her mind. "You haven't asked my name or who I am," she said, "but I'll tell you anyway. I'm sure you won't betray me. My name is Mae Pia and my home is in Chiengmai. The name of my father is Manitho, and he is one of the most trusted councillors of Prince Sarawong, although he is a slave, too. My mother was a slave in the family of the prince when my father secured her for his wife, and I was only a month old when she was asked to nurse the baby daughter of the prince, whose own mother died when she was born. We grew up together, and that is how it happened that I became the companion and friend of my foster-sister." She paused briefly, then abandoned her last reserve. "She is the Princess Sunatda Wismita."

It was Anna's turn to start. The mysterious Princess of Chiengmai! She had heard just yesterday that the Prince of Chiengmai had come to Bangkok with a retinue of twenty-five boats to pay the triennial tribute. He was earlier than expected.

As usual his turbulent personality had involved him in controversy. He was the defendant in a lawsuit over some extensive teak forests in his principality. The plaintiffs were an English firm from Moulmein, and the case was of such proportions that Mr. Knox had gone to Burma the year before to see about it personally. There had been a rumor afloat in Bangkok for some months that the prince was flirting with the idea of transferring his allegiance to the King of Burma. He was known to have sent a gift of two elephants to Ava just recently. They were not white elephants —that would have been open treason—but they had white patches around their eyes and peculiar tails. The King of Burma had been enchanted with them and had more than repaid the value of the gift with a present of gold jewelry set with rubies. This cordial rapprochement had not pleased King Mongkut. Now the Prince of Chiengmai had appeared boldly in the capital. Mae Pia had undoubtedly come down the river in his retinue.

The slave continued her story: *"Phutho! Phutho!* Mem *cha,* the princess has been a prisoner in the Palace of the King ever since the death of her husband. Two of her serving women are with her, we think, but we have heard nothing from any of them for almost a year."

Anna was sitting up straight now, her pulse beating rapidly. Could it be true that the princess was in the Palace? And if so, why had she not heard about it? She had been very much interested in the princess because of her rumored defiance of the King. Surely if the princess had been transferred to the regular prison the whole Inside would have seethed with the news, for little was ever concealed there successfully.

Mae Pia was speaking: ". . . and no one knows, not even her brother, whether she is alive or dead. This letter is for her, Mem *chao kha.* There is nothing in it that will bring you any trouble, even if it falls into the wrong hands. It is only a little note of greeting and sympathy from her brother, Prince Othong Karmatha, who is my master. Oh, Mem *chao kha,* the gods will surely reward you if you will deliver it to her! Sooner or later, it doesn't matter when. But it must be done with the greatest caution and secrecy! It may be the means of saving her life, at least it is our only chance. That is, if she is still living." As Anna looked incredulous at the contradiction between the importance the slave attached to the letter and its supposedly innocuous contents, Mae Pia hurriedly added: "Because she must be dying of grief and pain to think that we have never answered the letter she wrote us from Ban Sita before the Second King died."

Anna did not commit herself at once. The letter was thick, much too thick to be merely a note of greeting. Furthermore, the slave's unguarded words about "saving her life" were more suggestive of a scheme to effect the princess' escape than of condolence and encouragement. This was not a simple rescue like Son Klin's or even L'Ore's. Considering the importance of the people concerned, it was difficult to guess the extent of the intrigue lying back of the request that she deliver the letter. Mae Pia was acting for the royal family of Chiengmai. They were a haughty clan who chafed under King Mongkut's sovereignty. They must resent bitterly the imprisonment of the princess. Was King Mongkut actually holding her as a hostage? Was the gift of the elephants to the King of Burma a tacit threat to King Mongkut to release her or suffer the consequences of civil war? Something was afoot, and Anna hesitated to involve herself without knowing a good deal more.

"Where is the prince, your master?" she asked tentatively.

"He is on a visit to the Governor of Paklat." Hmmm! Anna thought. He was Lady Son Klin's father—another potential rebel—who had little reason to love King Mongkut.

Anna's indecision was apparent, but before she could ask another question, or accept or refuse the dangerous commission, Mae Pia was gone. With a swift, graceful movement she leaped through the window. As she jumped Anna saw in the folds of her skirt a short Lao dagger attached to the English belt.

The storm which had been gathering all day now burst in fury. For three hours thunder, lightning, and rain were all that could be seen or heard. Anna did not move from her chair. She sat full of a turmoil that matched the storm, revolving endlessly her new quarrel with the King, the interview with Mae Pia, the meaning of the red velvet envelope still lying at her feet, the curious fate of the Princess of Chiengmai and her own responsibility, if any, to a woman she had never seen. She wondered if the Lao woman were battling the storm on the tremendous currents of the river.

When the storm ended at last, well after midnight, Anna picked up the letter, closed the shutters, and went up to her room. She had reached no decision. For the time being she locked the letter in her leather trunk. Then she went to bed.

37

## THE TRIP TO PAKLAT

ANNA WOKE tired and unrefreshed. She debated the wisdom of staying at home until her status was clarified, but after careful thought decided that it would be better to continue with her normal routine as if nothing had happened. In her absence her assistant, Mae Prang, carried on very well. But if she did not go to school, her failure to appear would be reported to the King and might lead him to believe that he had succeeded in overawing her. Her success in dealing with him had been the result of her apparent fearlessness. More than once her friends of the harem had remarked on her temerity almost enviously. "Only a *farang* could do that!" they would exclaim. "*Farangs* are so bold!" Anna knew very well that she was not bold, but she had schooled herself to resist the appearance of weakness on the ground that her position and even her safety depended upon her ability to show always a cool and confident front.

She started out with Louis at the regular time and passed quickly within the wall of the Palace. A crowd of poor slaves, who lived outside the royal confines, was squatting near the inner gate waiting for it to open. They knew her well and greeted her with profound salaams. Lounging about the gate was a group of soldiers and rough-looking men whom Anna had never seen there before. It was broad daylight. Nervous as she was, there was nothing about them to warn her except their churlish appearance. She walked toward them confidently, never doubting that they would give way before her. Instead the whole group, including the soldiers, rushed at her shouting threats, thrusting her back violently. Stones appeared in their hands and their arms swung up. Anna was too taken by surprise to feel anything. She saw the jagged pieces of rock, the upraised arms, and in some distant area of her mind supposed she would experience their impact against her face and body almost immediately. Then suddenly she was surrounded by a warm rush of humanity. The crowd of slaves had leaped shouting to her defense. They pressed close to her and Louis on all sides, interposing their own bodies between them and their attackers. They began to edge her away from the gate. Still close around her and Louis they worked them out of the Palace and to their home, where they pushed them through the door, and shouted to the servants to come quickly. A few minutes more and the house was in a state of siege, all the doors and windows locked and barred.

As the anesthetic of shock wore off, Anna found herself very much shaken. Beebe hovered around her solicitously, never leaving her alone in the room. At lunch she tried to eat in order to reassure Louis, who was still frightened, but she had the greatest difficulty to keep from dropping her knife and fork. The water glass trembled in her fingers. Whenever Anna looked through the slats of the shutters she could see people idling near the house. Several men squatted for more than an hour at the edge of the road not far from her front door. She thought she saw someone hiding in the bushes. A few people came boldly to the door and knocked, but she had forbidden her servants to let anyone in.

Her first impulse was to write to the British Consul and tell him what had happened. She hesitated for several reasons. She had never yielded to the temptation to depend on consular protection in her dealings with the Siamese. It would look cowardly, and therefore contrary to her practice of outfacing her enemies, to do so now. Then, too, there would be complications if she invoked Mr. Knox's assistance. She and Louis often rode horseback with him on fine mornings along New Road, and regarded him as a friend. But the King disliked him and anything he said might only inflame the King against her further, while it was possible that by keeping perfectly quiet she could ride out the storm.

She did sit down at her desk and prepare a letter, in which she explained all that had happened since the previous morning—her quarrel with the King; the word that had come from the Palace that the King had openly incited his courtiers to attack her; the assault of the men at the gate, and the fact that people were lurking near the house. She sealed and addressed the letter, ready to send if any attack were made on her.

Then she had one of her servants go for a carpenter to install iron bars at all the windows, so that she could resist entry long enough to send for help—if it came to that—and also get some sleep at night. She had never felt the need of bars before, but the ease with which Mae Pia had jumped into her living room had convinced her that they were a wise precaution.

After that she wrote to Captain John Bush. The circular referred to in the King's list of accusations had been in Captain Bush's hands. In fact, it had annoyed the American Consul very much. Mr. Hood had come to Bangkok only the fall before, and was extremely careful to maintain the dignity of his position. He had felt insulted by having his name written at the bottom of the circular while the British Consul's and Mrs. Leonowens' names appeared at the top. Anna recalled the incident because she had had a good deal of sympathy with the American Consul's resentment. Her own name certainly should not have appeared above his. She knew that she had not been responsible, and that her handwriting appeared nowhere on the circular. She thought she had a clear memory of whose hand-writing did. In her note she asked Captain Bush merely to try to find the circular, if it was still in his possession, since some trouble concerning it had come up between herself and the King.

He arrived that evening, still her cheerful, red-faced friend of the first day in Bangkok. "Here it is, Mem," he said, holding it out to her. Ah, good! She had been right, she saw. "But what do you want it for?"

"All I want you to do is to take it and give it to the King."

Mystified and somewhat amused, he agreed. With difficulty she per-suaded Phra Alak, who lived nearby, to arrange an immediate audience for Captain Bush. Phra Alak was still annoyed by her refusal of his request on the day before. She reminded him rather sharply of the number of times she had befriended him when he was in trouble with His Majesty, and at last he consented.

Admitted to the King's presence, Captain Bush handed him the cir-cular. "Mem Leonowens tells me that you want to see this," he said simply.

The King looked at him questioningly, but the smiling Englishman had no explanation since Anna had given him none. His Majesty took the circular and examined it carefully. His face went blank, then bewildered, then a disgruntled expression appeared. He put his hand to his brow. The handwriting was his own!

"I have forgotten," he said bemused.

Captain Bush was back at Anna's house in a short while, chuckling at the discomfiture of the King. "Now tell me what it's all about," he de-manded. And Anna did. "And was there something about a book, too?" he asked.

"Yes," she said, "the King accused me of stealing a book from his library."

"That makes it perfect!" And Captain Bush threw back his head in a roar of laughter. "While I was there a little princess came crawling into the room with a book in her hand, and said something about finding it in one of the sleeping apartments. His Majesty looked more upset than ever and made a remark about thinking that you had it. I didn't get the connection."

The captain had brought assurance from the King of a cordial reconciliation. But Anna hesitated. Surely it would take a little longer for such titanic anger to wear off!

She reopened her doors and windows cautiously, but she did not enter the Palace for several weeks.

When the *Chow Phya* arrived with foreign mail, the King summoned her to return to her duties. She obeyed quietly, saying nothing. She sat down at her familiar table and began copying the pile of letters that the King had written. After a little he approached her. She did not look up.

"Mem, you are one great difficulty!" he said in a reproachful tone. "I have much pleasure and favor on you, but you are too obstinate. You are not wise. Wherefore are you so difficult? You are only a woman. It is very bad you can be so strongheaded. Will you now have any objection to write to Sir John and tell him I am his very good friend?"

Anna could not help but smile at this evasion of the issue between them. "None whatever, Your Majesty," she answered pleasantly, "if all you want is a letter of good wishes."

She wrote the letter and handed it to him for his perusal and signature. He wasn't satisfied. He had hoped that she would yield. His face showed it. With a grunt he returned the letter to her and left the apartment to vent his annoyance on someone less stiff-necked than his "one great difficulty."

In spite of this not-too-hopeful beginning the reconciliation was complete so far as the King was concerned. He took Anna into greater confidence than ever before. He had one of his recurring bouts of illness and was confined to the topmost chamber of the Palace for weeks. She was summoned there every day to write notes, or to translate English documents into the vernacular with the help of a Siamese woman secretary.

All this time the letter that Mae Pia had left at Anna's feet lay in its red velvet envelope in the leather chest. In the gossip that floated around her as she went her way in the streets and homes of the Inside there was no hint of the imprisonment of the Chiengmai princess. Anna began to wonder if Mae Pia had not been misinformed, and if the princess were not confined in the palace of the Second King—if she still lived. Anna was afraid to say much to her friends of the harem about the matter. There might be danger to herself and to the princess in any undue interest on her part. She went only so far as to inquire of Lady Son Klin whether anything had ever been heard of the Princess Sunatda, and she said no in a hurried, uncertain way that showed she did not wish to discuss the subject. The Prince of Chiengmai was still in Bangkok. His retinue was anchored across the river at Wat Arun (Temple of the Dawn), where they always stayed.

Then one day when Anna was working in a room that adjoined the royal bedchamber she heard Mae Ying Thahan come up to wait upon the King. Anna had been struggling with a mass of perplexing documents in the King's own handwriting, which she had been ordered to prepare for publication in the Bangkok *Recorder*. His Majesty had been in the best possible humor all morning. The manuscript on which Anna was working was a reply to Dr. Bradley's theory of Original Depravity. These two crusty gentlemen of advanced years, the King and the doctor, were sparring through the columns of the newspaper.

Dr. Bradley had come to Bangkok in 1835 and had been intimate with the King during his long seclusion in the priesthood. From their first meeting they had had long and involved theological arguments, each determined to convince the other of the flaws in his religion. The King was delighted with the idea that his newest paper completely refuted Dr. Bradley's theory and would put the reverend gentleman properly in his place. He had been chuckling to himself all morning at the thought of the devastation he was making of the doctor's arguments.

Through the thin walls Anna heard the chief of the Amazons crawl into the room next door, and without approaching too close to the sacred person of the King, tell him in a voice which carried clearly that the prisoner, Princess Sunatda Wismita, was very ill. "Let the princess be taken for an airing in the gardens, then," he replied cheerfully. "And transfer her to a better cell. Also order the chief physician to attend her."

The Amazon crawled out backward and started down the stairs. Noiselessly Anna rose from her table and tiptoed after her, being careful to keep the Amazon in sight without letting her know that she was being followed. Mae Ying Thahan walked through the harem streets rapidly, only pausing now and then to drop to her knees as some great lady approached and passed. Anna saw that she was moving toward the central prison where long ago Anna had gone for the first time to find Lady Son Klin. The Amazon disappeared through the gate of the rambling structure. Anna did not try to enter, but stood a little distance from the door and waited.

An idle crowd of slave women and girls were lounging about. Any opening of the prison door attracted their interest. Other slaves passing on errands pressed close to swell the group. No one seemed to know what was about to happen, but all welcomed the slightest event that broke the monotony of their lives. The street was soon choked with spectators. Anna stood back and watched until a guard of Amazons appeared from the prison, marching in file. In the center of the group moved a Lao woman, obviously the princess, followed by two of her countrywomen. She did not seem to notice the sensation which her appearance created, but walked composedly as if she were alone. She looked depressed and ill, withdrawn into the privacy of her sorrow.

The crowd fell in behind her and Anna with them. When the procession reached the nearest garden, which was laid out in Chinese style, the princess intimated with a proud gesture that she could go no farther. She sat down on the edge of an artificial rock beside a pond of water in which goldfish were swimming. She hung her head indifferently, as if the air had no power to revive her. Her beautiful features were set in stern lines, her face stamped with sadness.

A murmur of compassion arose from the crowd of women and girls, who were gazing awe-stricken at the face of the princess about whom everyone had heard for years. Even the Amazons were expressing guarded sympathy. For the first time the princess seemed to become aware that she was surrounded by people. Anna could just see that she raised her dark eyes to the crowd and then lowered them again.

After an hour the procession re-formed, and the crowd stirred. They had exchanged looks and whispers of pity to their hearts' content. Some half-palsied and aged slave women had lifted up their hands and prayed aloud for the ill-fated princess. As the Amazons moved off, the crowd of slaves fell in behind until they saw the prison doors open and close once more. Then at last they hurried away to their homes with the news.

When Anna returned home to lunch she could not put the picture of the princess out of her mind, the utter friendlessness expressed in her few slight actions. She knew now the princess was alive and where she was. This reopened the question of the red velvet letter. If the message had been oral Anna would have felt that she could undertake delivering it, but a written message might be anything. She did not believe Mae Pia's assurance that the letter was merely one of greeting and encouragement. The Prince of Chiengmai, Mae Pia herself—who could guess what reckless scheme they were plotting? Did Anna want to be their intermediary? If she carried the letter to the princess she must do it with her eyes open to the fact that she was conniving against the King. What sort of end would justify that means? Or was human need such as she had seen in the face of the princess justification enough?

When Anna started back to school the letter was pinned in her pocket. She had decided to call on Lady Thiang, and perhaps consult with her. But how was she to broach the subject to the head wife in the presence of the women who attended her at all times?

Anna turned in at the house with the quaint stuccoed front and the pleasant garden, her problem of seeing Lady Thiang privately still unresolved. They had been confederates in many little plots, but never in one where the stake was so large, or the person involved so important. Lady

Thiang might be quite unwilling to interfere between the King and the princess. It was not difficult, however, to make an occasion for a call and then trust to intuition. Lady Thiang was expecting her tenth child and Anna often stopped by to see how she was.

She received Anna with her usual bright smile. She put down one of her younger children, Prince Chaiyanuchit, who had been a tiny baby when Anna came to the Palace for the first time, and embraced Anna heartily. Little Chai settled himself in Anna's lap as usual. When he was two she had begun to teach him bits of English nursery rhymes and sentences, and he always greeted her, "Mem, Mem, how do do?" or "Mem, make a bow, make a bow," and bobbed his little head, blinking his bright eyes at her to the infinite delight of his mother and her maids.

The women in the room gathered around Anna's chair to listen to her English baby talk with Chai. "Baa-baa black sheep . . ." she began, and "Baa-baa black sheep . . ." Chai repeated after her. There was a roar of laughter when he followed her line by line through a little song, and then stopped her mouth with an orange. His offering! He jumped from her lap and put on her hat and cloak and strutted up and down the room saying, "How do do? How do do?" His mother snatched him up and covered him with kisses. And the women whispered, audibly to please Lady Thiang, that he was as clever as his father, and would surely come to the throne some day. In the midst of the laughter one of the physicians was announced.

Lady Thiang retired at once to an inner room with the physician, carrying Chai in her arms and beckoning Anna to follow. There she gave Chai to Anna and lay down to be massaged. Here was the opportunity that Anna had hoped for, almost miraculously provided. But she waited a little in order to make sure whether the doctor was to be trusted.

The women were silent for several minutes. Lady Thiang sighed and grunted a little, as the physician manipulated first one part of her body and then another. Anna waited, then suddenly realized that the women were also waiting. From their glances she saw that the physician had something to say to Lady Thiang, and that the latter had not given her the signal to proceed. She, too, seemed to be waiting—no doubt for the end of Anna's visit. Anna pretended not to see the interplay. She bounced Chai on her lap and sang a little song to him. After a while, seeing that Anna made no move to go, Lady Thiang said to the doctor in Siamese, "Never mind, speak out. It's perfectly all right. You don't need to be afraid!" which of course Anna understood perfectly.

The doctor ceased her manipulations, and after a cautious glance around the room, shook her head. "I don't think she'll live much longer," she said.

Lady Thiang sat bolt upright and clasped her hands together. *"Phutho!"* she exclaimed.

"It's impossible!" the doctor added in a low, earnest voice. "It would be better to put her to death at once than to kill her by inches the way they are doing."

"Great Buddha in heaven, help us!" Lady Thiang cried softly in profound agitation. "What shall I do? Can she be saved?"

"Something will have to be done at once if at all," the doctor replied.

"Well, why don't you draw up a paper and give it to Mae Ying Thahan? And be sure to say that she can't live twenty-four hours longer unless she's removed from that closet and allowed to have an airing every day. Poor child! Poor child!" Lady Thiang repeated. "With such a noble heart, and now to die like this. We must find some way of helping her live a little longer, until things look brighter. There must be something we can do!"

"He's forgotten all about her by this time," rejoined the doctor with a sniff, preparing to go.

Anna had been playing with Chai as if she had no concern with the conversation. After the doctor had closed the door she turned to Lady Thiang and spoke softly but directly. "Were you talking about the Princess Sunatda Wismita?"

The head wife jumped up in alarm and looked at Anna as if she supposed the Englishwoman was endowed with supernatural power to unravel mysteries. "How did you know her name?" she demanded. "We never mentioned it."

Anna told her swiftly about Mae Pia's visit and the red velvet letter. "If she's really dying, as the doctor says, surely there'd be no harm in letting her have the letter. Couldn't you send it to her? You spoke just now of finding some way to stimulate her interest in life until you could help her." Lady Thiang shook her head. "Then let me take the letter to her myself!"

Lady Thiang sat on the edge of the couch, sunk in thought. "We are all prisoners here, dear friend," she said at last, "and we have to be careful what we do. But if you promise never to say a word on this subject to anyone, and in case of discovery to take all the blame yourself, whatever it may be, I'll help you."

"Of course," Anna said. "I promise gladly."

Lady Thiang looked at Anna steadily. Her black hair made her ivory face even whiter than it was. It was a broad face, not pretty, but charming, with soft, very dark eyes, and a firm pleasant mouth. "You mustn't think that I'm just weak and selfish, Mem *cha*," she said after reflecting a little, laying her hand on Anna's as if pleading for understanding. "You are a *farang*, and HE hasn't the same power over you. You can go away whenever you like. But we must stay here and suffer HIS will and pleasure, no matter what happens."

Anna nodded. "I know," she said, "oh, certainly I know."

**317**

"Come back after sunset, and I'll tell you whether it is safe to deliver the letter tonight."

When it was quite dark Anna returned to Lady Thiang's house. The head wife hurried out to meet her before the household should see her.

"It's arranged, Mem *cha*," she whispered in an exulting voice, "and the doctor's report has made things much better. The princess has been moved into a good cell where there is some air from a window." She summoned two slaves and told them to go with Anna and instruct the Amazons that Anna might visit the princess. This was a courageous thing for her to do. Anna had expected only that the Amazons would have been prepared in a roundabout way for her visit and would admit her as they had before on the payment of a small sum to each guard.

The slaves moved rapidly and silently through the quiet streets, Anna following. At the door of the prison they said a few hurried words and melted into the night. Quickly and without ceremony Anna was conducted to a small apartment. The Amazon ushered her in, not having spoken at all, and closed the door. The room was dimly lighted by a wick burning in an earthen vessel. There was one window, heavily barred. The shutters had been thrown open and a little warm air stirred feebly. Beneath the window on wooden trestles a narrow plank had been laid and covered with a flowered mat and satin pillow. On this lay the wasted form of the Princess Sunatda.

Her dress was that of a Lao lady of high rank. She wore a scarlet silk *pasin*, gold encrusted, reaching to her feet, and a flowered black silk vest. A long veil of Indian gauze was across her shoulders. Around her neck was a heavy gold chain, and on her fingers several rings, obviously of great value. Her hair was combed smoothly back from her forehead and bound in a massive knot behind. This was circled by a tiara of diamond-headed pins. She was not nearly so beautiful as the slave Mae Pia, to Anna's way of thinking. But when the Englishwoman looked closely she caught the defiant, heroic pride that flashed from the princess' melancholy eyes. Whether the face was beautiful or not, it was one never to be forgotten.

At her feet were two other crude beds, and seated on them were the women who were her maids-in-waiting. Anna walked across the cell and took a seat near the group. The princess, who had been gazing at the little glimpse of sky which could be seen through the iron bars, turned to Anna. Her look was quiet and self-absorbed. She showed neither interest nor displeasure at seeing that a stranger had entered her apartment. No one said anything. Anna was at a loss how to start the conversation. She began in the conventional way by inquiring after the princess' health.

"I am well," the princess said indifferently. "Pray, why have you come here?"

"I have an important private message for you," Anna replied.

"Is that true?" the princess asked, looking for confirmation at the women rather than Anna.

Anna herself answered unhesitatingly. "Yes, it is. I've come to you as one woman to another, because of your trouble."

The princess looked at her strangely as if the words made no sense. "How can that be?" she asked in a haughty tone. "You must know, madam, that women are not just women. Some are born to high station, and some are born slaves." She pronounced the words slowly in the court language of Siam.

Anna took no umbrage at the words. "Yes, that's true," she said gently. "We're not all alike. There are many kinds of women. And I have come here because a very brave one asked me to. It wasn't out of any idle curiosity I might have felt about you, but because I didn't see how I could refuse Mae Pia's request."

"Mae Pia? What did you say?" The princess jumped up from her bed, her whole face illuminated, and threw her arms around Anna's neck as if they had been friends for years. She laid a hot cheek on Anna's and whispered, "Tell me! Tell me! Did you say Mae Pia?"

Anna drew the red velvet envelope out of her pocket and put it into the princess' hands. Such a look of joy came into her face that it was as if a crystal chandelier had suddenly bloomed with light in a dark room. The change from despair to joy made her supremely beautiful. With nervous movements she tore open the velvet covering and pulled out the letter, leaning toward the earthen lamp to read it. There was a soft flush on her pale face in the flickering lamplight. She smiled as she finished and turned to speak to the other women in a language unknown to Anna.

After this the three Lao talked together for a long time, the two attendants obviously urging their mistress to do something that she apparently would not consent to do. At last she threw the letter angrily away and covered her face with her hands, as if she were unable to resist their arguments but refused to hear them longer.

The elder of the women took up the letter quietly and read its contents several times aloud to her companion. She then opened a betel-box and drew out an inkhorn, a small reed and a long roll of yellow paper. In a labored script she began a letter, now and then rubbing out words with her finger and beginning again. She seemed to go on endlessly, consulting her companion several times. The princess lay on the bed looking out of the window as before. When the letter was finished it was unsightly and so blotted that Anna wondered if anyone could decipher its message. The woman folded it carefully, and put it into a blue silk cover which she took from the betel-box. Then she stitched the bag shut and sewed a piece of paper on the outside. This she addressed in the same characters that the red velvet envelope had borne. When her work was finished she handed it to Anna with a hopeful smile.

Only then did the princess turn and speak to Anna again. "Did Mae Pia promise you any money?"

"Certainly not!"

"Do you want any money?"

"No, thank you," said Anna as haughtily as the princess herself. "But you'll have to tell me to whom the letter is addressed because I cannot read the writing. I'll do everything possible to see that it gets to its destination, and to be of service to you in any other way to the best of my ability."

The princess seemed quite overwhelmed. She got up from her bed again and embraced Anna in the most affectionate manner, thanking her again and again, and told her she would bless her continually in her thoughts. Then she asked Anna to deliver the letter into the hands of Mae Pia or her brother, Prince Othong, but to no one else.

"Where will I find them?"

The princess whispered her answer, evidently afraid that one of the Amazons might be eavesdropping. "They're at the house of the Governor of Paklat, in hiding. Or they were when they sent the letter to me. If they have gone, he will know where to find them."

The next problem was how to get to Paklat. It was a town many miles down the river from Bangkok, not far from Paknam where the River Chow Phya emptied into the gulf. Anna had been there before. It was a picturesque village with six or seven thousand inhabitants. The most important section of the town faced a bend of the great river. A magnificent temple was gradually rising beside an ancient one so crumbled to decay that the sun poured down unchecked on the tapering crown of the huge brass Buddha, which sat undisturbed, its hands folded. As far as the eye could reach stretched groves of bananas, plantations of coconut and betel palms; gardens of mango and tamarind; banyan and box trees so old that they seemed to have weathered a thousand summers.

Paklat had one drawback, however, a very serious one. There was an open *sala* in the village which had long been a rendezvous for rough seamen from the English and American vessels that traded with Bangkok. In consequence it was set down in the code of etiquette of the élite of Bangkok that Paklat was "a dreadfully improper place for a lady to visit alone."

It was out of the question for Anna to go there without an escort, and she didn't want to attract attention by asking anyone to accompany her. Some chance remark from an English friend might arouse suspicion in the minds of the Siamese. She had known for a long time that she was closely watched, although she had never discovered who among her acquaintances were the spies reporting on her every move to the King.

Luckily, one of the Frenchmen in Bangkok, M. Louis Malherbe, who had been ill, had been sent to Paklat for a change of air by Dr. Campbell of the British Consulate. Louis was very fond of Mme. Malherbe, and had written Avis the year before:

> I know a pretty lady and her name is Madame Malherbe. She cannot talk English. She calls me *le beau* Louis. When Mama crys and is naughty and wont do as I tell her I call her *une Mauvaise Sugete*.

Unfortunately Mme. Malherbe was now in France, which made calling on her husband less easy in the tight little circle of Bangkok. But Anna could not invent a better excuse. M. Lamache, the drill master, was planning to go down the river to see M. Malherbe. His wife was going along and Anna asked permission to accompany them, pleading her desire to take Louis on a little excursion, and exhibiting polite interest in M. Malherbe, since "Louis is devoted to Madame, as you know." It was not quite good enough, and Anna had to endure a great deal of teasing from her friends. They made themselves very gay at her expense, accusing her of having designs on the invalid, warning her facetiously that his wife would be back presently. She accepted the teasing in good grace and explained nothing.

At five o'clock on the morning of the day M. Lamache had set, with the blue letter pinned in her pocket, she and Louis climbed into the launch with their host and hostess and set out. The trip down the river was very pleasant. They arrived at Paklat in time for breakfast with M. Malherbe. Anna ate quickly, rather enjoying the feeling of intrigue. It couldn't be real, this thing she was doing. It was going too smoothly, like something out of a book. She had even been able to devise a natural reason for leaving the party. She explained that she had promised to call on Lady Son Klin's father, the governor, and excused herself easily. She left Louis in charge of Mme. Lamache and hurried off to the governor's house.

He received her very kindly, inquiring for his daughter and grandson. She told him immediately the object of her visit, and learned that the prince and Mae Pia were still in hiding with him. He led her through long halls and corridors, which brought them out of the mansion to an old tower, covered with moss and black with age, surrounded by a deep moat full of stagnant water. There were only narrow loopholes for windows. From the roof two flights of steps built into the wall led down to ruined drawbridges. One was connected with the governor's palace, and the other with a low arched gateway which opened on a canal that in turn had access to the river. It was easy to see the tower had been designed for a refuge, or at least that it was a good one. Two boats were tied on the moat at the foot of the stairs as if ready for an emergency.

The governor left Anna standing at the low wall that skirted the moat and crossed the crumbling drawbridge. He entered the tower through an arched doorway. The door was ponderous and thick, and looked scarred and pitted as if it had already withstood more than one siege.

In a few minutes Mae Pia came running out, crying, "Oh, Mem *cha,* Mem *cha!* I'm so glad to see you! Oh, I love you! I love you dearly for coming! Here, you must come in and see the prince himself!"

She pulled Anna after her into the toppling fortress. They passed through a large room that had once been painted vermilion, but was discolored where the rain had beaten in. The walls were hung with rusty Indian armor of an antique style—shields, banners, spears, swords, bows and arrows, lances. They were so immense that Anna thought they must have been wielded by the Yak of the *Ramayana* long before the epoch of the present race. It was like something out of a fantastic dream. Passing from the hall they entered a smaller room, the walls of which had been painted with gigantic flowers, birds, and animals. The crocodile was the most conspicuous. This room contained a bed of state that looked like the workmanship of Bombay craftsmen. It reached to the ceiling and had a curtain of flowered kincob. The glimmering light and the reflections from the dark green water of the moat shifted across the walls in waves of iridescence that increased the feeling of unreality which gripped Anna. First one and then another of the mammoth flowers or birds or animals on the wall would be caught for a second in the rolling illumination.

One of the three dark young men sitting in the room stood up and came to greet Anna. She recognized him at once from his likeness to Princess Sunatda. "Welcome, brave friend, welcome!" he said bowing gracefully. With an excitement he could not quite control he inquired whether Anna had seen his sister.

"Yes, I saw her just a few days ago. She has been moved into an upstairs cell with a window, and her two maids-in-waiting are with her." As Anna began to speak Mae Pia drew near to listen, intense anxiety in her face. "She has been ill, but I think that she will be better now that she has heard from you. And she is to be permitted an occasional airing in the Palace gardens." They pressed Anna for every detail of her visit, and when she produced the blue silk envelope they were inexpressibly delighted.

As the prince read the letter to himself the others watched him apprehensively. When he had finished he read it aloud. "Mae Pia" were the only words that Anna understood, but she saw two big drops fall from the eyes of the prince on the blotted yellow paper, and his voice died away in a whisper as he concluded his reading and sat down again. The whole party was silent, each absorbed in his own thoughts, for what seemed like an hour. The prince sat with his eyes on the ceiling as if in prayer. Mae Pia crept to his side and kept her eyes fixed on his face. It was a weak face, impetuous and vacillating, deeply troubled now. It made a striking contrast to Mae Pia's, which was strong with an unshakable determination. There are times when one almost knows what is passing through the minds of other people, Anna thought. In the silent room ripples of green light shifted along the wall while an argument took place, although not a word was spoken. The prince's position made the final decision his, and he was afraid. But Mae Pia was not! She knelt beside him, willing him to agree to something that had been discussed so many times that it did not need to be framed in speech again. The force of her spirit stirred the prince uneasily. Anna knew how powerful that spirit was. She had felt its impact on herself. She watched Mae Pia with admiration. What a woman she was!

It was time for Anna to go. She had expected to be asked to carry a reply to the princess, but nothing had been written. The prince begged Anna to take something from him by way of compensation. She declined. He asked her to see his sister again, if it were possible, and tell her about the trip to Paklat. He sent also a message of love, comfort, and hope, but no letter.

Mae Pia conducted Anna to the governor's residence. She thanked Anna again and again for delivering the red velvet letter and bringing the reply. "Tell the princess to keep up her courage," she pleaded. "I don't know exactly what I'm going to do next, but something is going to be done to save her, even if I die for it. Tell her that!"

"Oh, Mae Pia," Anna objected, "be careful! You mustn't do anything rash. It would be better to wait patiently a while longer and see how things come out."

Mae Pia shook her head. "No, I'm going to do something. Soon, I hope. But sooner or later, anyway. Tell her that!"

"But, Mae Pia, she's in the prison. Even if you could get into the Palace, you couldn't get into the prison."

The slave only smiled.

The day that had begun brightly was now overcast. The tide had turned and was running toward Bangkok. M. Lamache would be impatient to start the trip back. Anna could wait to argue no longer, and besides it seemed futile. Mae Pia would make her attempt, whatever it was, unless the prince forbade it. If diplomacy and bribery failed, the slave would try one desperate gamble to free her mistress. It could only fail, Anna thought sadly.

She looked back once at Mae Pia standing in the long corridor of the governor's palace with her hands folded and raised high above her head in salutation. "She's magnificent!" Anna thought, and tears brimmed her eyes, for she did not expect to see the slave alive again.

## 38

## THE PRINCESS OF CHIENGMAI

ANNA HAD little difficulty in arranging another interview with the princess through Lady Thiang. Apparently no harm had come from the first one, and if the King had learned of it through his omnipresent spies he had made no objection. The princess was still in the same cell, but she looked much stronger and happier.

"Did you see my brother and Mae Pia?" she asked excitedly as soon as the Amazon had withdrawn.

"Yes, I did. And they were very glad to have news of you. They are still at Paklat, and they send you their love." Then she told the princess and her serving women all that had happened on her visit downriver. They talked it over with great animation in their own language, and the princess asked Anna a number of questions. When Anna told her of Mae Pia's promise to try to rescue her, she shook her head. "No, that's impossible!" she murmured, and for a moment she drooped again. But with a quick return of her high spirits she began to tell Anna about Chiengmai and herself.

"It takes six weeks up the river by boat against the current to reach the city, although one can come down in a month at some seasons. Chiengmai is tributary to Siam now, but there was a time when my ancestors were the sovereigns of all the land lying between Burma and China and Siam. Chiengmai was a great kingdom in those days. It was King Phra Chao Othong Karmatha, after whom my brother was named, who founded the city many centuries ago. He built the great waterworks that still brings water to the people from the mountains.

"My brother and I are the only children of Prince Sarawong, the brother of the present King of Chiengmai. My mother died when I was born and Mae Pia's mother brought me up. So Mae Pia and I are sisters of the flesh, as well as of the spirit. My brother is seven years older than I. He is fond of all kinds of pleasure and sport, but he loves glory and honor and independence more. It makes him angry and humiliated whenever he remembers that our house has to pay homage to the King of Siam, whose grandfather, after all, was only a general. But we are no longer independent, and so every three years we are required to send down gold and silver trees as our homage of fealty.

"Three years ago my uncle did not come himself with the trees, but sent my brother instead. That was when my brother became friendly with the Second King of Siam. The Second King had been on good terms with our house for a long time, but my brother did not know him intimately before. They were both very fond of hunting, and while my brother was in Bangkok they became close friends.

"Buddha forbid that I should disparage the First King, but everyone who knew them both will tell you that the younger brother was much superior in every way," the princess continued proudly. "Soon after this the Second King came to our home on a visit, and went with my brother on many hunting expeditions. I wish I could describe to you my first meeting with the King. But there are no words for it. I had heard about him for years, and I loved him from the minute I saw him. If I could learn the language of the angels perhaps there would be adjectives in it to fit him. There is none good enough in any language I know.

"When he left us and returned to his palace at Saraburi, I had lost the key to existence. My brother seemed to understand what was wrong with me, and unknown to me he sent Mae Pia to Ban Sita to get employment in the prince's palace and try to learn whether he had the same feeling for me that I had for him. Mae Pia's mother went with her, and when they got to the palace they managed to get into the harem on the pretext of visiting some of their friends, for there were many Lao in the prince's entourage. While they were there Mae Pia took out her silver flute and began to play. Have you ever heard her play? No? She is the best musician in our country, and can perform on ten different kinds of instruments. And sing! You have never heard anything so exquisite as her music. Everyone gathered around to hear her and she charmed them all. Khun Klip happened to pass and she was enchanted, too, so she purchased Mae Pia from her mother for the prince's orchestra.

"In a few days Mae Pia was taken to perform before the prince. He was delighted with her wonderful skill. He was ill and confined to the palace, and he grew so fond of Mae Pia's singing and playing that he kept her beside him all the time where she could entertain him when he was too wretched for anything else. Then one day when she saw that she had been unusually fortunate in soothing the prince with her melodies, she asked him if she could sing him a song that she had written herself, which she had set to his favorite air, *The Lament of the Heart*. The prince was surprised by her boldness, as he told me afterward, for who was she but a simple country girl? Or so he supposed. What could she know about poetic compositions? He was afraid that his courtiers would laugh at her effort, but he smiled and gave her permission to sing. 'And then,' to use his own words, 'she sang her wonderful song about you, my beloved, with such power, and with such a blending of the melodic theme and the eloquence of the heart's longing that it lingers with me still as a memory out of paradise. When she was through I snatched the lute from her hand, and poured out the burden of my love for you, Sunatda, in wild and imperfect measures.'

"By the time Mae Pia had been gone three months I had become disconsolate. And then one day she returned home with letters and presents from the prince, and a month afterward I set out for Ban Sita, a bride, and such a happy one, Mem *cha!* When we came close to Ban Sita my brother went on ahead to announce my arrival to the prince. . . ." She stopped talking suddenly and burst into passionate tears. Anna sat perfectly still, afraid that anything she said might stop the flow of the princess' narrative. After a little while she resumed. "And so we were married privately. We had a few months of happiness. Then he became seriously ill. He wanted me to return to my father because he was afraid that if he died I might fall into the hands of his brother, but I couldn't leave him. When he was brought to Bangkok I came with him.

"His last words to me were, 'Farewell, my beautiful Sunatda. You have been the light of the setting sun to me. The glory of your love has dispersed the dark clouds that overshadowed my life and the memory of your face will be bright before my fading eyes to the end.'

"A short time after my husband's death I found myself a prisoner in his palace. Then in a little while I was brought here to this Palace. I was appointed a residence suitable for a queen. The King waited on me there. He ignored the deep love I had for my husband and the sorrow of my bereavement and offered me his royal hand in marriage. Well, I rejected his cruel offer openly and proudly. And so I am a prisoner here, as you can see, and will probably remain one as long as I live."

326

She ceased speaking. Anna moved at last on the uncomfortable bench, stretching the cramped muscles of her back. One of the guard entered to say it was time to lock the prison doors. Anna rose to go. The princess sat with her lips pressed firmly together, her nostrils quivering. Her head was bowed with fresh grief, as if she were living again the bitterness of her loss and humiliation. She motioned her adieu, but did not turn.

Anna saw her occasionally after that, sitting in one of the Palace gardens under the watchful eye of the Amazons. She was always self-absorbed and withdrawn, but Anna thought that there was a difference about her, as if she had found new strength to live at least a little while longer.

By October the King seemed entirely well. On the twenty-sixth Prince Chulalongkorn was to leave the novitiate and return to the Palace. It had been decided that Anna was to teach him evenings from seven to ten in his new home, since he would no longer be a pupil in the temple schoolroom. The King was busy with final preparations for sending a display of Siamese art and craftsmanship to the Paris Exhibition. M. Daniel Windsor, a French merchant, and several Siamese nobles were to accompany it from Bangkok early in November. It was the first time that Siam had participated in anything of the sort. M. Aubaret was still pressing for a repeal of the fourth article of the 1865 treaty, but the King was refusing to commit himself to more than his promise to send an embassy to Paris.

On the last day of October the whole court, with the most favored of the royal family, and Anna and Louis, set out for Petchaburi. The city was about ninety miles southwest of Bangkok on a river of the same name. The countryside around it was much more picturesque than that of Bangkok. Ranges of low mountains ran from north to south in folds back to the horizon, and on the slopes and in the valleys were forests of magnificent trees. Between the mountains and the Gulf of Siam lay a plain like a patchwork quilt, with squares of rice land stitched around by betel and sugar palms to make a pattern in varying shades of green and yellow and golden brown. The King had had the ramshackle buildings on the main street of the town removed. The street was now a wide avenue lined for half a mile with brick stores like those at Singapore.

On the Royal Mountain near the town he had had an elaborate palace built. Five hundred slaves had been working on it for ten years and improvements were still being made. There were temples and *prachedis* on the peaks of several adjoining mountains. All over these slopes workmen were laying out gardens. In the center of several of them stone vases, Egyptian in form, had been carved from the natural rock. They were kept filled with flowers. Attached to the palace was a schoolhouse, a residence for the teacher, and a private chapel for the women. But there was no distinct women's city as in Bangkok. Those of the harem who accompanied the King on his annual visits had rooms in the western wing of the palace, which was separated from the rest by a wall and guarded by Amazons.

Prince Chulalongkorn, Anna, and Louis loved to wander over the mountainside, along the ravines and through the forests, gathering wild flowers and visiting the hot springs, the caves and grottoes. The latter were very beautiful. Stalactites like carved pillars and the wonderful colors of the roofs and walls made them seem like temples. One was, in fact, used as a temple. The others had been left as they were except that steps had been cut into them so they could be entered easily. Farther down the mountain was a small lake with a smooth silvery surface. From the palace there were many paths through groves of dark green trees, opening upon wide terraces which commanded views of the countryside or the fertile valley through which wound the thread of the river.

The whole court spent a happy two weeks. Anna taught her school mornings, and spent the afternoons exploring with the prince and Louis. She had enjoyed no place in Siam so much. Life was relaxed and simple, the air cooler and cleaner than that of Bangkok. She was glad when the King decided they would stay two weeks more. As Anna went to bed that night she chanted happily to herself:

> Genii in the air,
> And spirits in the evening breeze,
> And gentle ghosts with eyes as fair,
> As starbeams through the twilight trees.

It was three o'clock in the morning when she was awakened by the sound of tocsins and gongs. Trumpets blared over the distant hills, re-echoing from the rocks like the wail of demons. Lights were on in the royal palace. Torch-bearing phantoms issued from dark doorways and wove among the trees. Sedans and shadowy horsemen were picking their way along the paths.

The torch-bearers turned out to be Amazons sent to arouse everyone. The court would return to Bangkok within the hour.

"Why?" Anna asked, deeply disappointed. "The King told me just today that we were staying another fortnight." But the Amazons refused all explanation. "You have one hour to get ready," was all they said. "His Majesty has ordered everyone to return to Bangkok tonight."

No explanation was given all the way back, even on shipboard. His Majesty had ordered it, that was enough. Three days later Anna found herself settled again in her home in Bangkok, thinking wistfully of the pleasant mountain top at Petchaburi with its fresh air and lovely view.

The next morning Anna and Louis set out once more to resume their school routine. As they walked toward the gate they saw clusters of people reading with absorbed interest huge placards written in Siamese, Pali, Cambodian, Burmese, and Peguan, posted along the Palace walls. Anna could read the printed Pali and Siamese, but these proclamations were written in an elaborate orthography that baffled her. She asked several people what the proclamations said, but their fear of even mentioning royalty was so great that none of them would answer. They shook their heads and backed off from her in alarm. She went on to the school, only to find the same mysterious announcements, running zigzag over all the walls up and down the narrow streets and lanes.

No one would tell her what they meant. The women whom she asked looked at her strangely and moved away in haste. She began to wonder if she herself were in some way connected with the proclamations. She seemed to be on good terms with the King. Still, she was treasonably disposed toward slavery and polygamy, and had been from the beginning. No, it could hardly be that.

The schoolroom was deserted. After an hour's wait it was obvious that the royal children were not coming for classes. Anna hurried off to find Lady Thiang. But she was even more mysterious than the hieroglyphics on the walls. She looked at Anna curiously, shaking her head solemnly. Then she felt Anna all over carefully, as if to reassure herself that the Englishwoman was flesh and bones like herself. "Mem *cha*," she asked gravely, "have you ever practiced sorcery or witchcraft?"

This was so unexpected that Anna's lips trembled with irrepressible laughter. "Of course not! What a funny question. Why do you ask?"

Lady Thiang looked affronted and said sternly, "Mem, this is not a laughing matter. This is deadly serious, maybe for both you and me. While we were all at Petchaburi there was a powerful sorceress in the Palace. No one knows who she was, no one saw anything out of order. But all of a sudden, although every door was locked and guarded as usual, and no one passed in or out, the Princess of Chiengmai vanished in the night." At Anna's look of incredulity, she went on, "Yes, right out of her cell in the prison. The cell was locked, and the prison was locked, and the gates were locked and barred. There were guards at all the doors and gates as there always are, but the princess was conjured through them all in the dead of night. No one saw the witch come. No one saw her go. She was just there. When the Amazons opened the princess' cell they found in her place a deaf and dumb slave girl that the sorceress had substituted for her. There she lies on the princess' bed like a clod, not seeming to know anything, and nothing has been seen of the princess at all."

Anna was taken completely by surprise. Mae Pia! She remembered her last words: "Something is going to be done to save her, even if I die for it." Well, she had done the impossible! But how? She had chosen her time well, with the King out of the city and the harem vigilance somewhat relaxed. Nevertheless, it was beyond imagination to figure out how she had spirited her mistress from the prison and away from the Palace. No wonder Lady Thiang thought it was the work of a sorceress!

"I wish," Lady Thiang burst forth, her face working, "oh, I wish that this dumb girl could be exorcised and made to speak, and then we might know how it happened, and how the old witch looked, perhaps, and who she was. And then she could be caught, and you and I would be safe. Mem *cha,* I'm afraid for my life and the lives of my children, and even the very stones of this dismal city fill me with dread and horror. And do you know," she asked, her eyes growing rounded as her panic mounted, "that HE has shut HIMSELF up in HIS topmost chamber, and guards are set at all the doors and windows, to keep out suspicious-looking people, because the witch may still be around disguised in human form. And no one is allowed to enter but an old lady doctor, Khun Mo Prang. She serves HIM all HIS meals, and HE won't come down until the Palace and the whole city has been exorcised. Oh, and there will be no school tomorrow. I almost forgot to tell you. Because HE has ordered all the royal children to be shut up in their houses until noon. The Brahman priests will exorcise the city in the morning, and in the afternoon the priests of Buddha will purify it with burning incense and sprinkle the houses and the walls and all of us with holy water."

Anna breathed a little sigh of relief. A natural cause for the disappearance of the princess did not seem to have presented itself to the mind of the head wife, nor to the King, if what Lady Thiang said was correct. Anna was comforted to think how widespread the conviction seemed to be that the spiriting of the princess from the Palace was supernatural. This did not promise much hope for Mae Pia's safety, but it was better than nothing. Sooner or later some cool head like the Kralahome's would deduce the real course of events, and when that happened Mae Pia's life would be forfeit. Anna had come to love and admire the slave far more than her mistress, and she knew that the slave's situation was one of deadly peril.

Lady Thiang went on nervously to tell Anna that the court astrologers were trying to unravel the mystery and that large rewards had been promised to them if they could throw any light on it. Lastly, the two Lao captives and the deaf and dumb changeling were to be exorcised and examined in the ecclesiastical court by the wise men and women of the country.

The head wife put her face in her pillow and wept, terrified. Anna tried to comfort her, but it was useless. She was afraid that in the course of the trial her own small efforts to alleviate the suffering of the princess would come out, and would connect her with the princess' disappearance. Between her fears of the supernatural and her fears of being denounced in court she was completely demoralized and quite inconsolable.

The only thing Anna could say that seemed to be of any comfort to her was that she herself would go to the ecclesiastical court and attend the exorcism, and that she would come back to the Palace afterward and tell Lady Thiang all that had been said and done there.

The next morning—November 20, 1866—Anna set out on horseback for the scene of the exorcism. She was accompanied only by an Indian groom. She had managed to learn that the three women who were the central figures in the case had been taken from their cells, half stupefied by the foul air of the damp holes in which they had been thrust, and conducted through the silent streets while the city was still asleep. Only after their contaminated persons had been removed could the work of purifying the Palace and its environs begin. Since these were to be completed before the trial Anna had plenty of time.

It was the pleasantest month of the year and the morning sun shone brightly but not warmly. She rode toward the northeastern wall of the fortified town, enjoying the golden air and the leisurely motion of the horse. The section into which she came was occupied by Brahmans, to whom it had been allocated by the kings of Siam when the city was laid out. There was not a modern building in sight. Anna thought that she had never seen, even in her travels in India, so perfect a historical picture of ancient Brahminical architecture, unaltered by modern ideas. India itself had changed and become hybrid with the advent of British culture, but here in this little corner of Bangkok the traditional was scrupulously preserved. The varied gables, the quaint little windows, the fantastic towers and narrow doorways, the endless effects of color were all here. The Brahmans who occupied the houses still clung to the costume of their forefathers, which made the picture complete.

She came at last to the temple called Wat Bawonniwet within which was the court where the exorcism was to take place. Part of the temple seemed new, and part very old, with stained walls and huge trees covered by parasitic plants. A deep, narrow valley through which a tiny stream ran over a stony bed was crossed by a stone bridge black with time. Anna stopped her horse on the bridge and looked down at the mad little stream. Its steep banks were covered with grass and furze. There was a loneliness about it, and a sort of darkness, too, whether because of the shadow of the trees or not, it was hard to say.

Deep in the glen stood an old shrine to Phra Kan, god of death. Running along behind it, like a jagged shadow gloomy even in the brightest sunlight, were the blackened roofs of the monastic dwellings of the Brahman ascetics.

Anna alighted from her horse and handed the reins to the syce. "Keep the horse outside the temple grounds until I'm ready to go home," she said, and sat down on the bridge to wait. The syce walked off, but in a quarter of an hour returned with oil and fresh flowers and sweetmeats. He tied the pony carefully and went into the temple with his offering. Anna followed him. There were a great many gods in the temple, and he prostrated himself in front of each one. Anna took the notebook and pencil she had brought and began to make sketches and memoranda.

Vishnu, Siva, Krishna, and the black wife of Siva were the chief deities of the temple. They were the heroes and heroines of the numerous grotesque myths sculptured on the walls. Here was Vishnu lying comfortably on the thousand-headed snake, Shesha, or sporting as a fish, or crawling as a tortoise, or showing his fangs as a wild boar, or shaking his head in his last and fifth avatar as a dwarf. The carvings were admirable. Here, too, was Krishna, like another Apollo, whipped out of heaven for playing tricks on the lovely shepherdesses of Mathura, whose tender hearts he stole away, and whose butter he found so tempting that he perpetually ran off with it secretly, and whose jars of milk it was his madcap pleasure to upset. In another compartment, crumbling with age, he was seen again in his last prank, perched on a stony tree with the milkmaid's stony habiliments under his arm, and an unmistakable grin on his face, made greasy by worshipers with their offerings of oil, while the owners of the dresses were standing below in various attitudes of bashfulness imploring their restoration. Before the gods and goddesses in various places stood the Lingam. Here also was a sculpture of Siva and his wife Parvati, with the sacred bull, Nandi, lying at their feet, and Kali in combat with the monster Mahishasura; and close by again caressing an antelope, or Nilgau, that lay on the ground looking up at her.

How long it had been since she and Leon had set out one morning to see the Kali Ghat in Calcutta! It had been during the festival of the Juggernaut. There had been something enchanted and demoniac about that temple as there was about this. The black face of the goddess had been surmounted by long hair which had the appearance of innumerable serpents. A red tongue had protruded from the hideous mouth. The expression of the eyes had been strange, almost to madness. She had had four arms, in one of which she grasped a knife. In the second was the head of a man, in the third a lotus, and in the fourth a wheel. Around her neck had been hung the skulls of murdered victims, and she stood on the body of a prostrate worshiper, who was represented as shouting her praises while she crushed him to death.

How long ago it had all been, yet how clearly it came back to her now! Anna sighed and went out into the fresh air. She rambled about in the grove but there was little else to see. The procession had not yet appeared and she had begun to be hungry. She called the syce and sent him into the village for an earthen lota of milk and a flat cake of Bajri bread. These she ate sitting under the deep shadow of the temple and trees.

Very soon after she was through she heard the sound of drums and the shrilling of music. She rushed to the place where the sound seemed to come from and saw a weird-looking procession approaching. There were old women dressed in scarlet and yellow, and old gray-headed men in every variety of costume out of the past. Some were on foot and some on horseback, with embroidered flags flying in the wind. In the center, dressed in black and crimson vestments and riding on white mules, were about twenty men and women, some quite young and others extremely old, advancing with slow, solemn steps. These were the royal astrologers, wizards, and witches, attached to the court. They received salaries from the Crown. Anna had never seen them all in one place before, although on several occasions individuals had been pointed out to her with awe. She saw that they were all Hindus, or if of mixed blood, as seemed likely, had adopted the Hindu dress and religion.

In the rear came some Chinese coolies hired for the occasion, carrying two boxes and two long planks. Were they to be used in the ritual, she wondered? More likely they were what Mae Pia had used to get the princess out of the Palace. In the wake of the procession came a motley group of well-dressed Siamese and a crowd of ragged slaves.

The court was to be held in the grand hall, the roof of which was badly crumbled away. In spite of its dilapidation its shape bore a strong resemblance to the wonderful temple of Angkor Wat, although on a much smaller scale. Anna stepped out of the deep shade in which she had been standing beneath the bo trees and took a seat on a broken stone pillar, still under the shelter of the trees, but close enough to the hall so she could both see and hear clearly.

As soon as the procession entered the portal of the temple it halted. The men and women threw up their hands, folded them above their heads, and repeated the words of Krishna:

O thou who art the life in all things, the eternal seed of nature, the understanding of the wise and the weakness of the foolish, the glory of the proud and the strength of the strong, the sacrifice and the worship, the incense and the fire, the victim and the slayer, the father and the mother of the world, gird thy servants with power and wisdom today to slay the slayer and to vanquish the deceiver!

After this they marched into the temple to music, and offered their sacrifices of wine and oil, wheaten cakes and fresh flowers. With their eyes lifted to the dark vaulted roof they prayed again, calling upon Brahma the father, the comforter, the creator, the tender mother, the holy way, the witness, the asylum, the friend of man, to illumine with the light of his understanding their feeble intellects to discern the devil and to vanquish him.

It was only when the long prayers were complete that the astrologers, wizards, and witches took their places in the hall, with the eager crowds all around them, standing in rows on the steps of the building. Then two officers stepped forward with a royal letter from the King. They were the chief judge of the high court, Phya Phrom, and his secretary, who were to record the proceedings for the King. When they were seated the prisoners were brought—Mae Pia, and the two maids-in-waiting of the princess. They were placed at the end of the hall, strongly guarded by fifty Amazons, while soldiers scattered themselves around the building. There was utter silence. The strange assembly looked fearfully about, eyeing Mae Pia as if she were indeed a witch. The three prisoners sat motionless, waiting apathetically to hear their doom. The "deaf and dumb changeling" was deadly pale. Her eyes burned with a strange light, almost of insanity, or perhaps of intense suffering.

Anna grew restless. Why didn't the trial begin? There were the boxes and planks. She saw that there were little niches cut in the planks, deep enough to make it possible for a nimble person to climb with the tips of the toes. Obviously these were what Mae Pia had used to scale the walls. Even so, the feat was no mean physical performance! How had she managed to get the planks up and over the first wall so that she could use them again on the inner wall? And how had she escaped unseen? How had she got the princess, weak after her long confinement, over the wall? And how had she got into the prison? It was still incredible.

Anna turned to a soldier standing near and asked him why the trial was being delayed.

"They are waiting for the holy man of the woods," he explained. "They have blown the conch shells for him three times, but he has not come yet. And they will not begin the trial until he does, no matter how long they have to wait." He told her about the yogi who lived all alone in a cave in the rocks adjoining the temple grounds. He rarely emerged during the day, but pious Hindus bathing in the stream in the evening could sometimes see him moving in the moonlight, and hear him calling upon God. He fed on tamarinds and wild fruits, sleeping all day like an animal. All night long he prayed aloud, oppressed by his longing and yearning after the Invisible as by some secret grief that knew no balm. Anna was reminded of the words:

> . . . At night the passion came,
> Like the fierce fiend of a distempered dream;
> And shook him from his rest, and led him forth
> Into the darkness, to pray and pray forevermore.

After an hour's wait a man appeared on the opposite bank of the stream. He stood a moment looking and listening with the intentness of a deer. Then he plunged into the stream and emerged on the side of the temple. He was dressed only in a loin cloth. His thin brown body was heavily muscled and wiry, and his hair was long and unkempt. He shook the water from it as a dog will shake itself and came toward the hall, where he sat down almost shyly close to the prisoners. Anna got a clear view of him. He had a fine face, sensitive and gentle, and his head was noble in spite of the matted hair.

The soldier whispered to Anna. "This man's eyes are opened," he said reverently, "so that he can see things which the paid wizards of the court cannot. That's why they make it a point to invite him to help them in their spiritual examinations."

The trial began. The judge read the King's letter, which spoke of the mysterious and important nature of the accusation made against a person or persons unknown, who had abducted from the Palace a state prisoner, a lady of high rank and unflinching integrity. It called upon the assembly to do their utmost to unravel the affair and determine the guilty person or persons.

After the royal letter had received the customary salutation—three profound salaams from the assembly—the judge commanded the two Amazons who had been on duty at the door of the prison when the princess disappeared to speak. Their testimony followed. "On the night of the fifth day of the rising moon in the twelfth month a sudden strong wind arose that extinguished our lanterns, leaving us in utter darkness. And immediately afterward we were aware that a great tall figure enveloped in a black veil had entered the hall. As she approached us we saw that she was more than human in size, and held a short dagger in one hand and a great bunch of keys in the other."

They went on to explain that the horror which fell upon them deprived them of all power of speech and action, and they could move not even a little finger, so powerful was the spell cast upon them. As the strong being stood over them brandishing her glittering knife, there had flashed all around her a hideous light. By this light they saw her proceed to the cell in which the Princess Sunatda was confined, open it with one of her mysterious keys, and lead the princess forth, dragging her by the hand. Then the flashes had died away and a double darkness fell upon them so the prison had the terrible unearthly blackness of the tomb. After nearly two hours, while they were still paralyzed and unable to move, the strange figure reappeared, pallid and more ghastly than before but without the veil or the dagger, or the bunch of keys. She passed quickly by them and shut the prison door after her so hard that it closed with a dismal cry of pain.

The two Lao attendants of the princess were called next. Their story was brief. They said: "On the night of the fifth of the rising moon we were awakened by the slamming of the cell door. When we looked toward the bed where the princess had been sleeping we saw a figure sitting on it. We called out to the princess but she did not answer us, so we lit the lamp and found that our mistress was gone. This dumb slave girl was sitting there on her bed. We shrank away from her in horror because we were afraid that she might change us also into some unnatural thing."

It was plain to Anna that the Amazons believed their own story and in this there was a shred of hope for Mae Pia. They had been so frightened and so vividly impressed by the apparition they thought they had encountered, that they were prepared to swear solemnly that they had seen a supernatural being twice human size and altogether unlike the deaf and dumb slave before them. "It was a spirit," they insisted, and the assembly nodded sagely, for there was no one present who did not accept this explanation as logical under the circumstances.

Mae Pia was called next. The unnatural light of pain, madness, or frenzy—whatever it was—seemed to burn still more brightly in her eyes. Her crude brown clothing was stained here and there with darker spots, and her face seemed to grow more colorless every moment. The examiners asked her question after question. The crafty wizards and witches put innumerable inquiries to her. She did not reply. Her lips, ashy pale, seemed to have been closed by a supernatural agency.

Anna recalled her volubility and the impassioned song by which she had won for her mistress the acknowledgment of the Second King's love. What had happened to her eloquence? Surely she could invent a story that would deceive this credulous audience prepared by the testimony of the Amazons to accept the fantastic. "Is it possible that she's acting?" Anna wondered. She doubted it, unless Mae Pia were heavily drugged.

At a signal an alarm gong was struck suddenly just behind the slave. The whole assembly started and Mae Pia, taken by surprise, turned to see what had made the sound. "Ha!" shouted Phya Phrom triumphantly. "You aren't deaf! You can hear plainly! And you can probably speak, too." The feeling of sympathy that had extended to all the supposed victims of the sorceress now turned against Mae Pia. The crowd stirred and muttered, and the judge condemned her immediately to the torture of the rack.

But the yogi raised his bare arms on high and uttered a shrill cry. "Forbear! Forbear!" he cried so commandingly that it rang through the temple and arrested the movements of everyone in it. He turned to Mae Pia and placed his huge bony hands on her shoulders. He whispered something in her ear that seemed to move the girl, for she raised her eyes to his and they were filled with tears. Then she shook her head sadly, and laid her finger on her lips, apparently trying to make it clear to him that she could not speak. A sympathetic look kindled in the dark face of the yogi. He turned to the assembly and said, "This woman is not a witch and she is not even obstinate. She is powerless to speak because she is under a spell."

The tide of the feeling turned again to the prisoner.

"Let her be exorcised then," said Phya Phrom, accepting the yogi's judgment without question.

At this, the woman whom Anna had picked out as the queerest of the whole group, an old, toothless dame, drew out from her girdle a key and opened the wooden boxes. From them she took a small boat, a sort of coracle not unlike the boats used by the ancient Egyptians. Anna had seen boats similar to it in parts of Wales, made by covering a wicker frame with leather. Then she took out a long gray veil of some unusual material, an earthen stove, and some charcoal. From the second box she produced herbs, pieces of flint, the cast skins of snakes, feathers, the hair of various animals, human bones, short brooms, and a number of other things.

With the charcoal and flint the old woman lighted a fire in her earthen stove. When it was red hot she opened several jars of what appeared to be water, and muttering incantations threw into them portions of her herbs, repeating over each a mystic spell, and waving a wand that looked like a bone taken from the arm of a stalwart man. This done she seated the prisoner in the center of the group of wizards and witches and covered her with a veil of gray stuff. She passed the short handbrooms to a number of the witches. Then to Anna's intense horror she began to pour the burning charcoal over the veiled form of the prisoner. The other women danced around with wild gestures, repeating the name of Brahma and sweeping the coals off as fast as she poured them on. This was done without even singeing the veil or burning a hair of Mae Pia's head. Afterward they emptied the jars of water on her, still repeating the name of Brahma. Mae Pia was then made to change to entirely fresh clothes of the Brahminical pattern. Her dressing and undressing were effected skillfully without disclosing her person at all.

Once more the yogi laid his hands on her shoulders and whispered first in her right ear and then in her left. But Mae Pia still shook her head and pointed to her sealed lips. Then the oldest wizard, Khun Phikhat (the lord who drives out the devil), prostrated himself before her, and prayed with a wild energy of manner. Rising suddenly he demanded in a stentorian voice, full in the prisoner's face, "Where did you drop the bunch of keys?"

The glaring light of late afternoon illuminated the fine face of the Lao slave, as for the third time she moved her head from side to side in solemn assurance that she could not or would not speak. Some of the assembly began to whisper that the same witch who spirited the princess away had struck this poor girl dumb. The majority, unconvinced, grumbled that the judge ought to apply the rack. Anna herself was beginning to have the illogical conviction that Mae Pia could not speak even if she would.

"Open her mouth and pour some of the magic water into it," suggested one of the wise women. This was agreed to, and several stepped forward. One woman took hold of her lower jaw, one of her forehead, while a third stood ready with the water. Then as her mouth opened they fell back in horror, screaming, "Brahma! Brahma! Brahma!"

"What is it?" shouted Phya Phrom half rising from his place. One of the women turned to him, her face green and sick. "Brahma! Brahma! The evil fiend has torn out her tongue!"

Pandemonium broke loose. Immediately Mae Pia ceased to be an object of fear and dread and became one of pity, even—by some incomprehensible metamorphosis—of adoration. The transition from fear and loathing to compassion was so sudden that many of the men as well as the women wept at the thought of the dreadful mutilation to which the fiend had subjected the slave girl.

In slow, grave tones the final question was asked—was the exorcism effectual? A small taper was lighted and put into the wise woman's boat. The whole company followed her out to the borders of the stream to see it launched. The boat swept gallantly down the current, the feeble light burned brightly without even a flicker, until it was stopped by some stones that were set across the stream.

The yogi raised a shout of delight, and the whole company echoed it with satisfaction. The answer was yes—the exorcism had been effectual. In accordance with the King's instructions the trial was brought to a swift close. The prisoners were acquitted of any complicity with the devil in the abduction of the princess. Each received a sum of money and was set at liberty. The planks—damning evidence which showed so clearly that some person had scaled the Palace walls—were not brought into the trial at all. As the whole company set out for home, no longer in procession but each going his own way, they were left unheeded and forgotten where the coolies had dropped them.

It was sunset by this time. Anna sent her syce home and remained behind under the tree to which her horse was tied. The yogi splashed back through the stream to the solitude of his unknown cave, to sleep by day and pray alone by night. Still the women lingered sympathetically about Mae Pia in the hall.

Finally they were gone, and the slave who had been sitting dully on the floor stood up and came out. She caught sight of Anna under the tree and ran to her. She threw herself into the Englishwoman's arms and laid her head on Anna's shoulder. She made pitiful noises that Anna thought at first were cries of sorrow, but when Mae Pia raised her head she saw they were expressions of joy. There was nothing but gladness in the slave's face. Anna was too shocked by the lengths to which Mae Pia had gone to save her mistress to do more than embrace her with the tenderness a mother might feel for a brave and reckless child. She could not keep back the tears as she remembered how the princess had told her that Mae Pia was the finest musician in the North. Those bloodless lips would sing no more!

Mae Pia's two friends joined them and in whispers told Anna the rest of the story. Mae Pia had scaled the walls by means of the planks, pulling them up and over the first wall to use on the second. She had studied the Palace carefully and had chosen for her entry a dark spot between two gates on the river side. She had provided herself previously with the great bunch of keys—they did not know how she had come by them. She had opened the prison doors with them and terrified the Amazons. The wind that blew out the lanterns was her one great piece of luck. From her early questioning of Anna she was able to go directly to the cell in which the princess was. It was true that she had had to drag the princess away by force. After assisting the princess to climb the walls on the inner side, she had sat on the top of the outer wall until she saw the princess safely down. The prince and his two friends had been waiting in a small boat at the river's edge.

It was the dark of the moon and they had had no difficulty remaining undetected. Mae Pia had dropped the keys to the princess to be thrown into the river. In vain the prince and princess had begged, entreated and pleaded with Mae Pia to come down from the wall and join them in their flight. She had refused to leave the two companions of her mistress alone in their peril. So at last, afraid they would be discovered and unable to persuade Mae Pia, they had turned toward the river. A small ship waited at its mouth to receive the princess and take her with her brother and his friends to Moulmein.

Mae Pia had feared that in the terrible ordeal of torture to which she knew she would be subjected she might reveal the truth. So by one stroke of the dagger she had deprived herself of the power of ever again uttering a single intelligible sound.

"But why didn't all of you go with the princess?" Anna asked the women.

"Because we were too many," they answered, "and would surely have been discovered. And Mae Pia had promised not to leave us to bear the penalty alone."

There was nothing more to be said, nothing more even that Anna could do for them. Their plans were made. They were going downriver immediately to Paklat where they would take the next boat for Moulmein to rejoin the princess. It was getting dark, but Anna could hardly tear herself away from the slave even to fulfill her promise to Lady Thiang. The head wife had nothing to fear and she could wait. At last there was no further excuse for staying. The women would be anxious to find a boat before it was too late.

Anna untied her horse and mounted it. As she moved away Mae Pia raised her hands high above her head, and waved them to and fro. She was smiling. Anna smiled too, but faintly, for she was deeply shaken by the heroism she had witnessed that day.

39

## THE SHADOW BEFORE

ANNA HAD decided to accompany Louis to England. It had taken her many months to reach this decision, but when it was made she felt relieved. The King rejected it completely, refusing even to discuss the possibility of her leaving Bangkok.

"Mem, you are lazy! You are ungrateful!" he reproached her every time she brought the matter up. Why he should consider her ungrateful since he had never fulfilled his early promise to raise her salary, it was hard to say. "I have need of you," he argued, and to him that was conclusive. It took her six months to win his grudging consent, and even then he would not permit her to go unless she promised faithfully to return in six months. This she could do only conditionally, for her health was so undermined that it was doubtful whether six months would be sufficient to recover it.

Five years had passed since she had seen Avis, who was now twelve. Louis, who was only a year younger, needed to be placed in a boarding-school with a regular routine. An Oriental court full of enervating influences was no place for an English boy to spend his adolescence. She

340

and Louis had been in the tropics ten years, hard years indeed for her, and they both needed the bracing air of a temperate climate.

Against her going was the indubitable fact that her influence with the King was greater than it had ever been. Her quarrels with him seemed to have enhanced her position rather than otherwise. The three hours she spent with Prince Chulalongkorn every evening in the library of his new Rose Garden Palace were in themselves an inducement. He was not the impressionable child he had been before his period in the novitiate, but he still responded to her teaching. There was one occasion during the seven happy months that she taught him there which she was to remember often years later.

The prince and she had been talking about the life of Abraham Lincoln. The story of the great humanitarian was familiar to the prince from the constant references she had made to it through the years. He, like the other older pupils, had read the Emancipation Proclamation, and followed the course of the Civil War to its conclusion. On this evening Anna and he were talking about the tragic death of the President. It had made a deep mark on the young prince's thinking. He leaned across the table, his eyes shining with a determination she was not to forget.

"Mem *cha*," he said, "if I live to reign over Siam I shall reign over a free and not an enslaved nation. It will be my pride to restore this kingdom to the original constitution under which it was founded by a small colony of Buddhists many centuries ago. They fled from Magadah, their native country, to escape the persecution of the Brahman priests and came to Siam and established themselves here under one of their leaders, who was both priest and king. They called the country they had chosen '*Muang Thai*,' which means 'The Country of the Free.' Maybe some day I can change it back into 'The Country of the Free.' "

Anna looked at the ardent face of the boy in front of her and hoped that he would live to accomplish his dream. Even though his interpretation of Siam's early history was faulty his plans for the future were good. He was steady and quiet. Unlike his father, who was half of the old world that was passing and half of the new, Chulalongkorn was all of the new. He was facing squarely into the future. This was partly Anna's doing and she was glad. Whether there would be any kingdom left for him to rule when the time came was something that no one could have determined in that winter of 1867. There were the English in the south and west, and there were the French, always the French!

In December M. Aubaret had made another great scandal. He was still determined to force the King to relinquish specific claim to Battambang and Siemreap. He had become convinced that not the King but the Kralahome was the obstacle to his purpose. The Kralahome stood inflexible against any weakening of the Siamese position. The consul had demanded, therefore, the removal of the Kralahome from the commission

341

which was formulating Siam's reply to French insistence. This reply was to be carried to France by the Kralahome's son, Phya Suriwong. The King had answered that it was not in his power to remove the Kralahome since he was *ex officio* a member of the commission. This had infuriated M. Aubaret. He had had difficulty securing an interview with the King after that, and suspected that the King was putting him off until the embassy had sailed.

On December 14 M. Lamache sent him word that the King would appear during the late afternoon on the commons outside the eastern gate of the Palace, going and coming from a nearby temple. M. Lamache would be there with three hundred of his soldiers in their best uniforms, drilling for a time, and then parading before the King. M. Aubaret, who had nursed his wrath to keep it warm, "happened" along and watched the soldiers at drill. He was still standing there casually, as if he had merely chanced to be passing, when the King and court emerged. The King was surprised to see the French Consul. He ordered his palanquin bearers to halt. "Why for have you come?" he demanded.

The consul replied that he had only come on a pleasure stroll, but since His Majesty had so opportunely appeared there was a matter he did want to discuss with him, and perhaps this was as good a time as any. He drew a paper from his pocket and launched into a diatribe against the Kralahome, the burden of which was that it would be in the interests of both nations to have him replaced by someone less likely to disrupt the relations between them. Some of the listening courtiers reported afterward that M. Aubaret added in an aside that he had come to the conclusion a suitable person was available and he would be glad to supply His Majesty with the name when His Majesty agreed to the removal of the Kralahome. Finally, he bluntly threatened the King with war if His Majesty refused to comply with French demands in both the matter of the Kralahome and the Cambodian question.

The King's anger, as mercurial as M. Aubaret's own, had risen instantly, obliterating for the moment his fear of the French. He had ordered the consul out of his way, refusing any discussion. M. Aubaret, fully aware of the irregular nature of his procedure, tried to close the interview with some show of good will. He extended his hand to the King but the King ignored it. Pretending not to be aware of the King's action he then turned to a group of the King's children, who were close behind their father's palanquin, and tried to shake hands with them. They, too, rebuffed him with the haughty manner they as well as their father knew how to adopt.

The consul turned and walked away toward the north, his hat in his hand, his head bent apparently in deep thought. After he had gone perhaps three hundred feet, he turned back, whether to try again or to apologize it was impossible to know. But by that time the King and the whole court had retreated within the Palace, abandoning any plan of going to the temple. The Bangkok *Recorder* commented on the incident:

> In view of what M. Aubaret has already done, we should not be much surprised to learn that he will take this occasion to "move heaven and earth," as it were, to make it appear that His Majesty has in this affair insulted the Emperor of the French, and that it is a substantial *casus belli*—that a French army must be ordered forthwith to put "His Excellency the Prime Minister" out of the way, and thus remove every serious obstacle in the way of French domination in Siam. Why, the demand he made in that interview with the King appears to us tantamount to requiring him to cut off the right arm of the government—to pluck out its right eye and stop both the ears. . . .

Within the Palace panic reigned. The astrologers, magicians, and wise men of the court were called. After consulting the stars and the oracles they said: "The times are full of omen. Danger approaches from afar. Let His Majesty erect a third gate on the east and on the west."

At the close of every year a thread of unspun cotton of seven fibers, consecrated by the priests, was reeled around all the walls of the Palace. From sunset until dawn a continuous cannonading was kept up from all the forts within hearing to rout the evil spirits that had infested the departing year. This was not considered enough, however, in view of the serious situation, so the gates were to be constructed. Pick and spade dug deep trenches outside the gates that already protected the Palace on the east and west. When all was ready the San Luang set twelve officers to hide near the excavations until dawn. Two were stationed within the entrance to call loudly to passers-by, using familiar names, as if they were neighbors or friends greeting individuals among the peasants or market folk who were always passing just before dawn. Hearing their names, some paused and asked what was wanted. Others stopped out of curiosity. Immediately the officers dashed from concealment and arrested six indiscriminately. From that moment their doom was sealed. No petitions, payments, or prayers could save them.

On the appointed day they were mocked with a banquet at which they were the guests of honor, and conducted ceremoniously to the excavations. The King and all the court made profound obeisance before them as they stood trembling in the deep fosse that had been dug at the center of the new gateways. His Majesty charged them earnestly:

"Guard with devotion the gate, now about to be entrusted to your keeping, from all dangers and from all calamities! Come in season to forewarn me if either traitors within or enemies without conspire against the peace of this people or the safety of this throne!"

As the King spoke the last words a heavy beam that had been suspended by two cords above the "hinds and churls" selected for this doubtful honor was released, so transforming six Bangkok ragamuffins into guardian angels—three for each gate.

It would have been difficult to persuade most of the court that this precaution had not been effective, for M. Aubaret either forgot his threats, or cooled off after thinking over the angry scene with the King. Perhaps a dose of the King's English had reduced him to a sense of his situation. The King had written to him as follows:

To the Hon. the Monsieur Aubaret, *the Consul for* H.I.M.
Sir:—
The verbal insult or bad words without any step more over from lower or lowest person is considered very slight & inconsiderable.

The person standing on the surface of the ground or floor Cannot injure the heavenly bodies or any highly hanging Lamp or globe by ejecting his spit from his mouth upward it will only injure his own face without attempting of Heavenly bodies—&c.

The Siamese are knowing of being lower than heaven do not endeavor to injure heavenly bodies with their spit from mouth.

A person who is known to be powerless by every one, as they who have no arms or legs to move oppose or injure or deaf or blind &c. &c. cannot be considered and said that they are our enemies even for their madness in vain—it might be considered as easily agitation or uneasiness.

Aubaret said nothing more to the King and the Siamese embassy sailed for Paris without further interference. The only unfortunate person was Dr. Bradley, whom M. Aubaret was suing for libel for printing in the *Recorder* the story of his interview with the King. The latter in his anxiety to have no further trouble forbade all government employees and courtiers to testify on Dr. Bradley's behalf. Mr. Knox offered to serve as counsel for Dr. Bradley; and Anna, who with Louis had witnessed the incident, wrote a letter confirming the story as it had appeared in the paper. Unaccountably this was not admitted as evidence by the American Consul, in whose court the trial took place. The consul, who knew very little law, required Dr. Bradley to prove his innocence rather than insisting that M. Aubaret prove Dr. Bradley's guilt. When Dr. Bradley, taken unawares by this development, could not produce the witnesses who had supplied his paper with the story, he was convicted and fined. The foreign community indignantly collected a subscription of three hundred dollars and sent it to the doctor to pay the expenses of the trial and the fine.

Light and darkness! So it had been from the beginning and so it was to the end. Was the small good worth its cost, the cup of cold water, the binding of a wounded spirit, the occasional rescue, the word of teaching? L'Ore Anna had saved. Tuptim she had lost. Sometimes it was hard to decide whether the little she accomplished outweighed the pain of seeing continually evils she could not rectify. One day she would feel utterly futile, depressed; the next strong with the satisfaction of accomplishment.

As for the condition of the nation itself, here is her conclusion as she prepared to leave Siam:

> The King was fast failing in body and mind, and, in spite of his seeming vigor, there was no real health in his rule, while he had his own way. All the substantial success we find in his administration is due to the ability and energy of his accomplished premier, Phya Kralahome, and even his strength has been wasted. The native arts and literature have retrograded; in the mechanic arts much has been lost; and the whole nation is given up to gambling.
>
> The capacity of the Siamese race for improvement in any direction has been sufficiently demonstrated, and the government has made fair progress in political and moral reforms; but the condition of the slaves is such as to excite astonishment and horror. What may be the ultimate fate of Siam under this accursed system, whether she will ever emancipate herself while the world lasts, there is no guessing.

Whenever she looked at Prince Chulalongkorn and others of her pupils, who were the new generation, the tomorrow of the country, she felt encouraged to hope. Whenever she thought about the heroism of women like Mae Pia and Tuptim, the consistent kindliness of Lady Thiang, the idealism of Lady Son Klin, she knew that they were not surpassed by the women of any nation in the world. But the system under which they lived! That was the crux of the matter!

Her own personal triumphs seemed small as she totaled them, yet she found on reflection she was glad of each one. She was glad to have been able to restore little Mae Khao to her father. The white baby whom she had bought at auction, only to lose by her own fall in the river, had reappeared unexpectedly. Anna and Boy had been riding down New Road one evening when they met Monthani with Mae Khao in her arms. She was now married to a Chinese merchant who was kind to her and fond of the child. Anna urged Monthani to bring Mae Khao to see her and the very next Thursday they had appeared. She washed and dressed the little girl in English clothes she had prepared for her, put shoes and stockings on her feet, and bound her head with a blue ribbon. Both mother and child were delighted, and came again and again. In the end Anna located Captain George Davis through J. C. Campbell, the inspector of customs, and he persuaded his former wife to relinquish their little daughter to him. He then resigned his position and took her back to his mother in England. A year later Anna had a letter from him dated Liverpool, telling her that he and his daughter were in his native land, and his little girl was happy under the care of his mother. A few Sundays before she had been christened "Anna Harriette" after the woman who had restored her to her father. She had behaved beautifully at the christening. When she grew up he intended to tell her how she had once been auctioned off in the

Palace of Bangkok, and bought by the English lady whose name she bore. He added that he would never forget Anna's kindness.

In her final year in Siam the event which meant more to Anna than any other occurred. On the third of January Lady Son Klin invited Anna to dinner. As usual she signed her note "Harriet Beecher Stowe." The invitation itself was not unusual, but the importance Lady Son Klin attached to it was. She kept sending messengers all day reminding Anna of the appointment, and telling her to be sure to come, until Anna was certain she must be planning some very grand entertainment.

Anna was amused at the childlike concern. This childlike quality was one of Lady Son Klin's chief characteristics. She was a highly intelligent, thoughtful woman, but she had never outgrown a naïveté that contrasted oddly with the keenness of her mind. Thus her translation of *Uncle Tom's Cabin* was a sustained piece of good workmanship. But when she learned that Pegu, the country over which her ancestors had ruled, was now a British colony she urged Anna again and again to write to Queen Victoria that she, Princess Son Klin, was a British subject and could read and write English. Nor could she see any incongruity in her request. She was confident that Queen Victoria would be interested.

Neither could she ever make any clear line of demarcation between her own religion and Anna's. When she had read and translated the Sermon on the Mount, she suddenly exclaimed: "Oh, your sacred Phra Jesu is very beautiful! Let us promise one another that whenever you pray to him you will call him Buddha, the Enlightened One, and when I pray to Buddha, I will call him Phra Jesu Karuna, the tender and sacred Jesus, for surely these are only different names for the same God!"

On that day in January after school Anna dressed herself and Louis in their finest to do honor to the occasion that her friend thought so important. Lady Son Klin had her head and shoulders out the window, looking down the street for them. As they appeared she rushed to greet them in her curiously sweet, cordial manner.

Dinner was served in the "study." Two of Lady Son Klin's sisters who lived with her were present, and the party numbered six. Since there were only five chairs around the table Prince Krita and Boy squeezed into one together. They were served by slave girls in the Peguan fashion, on little silver plates, the slave girls kneeling around the table. Fish, rice, jelly, and a variety of sweetmeats came first; then different kinds of vegetables; after them a course of meat, venison, and fowl of all kinds. The meal ended with sweet drinks, preserves, and fruits.

After this truly sumptuous feast the entertainment followed. It was a program of music provided not only by trained slaves but also by Lady Son Klin and her sisters. The air of suppressed excitement that had pervaded the dinner continued. Anna gathered that even the music was only preliminary to something else. As it ended Lady Son Klin rose and led Anna out to her garden.

There in rows knelt all her slaves, one hundred and thirty-two men, women, and children. Each of them was dressed in entirely new garments, and seemed to be palpitating with the same secret stimulation that made Lady Son Klin's hand tremble on Anna's arm. Lady Son Klin stood looking down on them from her verandah, smiling at them as they knelt below her, the women in flowered chintz panungs, the men in colors as bright but without the flowers, the children in the gayest outfits the local markets could provide.

With a look at Anna out of shining dark eyes she began to speak. "I am wishful," she said in her sweet voice, "to be good like Harriet Beecher Stowe. I want never to buy human bodies again, but only to let go free once and for all. So from this moment I have no more slaves, but hired servants. I give freedom to all of you who have served me, to go or to stay with me as you wish. If you go to your home I am glad. See, here are the papers, which I shall give to each of you. You are free! If you stay with me, I am still more glad. And I will give you each four ticals every month after this day and your food and clothes."

Anna stood silent. There was a lump in her throat. She had been taken completely by surprise. If she had done nothing more than teach this one woman, she knew now that her five hard years had been amply repaid by what she had seen this night. Surely it was only a token of the future!

Anna had put off telling the women and children that she was going until the time was near. The day she made her announcement she had hardly the courage to face them. For some time most of them refused to believe she was really leaving. When they could doubt it no longer they gave her such a demonstration of their love and devotion that she was overcome. Gifts of every sort poured in with embarrassing profusion. Many sent small sums of money to help Anna on the journey. The poorest and humblest slaves brought rice cakes, dried beans, sugar. In vain Anna tried to tell them as gently as possible that she could not take all these things with her. Still the gifts came until she thought she would have enough to provision the whole ship. Even Nai Lek, the dwarf, brought his little contribution, a coconut.

The King himself had been silent and sullen until the morning of her departure. At the end he relented. He embraced Boy and gave him a silver buckle, and a bag containing a hundred dollars to buy sweetmeats on the way. Then turning to Anna he said: "Mem! you much beloved by our common people, and all inhabitants of Palace and royal children. Everyone is in affliction of your departure. And even that opium-eating secretary, Phra Alak, is very low down in his heart because you *will* go. It shall be because you must be a good and true lady. I am often angry on you, and lose my temper, though I have large respect for you. But nevertheless you ought to know you are difficult woman, and more difficult than generality. But you will forget, and come back to my service, for I have more confidence on you every day. Good-by."

Anna could not reply. Her eyes were full of tears. She realized that what she had not thought possible had taken place. She and the King were more than employer and employee, King and governess—they were friends.

He accompanied her to the temple to say farewell to the women and children. They knelt before her, filling the great room, weeping. This was hard enough, but when the King withdrew they were up and around her, embracing her, pressing little notes and last-minute gifts into her hands, reproaching her with tears for leaving them, princesses and slaves alike. Anna could stand it no longer. She rushed out and through the gate where they could not follow. But their voices floated after her, the women calling, "Come back! Come back!" and the children, "Mem *cha,* don't go! Don't go away and leave us!"

She hurried to Prince Chulalongkorn for her final and most difficult leave-taking. She had already bequeathed to him many of her poor "clients," particularly the Chinese boy whom she had christened Timothy. The prince had written her a little note in his most careful English only a few days before:

Bangkok
July 1st, 1867.

My dear Mrs. Leonowens

I herewith send you a photograph of myself which I trust will meet with your approbation, and which I hope you will keep in remembrance of your pupil, whom you have had the honour of instructing for such a length of time.

Enclosed is a small present of $30 (dollars) for your kind acceptance; and in conclusion I can only wish you a pleasant and quick voyage to Europe, and that you may meet with every enjoyment on your arrival.

I beg to remain
Your faithful friend
CHOWFA CHULALONGKORN

His regret seemed too deep for words and he managed only a few. Taking both her hands in his own and laying his brow upon them he said, after a long interval of silence, "Mem *cha,* please come back!"

"Keep a brave and true heart, my prince!" was all that she could say.

On the fifth of July, 1867, Anna and Boy left Bangkok in the steamer *Chow Phya.* Uncertain of the future, she had sold her household goods at auction. All her European friends accompanied her down the river to the Gulf. Then they were alone, she and Boy, on the same ship that had brought them five years before, watching the shore line fade to a thin gray shadow.

## 40

## FULFILLMENT

ANNA REACHED England in September. By the end of October she had visited her husband's Irish cousins at Enniscorthy, County Douglas, placed Louis in the Kingstown School, and sailed for New York with Avis. Her doctor had told her she needed a more bracing climate than either Ireland or England, and the Cobbs—for Mr. Cobb had married—were urging her to come to the United States. She had decided that she could return to Siam from there as well as from England.

After a visit with the Cobbs and one with the Mattoons, her old friends from Bangkok, Avis and she went to the Catskills for the mountain air. Anna had been burned very dark by the tropical sun. Her clothes, too, were different from the current fashion. The villagers whispered among themselves that she was the ex-queen of Syria living among them incognito, and fabulously rich! It was the first experience that either Anna or Avis had had of real snow and ice. They felt the cold acutely, but the scenery enchanted them—the partly frozen Hudson, the endless white with blue shadows, the evergreens. Anna was already at work on a book of her Siamese experiences.

She had written to the King setting forth the terms under which she would return. After deliberation she had concluded that she could not go back unless her salary was adequate and the arrangements clear. Louis was not at all enthusiastic about having her return without him. He wrote from Ireland:

April 28, 1868.
". . . I hope you wont go back to Siam because you will be in such a dangerous place and I will awals feel so unhappy thinking of you being among all those French peapel who hate you or praps a rober might come and may be do some thing to you or if you were walking up that green and one of those priests comeing up to you and saying something to you rudely or praps a cow or some strange thing come at you all those thing if any of them hapened to you what would I do the only thing is that I would die."

The King's letter when it came late in May was not entirely satisfactory. It was the last letter she was to have from him.

8th February 1868
To Lady A.H.Leonowens and her son Dear Louis
My Dear Maam & Louis
I have just received your letter under the date of 2nd. November on the 7th. Inst. I am very busy on these week as said in the preceding printed lines. My late lamented son's remains were just in cremation on 6th Inst. and the ceremony of inauguration of his relicks is yet continuing until the present date his Nadial relicks will be returned to his Palace today Evening.
Regarding your request I have given verbal reply through Mr. D. K. Mason, Phra Siam Thurabat, the consul for Siam in London, who will return to his post from hence tomorrow morg. I cannot write you fully as I am very busy and much engaging. I beg to say briefly that I am very desirous of complying with your desire, but fear lest you by any cause would not be able to return to Siam soon, and many foreigners may rumour more and more that I am a shallow-minded man and rich of money &c. &c. as usual general rumour, many and many trouble me in various ways.—You had better be indebted to anyone in London yourself, when you was arrived here I can give you the required Loan at once and moreover if you please to—I can allow the Loan of $200 to you freely but it may be not.
I beg to remain your faithful
S. P. P. M. MONGKUT R. S.
in 6115 days of reign

Avis was ill, so that the return to Siam would have had to be delayed a few months in any case. Anna wrote again to the King and postponed her decision until her status should be clear. His Majesty was engrossed all that summer with preparations for an expedition to Hua Wan in the southern peninsula of Siam for the purpose of observing a total eclipse of the sun. The French government had asked permission to send a group of scientists to that point, since it was expected that the eclipse could be seen best from there. Sir Harry Ord, Governor of the Straits Settlements, and Lady Ord were coming with a suite from Singapore. The British and French Consuls, and other prominent Europeans from Bangkok, were also attending. They were all to be guests of the Siamese government. The eclipse occurred on August 18. After the King and his party had returned to Bangkok he complained of a headache. A few weeks later it was evident that he was seriously, perhaps mortally, ill. Dr. William Campbell, who had succeeded Dr. James Campbell, his cousin, and Dr. Dan Beach Bradley were called. But they were not allowed to prescribe for the patient. They both felt strongly that the fever would yield to quinine. But none was used. On October 1, 1868, the King died—so suddenly that he was alone except for his adopted son, Phya Burut, who had attended him as a priest boy years before, and whom he had called Pheng Napoleon.

Earlier in the evening the chief ministers of state and Krom Luang Wongsa had been at the bedside. The King had already dictated in Pali a farewell to the Buddhist Order. Feeling sure that death was close, the King had solemnly imposed upon his chief ministers the care of his eldest son, Prince Chulalongkorn, and of the kingdom. He had not asked them to elect the prince to succeed him, but his wishes in that respect were well known. All he had said was that he hoped the Senabodi would choose as his successor someone who would conciliate all parties in the kingdom so that civil war would not follow his death.

He then told them that he was about to finish his course, and implored them not to give way to grief "nor to any sudden surprise" that he should leave them so, since it "is an event that must befall all creatures that come into this world, and may not be avoided." Then he turned to a small image of the Buddha and lay absorbed in contemplation. His voice was so strong and he seemed so far from death that they retired. The Krala-home even ventured to go home for a few hours' rest. Phya Burut sat alone beside the dying King. Suddenly the King raised his hands before his face in the attitude of devotion. His head dropped back, and he was gone.

Anna never returned to Siam.

The King had remembered Anna and Louis generously in his will, but neither of them was to receive the inheritance. The executors withheld it, and she knew of it only because her friends at court wrote and told her the circumstances.

The night that the King died the Senabodi elected Prince Chulalongkorn to succeed his father. The prince, now fifteen, was ill with the same fever. Gradually his strength returned and on November 11 he was crowned. Everyone who saw him was impressed with his dignity, his quiet assurance, and his lack of arrogance.

Actual power was not to be his until he attained his majority five years later. Nevertheless he was permitted by the Senabodi and the Regent, who was the Kralahome, to proclaim an amnesty of all political prisoners, three hundred and sixty-two of them. He began at once, quietly and with determination, to set forth his views on the future of the kingdom. His second proclamation established religious liberty. In it he declared:

In regard to the concern of seeking and holding a religion that will be a refuge to you in this life: it is a good and noble concern, and it is exceedingly appropriate and suitable that you, as a nation, and each man individually, should investigate for himself, and according to his own wisdom, which is the right and which is the wrong; and if you see any religion whatever, or any body of men professing any religion whatsoever who seem likely to be an advantage to you,—a true religion in accordance with your own wisdom,—hold to that religion with all your heart. . . .

The question of slavery was more difficult, woven as it was into the warp and woof of the system of privilege. The great nobles of the country whose fortunes were based on the thousands of serfs and slaves at their disposal did not look with favor on any attempt to disrupt a system so profitable to themselves. According to the letters that reached Anna, young King Chulalongkorn undertook the matter courageously but discreetly. She heard that he had said to the San Luang, "I see no hope for our country until it is freed from the dark blot of slavery."

They were impressed by the vehemence of the King, but not persuaded. The Kralahome replied: "It is impossible to free a nation of slaves without incurring much risk and danger to the state and to the slaveholders. Under the existing laws, Siam could not abolish her system of slavery without undermining at the same time her whole constitution."

"Well," the King answered, "let it be so for the time being then. But my slaves, my soldiers, and my debtors are my own, and I will free them at least, whatever my ministers may see fit to do. For my part, no human being shall ever again be branded in my name and with my mark!"

After much further discussion the Regent and the Senabodi agreed to a gradual termination of slavery. The first public pronouncement was made by the King. Standing on the lowest step of his glittering throne before the chief rulers, governors, and judges of the people he read his declaration:

Let this our royal message to our people be proclaimed, and not as if we were doing a great and lordly thing, but our simple duty to our fellowmen and subjects, that from the first day of January, 1872, slavery shall cease to be an institution in our country, and every man, woman, and child shall hold themselves free-born citizens; and further let it be made known, that a tax, according to circumstances of each and every man, shall be levied on the nation to remunerate the slaveholders for the loss of their slaves.

It was to be 1905 before the final proclamation was issued, absolutely and finally terminating serfdom and slavery. The length of the process was necessary in the transformation of the country from feudalism to freedom. In the end, however, the King had kept his solemn determination as he had made it long ago to Anna—"If I live to reign over Siam I shall reign over a free and not an enslaved nation."

Lady Son Klin wrote excitedly from Bangkok:

> Grand Royal Palace
> Nov. 11th, 1872.

To Lady Leonowens

My dear Friend & Teacher. My goodness gracious.

You will not know us any more, we are all so changed, a freedomed people; some of the free like not to leave their master and mistress so they weep for gladness, but most run off like wild deer from shot-gun and are for joy like one mad.

Me and my two sisters are too happy we fear almost to say how happy for fear perhaps it will all vanish.

I pray to my God to be very tenderly of you and your children and bless your good work.

Do come back to us very soon, we are in great need of you. I am like one blind. Do not let me fall down in the darkness. Come and lead me on the right road.

> Your loving pupil
> SON KLIN. HARRIET BEECHER STOWE.

In 1873 when he attained his majority King Chulalongkorn temporarily resigned his crown and kingdom to enter the priesthood for fifteen days, as was the custom. This act entailed—also according to custom—a new coronation, which took place on November 16, 1873.

On that morning the sudden blaring of bands from behind the high white walls of the Palace, the roar of cannon, told the people of Bangkok that their King had been recrowned. In the Hall of Audience the princes and nobles were prostrate on the carpeted floor. Every head was bowed. As the deafening noise quieted His Majesty stepped upon the platform of the throne to read the first proclamation of his new reign. It was an edict to end prostration:

> Siamese civil era, 1235, in the year of the Cock, the 12th moon, the 12th day of the waning.
>
> His Majesty Prabat Somdet Phra Paramenthara Maha Chulalong-korn . . . and the greater and lesser princes, the Senabodi, the Ministers of State, greater and lesser, military and civil, being in solemn audience in their respective places, His Majesty announced the royal mandate. . . . Whatever is oppressive and burdensome, it has been the Royal purpose to remove from the people, and abolish from the state. . . . In this kingdom of Siam there are some national customs that are rigorous, hostile to good usage, and ought to be

modified; but the changing and modifying of customs cannot be effected at once; such changes must be the subject of much thought and gradual modification. . . .

The custom of prostration and human worship in Siam is manifestly an oppressive exaction which an inferior must perform to a superior, causing him embarrassing fatigue. . . . This custom His Majesty perceives is a primary cause of many existing oppressive exactions, therefore, this ancient national custom, which made prostration the prescribed method of demonstrating respect in Siam, must be abolished; . . . His Majesty proposes to substitute in the place of crouching and crawling, standing and walking; and instead of prostration on all-fours and bowing with palm-joined hands to the ground, a graceful bow of the head. . . .

When the King concluded the reading, princes, nobles, and ministers performed three profound salaams, as had been the custom, and then in perfect order rose to their feet and stood before their sovereign for the first time.

With these reforms the King fulfilled Anna's early hopes of him and set the seal of final accomplishment on her efforts in Siam.

Anna herself was busy with a new life. Her first article describing some of her experiences at the court of King Mongkut appeared in the *Atlantic Monthly*, in June, 1869, and was followed by *The English Governess at the Siamese Court* and *The Romance of the Harem*. Instantly she was in demand as a lecturer. The way was open for her to meet the most distinguished literary personalities of New York. She became acquainted with Sarah Orne Jewett, James Russell Lowell, Oliver Wendell Holmes, William Cullen Bryant, Henry Wadsworth Longfellow, Julia Ward Howe, and Ralph Waldo Emerson, whom she had so long admired. In 1872 she met Harriet Beecher Stowe at the home of Mr. and Mrs. James T. Fields. She wrote to Avis that Mrs. Stowe, "a strong but plain woman, very handsomely dressed," embraced her as if she had known her for a lifetime.

The years passed swiftly. There were financial worries, but many compensations. Avis graduated from school and opened a kindergarten in New York. Anna continued to write, teach, lecture, until Avis married Mr. Thomas Fyshe, a young Scottish banker, and went to Halifax to live in 1878. In their Canadian home Mrs. Leonowens spent the rest of her life.

Louis, in the meantime, left school in Ireland and came to the United States. But he was not satisfied. He told his mother that "America is played out," and departed for Australia where he entered the police force. But his was a restless spirit, and in 1882 he returned to Siam. King Chulalongkorn made him an officer in the cavalry, and sent word to Mrs. Leonowens through the Siamese Consul that he had been happy to do so for her sake.

In 1881, after the assassination of Alexander II, she was sent to Russia by *The Youth's Companion* to write a series of articles. The editors offered her a permanent position on their staff but she declined. She had found that, much as she liked New York and Boston, she could not bear to be away from her new grandchildren for more than a few months.

It was on a trip to New York that she had the joy of meeting again Prince Krita, Son Klin's son, now H.R.H. Prince Nares and Ambassador to England. He had come on a special embassy to the United States and had sent word ahead that he wished to see her. She wrote to Avis in Halifax from New York on May 19, 1884, describing her meeting with the prince:

I went immediately after breakfast this morning to the Fifth Avenue Hotel, where the Embassy is staying, and sent up my card. Presently Mr. Loftus, a very polite English gentleman, interpreter and private secretary to the prince, came down and conducted me to the prince's private drawing room. Here I had hardly taken my seat when in rushed dear Krita Phinihan, and, putting his arms around my neck, embraced me just as he used to do when a little boy. I was quite overcome with joy at his enthusiastic reception of me. . . . After the first eager greetings were over, the prince and I talked about Siam. He said that if I went back there now I would hardly know the place, or the people, so changed were they in almost every respect: prostration, slavery, imprisonment of wife or child for the husband or father's debts were all abolished; that new roads and canals were built, schools endowed wherein all European and Oriental instruction was taught. . . . He also added that all this was the result of my teaching the present King and the royal family. You can imagine my delight in listening to him, hearing him converse thus; partly in Siamese and partly in English. . . . I enquired by name for most of my late pupils, and I rejoiced to find that no less than ten of the princes occupied at this moment high official positions under the present King and that he himself held one of the very highest—Minister of Foreign Affairs. He told me to my great delight that Louis was doing good work and making himself useful to the King in every way, that his men were devoted to him and that he now not only spoke but read Siamese quite fluently. . . . He told me that the King had desired him to enquire for me, and to try to see me, adding: "Mem, if you want any money at any time you must let His Majesty know for he says that all that he ever learned of good in his life you taught him."

Thirty years after she left Siam in 1867 Anna Leonowens saw her most distinguished pupil again. She was on her way to Leipzig with the older of Avis' children when King Chulalongkorn arrived in London. She had an interview with him there on August 19, 1897, at two-fifteen in the afternoon. It was another memorable day in her life.

The King had reigned for twenty-nine years, a grave, quiet, determined man who had accomplished much against great odds. The nobles whose privileges he had curtailed had secretly opposed him. The French had continued their depredations, seizing further territory on the slightest pretext. Nevertheless the work of reform had gone on. Schools had been established all over the kingdom. Missionaries had been encouraged in their efforts to start hospitals and schools. Transportation facilities were improved. The law courts had been reorganized. Gradually, educated officials were taking the places of the old feudal administrators. The whole system of government had been reorganized. The military forces were being modernized. Young men were being sent abroad for study, and teachers from Europe and America were being imported. Already in his lifetime the Siamese were beginning to say that Chulalongkorn was their greatest king. When he moved about Bangkok in formal procession they scattered rice mixed with flowers in his path—their highest tribute.

It was thus with a feeling of deep gratitude and humility that Anna heard him say it was through the principles laid down in her teaching that he had formed the plans by which he had transformed his kingdom. He had kept his determination to recreate a free Siam. It had not been easy. There was much still to do. But in Siam the current of change was running deep and strong and true, full of promise for the future, because it was a change based on the idea of the worth of a human being as Anna had helped instill it into the monarch—a change based on democratic principles.

Anna looked into the future of the country where she had spent the most difficult years of her life and was content.

# AUTHOR'S NOTE

ANNA LEONOWENS was introduced to me by the late Dr. Edwin Bruce McDaniel who extracted *The English Governess at the Siamese Court*[1] from behind a row of books in his bookcase and handed it to me with the remark: "Here's something you ought to read. The Siamese government did everything in their power to keep it from being published. I've been told they even tried to buy the whole edition to prevent its distribution. In fact there has been so much feeling against the book that I still keep my copy out of sight, just to be on the safe side." I took the book and sat down. Outside on the one long street of Nakon Sritamarat in south Siam automobiles honked continuously. There was the jingle of horse-drawn gharries and bicycle bells. An occasional elephant padded by in ponderous majesty. But as I read all of this dropped away.

Hours later I came up from the story in a daze, surprised to find myself still in the world of today. Dr. McDaniel also had Mrs. Leonowens' second book, *The Romance of the Harem*,[2] and that too I devoured. This happened almost fifteen years ago.

My efforts to secure copies were unsuccessful. Both books had been out of print for more than fifty years. But my enthusiasm for them led me to urge various American friends to read them, since copies were in the New York and Chicago Public Libraries. It was my college roommate and close personal friend, Muriel Fuller, who said to me in 1937: "Why don't you combine the biographical parts of the two books to make one? Omit the long discussions and descriptions. They only bore people who aren't students of Siamese history. Then fit the various incidents together in sequence."

I liked the idea of trying to introduce Anna Leonowens to modern readers. The story of her life in Siam was more than interesting: it was the record of an amazing person. I had found the long descriptions far from dull, but I could see how they might be so to people without a special interest in Siam. In fact, a reviewer of Mrs. Leonowens' time had made

[1] Leonowens, Anna Harriette, *The English Governess at the Siamese Court,* Boston, Fields, Osgood and Company, 1870.

[2] Leonowens, Mrs. Anna H., *The Romance of the Harem,* Boston, James R. Osgood and Company, 1872.

357

just this criticism of her book in *The Nation* for March 9, 1871. He gave it as his opinion that:

> Whenever the author is occupied with the story of her intercourse with the royal family, she is very lively and every way admirable. . . . What she has told us about the King, and what she saw in the process of "doing her education" on his household, is so interesting that we cannot help wishing she had recorded it more in detail. . . . As it is the book is half-filled up with geographical, historical, and other padding not very skillfully inserted, and very disorderly in its arrangement. Indeed, when the author comes outside of the palace gates, and away from the immediate care of her pupils, she grows uninteresting.

I was still faced with the seeming impossibility of finding copies of the books. Then on March 17, 1938, while my husband was looking for an obscure book on China in the Economy Bookstore in Chicago I strolled into the section marked OUT OF PRINT NOVELS. I could hardly believe my eyes when under "L" I found *The Romance of the Harem.* I was almost afraid to look at the price for one of my acquaintances had paid three pounds for a copy of *The Governess* in London! Inside the back cover was penciled "$1.00." Only a few weeks later I read in the paper that Marshall Field's was to put on its counters fifty thousand unsorted books. Incredible as it seems, I found *The English Governess at the Siamese Court* for fifty cents and half an hour's search!

A careful rereading of both books showed that I should need more information than they contained if I were to make a connected narrative. I knew nothing of Mrs. Leonowens' descendants except that her son had had a lumber firm in Siam and had died there. The final coincidence occurred in the winter of 1939 when my husband was having lunch with a group of ministers in Evanston, Illinois.

He was introduced as from Siam, and the Very Reverend Doctor Gerald G. Moore, then Dean of St. Luke's, leaned across the table and remarked:

"Mother would like to meet you. She had a friend—the wife of a cousin, in fact—who used to live in Siam many years ago. Mother still talks about Aunt Annie and her letters from Siam."

"Not Anna Leonowens, surely?" my husband asked in astonishment.

"Why, yes," Dr. Moore said, equally astonished, "that was the name!"

My husband quickly revolved the fact that it was more than seventy years since Mrs. Leonowens had left Siam and said:

"It would have been pleasant to have met your mother. My wife and I are interested in Mrs. Leonowens and would have liked very much to have met someone who had actually known her."

Dr. Moore's eyes twinkled as he said, "Mother lives only a few blocks from here. Would you care to come with me and see her now?"

358

As a result of this chance encounter we met Dr. Moore's sister, Miss Kathleen Moore, and his mother, Mrs. Lizzie Avice Moore, who had been a young girl in Enniscorthy, Ireland, when Anna Leonowens came home from Siam in 1867, and who remembered her clearly. The Moores arranged my meeting with Miss Avis S. Fyshe of Montreal, Canada, Mrs. Leonowens' granddaughter, who supplied me with copies of letters and other pertinent material in her possession. I should like to express here my gratitude both to the Moores and to Miss Fyshe. I am indebted to Miss Fyshe not only for her material and for permission to use it in this book, but also for her kindness in answering my many questions.

In the fall of 1939 I began the book. It proved to be a much more intricate and difficult task than I had supposed it would be. I had been interested in the reign of King Mongkut for some time and as a result had read a good deal on the history of nineteenth-century Siam. Then, too, in the ten years I had lived in Siam, all but one of them in the provinces where I was usually the only white woman, I had listened to endless stories out of the past which served to illuminate the world of yesterday that has disappeared from modern Bangkok. But I found when I began to fit the story of Anna Leonowens together that there were hundreds of specific questions which would have to be answered if it was to be a coherent whole.

The Siam of 1927–1937 which I had known was different in endless detail from the Siam of 1862–1867 that she had known. For instance, in the time that I lived in Siam I never saw a single person who had been branded. But in the period that Anna Leonowens lived there it was the rare man who did not have on his left wrist the brand of the great noble to whom he owed allegiance, and if he had lived under two reigns his brand would appear both on the outside and the inside of the wrist.

Then, too, in attempting to set in order the various experiences which she had recorded so vividly I found it necessary to search for specific information on obscure historical events. As an example, there is the story of the reception of Lord John Hay by the ladies of the harem. Both the date and the occasion for Lord John's visit to Bangkok were extremely difficult to find. It was not until I discovered in the Library of Congress among the then unlisted books in the Siamese language the first volume of King Mongkut's letters that I was able to find either. King Mongkut himself in the eighth letter of this series had written a long description of the occasion and circumstances of the visit—though not the incident that Anna Leonowens recorded. It was then possible to find also several letters of Lord John Hay's relating to the so-called Trengganu incident, in which in the careful language of diplomacy he deprecated the actions of Governor Cavenagh.

I am especially indebted to Dr. Philip M. Hamer of the National Archives and Dr. Horace I. Poleman of the Library of Congress for making available to me material that helped in the reconstruction of the historical background for the book. I should like to express my appreciation also of the help given me by Luang Dithakar Bhakdi, First Secretary of the Royal Thai Legation, in finding the correct form of obscure Siamese names and words, from which the English transliterations have been made in accordance with the official system used by the Thai government.

The method of presentation was determined by the form of the incidents as recorded by Anna Leonowens herself. While it was not possible to do what I originally intended—that is, piece together her own writings without alteration in language or style—as little change has been made as seemed consistent with the change from a first-person to a third-person narrative, and from the 1860's to the 1940's. If I were asked to give the fabric content of the book I should say that it is "seventy-five per cent fact, and twenty-five per cent fiction based on fact."

There are two people who have helped and encouraged me throughout the four years that I have been writing, and to them I am especially grateful. Both of them have pushed and pulled me over apparently insuperable difficulties. One of them I have already mentioned, my friend Muriel Fuller. The other is my husband, Kenneth Perry Landon, who encouraged me to write the story of Anna Leonowens, has shared in the research, has turned up new sources of material when none seemed available, and who has in other ways served as midwife in the long, slow effort of bringing this book into being.

Washington, D. C. MARGARET LANDON